D0073431

Monetary Economics

Monetary Economics

Theory and Policy

Bennett T. McCallum

Carnegie–Mellon University

Macmillan Publishing Company
New York

Collier Macmillan Publishers
London

Macmillan Publishing Company
866 Third Avenue, New York, New York 10022

Collier Macmillan Canada, Inc.

Library of Congress Cataloging in Publication Data

McCallum, Bennett T.
    Monetary economics: theory and policy/Bennett T. McCallum.
        p.   cm.
    Includes index.
    ISBN 0-02-378471-7
    1. Money.   2. Monetary policy.   I. Title.
    HG221.M423 1989
    332.4--dc19

PRINTING   9   Year: 7 8

PREFACE

The object of this book is to present a systematic treatment of monetary economics in a manner that is clear and nontechnical, yet accurately reflective of important research developments of the past 20 years. Such a task is not an easy one, since recent research has emphasized dynamic and stochastic aspects of economic behavior—aspects that involve analytical difficulties. My strategy for accomplishing the task has been to begin with simple models, to introduce complexities only as needed, to focus selectively on matters of fundamental importance, and to relate the discussion at each point with what has gone before.

By proceeding in this fashion, I have found it possible to handle in a satisfying manner numerous topics not usually included in textbook discussions. In particular, the book is novel in its emphasis on severe inflation, on monetary standards (including commodity-money arrangements), and on realistic descriptions of central-bank operating procedures. Also, there is a discussion of United States monetary history that is unusual in its coverage, as three-quarters of its length is devoted to periods *before* the creation (in 1914) of the Federal Reserve System. In terms of technique, moreover, the book includes extensive expositions of inflationary steady-state analysis, dynamic analysis with adaptive and rational expectations, and a systematic procedure for solving linear stochastic models with rational expectations.

The book does not, on the other hand, include much institutional detail or any substantial amount of material on the subject of finance. These omissions do not in my opinion constitute a weakness; an important ingredient of effective instruction is selectivity in terms of coverage.

Because the book emphasizes recent research topics but strives for analytical simplicity, it should be appropriate for textbook use in a variety of settings. Preliminary versions have been used successfully in advanced undergraduate and MBA courses, yet much of the material could be helpful to beginning graduate students in economics. The book is primarily designed for courses in monetary economics, but could alternatively serve as a textbook in macroeconomics or money and banking with analytical emphasis. It would need to be augmented with additional material on consumption, investment, and fiscal policy (in the former case) or on financial markets and institutions (in the latter). A synopsis of the material in each chapter is provided in Section 1.4 on pp. 12–15.

In expressing thanks to those who have been helpful to me in writing the book, I will begin with two organizations. First, the Graduate School of Industrial Administration (GSIA) at Carnegie-Mellon University has provided an excellent intellectual atmosphere plus the possibility of combining research and teaching activities. Second, the Research Department of the Federal Reserve Bank of Richmond, with which I have been associated for several years, has provided the opportunity of learning from its members about monetary issues in general and the Federal Reserve System in particular. Needless to say, none of the views expressed in the book should be attributed to either of these institutions.

Many individuals have contributed in a variety of ways. Excellent typing was provided by GSIA's word-processing department and by my secretaries, Sue Sholar and Gerri Carrozzi. At Macmillan, Ken MacLeod and Elaine Wetterau were helpful in their roles as Editor and Production Supervisor, while special thanks go to Jack Repcheck for crucial support and encouragement in the initial and intermediate stages of the project.

Helpful comments on various chapters have been provided by a number of economists. My thanks go particularly to those who read large portions of the manuscript, including David Aschauer, Michael Bordo, Martin Eichenbaum, Richard Froyen, Marvin Goodfriend, John Huizinga, and Dean Taylor. I regret that time pressures have kept me from incorporating more of their thoughtful suggestions.

Final thanks go to my wife, Sally, whose support has been extraordinary. She deserves substantial credit for anything that I manage to accomplish.

B.T.M.

CONTENTS

Preface   v

———————————————————— PART I ————————————————————
Rudiments of Monetary Analysis

1 An Introduction to Monetary Economics   3

   1.1 Preliminary Remarks   3
   1.2 A Few Historical Facts   5
   1.3 The U.S. Monetary Experience of 1979–1982   9
   1.4 A Look Ahead   12
       Problems   15   References   15

2 Basic Concepts   16

   2.1 The Functions of Money   16
   2.2 Empirical Measures   19
   2.3 Monetary Standards: Fiat Versus Commodity
       Money   22
   2.4 Legal Tender   24
   2.5 Money, Credit, and Financial Intermediation   25
       Problems   30   References   32

3 The Demand for Money   33

   3.1 Informal Discussion   33
   3.2 A Formal Model   35
   3.3 Uncertainty   41
   3.4 Empirical Money Demand Functions   42

3.5 Velocity 47
3.6 The Baumol–Tobin Model 48
3.7 Conclusions 52
     Problems 53   References 54

4 The Supply of Money   55

4.1 Introduction 55
4.2 Basic Relationships 56
4.3 Monetary Control 60
4.4 Alternative Control Procedures 63
4.5 Algebraic Analysis 67
4.6 Conclusions 71
     Problems 72   References 73

────────────────── **PART II** ──────────────────
Monetary Macroeconomics

5 The Static Classical and Keynesian Models   77

5.1 Introduction 77
5.2 The *IS* Function 78
5.3 The *LM* Function 83
5.4 The Aggregate Demand Function 85
5.5 The Classical Aggregate Supply Function 89
5.6 The Classical Model 93
5.7 The Keynesian Aggregate Supply Function 96
5.8 The Keynesian Model 100
Appendix: *IS–LM* and Maximizing Analysis 102
     Problems 107   References 108

6 Steady Inflation   109

6.1 Introduction 109
6.2 Real Versus Nominal Interest Rates 112
6.3 Inflation in the Classical Model 113
6.4 Comparative Steady States 117
6.5 Analysis with Real-Balance Effects 120
6.6 Analysis with Output Growth 122
6.7 The Welfare Cost of Inflation 124
6.8 Concluding Comments 130
     Problems 131   References 131

7 Inflationary Dynamics   133

7.1 The Cagan Model   133
7.2 Hyperinflation Episodes   135
7.3 Cagan's Estimates   136
7.4 Stability Analysis   139
7.5 Weakness of Adaptive Expectations   142
      Problems   144   References   144

8 Rational Expectations   145

8.1 Basic Properties   145
8.2 Application to the Cagan Model   148
8.3 Solution Procedure   151
8.4 Properties of the Solution   153
8.5 Examples of Rational Expectation Solutions   155
8.6 Models with Lagged Variables   157
8.7 Multiple Solutions   158
Appendix: Mathematical Expectation: A Review   160
      Problems   172   References   173

9 Inflation and Unemployment: Alternative Theories   174

9.1 Dynamics and the Keynesian Model   174
9.2 The Original Phillips Curve   177
9.3 The Augmented Phillips Curve   181
9.4 Lucas's Monetary Misperceptions Theory   185
9.5 Taylor's Relative-Prices Theory   188
9.6 Fischer's Sticky-Wage Theory   189
9.7 Real Business Cycle Theory   192
9.8 Conclusions   196
      Problems   197   References   199

10 Money and Output: An Analytical Framework   201

10.1 Introduction   201
10.2 Aggregate Supply: Basic Model   203
10.3 Normal Output   208
10.4 Multiperiod Pricing   211
10.5 Rationale for Price Stickiness   214
10.6 Conclusions   215
       Problems   217   References   217

──────────── **PART III** ────────────

Monetary Policy

11 Analysis of Alternative Policy Rules   221

    11.1 Introduction 221
    11.2 Monetary Policy Ineffectiveness? 221
    11.3 The Lucas Critique 228
    11.4 Money Stock Control 230
    11.5 Conclusions 235
          Problems 236   References 236

12 Rules Versus Discretion in Monetary Policy   237

    12.1 Fundamental Distinctions 237
    12.2 Rules Versus Discretion: An Example 239
    12.3 Effects of Rules Versus Discretion 241
    12.4 Extensions of the Basic Model 244
    12.5 Evidence 245
          Problems 248   References 248

13 The Gold Standard: A Commodity-Money System   249

    13.1 Introduction 249
    13.2 Basic Model 250
    13.3 Analysis with Basic Model 255
    13.4 Dynamic Analysis with Rational Expectations 258
    13.5 Bimetallism 263
    13.6 Conclusions 267
          Problems 267   References 268

14 Open-Economy Monetary Analysis   269

    14.1 Introduction 269
    14.2 Basic Open-Economy Model 271
    14.3 Properties of the Model 275
    14.4 Extensions 280
    14.5 Fixed Exchange Rates 285
    14.6 The Balance of Payments 288
    14.7 Fixed Versus Floating Exchange Rates 293
          Problems 296   References 297

15 Episodes in U.S. Monetary History   298

    15.1 Introduction 298
    15.2 Money in Colonial America 299
    15.3 From the Revolution to the Civil War 309
    15.4 From the Civil War to World War I 317
    15.5 From 1914 to 1944 324
    15.6 Conclusion 331
          Problems 333   References 334

16 A Strategy for Monetary Policy   336

    16.1 Basic Considerations 336
    16.2 A Specific Rule 339
    16.3 Performance of Proposed Rule 343
    16.4 Conclusions 348
          Problems 350   References 350

Index   352

Rudiments of Monetary Analysis

An Introduction to Monetary Economics

1.1 Preliminary Remarks

Monetary economics is concerned with the effects of monetary institutions and policy actions on economic variables that are of importance to individuals and organizations. Among these variables are commodity prices, wages, interest rates, and quantities of employment, consumption, and production—all considered at various levels of disaggregation but especially on an economy-wide or aggregate basis.

Given the foregoing definition, it would be natural to ask why this topic warrants designation as a special field or area of study within economics. "Money is just one of many commodities," some persons would say, "so why emphasize it rather than bicycles or suitcases or five-year government bonds?" Part of the answer to this question is that money is quite special in its role as a crucial intermediary object that is involved on one side of most transactions that take place in today's market economies. A second part of the answer, moreover, stems from the fact that a majority of analysts—including professional economists, journalists, policymakers, and financial market participants—believe that monetary policies have an overwhelmingly important impact on the economic life of a nation. Indeed, for this reason Paul Volcker was frequently described during the years 1979–1987 as the "second most powerful man in the United States" (i.e., second only to the President).[1] Such statements were, of course, made about him not

---

[1] See *The Economist*, September 22, 1984, p. 5.

because of his height—although it is 6 feet 7 inches!—but because Volcker occupied the dominant executive position in the Federal Reserve System, which is the central institution in the country's current monetary system. (In August 1987, Alan Greenspan replaced Volcker as Chairman of the Board of Governers of the Federal Reserve System.)

Mention of the Federal Reserve System, typically referred to as "the Fed," is a useful reminder that recent U.S. monetary experience has been both eventful and contentious. A brief overview of some aspects of that recent experience will be provided momentarily, in Section 1.3. Before turning to the recent period, however, it will be useful to take a look at certain features of U.S. monetary experience over a longer historical span of time.

Table 1-1.   U.S. Price-Index Numbers

Date	WPI W&P[a]	WPI BLS[b]	WPI W&P[c]	CPI BLS[d]
1749	68		24.0	
1776	86		30.3	
1800	129		45.5	51
1820	106		37.4	42
1840	95		33.5	30
1860	93		32.8	27
1865	185		65.2	46
1890	82	28.9	28.9	27
1900		28.9		25
1915		35.8		30.4
1920		79.6		60.0
1929		49.1		51.3
1933		34.0		40.9
1940		40.5		42.0
1946		62.3		58.5
1960		94.9		88.7
1970		110.4		116.3
1980		268.8		246.8
1987		307.6		340.4

[a] Base year 1910–1914. See *Historical Statistics of the United States*, pp. 201–202.

[b] Base year 1967. *Historical Statistics of the United States*, p. 199, and *Survey of Current Business*.

[c] Base year 1967. The first column multiplied by 28.9/82.

[d] Base year 1967. *Historical Statistics of the United States*, pp. 210–11, and *Survey of Current Business*.

1.2   A Few Historical Facts

"The price level" is a term used to refer to some average of the money prices of a broadly defined group of commodities—in other words, the price (in monetary units) of some "representative" bundle of commodities. The inverse of the price level, then, is a measure of the commodity value of a unit of money. Probably the most striking fact about U.S. monetary experience of the past 40 years is that the price level has risen since the end of World War II by a factor of about 5.8. Equivalently, the value of a U.S. dollar in 1987 is only 17 percent of what it was in 1946.[2] Now, to some readers this fact may not at first seem striking, as it reflects an average inflation rate of only a few percentage points a year.[3] But in that regard it is important to realize that the U.S. price level at the *start* of World War II was only a little higher than it had been at the nation's inception (i.e., at the outbreak of the War of Independence). More specifically, the price level in 1940 was approximately 1.3 times its level in 1776.[4] Never in the nation's history, until the last 40 years, had major movements in the price level occurred without being substantially reversed within one or two decades. Some pertinent statistics concerning U.S. price-level history are reported in Table 1-1.

Mulling upon these facts, one tends naturally to ask: What is the explanation for this vastly different inflationary experience of the postwar period as compared with previous historical eras?[5] There are various levels at which an answer could be attempted, but one possibly significant difference is provided by the complete abandonment since World War II of any attachment to a commodity-money standard. There is no single point in time at which this abandonment took place; nevertheless, the following facts are clear. First, before 1933 the nation

[2] This calculation is based on one well-known measure of the general price level, the U.S. Bureau of Labor Statistics's Consumer Price Index (CPI) for all items. Its value was 340.4 in 1987, on a scale that makes the 1967 value equal to 100, as compared with 58.5 for the year 1946. The ratio 340.4/58.5 is 5.82; its inverse is 0.172.

[3] Solving $(1 + \pi)^{41} = 5.82$ gives $\pi = 0.0439$, or an average inflation rate of about 4.4 percent per year.

[4] This calculation is based on a Wholesale Price Index (WPI) comparison, rather than one involving consumer prices, because the CPI is available only back to 1800. Actually, the Bureau of Labor Statistics's WPI measure only goes back to 1890, but there is also an index of wholesale prices created by the economists Warren and Pearson [see p. 186, vol. 1, of U.S. Department of Commerce, Bureau of the Census, *Historical Statistics of the United States* (Washington: U.S. Government Printing Office, 1975)]. The Warren and Pearson index is 86 for 1776 and 82 for 1890; the Bureau of Labor Statistics WPI figures are 28.9 for 1890 and 40.5 for 1940. The calculation in the text in effect "splices" the series as of 1890, using the two values for that year. A qualification to this comparison is mentioned in Chapter 15.

[5] A similar contrast is present in the data for other nations; see Chapter 12.

was officially on the *gold standard* in the sense that a dollar was a legal claim to 0.0484 ounce of gold. In particular, Federal Reserve Notes, which were the main circulating currency, were convertible into gold: the Fed was obligated to exchange its Notes, if presented at certain specified locations, for gold in the quantity mentioned above.[6] Second, since 1971 there has been no link whatsoever between dollars and gold or any other commodity. The Fed now makes no promises about what its Notes are worth in real terms; they are not legal claims on anything (except other dollars!).

The implicit suggestion of the preceding paragraph is that the absence of a commodity-money standard has permitted the Fed to expand the nation's money stock excessively, thereby inducing the fall in the value of a dollar that has in fact taken place. As a partial test of this suggestion, one might examine the data pertaining to the U.S. money stock to see if in fact it has grown rapidly in the postwar period. Doing so, it is found that the stock of money was approximately $40 billion in 1940 and about $750 billion at the end of 1987, a ratio of 18.7 to 1.[7] So, at least in this rather rough way, the facts are indeed consistent with our supposition.[8]

A second important difference in postwar U.S. monetary arrangements, as compared with previous periods, is the extent to which responsibility for real macroeconomic conditions has been accepted by the Fed and by the federal government more generally. In this regard, too, the change did not occur entirely at a single point in time. But it is certainly true that before World War II the use of activist monetary policy to smooth out fluctuations in aggregate output and employment was not generally regarded as an important part of the Fed's duties. For the past 40 years, by contrast, monetary policy has been conducted in an environment significantly affected by the Employment Act of 1946, which declares that

> It is the continuing policy and responsibility of the Federal Government to use all practical means consistent with its needs and obligations...to coordinate and utilize all its plans, functions, and resources for the pur-

---

[6] Actually, this statement is accurate only for the period 1900–1933. Before 1900, the country was officially on a bimetallic—gold *and* silver—standard. That type of arrangement will be discussed in Chapter 13.

[7] The two figures pertain to slightly different variants of M1, the basic money stock measure. The earlier is taken from Gordon (1984), the latter from the *Federal Reserve Bulletin*.

[8] The main reason why the price-level increase was proportionately less than that of the money stock is that real income has grown and led to a growth in the real value of transactions. This type of effect is discussed in Chapter 3.

pose of creating and maintaining . . . conditions under which there will be afforded useful employment opportunities . . . and to promote maximum employment, production, and purchasing power.[9]

It seems almost certainly the case that the existence of this expansion in the macroeconomic policy role of the federal government has affected the Fed's conduct of monetary policy, and it is at least conceivable that the effect would be of a type that is conducive to inflation. Indeed, some formal analysis presented in Chapter 12 suggests that such is the case—that discretionary policy has had an inflationary bias.

In other words, a plausible suggestion is that increased emphasis on real objectives such as output and employment has contributed to the inflationary character of the postwar period. A natural question to ask, then, is whether there has been any compensating improvement in the behavior of output and employment, relative to earlier eras. In that regard, a mere glance at the unemployment data reported in Table 1-2 suggests that cyclical fluctuations may have been less severe in the postwar period than before. To examine the data in a slightly more informative way, let us consider the behavior of the difference between UN_t (the measured unemployment rate in year t) and UN_t^* (the "natural" or "normal" unemployment rate for that year). If real employment fluctuations have been less severe in the recent period, the absolute value of $UN_t - UN_t^*$ should on average be smaller than before. In fact, if we use estimates of UN_t^* developed by Gordon (1984), the average of annual values of $|UN_t - UN_t^*|$ over three major periods is as follows:

Time Period	Average Value of $|UN_t - UN_t^*|$
1890–1915	3.9
1920–1940	8.0
1946–1985	1.2

Thus this measure, in agreement with a simple glance at Table 1-2, suggests that fluctuations in output and employment have been *considerably* less severe in the postwar period than before. Thus it might be possible to argue that the change in monetary policy arrangements has on balance been desirable, even if it induced more inflation. But that position is debatable; whether the improvement in unemployment

[9] The three omitted phrases are as follows: (1) "and other essential considerations of national policy, with the assistance and cooperation of industry, agriculture, labor, and state and local government"; (2) "in a manner calculated to foster and promote free competitive enterprise and the general welfare"; and (3) "including self-employment for those able, willing, and seeking to work."

Table 1-2.   U.S. Unemployment Rates, 1890–1985

Year	UN_t (%)[a]	Year	UN_t (%)[a]	Year	UN_t (%)[a]
1890	4.0	1930	8.9	1960	5.5
1	5.4	1	16.3	1	6.7
2	3.0	2	24.1	2	5.6
3	11.7	3	25.2	3	5.6
4	18.4	4	22.0	4	5.2
5	13.7	5	20.3	5	4.5
6	14.4	6	17.0	6	3.8
7	14.5	7	14.3	7	3.8
8	12.4	8	19.1	8	3.6
9	6.5	9	17.2	9	3.5
1900	5.0	1940	14.6	1970	5.0
1	4.0	1	9.9	1	6.0
2	3.7	2	4.7	2	5.6
3	3.9	3	1.9	3	4.9
4	5.4	4	1.2	4	5.6
5	4.3	5	1.9	5	8.5
6	1.7	6	3.9	6	7.7
7	2.8	7	3.9	7	7.0
8	8.0	8	3.8	8	6.0
9	5.1	9	6.1	9	5.8
1910	5.9	1950	5.2	1980	7.2
1	6.7	1	3.3	1	7.6
2	4.6	2	3.0	2	9.7
3	4.3	3	2.9	3	9.6
4	7.9	4	5.6	4	7.5
5	8.5	5	4.4	5	7.2
6	5.1	6	4.1	6	7.0
7	4.6	7	4.3	7	6.2
8	1.4	8	6.8		
9	1.4	9	5.5		
1920	5.2				
1	11.7				
2	6.7				
3	2.4				
4	5.0				
5	3.2				
6	1.8				
7	3.3				
8	4.2				
9	3.2				

[a] UN_t denotes the unemployment rate for all U.S. workers, during year t. Data for 1900–1982 come from Gordon (1984, Table B-1); earlier values appear in *Historical Statistics of the United States* and more recent ones are reported in numerous publications.

behavior has been attributable to improved monetary policy is a leading unsettled issue in macroeconomics. Indeed, a major objective of this book is to develop the tools necessary for the reader to reach an informed conclusion of his or her own on that question.

1.3   The U.S. Monetary Experience of 1979–1982

Having briefly highlighted some contrasts between the pre– and post–World War II record, let us now consider a recent episode that has received considerable attention. As a result of the relatively severe inflation of the late 1970s, Volcker and other officers of the Fed became convinced during 1979 that to prevent an extremely unhealthy situation they would need to exercise tighter control over growth of the money stock than in previous years. To facilitate such control,[10] they publicly adopted on October 6, 1979, a new set of operating procedures, procedures that featured increased emphasis on a particular measure of bank reserves (i.e., nonborrowed reserves) and reduced emphasis on short-term interest rates. Their new procedures were supposed to be helpful to the Fed in achieving its targets for money supply growth—targets that it had been announcing since 1975 but failing to achieve in most years.

The practice of announcing these money supply targets, it should be explained, had been reluctantly adopted by the Fed at the insistence of the U.S. Congress.[11] As can be seen from Table 1-3, the targets were not highly precise. For the year ending with the fourth quarter of 1978, for example, the target consisted of a *range* of values for the money growth rate that extended from 4.0 to 6.5 percent. (The actual value turned out to be 7.2 percent in this year, as can also be seen from Table 1-3.) Given the modest degree of precision sought for, it appeared that the failure to achieve the official targets should in principle be correctible.

The new operating procedures begun in October 1979 were kept in place by the Fed until late 1982, with September 1982 usually regarded as the last month of the episode. Because so-called "monetarist" economists had for many years been recommending tighter money stock control as the best way of fighting inflation, and had often recommended operating procedures with a measure of bank reserves[12] as the

---

[10]   According, at least, to the Fed's public statements on the subject.
[11]   On this topic, see Weintraub (1978).
[12]   *Total* reserves, however, not the nonborrowed reserves measure actually emphasized by the Fed.

Table 1-3   Money Stock Growth Rates (percent)

Year Ending 4th Quarter of:	M1 Growth Rates[a]	
	Target Range	Actual Value
1976	4.5–7.5	5.8
1977	4.5–6.5	7.9
1978	4.0–6.5	7.2
1979	4.5–7.5	6.8
1980	4.0–6.5	6.9
1981	3.5–6.0	2.4
1982	2.5–5.5	9.0
1983[b]	4.0–8.0	10.3
1984	4.0–8.0	5.2
1985[c]	4.0–7.0	12.2
1986[d]	3.0–8.0	15.3

[a] Some adjustments to raw values have been made to reflect anticipated shifts into or out of NOW accounts. For the reason for these adjustments, and more detail concerning the figures, see Broaddus and Goodfriend (1984).

[b] In the second quarter of 1983 a new target range of 5.0–9.0 percent was set for the remaining half-year; the actual rate was 7.4 percent.

[c] During 1985 the target range was changed to 3.0–8.0 percent.

[d] During 1986 the M1 target was suspended.

key variable, this experience has frequently been termed a "monetarist experiment." Actually, for various reasons, that label is highly inappropriate.[13] But the episode did nevertheless constitute a policy experiment of a sort, and is therefore of considerable interest.

What, then, were the results of this experiment? In one respect the Fed's attempts were successful: by September 1982 the U.S. inflation rate had been reduced from around 11 or 12 percent (per year) to a magnitude in the vicinity of 4 or 5 percent. Other aspects of the outcome were not as planned, however, and were highly unpopular with the public and with most commentators. Of these undesirable side effects, four will be mentioned. First, short-term interest rates rose to levels unprecedented in U.S. history. Over the month of May 1981, for example, the 90-day Treasury bill rate averaged 16.3 percent. Second,

[13] In particular, monetarist prescriptions have typically stressed the importance of nearly constant money growth rates and the absence of activist attempts to vary these rates countercyclically. In fact, the Fed did not abstain from activism during 1979–1982 and—as we will see shortly—money growth rates were far from constant. For an elaboration on this argument, see Friedman (1983).

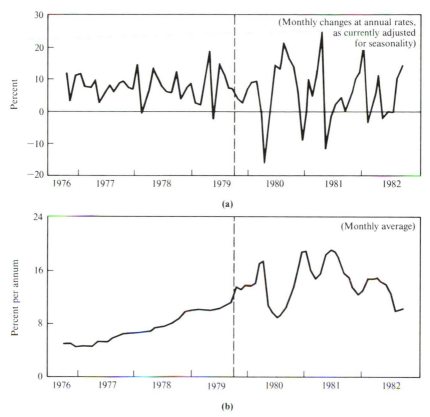

Figure 1-1.   (a) Growth rate of M1 money measure before and after October 1979. Source of primary data: Board of Governors, Federal Reserve System. (b) Federal funds rate before and after October 1979. SOURCE: Board of Governors, Federal Reserve System.

the extent of month-to-month *variability* of interest rates was greater than ever before. Third, in 1981 a recession began that was the most severe since the Great Depression of the 1930s; the nation's overall unemployment rate climbed over 10 percent in the second half of 1982. So while the economy was relieved—at least temporarily—of the inflationary pressures that it had been experiencing for about a decade, this relief was apparently[14] obtained at the cost of an unwelcome recession and the associated loss in output.

---

[14] The word *apparently* is inserted because a few economists would argue that the recession of 1982–1983 was not brought about by the monetary policy actions under discussion. The viewpoint of such economists is discussed in Section 9.7.

Perhaps the most interesting aspect of the episode, however, pertains to the fourth item on our list: the Fed did *not* succeed in improving its record of money stock control. Instead, the realized growth rates for the years ending in the fourth quarter of 1980, 1981, and 1982 were again outside the specified target range, as indicated in Table 1-3. And monthly values of the growth rate were highly variable, as can readily be seen from Figure 1-1. This is especially striking, of course, because the special operating procedures of 1979–1982 were designed precisely for the purpose of improving money stock control so as better to achieve the monetary growth targets!

The *facts* that we have just reported are not a matter of dispute—students of the episode agree that inflation came down, unemployment rose, interest rates became high and variable, and money stock targets were not met. What *interpretation* to place on the facts is, however, another matter. To some economists they suggest that it is unwise to pursue money stock targets, in part because of the putative unreliability of money demand behavior in an economy in which new payments practices and financial assets are constantly being developed.[15] To other economists, however, the experience illustrates how poorly the Fed's procedures were designed for money stock control and how dangerous it is to allow excessive money growth—and the inflation that it engenders—to become established in an economy.[16]

1.4   A Look Ahead

In the chapters that follow, we shall develop the theoretical and factual knowledge necessary to draw reasoned conclusions regarding issues—including, for example, the just-mentioned disagreement—relating to the conduct of monetary policy and the design of monetary institutions. The object will be more to enhance the reader's analytical skills than to reach specific conclusions, but the author's opinions will undoubtedly be apparent in several places.

The material begins in Chapter 2 with a discussion of the nature and role of money in a market economy, together with an introduction to the most important empirical measures of the money stock used in the United States. Also included is a section contrasting fiat-money and commodity-money *standards* and one on the significance of *legal tender* requirements. Chapters 3 and 4 are devoted to the demand for money

---

[15] For an expression of this view, see Blinder (1981) or Bryant (1983).

[16] These views are expressed by Brunner and Meltzer (1983) and Friedman (1983), among others.

and the supply of money, respectively, with the latter also including a preliminary analysis of the way in which the Fed attempts to control the U.S. money stock. Together, Chapters 1 through 4 constitute Part I of the book, a part that might be viewed as comprising the rudiments of monetary economics.

Part II of the book, which includes Chapters 5 through 10, concerns monetary macroeconomics—that is, macroeconomic analysis with a strong emphasis on monetary aspects. In Chapter 5 we review two models that have been extremely important in macroeconomic analysis and teaching over the last 40 years: the "classical" and "Keynesian" models. These two models can be used to provide various insights into the operation of actual economies, but they share the drawback of being essentially static (i.e., timeless) in nature. In Chapter 6, then, we begin the task of developing a framework for dynamic analysis. The first step is to consider situations in which some of the economy's variables are changing over time but at a constant rate. In particular, Chapter 6 is concerned primarily with steady, ongoing inflation—a process of steadily increasing prices. In Chapter 7 we turn to an analysis of inflation when its magnitude is not constant but is changing from period to period. As it happens, this generalization can be effected most easily for cases in which inflation is very severe, so part of Chapter 7 is devoted to a discussion of actual *hyperinflation* episodes that have occurred in Europe during this century. Some of the main concepts of dynamic analysis are introduced in this context.

Whenever variables are changing over time, the *expectations* held by individuals and firms about values in the future are important determinants of current demand and supply decisions. In the analysis of Chapter 7, a particular model of expectation formation is utilized. As it happens, however, that model—known as the model of adaptive expectations—is open to severe criticism. In Chapter 8, accordingly, we explain that criticism and then introduce a second hypothesis about expectations that is not open to the same criticism. The second hypothesis, known as the hypothesis of *rational expectations*, has been very important in recent macroeconomic discussions and is widely used today. Consequently, Chapter 8 provides a rather lengthy discussion of the concept and an introduction to the techniques of conducting formal analysis under conditions of rational expectations.

The analysis in Chapters 6–8 proceeds within a version of the classical model, a framework which implies that real output and employment are virtually independent of monetary policy actions. That assumption can be useful in developing an understanding of the basic nature of inflation, but must be reconsidered in the context of business cycle analysis for there are reasons to believe that, in reality, monetary policy actions have important effects on the cyclical behavior of real variables. The magnitude and nature of such effects are, however, matters that involve considerable disagreement among macro economists. Accordingly, in Chapter 9 we summarize today's leading alternative theories regarding real cyclical effects of monetary policy. As it happens, each of the theories possesses some empirical or analytical weakness, so it is unclear which model would be most useful for analysis of cyclical phenomena. A compromise model is, consequently, developed and exposited in Chapter 10. This model is designed to be compatible with the basic principles of economic theory, reasonably consistent with recent cyclical experiences of the United States, and comparatively easy to work with.

The last major portion of the book, Part III, stresses issues of monetary *policy*. In the setting of a dynamic model with rational expectations, analysis of policy options is conducted in a manner that differs from standard comparative static treatments. This difference is emphasized in Chapter 11, which takes up three specific policy issues that have concerned researchers in recent years. That discussion prepares the way for Chapter 12, which involves a topic of long-standing concern—the desirability of rules versus discretion in monetary policy—but in a new analytical form. Then Chapter 13 provides an extensive analysis of one particular type of a monetary rule, namely, a commodity-money standard. Since the version that has been most important historically featured gold as the monetary commodity, this chapter is entitled "The Gold Standard."

Recently, considerations involving trade and financial relations among nations have become increasingly important, even for the comparatively self-sufficient economy of the United States. Accordingly, Chapter 14 extends the macroeconomic analysis of Part II so as to be applicable to an open economy, that is, one engaged in international economic relationships. The analysis builds upon that of the preceding pair of chapters, as an international monetary system with fixed exchange rates entails adherence by each country to a particular monetary policy rule, while such a rule is in turn rather similar to a commodity-money standard. Our modeling of an open economy emphasizes, however, the currently relevant case of flexible (market determined) exchange rates.

In Chapter 15 several of the book's analytical points are illustrated by reference to actual occurrences in U.S. history, including some from the pre-1776 colonial era. The object here is not to provide a well-rounded monetary history of the nation but rather to concentrate on selected episodes that bear upon analytical points in enlightening ways. Enough of these episodes are considered, nevertheless, for the chapter to offer a coherent outline of the various monetary standards that have prevailed during the nation's history.

Finally, in Chapter 16 we discuss a specific and operational strategy for the conduct of monetary policy. This particular strategy has been promoted elsewhere by the present author, so there is no pretense that it represents the views of the profession in general. It is presented, rather, in the spirit of providing a response to the desire of many students for some concrete and constructive position regarding policy, rather than a mere string of criticisms. Whatever the reader's reaction may be to this proposal, its discussion provides an integrative review of several ideas developed elsewhere in the book.

Each chapter is accompanied by a few problems. These are of varying degrees of difficulty, but all are designed to illustrate significant points. In some cases the problems provide extensions or new applications of material covered in the text.

Problems

1. From figures reported in the most recent issue of the *Federal Reserve Bulletin*, determine the rate of growth of the M1 money stock over a six-month period ending (approximately) four months prior to the current date.
2. The Federal Reserve's annual reports to Congress are published in the *Federal Reserve Bulletin* each year, usually in the March issue. From the most recent report, determine which monetary aggregates are currently being targeted by the Fed.
3. What was the ratio of the WPI in 1940 to its level in 1840?

References

Blinder, Alan S., "Monetarism Is Obsolete," *Challenge* 24 (September–October 1981), 35–41.

Broaddus, Alfred, and Marvin Goodfriend, "Base Drift and the Longer Run Growth of M1: Experience from a Decade of Monetary Targeting," Federal Reserve Bank of Richmond, *Economic Review* 70 (November–December 1984), 3–14.

Brunner, Karl, and Allan H. Meltzer, "Strategies and Tactics for Monetary Control," *Carnegie–Rochester Conference Series on Public Policy* 18 (Spring 1983), 59–104.

Bryant, Ralph C., *Controlling Money: The Federal Reserve and Its Critics*. (Washington, D.C.: The Brookings Institution, 1983).

Friedman, Milton, "Monetarism in Rhetoric and Practice," Bank of Japan, *Monetary and Economic Studies* 1 (October 1983), 1–14.

Gordon, Robert J., *Macroeconomics*, 3rd ed. (Boston: Little, Brown and Company, 1984).

Weintraub, Robert E., "Congressional Supervision of Monetary Policy," *Journal of Monetary Economics* 4 (April 1978), 341–62.

Basic Concepts

2.1 The Functions of Money

Let us begin our discussion concerning the nature and functions of money by considering the workings of two hypothetical economies that are similar in most ways but different in one crucial respect. In each of these economies there exists a large number of individuals, each of whom produces only a few distinct goods—indeed, for simplicity, suppose that each person produces only one good. Each of these individuals desires to consume (at one time or another) quantities of a large number of different goods, but on any given day will want to make purchases of only a few. Suppose next that these people meet each other, when they go to make exchanges, in a random and unpredictable fashion. In most meetings, consequently, one or both of the individuals will have no desire to acquire the good that the other has to offer. In the words of J. S. Mill (1848): "A tailor, who has nothing but coats, might starve before he could find any person having bread to sell who wanted a coat: besides, he would not want as much bread at a time as would be worth a coat and the coat could not be divided." Clearly, in this economy people are forced to spend a large fraction of their time and energy in shopping about for exchange partners whose desires are such as to satisfy the condition, necessary for any trade to be made, of the so-called "double coincidence of wants."

In the second hypothetical economy, which is in other respects like the first, there exists a certain durable and transportable commodity that is generally acceptable in exchange for any other good. This special commodity is acceptable even by persons who have no wish for quantities of the commodity itself, precisely because they know it will be acceptable in exchanges with other people for other goods. Consequently, when going to make purchases, individuals carry with them not quantities of their own produce, but quantities of the special commodity that is generally acceptable. Their shopping problem is thereby drastically simplified; they need only to visit the locations of sellers of the products they desire that day. Those sellers will without question be glad to exchange their products for specified quantities of the special commodity—which is consequently referred to as this economy's *medium of exchange.* In this second economy, because of the existence of a generally acceptable medium of exchange, individuals are able to spend a much smaller fraction of their time and energy in shopping about. Consequently, they are able to use the released time and energy to produce greater quantities of goods and/or (as they choose) to enjoy increased quantities of leisure.

The first of the two hypothetical economies just described is one in which exchange is carried out by means of direct *barter* of goods and services, while the second, by contrast, features monetary exchange: the special medium-of-exchange commodity is termed *money.* Our comparison illustrates, then, the reason why money is used in actual economies, namely, because it facilitates transactions and thereby makes the individual members of the economy able to enjoy the consumption of greater aggregate quantities of goods and/or leisure. Thus the presence or absence of monetary exchange has important effects on the equilibrium quantities of the economy.

It should be noted, furthermore, that the saving in time and energy provided by the existence of a special monetary commodity does not depend on whether that commodity is intrinsically valuable (i.e., is desirable for consumption or useful in production). The monetary commodity might be paper tokens; all that matters from the point of view of saving time and energy is that it be generally acceptable in exchange. Indeed, there is one advantage to the use of paper or other intrinsically worthless material as the monetary commodity: no intrinsically valuable material is diverted away from consumption or productive uses.

There is a second important function provided by money in most actual economies, namely, that of serving as a *medium of account.*[1] If an economy includes N distinct commodities, there are $N(N-1)/2$ different relative prices denoting the ratios at which exchanges can be made for each pair of goods. Thus, if N is equal to (say) 10,000, the number of relative prices is 49,995,000. But if all transactions take

---

[1] It is often said that money serves as a *unit of account,* but that terminology is illogical since money is a tangible material, not a unit of measurement. Here we will say that the medium of account is the good some quantity of which serves as the unit of account (i.e., is used as the base for quoted prices). In nineteenth-century Britain, for example, gold was the medium of account while a quantity of gold called the "pound sterling" (approximately 0.2354 ounce) was the unit of account.

place through the intermediary of money, it is natural to express the prices of each of the 9999 other commodities in terms of money. In this case, knowledge of the 9999 money prices is all that is needed or useful for shoppers, a simplification that reflects the advantage of having a common unit of account.

There is no strict necessity, it should be recognized, for the same commodity to serve as the medium of exchange and as the medium of account. It would in principle be possible for prices in the United States to be quoted in terms of (say) ounces of copper, with U.S. currency continuing to serve as the medium of exchange. But each transaction would then have to be accompanied by an extra calculation; the quoted price in terms of copper would have to be converted into dollars before payment in U.S. currency would be made. Consequently, there is a strong tendency for the medium of exchange also to be used as the medium of account; unless there are special reasons why sellers would prefer to do otherwise, they will quote prices in terms of money (i.e., the medium of exchange).[2]

A third function of money is to serve as a *store of value*. Thus if someone wishes to save part of her current income for use at a future date, she can acquire money and hold it until the future date arrives, thereby "storing value" in the interval. There are many other assets, however, that serve as stores of value: bonds, stocks, real estate, and so on. Furthermore, money typically pays no interest to its holder, so is often inferior as a store of value to these other interest-bearing assets— even when the price level is not changing. This inferiority is increased, clearly, when money is falling in value (i.e., when the price level is rising) and decreased when it is rising in value. Consequently, there will be a tendency for less money to be held, other things equal, when the price level is rising (i.e., in times of inflation). This tendency will enter the discussion in many places in later chapters.

In summary, money typically serves three distinct roles: as a medium of exchange, as a medium of account, and as a store of value. Only the first of these is a distinguishing characteristic of money, however, for the medium-of-account role could conceivably fall to some other commodity, whereas there are many nonmonetary assets that serve as stores of value.

---

[2] On this topic see White (1984) and McCallum (1985). One reason why the medium of exchange might *not* be used as the medium of account occurs when the former is rapidly losing (or gaining) in value as time passes, making it difficult to know what prices to use for transactions that will be completed only in the distant future (e.g., loans). In other words, there will be some tendency for alternative media of account to arise when inflation or deflation is severe.

2.2 **Empirical Measures**

In the present-day economy of the United States, the principal medium of exchange is U.S. currency: coins and Federal Reserve notes ($1 bills, $5 bills, etc.).[3] Most empirical measures of the money stock also include, however, checkable deposits at banks and other financial institutions. There are various ways of arguing that this type of inclusion is appropriate. Our approach will rely on the fact that, given current regulations, a bank demand deposit of (say) $100 is a legal *claim* to $100 of U.S. currency: the deposit holder can demand payment from the bank in currency. Second, in part because they are claims to currency, deposits are very widely acceptable in exchange. Of course, a seller prefers not to be paid by check for very small transactions, but it is similarly true that sellers prefer not to be paid in coins or small bills for very large transactions, so that preference does not imply that deposits are not widely acceptable. It is a mistake, incidentally, to suggest that deposits are not generally acceptable simply because it is very hard to pay by check at certain times or in certain locations. This difficulty is usually attributable not to the seller's unwillingness to be paid in terms of bank deposits, but rather to his uncertainty as to the legitimacy of a check in its role as a device for transferring deposit balances.

In any event, the Federal Reserve compiles and publishes statistics on a measure of the U.S. money supply, a measure called M1, that is intended to reflect the medium-of-exchange concept of money. This M1 measure has been revised in recent years in response to changes in the types of deposits available. The composition of the current measure, and the magnitude of its components, are illustrated by the figures reported for some recent dates in Table 2-1. There it will be noted that the largest component is demand deposits, with currency and other checkable deposits each forming a substantial fraction of the whole, and travelers checks amounting to about 1 percent. Other checkable deposits (OCDs) are made up of NOW and ATS accounts, these letters standing for "negotiable order of withdrawal" and "automatic transfer service," respectively. These terms refer to deposit accounts that are in effect checkable yet earn interest, which is legally forbidden for ordinary demand deposits. NOW and ATS accounts represent claims to currency, however, from which transfers can readily be made. They are therefore appropriately treated as part of the medium of exchange.

---

[3] There are also some Treasury-issued notes in circulation, but the current quantities of these are so small that they can safely be neglected.

Table 2-1.   M1 Money Stock (billions of dollars)[a,b]

Component	Dec. 1984	Dec. 1985	Dec. 1986	Dec. 1987
Currency[c]	158.5	170.2	183.0	199.4
Demand deposits[d]	253.0	276.9	314.4	298.5
Other checkable deposits[e]	148.2	180.9	237.3	261.5
Travelers checks	4.9	5.5	6.0	6.5
Total	564.5	633.5	740.6	765.9

[a] Data from *Federal Reserve Bulletin*, June 1988.

[b] Monthly averages of daily figures (not seasonally adjusted).

[c] Currency outside the U.S. Treasury, Federal Reserve Banks, and vaults of commercial banks.

[d] Demand deposits at commercial banks and foreign-related institutions, other than deposits due to domestic banks, the U.S. government, and foreign banks or official institutions, less cash items in the process of collection and Federal Reserve float.

[e] Consists of NOW and ATS balances at all depository institutions, credit union share draft balances, and demand deposits at thrift institutions.

It is sometimes suggested that M1 magnitudes should in some way reflect the widespread use of credit-card transactions. The number to be included would in this case presumably be the sum over all credit-card holders of the credit limits—amounts that can be utilized without special negotiation. These amounts do not constitute unconditional claims to currency, however, but prenegotiated rights to borrow and repay. That a credit-card purchase does not itself constitute a transfer of the medium of exchange, as a purchase paid for by check does, is evidenced by the need for the purchaser later to repay the credit-card company and for the seller to collect from the credit-card company. For these reasons, it is more appropriate to think of credit-card arrangements as ones that reduce the quantity of the medium of exchange needed to effect a given volume of transactions, rather than as additions to the stock of the medium of exchange.

A second measure of the money stock that has played a significant role in economic analysis is M2, which adds to M1 the following items: savings account deposits, small-denomination time deposits, money market mutual funds and deposit accounts, overnight repurchase agreements, and overnight Eurodollars. The breakdown among these components is illustrated in Table 2-2. As this M2 measure does not correspond closely to the medium-of-exchange concept of money, yet is substantially less inclusive than a measure of all highly marketable assets would be, it might be wondered *why* it has played a significant role. The answer that this author would give, perhaps idiosyncratically, is that, by chance, historical records existed in the early 1960s that

Table 2-2. Alternative Monetary Measures (billions of dollars)[a]

	Dec. 1984	Dec. 1985	Dec. 1986	Dec. 1987
Total reserves	40.9	47.2	57.6	59.0
Monetary base	202.7	220.8	243.6	261.2
M1	564.5	633.5	740.6	765.9
Savings deposits	283.0	298.5	367.1	410.0
Small time deposits	885.1	881.5	855.0	914.5
MMM funds	230.2	241.0	292.4	310.7
MM deposits	416.8	513.6	572.5	525.2
M2	2373.2	2573.9	2821.5	2914.6
M3	2991.4	3211.0	3508.3	3677.4
L	3532.7	3841.4	4153.0	4343.5

[a] Data from *Federal Reserve Bulletin*, June 1988.
[b] Not seasonally adjusted.

permitted compilation of long time series for M2 but not M1. At that time, moreover, the study of U.S. monetary history was given a major stimulus by Milton Friedman and Anna Schwartz in their monumental book, *A Monetary History of the United States, 1867–1960* (Princeton, N.J.: Princeton University Press, 1963). In this book, Friedman and Schwartz compiled and used M2 figures in part because they could not do so for M1. Specifically, the M2 concept, which was somewhat different from the current one, consisted of currency in circulation plus all deposits at commercial banks. The available records included commercial bank deposits but did not distinguish between demand and time deposits, as would have been necessary for the compilation of a long series on M1. Subsequently, Friedman used M2 in his empirical work, and his enormous personal impact on the profession led to the popularity of the (somewhat illogical) M2 concept.

There are other measures called M3 and L, even more inclusive than M2, that are complied and published by the Fed. Instead of them, however, we shall emphasize a measure that is *less* inclusive, even compared to M1, but is of greater analytical importance than M3 or L. This measure is the stock of "high-powered money," alternatively termed the "monetary base." The stock of high-powered money consists basically of currency outside banks plus bank reserves, the latter including both currency held by banks and banks' deposits with the Federal Reserve. What this magnitude represents is currency plus claims to currency that are not offset by private liabilities. A demand deposit does not represent net wealth for the private sector of the economy, for the deposit-holder's asset is exactly matched by the bank's liability. Currency and reserves, by contrast, are net wealth to the private sector, since the Fed is not a private institution.

A second reason for emphasis on the monetary base is that its magnitude is an extremely important determinant of the quantity of M1 money in existence. Thus, if the Fed takes an action that increases the monetary base, it is typically the case that the quantity of M1 will increase. Indeed, a 1 percent change in the base will tend to produce approximately a 1 percent in M1. Since the magnitude of M1 is slightly over 2.5 times as great as that of the base, it then follows that a $1000 change in the base will tend to result in a change in M1 of slightly over $2500. This type of reaction does not occur mechanically, however, but is the result of purposeful behavior on the part of banks and money holders. Thus a much more extensive discussion is needed for understanding of the process; a beginning is provided in Chapter 4.

We conclude the present discussion by noting that there is in fact a minor difference, ignored in the previous sentences, between the monetary base and the stock of high-powered money. In particular, the former concept does (and the latter does not) involve adjustments designed to take account[4] of changes in reserve requirements, that is, the regulations that legally oblige banks (and other depository institutions) to hold reserves at least equal to certain required levels, with these levels specified in relation to deposit liabilities.

2.3 Monetary Standards: Fiat Versus Commodity Money

In the preceding section it was mentioned that the basic medium of exchange in the United States consists of U.S. coins and paper Federal Reserve notes. It should be emphasized that these items of currency do not constitute claims on gold or any other precious metal, or indeed on any commodity—U.S. currency is simply *fiat* money, money "by arbitrary order or decree."[5] This point deserves emphasis because it calls attention to the important distinction between fiat-money and commodity-money systems.

In its purest form, a commodity-money system is one in which the medium of exchange (and medium of account) is a good that would be valuable even if it were not used as money. Such a system may be put in

---

[4] From the perspective of effects on the normal ratio of M1 to the base.

[5] The coins, as well as the notes, are much more valuable than is the material from which they are made.

place by government decree or may arise naturally as the outcome of evolutionary experiments by private citizens and organizations. The government may or may not coin the designated material and may or may not discourage the use of other potential media of exchange. The fundamental characteristic of a commodity-money system is that the value of money—the inverse of the price level—is simply the price, determined by supply and demand, of a good whose production is costly. In particular, in full competitive equilibrium the value of the monetary commodity will be equal to the marginal cost (in terms of commodities in general) of producing that commodity. Thus in such a system the price level is determined by the technological conditions relating to production (perhaps abroad) of the commodity in conjunction with the factors governing its demand (these including but not limited to the desire to hold certain quantities of the medium of exchange).

In a less pure form of a commodity-money system, the commodity itself will not circulate as the medium of exchange; instead, token (e.g., paper) claims to the monetary commodity will serve as the actual circulating medium. In such a system it remains true, nevertheless, that the value of the monetary commodity (or its claims!) will not differ in equilibrium from the marginal cost of production of the commodity. Thus an economy can use paper claims to gold as its circulating medium, and yet have the price level determined as if gold coins were the actual money. Indeed, this type of arrangement prevailed in the United States, with occasional interruptions, from its inception until 1933. Under such an arrangement, or the more pure type mentioned before, the economy is said to be on a commodity-money *standard*. The most famous example of such a standard is, of course, the international *gold standard* that prevailed widely from the mid-nineteenth century until 1914.

Under a fiat-money system, by contrast, the circulating medium is paper or some such material that has extremely low costs of production and very low value in nonmonetary uses. Furthermore, it does not represent claims to other commodities of value. Now for something to be useful as a medium of exchange, its value must obviously be great in relation to the difficulty in transporting it from place to place. Therefore, since its value must also be consistent in some sense with supply–demand equilibrium, it follows that the medium of exchange must be clearly distinguished from other items made of paper (or whatever), and its supply artificially controlled in some fashion. The usual method is to have the quantity in existence controlled by the nation's monetary authority—controlled so as to keep the purchasing power of a unit of money very high in comparison to its cost of production. With this type of system, the economy is not on a commodity-money standard. What the standard amounts to, in this case, depends upon the precise way in which the monetary authority exercises its control of the quantity of money.

It may be of some incidental interest to mention that the framers of the U.S. Constitution almost certainly intended for this nation to have a commodity-money standard. In support of that opinion, it may be noted that there are only two clauses referring to monetary arrangements in the Constitution. First, Section 8 declares that "The Congress shall have Power ... to borrow Money on the Credit of the United States; ... to coin Money, regulate the Value thereof, and of foreign Coin, and fix the Standard of Weights and Measures." Second, Section 10 decrees that "No State shall ... coin Money; emit Bills of Credit; make any Thing but gold and silver Coin a Tender in Payment of Debts. ..." From these statements it seems clear that the presumption—apparently thought hardly worth mentioning—was that the basic money of the nation would be gold and/or silver coin. Indeed, from the way in which the Section 8 statement was combined with one pertaining to establishment of standards for weights and measures, it would appear that the writers regarded the two main tasks of monetary management to be (first) the selection of some quantity of a metal to be the unit of account and (second) the provision for the physical production of coins. Be that as it may, the analysis of a commodity-money system will be developed in a subsequent chapter and some of the experiences of the United States with metallic money will be discussed at length.

2.4   Legal Tender

In the current age of fiat money, it is easy to overestimate the role of government. For example, although it is certainly true that a government can give a very strong impetus to the acceptance of a certain entity as money, the government will not have complete control over the public's views as to what is "generally acceptable," and it is these views that will determine what prevails as the medium of exchange. If a government produces a paper currency and declares it to be money, but then mismanages this currency so that its value fluctuates wildly, it may happen that the citizens of the nation in question abandon that currency in favor of a metallic medium of exchange or even a paper currency issued by some other government. Except in an extremely authoritarian state, what will be used as money is not entirely under the control of the authorities.

As a related matter, it is not correct to view *legal-tender* legislation as the essential determinant of what serves as the media of exchange. Historically, legal-tender laws have typically had as their purpose the promotion of a secondary medium of exchange when a primary medium such as gold was already well established. The secondary medium would be denominated in units with the same name as that pertaining to the primary money (e.g., dollars) and the government would declare them to be legal tender in the following sense: any debts denominated *in these units* could be satisfied by offering payment of the secondary money; a creditor who rejected such payment, demanding payment in the primary money, would then receive no assistance from the court system in collecting. Now certainly such laws will tend to make a secondary money acceptable. But, even so, they do not, in most cases, require that loan contracts be written *only* in terms of legal tender. Contracts written in terms of other media will therefore also be enforceable. So legal-tender laws do not quite guarantee that some asset with legal-tender status will be the economy's medium of exchange.

A leading example of the nonprimacy of legal-tender stipulations is provided by the 1797–1821 Napoleonic Wars period in Britain, when convertibility of Bank of England notes was suspended. These paper notes became that nation's medium of exchange, even though they lacked legal-tender status.[6] Such status is helpful in making something become a generally acceptable medium of exchange, but it is neither necessary nor sufficient.

2.5 Money, Credit, and Financial Intermediation

From the discussion so far, it is probably apparent that this book is principally concerned with issues of *monetary* theory and policy, as contrasted with issues of *credit* conditions or the operation of financial markets. The distinction between issues of these two types is one that is frequently overlooked and/or misrepresented in writings by journalists and policymakers. Accordingly, a few pages can usefully be devoted to an explanation of the distinction and our lack of emphasis on financial matters.

---

[6] Here we are exaggerating somewhat to make a point; while Bank of England notes were not officially given legal-tender status during the episode, for practical purposes they might as well have had such status. For a description of the 1797–1821 episode, the reader is referred to Cannan (1925).

Let us begin by being explicit about the nature of monetary issues. Although other conceptions are possible, what is meant here by the term is issues regarding the determination of *nominal variables*, their movements over time, and their influences on real variables.[7] As a prominent example, consider the price level. It is a nominal variable and its rate of change is the inflation rate, so price level and inflation rate determination are both monetary issues. Furthermore, since the inflation rate exerts an important influence on interest rates charged on loans, the determination of interest rates is also a monetary issue.[8] Finally, our concept of monetary issues pertains to any effects that the monetary policy authority might have on real aggregate variables such as the level of employment or output.

Next we need to consider the meaning and measurement of "credit." In this regard, the main point is that any loan constitutes an extension of credit from a lender (or creditor) to a borrower (or debtor). Quantitatively, the amount of additional credit extended by any particular loan agreement is the same as the additional amount of debt—negative credit—taken on. If both parties are considered, therefore, the total volume of credit created by any loan will amount to zero. To obtain a usable measure of the aggregate volume of credit outstanding in a economy, consequently, it is necessary to limit coverage in some way. Thus it is necessary either to consider the position of only some limited group of market participants—some specific "sector"—or else to exclude from the calculated total some of the negative credits (debts) involved.

Clearly, there are many ways in which such totals could be calculated, depending on the sectors included, the extent of consolidation, and the types of financial instruments (loan contracts) recognized. To focus on any particular total seems, accordingly, quite arbitrary. Nevertheless, it may be of some interest to consider briefly one certain measure, not because it is the "proper" measure of credit, but because it is a measure that has received a large amount of attention during recent years. The measure is termed "domestic nonfinancial debt" and is defined as the total quantity of debt in the form of "credit market instruments" owed by households, nonfinancial businesses, and units of government.[9] Included as credit market instruments in the construc-

---

[7] Nominal variables are ones expressed in monetary units, such as dollars, dollars per bushel, or dollars per bushel per year, whereas real variables are expressed in physical units, such as bushels or bushels per year. Interest rates do not fall neatly into either category.

[8] This statement refers to so-called "nominal" interest rates, which (as mentioned above) do not fall into the category of nominal variables.

[9] This variable has been discussed most prominently in a series of articles by Benjamin Friedman; see, for example, Friedman (1983). In addition, the variable is currently listed among those that the Fed considers in its annual reports to Congress, although it is officially a variable that is "monitored" rather than "targeted."

tion of this measure are the following types of obligations: U.S. Treasury securities, Federal agency securities, tax-exempt securities, corporate and foreign bonds, mortgages, consumer credit, bank loans (not elsewhere classified), open-market paper, and other loans.[10] Figures compiled for some recent years are reported in Table 2-3 by type of debtor. From these figures it can be seen that the household and nonfinancial business sectors each have more debt outstanding than the federal government, whereas the latter has about four times as much debt as state and local governments. The table does not show, however, that households (unlike nonfinancial businesses) hold substantial amounts of credit market assets.

A related concept that has also received a considerable amount of attention is the volume of *financial intermediation*. This term refers to the loan activities of private financial institutions, firms that are called financial intermediaries because they "intermediate" between surplus spending units (ultimate lenders) and deficit spending units (ultimate borrowers). One measure of the volume of financial intermediation is provided by the sum of credit market claims (as defined above) that are held by intermediary firms. Some figures relating to this measure are reported in Table 2-4. There it will be seen that commercial banks provided about 36 percent of the volume of intermediation in 1986, with the remainder coming from nonbank financial intermediaries.

The importance of financial intermediaries in the U.S. economy has been stressed by many writers. An influential summary of the economic role of these institutions was provided by Tobin (1963, pp. 410–11):

> The essential function . . . is to satisfy simultaneously the portfolio preferences of . . . borrowers, who wish to expand their holdings of real assets . . . beyond the limits of their own net worth . . . [and] lenders, who wish to hold part or all of their net worth in assets of stable money value with negligible risk of default. . . . Financial intermediaries typically assume liabilities of smaller default risk and greater predictability of value than their assets. . . . The reasons that the intermediation of financial institutions can accomplish these transformations between the nature of the obligation of the borrower and the nature of the asset of the ultimate lender are these: (1) administrative economy and expertise in negotiating, accounting, appraising, and collecting; (2) reduction of risk per dollar of lending by the pooling of independent risks, with respect both to loan default and to deposit withdrawal; (3) government guarantees of the

---

[10] The measure does not, it should be said, represent either net or gross loans from the financial sector (i.e., banks and nonbank financial firms including insurance companies, pension funds, and savings institutions) to the nonfinancial sectors—even when foreign complications are ignored. Instead, the measure includes some loans between members of the nonfinancial sectors (e.g., mortgage loans from one household to another).

Table 2-3.   Domestic Nonfinancial Debt ($ billions, end of year)

	1967	1972	1977	1982	1987
Households	388	586	989	1657	2810
Nonfinancial business	371	617	1023	1703	2958
State and local government	117	181	243	323	554
Federal government	279	341	573	992	1959
Total	1155	1725	2828	4675	8281

Data from Board of Governors of the Federal Reserve System, *Flow of Funds Accounts, First Quarter 1988.*

Table 2-4.   Credit Market Claims Held by Private Financial Institutions ($ billions, end of year)

Claims Held by:	1967	1972	1977	1982	1986
Commercial banks	359	575	925	1478	2173
Savings institutions	205	335	594	809	1283
Insurance and pension funds	248	329	558	990	1544
Other financial intermediaries	53	99	160	408	946
Total	864	1338	2237	3685	5947

Data from Board of Governors of the Federal Reserve System, *Flow of Funds Accounts, Financial Assets and Liabilities, Year-End, 1963–1986.*

liabilities of the institutions and other provisions . . . designed to assure the solvency and liquidity of the institutions.

For these reasons, intermediation permits borrowers who wish to expand their investments in real assets to be accommodated at lower rates and easier terms than if they had to borrow directly from the lenders. . . . Therefore, any autonomous increase . . . in the amount of financial intermediation in the economy can be expected to be, *ceteris paribus*, an expansionary influence. This is true whether the growth occurs in intermediaries with monetary liabilities—i.e., commercial banks—or in other intermediaries.

From the foregoing statement, as well as general consideration of the role of intermediaries, it should be clear that financial intermediaries (and financial markets more generally) are of enormous importance for the efficient functioning of a developed economy. If their activities were severely disrupted, the flow of funds from lenders to borrowers would be seriously impaired and major macroeconomic consequences would probably ensue. How, then, can it be sensible to discuss monetary economics with little attention devoted to the workings of financial markets? That question warrants discussion, especially in light of this book's specialized focus.

The question's answer is, however, fairly straightforward. It rests basically on the fact that in making their borrowing and lending decisions, rational households (and firms) are fundamentally concerned with goods and services consumed or provided at various points in time. They are basically concerned, that is, with choices involving consumption and labor supply in the present and in the future. But such choices must satisfy budget constraints and thus are precisely equivalent to decisions about borrowing and lending—that is, supply and demand choices for financial assets. Thus, for example, a household that chooses to consume this year in excess of this year's income, equivalently chooses to borrow (or to draw down its assets) to the required extent. Consequently, there is no need to consider *both* types of decisions explicitly. The practice adopted in this book is to focus attention on consumption/saving decisions rather than on borrowing/lending decisions, letting the latter be determined implicitly. In adopting this modeling convention, we are not taking any radical position but are merely making use of an analytic device that is highly traditional in macroeconomics.

There is, moreover, a second point that is germane to our lack of emphasis on financial markets and institutions. This point stems from the fact that, in making their demand and supply decisions, rational households and firms are concerned with real (as opposed to nominal) variables. They care, that is, about the *quantities* of goods and services acquired or supplied in the present and in the future, not the dollar magnitudes involved. This basic postulate of neoclassical analysis will be familiar to all students of economics in the context of demand–supply choices of an atemporal type. The theory of consumer choice, for example, is concerned entirely with quantities and relative prices.[11] But there is no reason why the postulate should be any less appropriate for intertemporal decisions, that is, decisions involving choices between consumption (or labor supply) in the present and in the future. So, since these choices are equivalent to decisions about financial assets, it follows that rational households and firms are concerned with the real (price-level-deflated) magnitudes that they buy and sell of corporate bonds, Treasury bills, pension-fund rights, insurance claims, and so on.

But when it is recognized that these supplies and demands are

---

[11] It warrants emphasis that standard microeconomic analysis rests on the assumption that households and firms are ultimately concerned only with real variables; its basic results would be overturned if (for example) utility functions were assumed to include nominal variables.

formulated in real terms, it becomes clear that there is no *necessary* connection between financial and monetary issues. The ratio of domestic nonfinancial debt to GNP, for example, is a real variable that may be independent of monetary influences. The financial sector of the economy may be extremely important, but so is the transportation sector (for example). If the latter were to break down, the flow of goods from sellers to buyers would be seriously impaired and major macroeconomic consequences would ensue. But that does not imply that there is any close or necessary connection between monetary and transportation issues. Essentially the same reasoning applies with regard to the financial sector of the economy.[12]

From the perspective just expressed, it is seriously misleading to discuss issues in terms of possible connections between "the financial and real sectors of the economy," to use a phrase that appears occasionally in the literature on monetary policy. The phrase is misleading because it fails to recognize that the financial sector *is* a real sector. The proper issue of concern, instead, is the possibility of connections between "the monetary and real sectors of the economy."

In light of the preceding statement, a final word of clarification may be useful. In this section we have formulated and emphasized a distinction between monetary and nonmonetary issues. But this emphasis should not be interpreted as a presumption that real variables are independent of monetary variables or that monetary policy actions are without effect on real variables. That is a *possibility* admitted by our distinction but not an implication. On the contrary, our analysis will include a lengthy consideration of the extent of monetary policy effects on real variables and the nature of the mechanism that produces such effects. This consideration, which appears in Chapters 9 and 10, needs to be rather lengthy because the topic is one that is not firmly established. On the contrary, it is among the most unsettled and important of all topics currently being explored by researchers.

Problems

1. What was the U.S.–U.K. exchange rate in 1900 (i.e., the dollar price of a pound)?
2. Consider a hypothetical society in which all market transactions are

---

[12] It applies even though banks are involved with both monetary and financial issues, because banks are owned and operated by people who care about real magnitudes.

carried out by means of a nationwide computerized network of accounts; there is no currency. Prices in this economy are expressed in terms of "ingots," an ingot being a certain specified quantity of high-purity steel. Individuals hold their financial wealth primarily in the form of ownership shares in mutual funds, which themselves hold shares in various producing firms. The accounts of the different mutual funds are linked by the nationwide network. To make a purchase in this economy, the buyer keys her share-account number into the accounting network while the seller enters his number and the details of the transaction—price and quantity of the goods purchased. The buyer's share holdings in her mutual fund are then debited by the appropriate amount and the seller's are credited.

a. What is the medium of account in this economy?

b. What is the unit of account?

c. What is the medium of exchange?

d. Is this a monetary economy?

3. From some convenient source of U.S. monetary statistics, find the volume of demand deposits in December 1980. What accounts for the change between that month and December 1984?

4. Comment critically on the following passage, which comes from a famous article in the *Quarterly Journal of Economics* (February 1937, pp. 215–16):

> ... our first step must be to elucidate more clearly the functions of money.
>
> Money, it is well known, serves two principal purposes. By acting as a money of account, it facilitates exchanges without its being necessary that it should ever itself come into the picture as a substantive object. In this respect it is a convenience which is devoid of significance or real influence. In the second place, it is a store of wealth. So we are told, without a smile on the face. But in the world of the classical economy, what an insane use to which to put it! For it is a recognized characteristic of money as a store of wealth that it is barren; whereas practically every other form of storing wealth yields some interest or profit. Why should anyone outside a lunatic asylum wish to use money as a store of wealth?

5. In Section 2.1 it is mentioned that there are many assets other than money that serve as stores of value. Determine what fraction of wealth is in fact held in the form of money by the household sector of the U.S. economy. (A recommended source of information is the Federal Reserve Board's annual publication *Balance Sheets for the U.S. Economy*.) Repeat this exercise for the nonfinancial corporate business sector.

References

Cannan, Edwin, ed., *The Paper Pound of 1797–1821*, 2nd ed. (London: P. S. King & Son, 1925).

Friedman, Benjamin M., "The Roles of Money and Credit in Macroeconomic Analysis," in *Macroeconomics, Prices, and Quantities*, James Tobin, ed. (Washington, D.C.: The Brookings Institution, 1983).

Friedman, Milton, and Anna J. Schwartz, *A Monetary History of the United States, 1867–1960.* (Princeton; N.J.: Princeton University Press, 1963).

Jevons, W. Stanley, *Money and the Mechanism of Exchange.* (London: King, 1875).

McCallum, Bennett T., "Bank Deregulation, Accounting Systems of Exchange, and the Unit of Account: A Critical Review," *Carnegie–Rochester Conference Series on Public Policy* 23 (Autumn 1985), 13–45.

Mill, John Stuart, *Principles of Political Economy*, Book III. (London: John W. Parker, 1848).

Niehans, Jürg, *The Theory of Money.* (Baltimore: Johns Hopkins University Press, 1978).

Tobin, James, "Commercial Banks as Creators of 'Money'," in *Banking and Monetary Studies*, Deane Carson, ed. (Homewood, Ill.: Richard D. Irwin, Inc., 1963).

White, Lawrence H., "Competitive Payment Systems and the Unit of Account," *American Economic Review* 74 (September 1984), 699–712.

Wicksell, Knut, *Lectures in Political Economy*, Vol. 2. (London: Routledge & Kegan Paul, 1935).

3

The Demand for Money

3.1 Informal Discussion

The purpose of this chapter is to develop an understanding of the determinants of the quantity of money demanded by private agents (i.e., the amount they choose to hold at a point in time). To anyone except an economist, this may sound like a peculiar idea; doesn't everyone always want as much money as possible? But the answer to this hypothetical question is, of course, "no." To someone experienced in the economist's ways of thought, it will readily be recognized that there is an implied choice problem which involves the following consideration: for a given amount of wealth, individuals will normally wish to hold only a fraction of it in the form of money, with the remainder being held in the form of other assets—bonds, stocks, houses, cars, and so on. Almost anyone could be holding more money, more of the medium of exchange, at the present time if he chose to hold less of his wealth in these other forms.

In fact, the surprising thing from one point of view is that individuals hold any money at all. For it pays no interest—at least currency does not—while there are other assets that do pay positive interest. Why, then, hold "barren" money? But from our discussion in Chapter 2, it is clear that this point of view is excessively limited. In particular, it takes account only of pecuniary matters and thereby neglects the most important aspect of money—that it helps to facilitate transactions. But, as we have seen, someone who holds an adequate quantity of money is able to conduct her business—do her "shopping"—with a smaller expenditure of time and energy than one who tries to carry out her transactions without use of the medium of exchange. Consequently, the topic at hand involves an optimization problem—that of balancing the expected transactional benefits of holding an additional unit of money against the cost of doing so, which is the extra interest forgone.

From simply thinking about the tradeoff in this way, we can easily deduce the main characteristics of the demand for money by an individual at a point in time. First, since the purpose of holding money is to facilitate planned transactions, more money will be held the greater is the volume of transactions planned. Second, since it is the real quantities of goods and services that people care about, not their nominal values, the relevant quantity of money demanded will be expressed in real (i.e., price deflated) terms. That is, the behavioral relationship to be studied relates real money balances demanded to real transactions planned. Third, since the drawback to holding money—the cost—is the interest that is sacrificed, the (real) quantity willingly held will be smaller the higher is the rate of interest on alternative assets.

These three properties can be expressed formally in terms of a function relating the quantity of real money demanded by a typical person at time t, M_t/P_t, to her planned spending during period t, y_t, and the prevailing rate of interest on some relevant asset, R_t. Letting L denote the function, we then assume that the person's money demand behavior satisfies

$$\frac{M_t}{P_t} = L(y_t, R_t). \tag{1}$$

Because the left-hand-side variable is written as it is, this relation satisfies the second property mentioned in the preceding paragraph. The first and third properties concern the direction of response of the left-hand-side variable to y_t and R_t, respectively. For them to be satisfied, L must be increasing in y_t and decreasing in R_t. Let us then complete our specification by assuming that the function L possesses partial derivatives, and that the partial derivative with respect to (w.r.t.) y_t, denoted $L_1(y_t, R_t)$, is positive while the partial w.r.t. R_t, denoted $L_2(y_t, R_t)$, is negative. Or, to put it more briefly, we assume that $L_1 > 0$ and $L_2 < 0$.

Now, while we have expressed the conclusions of our reasoning about money demand in a somewhat formal way, the reasoning itself has been highly informal. It would accordingly seem to be desirable to work out some analysis in terms of a more explicit and specific optimizing model—one that is more concrete about the nature of alternative assets, transactional benefits from money holding, and so on. As it happens, there is a quite simple and highly specific model that is presented in most textbooks on macroeconomics or monetary theory, the Baumol–Tobin inventory model.[1] That model is *so* specific, however, that its assumptions seem highly artificial and almost unrelated to reality. For completeness we describe the Baumol–Tobin model in Section 3.6. But for our main discussion of money demand, it seems preferable to focus on a different model, one that is just as explicit as the Baumol–Tobin model but more general (i.e., less specific). The lessons it teaches are the same, but some restrictiveness is avoided by taking this more general approach.

3.2 A Formal Model

Consider a hypothetical household that seeks at time t to maximize the multiperiod utility function:

$$u(c_t, l_t) + \beta u(c_{t+1}, l_{t+1}) + \beta^2 u(c_{t+2}, l_{t+2}) + \cdots. \tag{2}$$

Here c_t and l_t are the household's consumption of goods and leisure, respectively, during period t. Note that at time t the household is concerned about its consumption of goods and leisure in future periods, as well as in the present. The function $u(c, l)$ is increasing in both c and l; formally, we assume that the partial derivatives u_1 and u_2 are both positive. In addition, we assume that these partials, which reflect marginal utilities, decrease with c and l; in particular, we assume that $u_{11} < 0$ and $u_{22} < 0$.[2] The parameter β in (2) is a discount factor that is positive but smaller than unity. Thus the household has positive time preference[3] and "discounts the future" in the sense that the utility it receives in t from a given c_t, l_t combination is greater than from the same combination if planned for $t + 1$: if $c_{t+1} = c_t$ and $l_{t+1} = l_t$, then $\beta < 1$ implies that $u(c_t, l_t) < \beta u(c_{t+1}, l_{t+1})$.

In making its choices, the household is of course restricted by its budget constraint. In fact, it faces a budget constraint currently in t and knows that it will also face such constraints in future periods $t + 1$, $t + 2$, ... To keep matters as simple as possible, we assume that the household receives in each period real income in the amount y, with

---

[1] That model was developed by Baumol (1952)) and Tobin (1956). Clear expositions are included in Barro (1984, Chap. 5) and Dornbusch and Fischer (1984, Chap. 8), among others.

[2] Here u_{11} is shorthand notation for $\partial^2 u / \partial c^2$ and u_{22} for $\partial^2 u / \partial l^2$. Our assumptions on u also include the stipulation that it be "well behaved," which implies that corner solutions will not be chosen for either c_t or l_t in any period.

[3] We can use $\beta = 1/(1 + \rho)$ to define the time preference parameter ρ, as in Barro (1984). Then $\rho > 0$ implies that $\beta < 1$.

this amount unaffected by the household's choices. The household does, however, have significant choices to make with regard to its borrowing or lending of wealth. Suppose that in t it can borrow or lend at the interest rate R_t, these loan agreements lasting for just one period. Notationally, let B_t be the nominal quantity of loans made ("bonds" purchased) by the household in t (which expire in $t + 1$). This formulation permits borrowing; if B_t is a negative number, the household is borrowing to that extent. Note, finally, that the household begins period t with assets in the amount $B_{t-1} + M_{t-1}$.

Given these assumptions, the household's budget constraint for period t alone can be written as follows:

$$P_t y + M_{t-1} + (1 + R_{t-1})B_{t-1} = P_t c_t + M_t + B_t. \tag{3}$$

Here the left-hand side (abbreviated l.h.s.) totals the resources (in nominal terms) available to the household from current income, money brought into the period, and bonds purchased (loans made) in the past. Similarly, the right-hand side (r.h.s.) totals expenditures on consumption and bonds during t, plus money balances held at the end of the period. Similar constraints will also be faced in each succeeding period. To take account of those constraints, first note that the constraint for $t + 1$ can be written as

$$B_t = \frac{P_{t+1}(c_{t+1} - y) + M_{t+1} - M_t + B_{t+1}}{1 + R_t}. \tag{4}$$

Now the latter can be used to eliminate B_t from (3). That brings in B_{t+1}, but then a similar step can be used to eliminate B_{t+1}, and so on. By successive eliminations of this type, we can finally arrive at the following equation:

$$\begin{aligned}
(1 + R_{t-1})B_{t-1} = {} & [P_t(c_t - y) + (M_t - M_{t-1})] \\
& + (1 + R_t)^{-1}[P_{t+1}(c_{t+1} - y) + (M_{t+1} - M_t)] \\
& + (1 + R_t)^{-1}(1 + R_{t+1})^{-1}[P_{t+2}(c_{t+2} - y) \\
& + (M_{t+2} - M_{t+1})] + \cdots.
\end{aligned} \tag{5}$$

This single equation then describes the household's entire intertemporal budget constraint, incorporating the constraints for each single period, when the planning horizon is infinite.[4]

---

[4] For a similar development, see Barro (1984, pp. 83–88). It should be said that formulation (5) assumes that the present value of B_T approaches zero as $T \rightarrow \infty$.

Next, we bring in the medium-of-exchange role of money by assuming that to acquire its consumption goods[5] the household must expend time (and energy) in shopping. The amount of time (and energy) so spent depends positively on the volume of consumption but, for any given volume, is reduced by additional money holdings. The reason, of course, is that these holdings facilitate transactions in the manner described in Chapter 2. It is the real quantity of money that matters in this regard; with higher prices, greater nominal amounts of money are needed for given real consumption quantities.

Now, the greater the time (and energy) spent in shopping, the smaller the amount left over for leisure. Thus the argument of the preceding paragraph indicates that leisure in period t, l_t, will be negatively related to consumption and positively related to real money holdings. [We are, as suggested by (3), holding constant the amount of labor performed by the household.] Let us then formalize that idea by assuming that the relationship can be expressed in terms of a function, ψ, as follows:

$$l_t = \psi(c_t, m_t). \tag{6}$$

Here $m_t = M_t/P_t$ is real money holdings.[6] The direction of dependence of l_t on c_t and m_t suggests that we would have $\psi_1 < 0$ and $\psi_2 > 0$, in notation that should by now be familiar. The general notion of diminishing marginal effects, moreover, suggests that $\psi_{11} > 0$ and $\psi_{22} < 0$.

We now have the household's situation specified in enough detail to permit the desired analysis. The household's object at t is to choose c_t, M_t, and B_t values, subject to the constraint (5), so as to maximize the value of

$$u\left[c_t, \psi\left(c_t, \frac{M_t}{P_t}\right)\right] + \beta u\left[c_{t+1}, \psi\left(c_{t+1}, \frac{M_{t+1}}{P_{t+1}}\right)\right] + \cdots, \tag{7}$$

---

[5] Formally, our model recognizes only one type of consumption good, a feature that appears to be inconsistent with our explanation (in Chapter 2) of the use of money, since the latter presumes that households each consume a large number of distinct goods. These notions can be formally reconciled, as explained by Lucas (1980), by assuming that there are many goods but that conditions for the construction of a composite commodity are satisfied. This strategy permits us to think sensibly about a monetary economy with many goods without worrying about relative price changes, or changes in the composition of consumption bundles, which are irrelevant to most of the important issues in monetary theory.

[6] It might be that the real money held at the start of t, rather than at the end, is the relevant magnitude. In that case the theory would be much the same as here presented, but slightly more awkward in appearance. (Actually, some average value of M over the period might be even more appropriate.) The theory would then include as a special case the "cash-in-advance" specification used by Lucas (1980) and in much recent theoretical research.

where we have substituted (6) into (2). To carry out the maximization problem, let us formulate a Lagrangian expression L_t as follows:[7]

$$
\begin{aligned}
L_t = u\left[c_t, \psi\left(c_t, \frac{M_t}{P_t}\right)\right] + \beta u\left[c_{t+1}, \psi\left(c_{t+1}, \frac{M_{t+1}}{P_{t+1}}\right)\right] + \cdots \\
+ \lambda_t\{(1 + R_{t-1})B_{t-1} - [P_t(c_t - y) + (M_t - M_{t-1})] \\
- (1 + R_t)^{-1}[P_{t+1}(c_{t+1} - y) + (M_{t+1} - M_t)] - \cdots\}.
\end{aligned}
\tag{8}
$$

Then by maximizing with respect to λ_t as well as the actual choice variables, we in effect impose the constraint (5) by way of the first-order condition $\partial L_t / \partial \lambda_t = 0$.

The maximization problem at hand requires in principle that we compute the partial derivatives $\partial L_t / \partial c_{t+j}$ and $\partial L_t / \partial M_{t+j}$ for $j = 0, 1, 2,$ ... as well as $\partial L_t / \partial \lambda_t$; set all of these equal to zero; and solve the resulting equations for the implied values of c_{t+j} and M_{t+j}. For the purpose of obtaining our money demand function, however, we need only to find $\partial L_t / \partial c_t$ and $\partial L_t / \partial M_t$. Doing so and setting the resulting expressions equal to zero, we have

$$
\frac{\partial L_t}{\partial c_t} = u_1[c_t, \psi(c_t, m_t)] + u_2[c_t, \psi(c_t, m_t)]\psi_1(c_t, m_t) - \lambda_t P_t = 0 \tag{9}
$$

and

$$
\frac{\partial L_t}{\partial M_t} = \frac{u_2[c_t, \psi(c_t, m_t)]\psi_2(c_t, m_t)}{P_t} - \lambda_t + \lambda_t(1 + R_t)^{-1} = 0. \tag{10}
$$

Eliminating $\lambda_t P_t$ from these two equations gives

$$
\begin{aligned}
u_2[c_t, \psi(c_t, m_t)]\psi_2(c_t, m_t) = [1 - (1 + R_t)^{-1}]\,\{u_1[c_t, \psi(c_t, m_t)] \\
+ u_2[c_t, \psi(c_t, m_t)]\psi_1(c_t, m_t)\}.
\end{aligned}
\tag{11}
$$

Careful inspection of the latter will reveal that although it is somewhat complicated, this necessary condition for household optimality involves only three variables: c_t, m_t, and R_t. Assuming that it can be uniquely solved for $m_t = M_t/P_t$, we then rewrite (11) as

$$
\frac{M_t}{P_t} = L(c_t, R_t). \tag{12}
$$

Now this equation is just like (1), the one we set out to rationalize, except that c_t appears instead of y_t. But even that difference is only apparent, for it is clear that in the present model c_t *is* the relevant

---

[7] For a very readable explanation of the Lagrangian technique, see Baumol (1977, Chap. 4).

transaction variable (i.e., the relevant measure of expenditure volume), which is what y_t stands for in (1).

As a theoretical justification for (1), the foregoing development is lacking in one way: we have not shown that c_t enters positively and R_t negatively on the right-hand side of (12). In fact, it is not true that those signs [i.e., $L_1 > 0$ and $L_2 < 0$ in (12)] are strictly implied for all functions satisfying the assumptions that we placed on u and ψ in (2) and (6). But the appropriate signs will, in fact, obtain except in cases with extreme and unrealistic specifications for u and/or ψ.

To illustrate this fact, and provide an example of a relationship like (12), let us consider a case with specific functional forms for $u(c, l)$ and $\psi(c, m)$. In particular, suppose that

$$u(c_t, l_t) = c_t^{1-\alpha} l_t^{\alpha} \tag{13}$$

and

$$\psi(c_t, m_t) = c_t^{-a} m_t^{a} \tag{14}$$

with α and a positive fractions ($0 < \alpha < 1, 0 < a < 1$). Then we have the partials

$$
\begin{aligned}
u_2 &= \alpha c_t^{1-\alpha} l_t^{\alpha-1} = \alpha c_t^{1-\alpha} (c_t^{-a} m_t^{a})^{\alpha-1}, \\
\psi_2 &= a c_t^{-a} m_t^{a-1}, \\
u_1 &= (1-\alpha) c_t^{-\alpha} l_t^{\alpha} = (1-\alpha) c_t^{-\alpha} (c_t^{-a} m_t^{a})^{\alpha}, \\
\psi_1 &= -a c_t^{-(a+1)} m_t^{a}.
\end{aligned}
\tag{15}
$$

Using these, we find that equation (11) becomes

$$
\begin{aligned}
a\alpha c_t^{1-\alpha} & c_t^{a(1-\alpha)} m_t^{a(\alpha-1)} c_t^{-a} m_t^{a-1} \\
&= [1 - (1+R_t)^{-1}]\{(1-\alpha) c_t^{-\alpha} c_t^{-a\alpha} m_t^{a\alpha} \\
&\quad - a\alpha c_t^{1-\alpha} c_t^{a(1-\alpha)} m_t^{a(\alpha-1)} c_t^{-(a+1)} m_t^{a}\}.
\end{aligned}
\tag{16}
$$

Simplifying the latter and solving for m_t, we finally obtain

$$m_t = \frac{a\alpha}{1 - \alpha - a\alpha} c_t \left(1 + \frac{1}{R_t}\right). \tag{17}$$

Now the latter will have the appropriate signs—a positive partial derivative w.r.t. c_t and a negative partial w.r.t. R_t—provided that the term $a\alpha/(1 - \alpha - a\alpha)$ is positive; and that will be the case as long as $1 - \alpha > a\alpha$. Looking back at (13) and (14), we see that this condition requires merely that a change in consumption has a *direct* effect on utility that is stronger than its *indirect* effect working through the shopping-time impact on leisure. Such would certainly be the case for any realistic specification of numerical values for α and a. So our formal model does result in a money demand function of the type postulated in (1).

Before continuing, however, we should pause to note that the "money demand function" that we have derived is in fact not a *demand function* in the proper sense of that term. Strictly speaking, that is, a demand function for an individual specifies the quantity chosen of some commodity as a function of variables that are exogenous to this person—taken by him as given beyond his control. Our relation (12) does not accord with that description since the "explanatory" variable c_t is not exogenous but is chosen by the household. It would, therefore, be more appropriate to refer to (12)—or to (1)—by some other name. In fact, the term "portfolio balance relation" is sometimes used for such equations. But the practice of calling relations like (12) money demand functions is extremely common. Indeed, this practice is so widespread that attempting to avoid it would probably cause more confusion than it would eliminate. Accordingly, we shall continue to use that terminology, improper though it may be.

Let us conclude this section by emphasizing the economic, as opposed to mathematical, content of our derivation of the money demand relation (12). That relation, it should be recalled, is based entirely upon the two first-order optimality conditions (9) and (10), which we rewrite for convenience as follows:

$$u_1(c_t, l_t) + u_2(c_t, l_t)\psi_1(c_t, m_t) = \lambda_t P_t \tag{9'}$$

$$\frac{u_2(c_t, l_t)\psi_2(c_t, m_t)}{P_t} = \lambda_t\left(1 - \frac{1}{1 + R_t}\right). \tag{10'}$$

Consequently, the money demand function (12) is simply the relationship between m_t, c_t, and R_t that holds when both (9') and (10') are satisfied. To appreciate the economic content of these, we begin by observing that the first term on the left-hand side of (9') is the utility provided by an extra unit of consumption, while the second term is the utility provided by an extra unit of leisure multiplied by the loss of leisure necessitated by an extra unit of consumption (a negative number). So the right-hand side of (9'), $\lambda_t P_t$, is equal to the *net* marginal utility of consumption, which is the utility obtained directly from an incremental unit of consumption minus the cost (in utility units) of the leisure sacrificed as a result of the extra consumption. We can then divide $\lambda_t P_t$ by P_t, which is the number of units of money that correspond to one unit of the consumption good, and find that λ_t is the net utility provided by an incremental unit of money holdings.

Turning now to (10'), we see that the left-hand-side numerator is the utility of an extra unit of leisure times the addition to leisure provided by an incremental unit of real money holdings. Division by P_t then makes this pertain to an incremental unit of nominal money holdings. On the right-hand side we have λ_t, the net marginal utility of a unit of money, times $[1 - 1/(1 + R_t)]$. But the latter is approximately equal to R_t, so equation (10′) can be interpreted as follows:

$$\left(\begin{array}{c} \text{utility from extra leisure provided} \\ \text{by an incremental unit of money held} \end{array} \right)$$

$$= \left(\begin{array}{c} \text{utility from an} \\ \text{extra unit of money} \end{array} \right) \left(\begin{array}{c} \text{interest earnings forgone} \\ \text{per unit of money} \end{array} \right).$$

In other words, the gain in leisure from holding an additional unit of money must, for optimality to obtain, equal the interest lost, both sides being evaluated in utility units. This is, of course, the type of equality "at the margin" that is characteristic of optimal choices in general, in the manner made familiar by basic microeconomic analysis.

3.3 Uncertainty

In Section 3.2 our discussion proceeded as if the values of *future* variables such as R_{t+1}, P_{t+1}, R_{t+2}, and so on, were known by the household when making decisions at time t. Such knowledge is, of course, impossible for anyone to have; they can only form expectations (which may be wrong) about the future. But our simplified way of conducting the analysis is probably harmless in the present context. The reason is that relations like (9) and (10) would hold in terms of expected values in the more realistic case in which the household is assumed to form expectations about future values and to maximize the expected value of (2). Furthermore, as long as the household has knowledge of the true *current* values of R_t and P_t, which is not so unreasonable to assume, its choices will continue to conform exactly to (9) and (10), even though future values can only be expected, not known. In this case, therefore, the derivation of (11) and subsequent equations would proceed just as above.[8]

---

[8] These statements would not remain true if the model were altered so as to make it the household's real money holdings at the *start* of period t, rather than at the end, that affect the shopping time required for its consumption during t. Indeed, the simplicity of the analysis of Section 3.2 would be diminished significantly by that one change. In actuality, of course, some average of the money holdings at various instants during the period would probably be more appropriate than either the start-of-period or end-of-period value, but recognition of this fact would complicate the analysis unduly without providing significant additional insight. For that reason, the formulation that yields the simplest analysis—of the type under consideration—has been adopted for use in this book.

Some other writers' descriptions of money demand behavior emphasize the existence of alternative assets whose rate of return (for current holdings) is uncertain,[9] in contrast to the case considered here in which R_t is known at t. In developed countries like the United States, however, there exist widely traded assets whose nominal returns are virtually free of uncertainty over relevant planning periods (such as a month, quarter, or year). In our analysis, R_t is to be thought of as the rate of interest on such assets. Furthermore, we are proceeding as if there were only this one type of relevant interest-earning asset. Consequently, the analysis itself should be thought of as pertaining to the division between money and (riskless) bonds of the portion of the household's wealth that is not devoted to risky assets. The other type of analysis, by contrast, is about the division of the household's wealth between this (riskless) portion and other assets that have risky returns but promise larger expected returns. The two types of analysis are about different subjects, with the one presented here being more specifically related to the demand for *money*.

The foregoing argument indicates that the recognition of uncertainty would not invalidate the development in Section 3.2, even though that development neglects uncertainty. This argument should not be interpreted as a claim, nevertheless, that uncertainty has nothing to do with money demand. In that regard, it is worthwhile to recall our discussion in Section 2.1 of the basic reason why individuals use a medium of exchange in making transactions. There the discussion involved uncertainty concerning the meeting of fruitful exchange partners when trying to conduct transactions by means of barter. In that sense, then, uncertainty lies at the very heart of money demand theory. But the *type* of randomness involved, that of making meetings from minute to minute or hour to hour that by chance satisfy the double coincidence of wants, is relevant at a much finer level of temporal and spatial disaggregation than is appropriate for monetary analysis of the macroeconomic type with which we are concerned.[10]

3.4 Empirical Money Demand Functions

In this section we switch gears. Here our aim is not theoretical but empirical. It is to describe the general approach that has been taken by researchers attempting to obtain econometric estimates of money de-

---

[9] The classic analysis of this type is that of Tobin (1958). For a textbook description of the approach, together with a judgment similar to the one presented here, see Dornbusch and Fischer (1984, pp. 262–63). See also Barro and Fischer (1976, pp. 139–40).

[10] On this topic, too, see Barro and Fischer (1976, pp. 149–55).

mand functions. Such studies have naturally focused *not* upon individual households—the behavior of any single household is of little interest in and of itself—but on the aggregate behavior of households in general. Indeed, these studies have typically considered money demand by the entire private sector of the economy, presuming (or hoping) that the behavior of firms and other organizations will be qualitatively similar—in terms of relevant variables, directions of response, and so on—to that outlined by models such as the one of Section 3.2.[11]

In our discussion it will be useful to begin with the example of a money demand function provided by equation (17), which we rewrite in the following simplified form:

$$\frac{M_t}{P_t} = \frac{\gamma c_t}{R_t}. \tag{18}$$

Here we have used γ to denote the composite parameter $a\alpha/(1 - \alpha - a\alpha)$ and have approximated $1 + (1/R_t)$ with $1/R_t$. The justification for the latter step comes from recognizing that in our model R_t is expressed in fractional, not percentage, units. A 10 percent interest rate is denoted, for example, by $R_t = 0.10$. Furthermore, we are concerned primarily with time periods that are measured as years, quarters, or months. Thus the relevant values of R_t will be figures like 0.1 or 0.025 or 0.0008, and the implied values of $1/R_t$ will be large in comparison to 1.0 which permits us to neglect the latter.

Next let us take (natural) logarithms of (18), obtaining

$$\log \frac{M_t}{P_t} = \log \gamma + \log c_t - \log R_t. \tag{19}$$

This last form is highly convenient for manipulation, as it is *linear* in the variables $\log M_t$, $\log c_t$, and $\log R_t$. Given this form, furthermore, it becomes natural to consider the following generalization, in which the coefficients attached to $\log c_t$ and $\log R_t$ are permitted to be different from $+1$ and -1, respectively:

$$\log \frac{M_t}{P_t} = \gamma_0 + \gamma_1 \log y_t + \gamma_2 \log R_t. \tag{20}$$

Here we have used y_t rather than c_t to denote the transaction variable and have denoted $\gamma_0 = \log \gamma$. In comparison to (19), the more general

---

[11] Obviously, our model would have to be revised to be applicable to a firm. But it would still be true that money would be held to facilitate transactions of some sort—no longer represented by consumption—and that higher rates of interest would induce lower levels of real money holdings.

form of (20) corresponds to the use of more general functional forms for $u(c, l)$ and $\psi(c, m)$ than those given in (13) and (14). Yet (20) retains the highly attractive feature of being linear and therefore easy to comprehend and to work with.[12]

When studying aggregate time series, there will be two obvious reasons for observed discrepancies from relations such as (20). First, different individual households (or other agents) would certainly have different values for behavioral parameters such as γ_0, γ_1, and γ_2, even if they all had the same functional form, and the relative importance of these different agents will change somewhat over time. Second, the values of each individual agent's parameters will likewise be prone to occasional changes as time passes. Thus even under the most favorable conditions conceivable, there will be sources of error in aggregate studies: discrepancies between actual and predicted values of M_t. What is assumed by researchers conducting these studies is that these sources of error are predominantly *random*, in which case they can be accounted for by a random "disturbance term" for each observation.

An example of an estimated money demand function of the form (20), based on annual observations for the period 1897–1958 for the U.S. economy, is as follows:[13]

$$\log \frac{M_t}{P_t} = \underset{(1.00)}{8.40} + \underset{(0.077)}{0.27} \ \log y_t - \underset{(0.095)}{0.32} \ \log R_t. \tag{21}$$

Here the figures in parentheses are standard errors, that is, estimates of standard deviations of the distribution of the estimators. The variables are measured as follows:

M_t = currency plus demand deposits (middle of year)
P_t = price index for consumer expenditures
y_t = real (deflated) net national product
R_t = 20-year corporate bond yield

Also, M_t and y_t are measured per member of the population. These variables correspond reasonably well to the concepts in our model, except that a long-term interest rate is used instead of the yield on some short-term security.[14] It should be pointed out, in addition, that the estimates in (21) were obtained not by ordinary least-squares regression, but by a technique designed to correct for serial correlation of the disturbances.

---

[12] It is worth mentioning that the Baumol–Tobin model is a special case of (20), one with $\gamma_1 = \frac{1}{2}$ and $\gamma_2 = -\frac{1}{2}$.
[13] These estimates were made by Lieberman (1980).
[14] It is also true that NNP figures do not include intermediate transactions and are in that way inappropriate. Such figures are typically used, nevertheless.

The signs of the parameter estimates in (21) are as the theory implies (i.e., $\gamma_1 > 0$ and $\gamma_2 < 0$) and the equation fits the data moderately well: the fitted residuals have a standard deviation of 0.04. But the estimated value of γ_1 is smaller than most studies suggest and the estimated value of γ_2 is larger (in absolute value). This leads to the thought that, while study of a long time period is desirable in many ways, it seems unlikely that the same behavioral parameters would have obtained in 1897 as in 1958! Consequently, most recent studies have used only data from the postwar (i.e., post–World War II) era. Let us then consider that type of study.

In working with postwar data, it has been standard practice to use quarterly, instead of annual, observations. This gives the researcher more data points to work with and a better chance of learning something from short-lived episodes. There are also disadvantages to using quarterly data, however, the most prominent of which is the apparent need to take account of sluggish adjustments by money holders to fluctuations in the determinants of money demand.[15] The most popular way of handing that matter has been to assume that agents behave as posited by the "partial adjustment" scheme. According to the latter, basic theoretical considerations such as those of Section 3.2 explain the determinants not of each period's money demand, but of a variable denoted m_t^* that reflects what (real) money demand would be if there were no adjustment costs.[16] Then the actual values of m_t are related to m_t^* by the partial adjustment formula

$$\log m_t - \log m_{t-1} = \lambda(\log m_t^* - \log m_{t-1}), \qquad (22)$$

where λ is a measure (with $0 \le \lambda \le 1$) of the speed of adjustment: $\lambda = 1$ represents full immediate adjustments, while smaller values represent slower, more sluggish, adjustments. Assuming that $\log m_t^*$ is given by an equation of the form (20), one can substitute (20) into (22) and obtain

$$\log m_t = \lambda\gamma_0 + \lambda\gamma_1 \log y_t + \lambda\gamma_2 \log R_t + (1 - \lambda) \log m_{t-1} + \varepsilon_t, \qquad (23)$$

where ε_t is the stochastic disturbance term that has been present in our discussion but not in our previous equations. The parameters of (23) can then be estimated by ordinary least-squares regression (OLS) or whatever technique the econometrician considers appropriate.[17]

---

[15] Another is the need to make some decision about the treatment of seasonality in the data series.

[16] This variable m_t^* is sometimes called the "desired" value of m_t, but that terminology is somewhat misleading (as it seems to suggest that agents' actions are inconsistent with their own choices).

[17] More details are provided in an influential paper by Goldfeld (1973).

Another (minor) complication is introduced by the widely held belief that the economy's transaction technology, represented by the ψ function in our formal model, is changing over time as innovations and improvements are made in the computer and telecommunications area. If such considerations are important, as they almost certainly are, a relation like (23) would not remain the same as time passes. One very simple way to take account of this fact is to add to (23) a trend term $\lambda\gamma_3 t$, where the variable is time itself and $\lambda\gamma_3$ is the associated coefficient. The value of γ_3 should then be negative, to reflect the need for smaller real money balances (for given y_t and R_t values) as time passes and technology improves.

As it happens, estimates of the formulation just described give rise to residual errors that are highly serially correlated (implying autocorrelated disturbances). The simplest way of taking account of that statistical problem is to work with first-differenced data. Thus if one adds $\lambda\gamma_3 t$ to (23), uses the same equation for period $t - 1$, and subtracts the latter from the former, the result will be

$$\Delta \log m_t = \lambda\gamma_1 \, \Delta \log y_t + \lambda\gamma_2 \, \Delta \log R_t$$
$$+ \, (1 - \lambda) \, \Delta \log m_{t-1} + \lambda\gamma_3 + \Delta\varepsilon_t, \tag{24}$$

where $\Delta \log m_t = \log m_t - \log m_{t-1}$, and so on. In this equation the $\lambda\gamma_0$ term has disappeared and $\lambda\gamma_3$ enters as it is equal to $\lambda\gamma_3 t - \lambda\gamma_3(t - 1)$. The main point, however, is that the disturbance term in (24) is $\Delta\varepsilon_t$ rather than ε_t. It turns out in practice that the former suffers from serial correlation to a much smaller extent than the latter, suggesting that the econometric estimates obtained with differenced data should be more reliable.

Equations similar to (24) have been estimated by a number of economists. Results obtained by the present writer, using data for 1952.2–1979.4, are as follows:[18]

$$\Delta \log m_t = \underset{(0.061)}{0.247} \, \Delta \log y_t - \underset{(0.004)}{0.010} \, \Delta \log R_t$$
$$+ \, \underset{(0.005)}{0.463} \, \Delta \log m_{t-1} - \underset{(0.0007)}{0.0015} \tag{25}$$

$$R^2 = 0.401 \qquad SE = 0.0055 \qquad DW = 2.11.$$

These values imply parameter estimates as follows: $\lambda = 0.537$, $\gamma_1 = 0.460$, $\gamma_2 = -0.019$, and $\gamma_3 = -0.0028$. Those figures suggest that money demand is less responsive to movements in y_t and R_t than most

---

[18] These use real GNP as the measure of y_t, the 90-day Treasury bill rate for R_t, and M1 deflated by the GNP deflator for m_t.

economists (including the author) would expect to be the case. That is one of several reasons for believing that attempts to provide reliable econometric evidence on money demand behavior have not yet been highly successful.[19] Another is that the econometric results are somewhat less satisfactory when estimated with data sets that include observations for years after 1979; residual variability is greater and an unexplained shift in the value of γ_3 seems to have occurred. (Estimates of γ_1 and γ_2 are not strongly affected when observations are included through 1986.) To some extent these difficulties can be rationalized by reference to regulatory changes, including the imposition and removal of selective credit controls in 1980 and the gradual relaxation of restrictions that made it difficult (in earlier years) for banks to pay interest on checkable deposits. Important issues remain unresolved, however, and significant research continues to be undertaken.

In conclusion, mention should be made of an alternative formulation that is often used instead of (20) to represent the basic money demand relation for m_t^*. That formulation is

$$\log m_t^* = \gamma_0 + \gamma_1 \log y_t + \gamma_2 R_t, \tag{26}$$

which differs from (20) in that the interest rate itself, rather than its log, is used as the relevant cost variable. In several contexts, theoretical analysis can be streamlined by the adoption of (26) instead of (20). Empirically, there is little basis for choice between the two formulations: reestimation of (24) with ΔR_t in place of $\Delta \log R_t$ leads to results that are neither better nor worse than those in (25). Consequently, we shall use specification (26) below in places in which its form is especially convenient.

3.5 Velocity

In discussions of monetary policy, one frequently encounters the term "velocity," which we have not yet mentioned. Although there are various concepts of velocity,[20] the one most frequently used is just the ratio

---

[19] One specific problem concerns the need for the partial adjustment specification; it is hard to believe that wealth reallocations between money and other assets would not be made more promptly than most estimates of λ suggest. Goodfriend (1985) argues that the actual reason for these estimates is not slow adjustments, but errors in measuring the transaction variable.

[20] These concepts differ in using alternative measures of the transaction variable, y_t. For more discussion, see Barro (1984, pp. 110–13) and, especially, Dornbusch and Fischer (1984, pp. 269–74).

of nominal income to the money stock,

$$V_t = \frac{P_t y_t}{M_t}. \tag{27}$$

Clearly, by using $M_t/P_t = L(y_t, R_t)$ in (27), we can obtain

$$V_t = \frac{y_t}{L(y_t, R_t)}. \tag{28}$$

This shows velocity to be dependent upon both y_t and R_t, unless y_t happens to cancel out between the numerator and denominator, as it would if money demand were of the special form $M_t/P_t = y_t\phi(R_t)$. The empirical estimates presented above suggest that M_t/P_t depends less strongly on y_t than this special form implies, however, so velocity is probably positively related to real income and is almost certainly related (positively) to the level of interest rates.

The foregoing considerations indicate that velocity is not cyclically constant and that to understand its behavior is no simpler than understanding the behavior of money demand. There is in logic, then, no strict necessity for using the concept at all. In fact, however, many leading monetary economists do find it convenient to utilize the concept, and for that reason it is necessary to understand its meaning, so as to be able to read the writings of those analysts. It will not be used frequently in the present work but will appear in a modified form in Chapter 16.

3.6   The Baumol–Tobin Model

It was mentioned above that there exists a theoretical model of money demand behavior that appears frequently in textbooks and other treatments of monetary economics. This model, which was developed by Baumol (1952) and Tobin (1956), is rather different in detail from the "shopping-time" model of Section 3.2 but is quite similar in spirit. The reader's understanding of money demand analysis should be enhanced, therefore, by a familiarity with the Baumol–Tobin model. In this section we begin with a description of the latter and then provide some comments on its relation to the empirical evidence and to the theoretical approach of Section 3.2.

In the Baumol–Tobin analysis it is assumed that the typical household's expenditure during a given period is c in real terms or cP in nominal terms. Also, its purchases are spread evenly in time throughout the period, and these purchases must be paid for entirely with money. Now suppose that the household's income for the period is received,[21] at the start of the period, in the form of an interest-earning deposit—a "savings account"—that pays interest at the rate R per period but which cannot be used for making purchases. In addition, assume that each "withdrawal" of money from this account or payment into it—that is, each transfer between the earning asset and money— costs the household the lump-sum amount δ in real terms (or δP in nominal terms). This cost is perhaps best thought of as involving an expenditure of time and/or energy, rather than an explicit charge, but that interpretation is not essential.

In the setting described, the household obtains cash for the period's purchases by making one withdrawal in the amount cP, or two withdrawals in the amount $cP/2$, or three in the amount $cP/3$, and so on. Such withdrawals are evenly spaced, so with a steady outflow of money for purchases the household's cash holdings will be as shown in the appropriate panel of Figure 3-1. The different cash-management strategies imply, as a glance at Figure 3-1 will indicate, different *average* levels of money holdings over the period. In particular, if the household makes n withdrawals per period, its average level of money balances during the period will be

$$M = \frac{cP/n}{2}. \tag{29}$$

Thus the larger the number of transactions (withdrawals) per period, the smaller will be the level of money balances held on average over the period.

We now ask: What is the *optimum* number of transactions for the household? This can be determined by noting that the relevant tradeoff is between the cost of making transactions and the opportunity cost of forgone interest that occurs when wealth is held as cash rather than in the interest-earning deposit. In particular, for n withdrawals the transaction cost over the period will be $n\delta P$ in nominal terms, while the interest forgone will be RM. Using (29), the transaction cost can alternatively be expressed as $n\delta P = (cP/2M)\,\delta P = c\,\delta P^2/2M$. Consequently, the magnitude of the two relevant costs together is

$$RM + \frac{c\,\delta P^2}{2M}. \tag{30}$$

To find the household's minimum-cost cash management strategy, we

---

[21] The model would work the same, but the explanation would be slightly more awkward, if the income were received in the form of money. Then the household for which $n = 2$, for example, would make one deposit into the earning asset (keeping $Pc/2$ in the form of cash) and one withdrawal—two transfers—and would have an average money balance of $Pc/4$, just as it would with the assumption of the text.

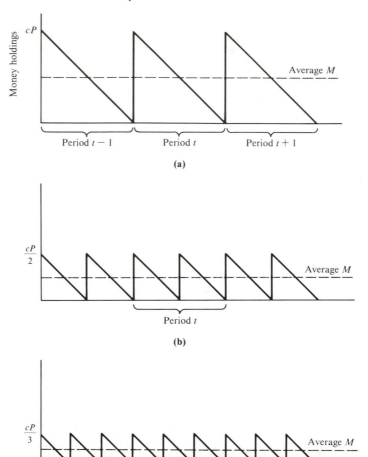

(a)

(b)

(c)

Figure 3-1

can then differentiate this expression with respect to M and set the result equal to zero.[22] Doing so, we obtain

$$R - \frac{c\,\delta P^2}{2M^2} = 0,\qquad(31)$$

---

[22] Since the second derivative is $\delta P^2 c/M^3$, which is necessarily positive, a minimum will be obtained.

and solving the latter for M/P yields

$$\frac{M}{P} = \sqrt{\frac{c\,\delta}{2R}}. \tag{32}$$

Introducing time-period subscripts and using exponential notation, we then have

$$\frac{M_t}{P_t} = \left(\frac{\delta}{2}\right)^{0.5} c_t^{0.5} R_t^{-0.5} \tag{33}$$

as the money demand formula implied by the Baumol–Tobin model. Taking logarithms, this formula can equivalently be expressed as

$$\log \frac{M_t}{P_t} = 0.5 \log \frac{\delta}{2} + 0.5 \log c_t - 0.5 \log R_t. \tag{34}$$

Inspection shows that the latter is a special case of equation (20), which verifies the claim of footnote 12.

At this point it is necessary to mention that there is actually a flaw—a logical error—in the foregoing derivation. The problem is that the number of transactions per period by a household, n, should be constrained to be an integer value—one cannot make (say) 1.37 trans-actions in a single period. But by using (29) to eliminate n in our derivation of the total cost expression (30), and then taking the deriva-tive with respect to M, we have implicitly treated n as if it were a continuous variable. Thus the final formula (32) cannot be exactly correct.

The main practical implication of this problem is, as it happens, one that makes the Baumol–Tobin model more nearly consistent with the empirical evidence than formula (34) would suggest. The point is that recognition of the integer restriction on n leads to the conclusion that many households will choose to make only one withdrawal, as in the first panel of Figure 3-1.[23] In this case, the household's average money balance during the period will be $M = cP/2$, which features no re-sponse at the margin to changes in R.[24] The implied expressions analo-gous to (33) and (34) are then $M_t/P_t = 0.5c_t$ and $\log (M_t/P_t) = \log 0.5 + \log c_t$. Thus the coefficient corresponding to γ_1 in expression

---

[23] Under the interpretation of footnote 21, these households will make either one or zero transfers, depending on whether or not they deposit part of their income in the interest-earning account. Either way, their average money holdings will agree with the formula given in the next sentence.

[24] There is also no response at the margin to changes in R for some households for which n is greater than 1. But a few such households will make substantial responses as they move to different values of n. For more detail concerning these issues, see Barro and Fischer (1976) and references provided therein.

(20) is 1.0, rather than 0.5, and the coefficient corresponding to γ_2 is zero rather than -0.5. So with some households falling into this category of making the fewest possible number of transfers between money and the interest-earning deposit, the measured economy-wide value for γ_1, which will be an average of the values for all households, will be greater than the value 0.5 given in (34). Similarly, the measured aggregate value for γ_2 will be closer to zero than -0.5. In fact, this is what has been found in the econometric studies mentioned above.[25]

3.7　Conclusions

Before leaving the subject of money demand, it is important to emphasize that the two theoretical models here described—the shopping-time model of Section 3.2 and the Baumol–Tobin model of Section 3.6—are quite similar in terms of their fundamental precepts.[26] Specifically, both of these models presume that money is held (even though higher-yielding assets are available) because it helps to facilitate transactions: in Section 3.2 increased money holdings serve to reduce the time and energy that must be devoted to shopping, while in Section 3.6 money is an absolute necessity for making purchases. And in each case there are ways of getting by with smaller average money holdings when interest opportunity costs are high. Consequently, both models lead to demand functions in which real money balances are positively related to the volume of transactions and negatively related to the interest opportunity-cost variable.

That is not to say that there are no differences between the models; obviously, there are. But these involve details of timing and the precise way in which transaction costs impinge on individuals. Choosing between the models on the basis of these details would seem to be unwise, for the precise ways in which money facilitates exchange are too complex and multifaceted to be represented accurately in any model that

---

[25] A remaining flaw is that the total amount of money held by households in the United States is larger than the model can account for even with the minimum value of n. But it is widely believed that the surprisingly large magnitude of the U.S. money stock is to be explained by large cash holdings on the part of participants in criminal activities, who wish to keep their transactions unrecorded. Such behavior cannot be explained by any theory that fails to take account of the special nature of criminal activities.

[26] There is, by contrast, a very different approach to money demand analysis known as the "overlapping generations model of money." This approach ignores the fact that money helps to facilitate transactions, emphasizing instead its role as a store of value. Consequently, the overlapping generations model fails to rationalize the observed tendency for agents to hold money even when there are other assets that are free of nominal risk and pay positive interest rates. A relatively nontechnical exposition of this approach is provided by Wallace (1977).

is simple enough to be manageable. Any manageable model, then, should be thought of as a potentially useful parable rather than as a literal description of the exchange process. Choice among different models must consequently be made on the basis of fundamental precepts, consistency with empirical evidence, and analytical convenience. In the case of the shopping-time and Baumol–Tobin models, there is no basis for choice provided by the first two of these criteria. The decision to use one in preference to the other should, therefore, be made on the grounds of relative analytical convenience—which will depend on the issue being studied.

Problems

1. What is the elasticity of money demand with respect to the interest rate, according to the functional relationship (20)? According to (26)? What is the elasticity with respect to transactions in each?
2. Suppose that the stock of (nominal) money balances in an economy grows steadily over time at a rate of 10 percent per period, with output growing at 5 percent and the interest rate constant. What would be the trend rate of growth of the price level if the economy's money demand function is of the form (20)?
   [*Hint*: The growth rate of any variable x between periods $t - 1$ and t is approximately equal to $\log x_t - \log x_{t-1}$ (see Chapter 6).]
3. The U.S. money stock was about \$114 billion in 1950 and about \$580 billion in 1985. Nominal GNP figures for those two years are \$288 billion and \$3992 billion, respectively. Using these values, calculate *velocity* magnitudes for the two years. What was the average annual (percentage) growth rate of velocity over the 1950–1985 period?
4. In the specific formulation of equations (13)–(17), what parameter reflects the sensitivity of "time and energy spent in shopping" to the quantity of money held? Consider a technological change in the payments process that reduces the value of this parameter. What effect would such a change have on the quantity of money held?
5. Suppose that transactions made during any period are facilitated only by money balances held at the *start* of that period. In this case the general model of Section 3.2 would be altered so that leisure during period t would be give by

$$l_t = \psi\left(c_t, \frac{M_{t-1}}{P_t}\right)$$

instead of (6). Making the implied modifications to the Lagrangian expression (8), evaluate the partial derivatives $\partial L_t / \partial c_t$ and $\partial L_t / \partial M_t$. From these, derive a relationship analogous to (11). What would be the effect on the "money demand function" analogous to (12)?

6. Some researchers have suggested that partial adjustment of money demand pertains to nominal holdings, as in

$$\log M_t - \log M_{t-1} = \lambda(\log M_t^* - \log M_{t-1}).$$

Suppose that this is the case and that the demand for $m_t^* = M_t^*/P_t$ is as given in equation (26). Describe an operational procedure for econometric estimation of λ, γ_1, and γ_2 using aggregate time-series data.

References

Barro, Robert J., *Macroeconomics*. (New York: John Wiley & Sons, Inc., 1984).

Barro, Robert J., and Stanley Fischer, "Recent Developments in Monetary Theory," *Journal of Monetary Economics* 2 (April 1976), 133–67.

Baumol, William J., "The Transaction Demand for Cash: An Inventory Theoretic Approach," *Quarterly Journal of Economics* 66 (November 1952), 545–66.

Baumol, William J., *Economic Theory and Operations Analysis*, 4th ed. (Englewood Cliffs, N.J.: Prentice-Hall, Inc., 1977).

Dornbusch, Rudiger, and Stanley Fischer, *Macroeconomics*, 3rd ed. (New York: McGraw-Hill Book Company, 1984).

Goldfeld, Stephen M., "The Demand for Money Revisited," *Brookings Papers on Economic Activity* (No. 3, 1973), 577–638.

Goodfriend, Marvin, "Reinterpreting Money Demand Regressions," *Carnegie–Rochester Conference Series* 22 (Spring 1985), 207–42.

Lieberman, Charles, "The Long-Run and Short-Run Demand for Money, Revisited," *Journal of Money, Credit, and Banking* 12 (February 1980), 43–57.

Lucas, Robert E., Jr., "Equilibrium in a Pure Currency Economy," in *Models of Monetary Economies*, ed. J. H. Kareken and N. Wallace. (Minneapolis, Minn.: Federal Reserve Bank of Minneapolis, 1980).

Tobin, James, "The Interest-Elasticity of the Transactions Demand for Cash," *Review of Economics and Statistics* 38 (August 1956), 241–47.

Tobin, James, "Liquidity Preference as Behavior Towards Risk," *Review of Economic Studies* 25 (February 1958), 65–86.

Wallace, Neil, "Why the Fed Should Consider Holding the Stock of M. Constant," Federal Reserve Bank of Minneapolis, *Quarterly Review* 1 (Summer 1977), 2–10.

4

The Supply of Money

4.1 Introduction

Having discussed money demand fairly extensively, it is natural for us to turn now to the topic of money supply. In that regard, a few words on terminology may be useful. The phrase "money supply" is frequently used, by economists as well as journalists, to refer to the nominal quantity of money in existence. A different use of the phrase is with respect to money supply *behavior*, that is, the behavior of banks and other organizations whose liabilities serve as part of the medium of exchange. It is primarily this second meaning of the term with which we are concerned in the present chapter. Thus for the sake of clarity we will normally use the term "money stock" instead of "money supply" to refer to the quantity of money in existence.

Throughout this chapter, our discussion will pertain to the present-day institutions of the United States (albeit in simplified form). The main relevant organizations are, of course, the Federal Reserve System and the nation's commercial banks. The Federal Reserve System is in actuality a large and complex organization with a variety of duties, including bank regulation[1] and a major operational role in the actual physical chores of distributing currency and clearing checks. But since our present concern is only with its role as the nation's monetary authority, we shall here treat the Fed as if it were a single entity whose only concern is the determination of the money stock. For an excellent introductory discussion of the Fed's activities, the reader is referred to Broaddus (1988).

---

[1] The Fed is, however, only one of several agencies with regulatory responsibility vis-à-vis banks.

4.2 Basic Relationships

To keep the analysis as simple as possible, without neglecting the essential issues, let us treat the money stock as being composed of only two types of assets, currency (C) and checkable deposits (D):

$$M = C + D. \tag{1}$$

Here it should be noted that C includes only currency held by the nonbank public; it does not include that portion held by banks in the form of vault cash. Under prevailing U.S. regulations, deposits are effectively claims to currency that can be exercised freely and with minimal delay by the (nonbank) public. Consequently, the currency-to-deposit ratio C/D is under the control of the public, rather than banks or the Fed. Let us denote that ratio by the symbol cr:

$$cr = \frac{C}{D}. \tag{2}$$

Next we recall the definition of the stock of high-powered money, H, which is the sum of currency in circulation and bank reserves (TR):

$$H = C + TR. \tag{3}$$

In addition, we recall that reserves include both currency held by banks (vault cash) and banks' deposits with the Fed. Also, since high-powered money and the monetary base are very closely related concepts, we may occasionally use the latter term when referring to H.

A major objective of this chapter is to determine how the money stock M is related to variables that are more directly under the control of the Fed. To begin that discussion, let us focus on the relationship between M and H. Now, clearly equations (1) and (2) permit us to write

$$M = (cr + 1)D. \tag{4}$$

Furthermore, if we define the banks' reserve-to-deposit ratio by $rr = TR/D$, we can also write

$$H = (cr + rr)D. \tag{5}$$

From (4) and (5) it follows immediately that M and H are related according to

$$\frac{M}{H} = \frac{cr + 1}{cr + rr}. \tag{6}$$

This last expression, it should be noted, is just an identity that follows from the definitions of M, H, cr, and rr. Thus to give it behavioral content, we need to specify the economic determinants of *cr* and *rr*. It has already been pointed out that *cr* is chosen by the nonbank public. Let us now add the behavioral assumption that the value chosen depends primarily on institutional features of the economy that change slowly and predictably over time in a manner that is unrelated to current economic conditions. In that case, *cr* will be basically a trend-dominated variable. For several purposes, moreover, it will be adequate to simply treat *cr* as a *constant*. We shall accordingly do so for the present, but must keep in mind that this is not literally correct.

Finally, we turn to *rr*, which is determined by the choices of banks. To understand that choice process, let us develop a highly simplified picture of a typical bank, viewing it as a profit-seeking organization whose balance sheet includes the following items:

Assets	Liabilities
Reserves (TR)	Deposits (D)
Loans (LB)	Borrowed reserves (BR)
Physical assets	Net worth

Here LB reflects "loans" made by the bank in question. This item includes not only specifically negotiated loans to customers such as households and firms, but also loans implicitly made to the government—that is, government bills and bonds held by the bank. On its holdings of all of these loan assets, the bank earns interest; for simplicity we assume that the same rate, R, is earned on all types. From its holding of reserves, by contrast, the bank earns no interest. It is therefore costly to the bank to hold reserves.

On the liability side of the balance sheet the main item is deposits. We are simplifying in this regard by pretending that there is only one type of deposit. We also pretend that this type is the old-fashioned demand deposit, which pays no interest to its owner.[2] Next, the second item on the liability side refers to borrowing by the bank from the Fed, so-called "discount window" borrowing. This item is in all cases quantitatively small, but needs to be recognized because of the important role it plays in money stock determination under some policy regimes (although not the ones discussed in this chapter).

The remaining items on the bank's balance sheet are physical assets and net worth. The former refers to the buildings, machines, and so on, owned by the bank and used in conducting its business. The latter is, of course, cumulated retained profits plus the initial investment in the

---

[2] Assuming that interest is paid on these deposits would complicate but not invalidate the analysis of this chapter. As the deposits provide transaction services to a greater extent than other assets, they will pay an interest rate that is lower than that on bank loans, and R could be reinterpreted as the difference between these two rates.

bank made by its owners. We will not need to refer explicitly to either of these items in our analysis, so symbols have not been assigned to their magnitudes.

The most important aspect of bank behavior, from our perspective, is the bank's choice of its reserve-to-deposit ratio, rr. In analyzing that choice, it will be convenient to recognize two categories of reserves. The first of these is *required reserves*, the quantity that a bank must hold at a point in time as required by law. This quantity depend on the bank's deposits: the greater are its deposits, the more reserves are required. As an approximation, we shall assume that the quantity of required reserves is proportional to the value of deposits. Letting k denote the proportionality factor, required reserves are then equal to kD. The other category of reserves is *excess reserves*, the amount of reserves held above the quantity required. Thus we have the decomposition

$$TR = kD + ER, \tag{7}$$

where ER denotes excess reserves.

Our main behavioral hypothesis concerning banks is that the quantity of excess reserves chosen obeys a relation of the form

$$\frac{ER}{D} = e(R), \tag{8}$$

with e a decreasing function: $de/dR = e'(R) < 0$. The logic of this hypothesis is simple. Any bank will normally hold a positive amount of excess reserves so that an unexpected loss of reserves, from (say) a large unexpected cash withdrawal, will not leave the bank with total reserves below the legally required minimum. But each dollar of excess reserves is costly to the bank in terms of forgone interest, as it represents assets that could be held in the form of interest-earning loans. Furthermore, the higher is the rate of interest, the more costly is each dollar of excess reserves. Thus a bank of a given size will hold a relatively small volume of excess reserves when the rate of interest is high and a relatively large volume when it is low. This aspect of behavior is reflected in our assumption that the derivative $e'(R)$ is negative. The role of D in (8), finally, is to normalize by using D as the relevant measure of bank size.

Together, relations (7) and (8) provide a simplified explanation of the reserve-to-deposit ratio rr. To see this, divide each term in (7) by D and note that the result is

$$rr = k + e(R). \tag{9}$$

Since $e' < 0$, we see immediately that rr will be smaller, for a given value of the legally determined k, the higher is the rate of interest.

It is now a trivial matter to substitute (9) into (6) and obtain

$$\frac{M}{H} = \frac{cr + 1}{cr + k + e(R)}. \tag{10}$$

Furthermore, we could express (10) as

$$\frac{M}{H} = \mu(R; k, cr), \tag{11}$$

where μ is a function with $\mu_1 > 0$, $\mu_2 < 0$, and $\mu_3 < 0$. That the signs of the first two of these partial derivations are as indicated should be clear from expression (10). For the partial with respect to cr the result relies on the fact that $k + e(R) = rr$ is smaller than 1.0. Therefore, if we express the right-hand side of (10) as

$$\frac{cr + 1}{cr + rr} = \frac{cr + rr - rr + 1}{cr + rr} = 1 + \frac{1 - rr}{cr + rr}, \tag{12}$$

the final term must be positive. But that term unambiguously decreases with any increase in cr, holding rr constant, which implies that M/H is negatively related to cr.

Equation (11), especially when written as $M = \mu(R; k, cr)H$, is an example of a money supply function. By that we mean that it describes how much money would be "supplied" for specified magnitudes of H, R, k, and cr. Since $\mu_1 > 0$, the function is increasing in R. Consequently, a money supply curve could be drawn as in Figure 4-1, where the symbols in brackets indicate determinants of the position of the curve. Also shown in Figure 4-1 is a money demand curve, downward sloping to reflect a negative dependence upon R, of the type discussed in Chapter 3. The symbols in brackets by the demand curve

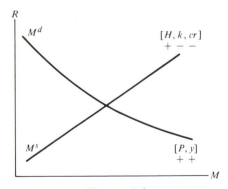

Figure 4-1

indicate that its position (in the M, R plane) depends on the price level (P) and the prevailing volume of transactions (y).[3]

In Figure 4-1, the "+" and "−" signs below the variables in brackets need to be emphasized. The meaning of these is as follows: a + sign indicates that the position of the curve in question will shift to the right if the value of the associated variable is increased. For example, if H were larger than is the case in Figure 4-1, the M^s (money supply) curve would be farther to the right than is shown. Similarly, the fact that $\mu_2 < 0$ in (11) implies that the sign associated with k in the bracket attached to the M^s curve is negative: an increase in k would move M^s to the left. Also, the + signs associated with P and y in the bracket attached to the money demand (M^d) curve indicate that M^d would be farther to the right if P and/or y were larger, which accords with the specification of the money demand function (1) of Chapter 3, where $L_1 > 0$.

4.3   Monetary Control

We are now prepared to consider how the Fed can exert control over the stock of money, in the event that it chooses to do so. Suppose that, at the beginning of period t, the Fed anticipates that the values of y_t and P_t will be y_t^e and P_t^e. (Here "e" means "expected.") Thus the Fed anticipates that the money demand curve will be in the position indicated in Figure 4-2.

Now, suppose that the value of the money stock that the Fed wishes to achieve for period t, the *target* value of M_t, is M_t^*. Then with M_t^* located as shown in Figure 4-2, the Fed can try to make the realized value of M_t equal the target value M_t^* by choosing H_t, which is under its control, to be that value which makes the money supply curve M^s go through point A. The location of M_t^s also depends on k and cr, of course, but these can be treated as known constants for the purpose of the present exercise. Consequently, the location depends primarily on the value of H_t set by the Fed.

Algebraically, this control process can be represented as follows. First, treating k and cr as constants, write the M^s function as $M_t/H_t = \bar{\mu}(R_t)$. Then solve the latter for R_t as

$$R_t = \bar{\mu}^{-1}\left(\frac{M_t}{H_t}\right), \tag{13}$$

---

[3] Note that the demand function drawn in Figure 4-1 pertains to nominal money balances. It is a plot of the right-hand side of $M = PL(y, R)$.

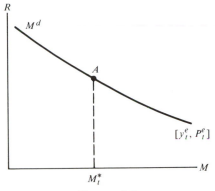

Figure 4-2

where $\bar{\mu}^{-1}$ is the inverse function to $\bar{\mu}$. Next, substitute (13) into the money demand function:

$$\frac{M_t}{P_t} = L\left[y_t, \bar{\mu}^{-1}\left(\frac{M_t}{H_t}\right)\right]. \tag{14}$$

Then set $M_t = M_t^*$, $P_t = P_t^e$, and $y_t = y_t^e$ in (14):

$$\frac{M_t^*}{P_t^e} = L\left[y_t^e, \bar{\mu}^{-1}\left(\frac{M_t^*}{H_t}\right)\right]. \tag{15}$$

Since the values of all other variables in (15) are determined, that equation can be solved for H_t. The resulting value will be the one that should result in the target value M_t^* being realized, given the anticipated values y_t^e and P_t^e. By choosing H_t in this manner, the Fed can attempt to make M_t equal M_t^*, even though it does not have direct control over M_t.

A process such as the foregoing is of course not going to work perfectly. One reason is that, as mentioned before, there are stochastic disturbances associated with money demand. Thus the M^d function will turn out to be located (in period t) somewhat differently than the Fed expects at the start of t, in part because the disturbance term—represented by ε_t in (23) of Chapter 3—turns out to have a value different from its average (expected) value of zero. In addition, the position of M^d will be different than expected because that position depends on the actual values of y_t and P_t, which will usually be different from the values expected (y_t^e and P_t^e). For these reasons it is useful to think of the curve M^d in Figure 4-2 as indicating the central tendency of a range of possible locations, such as those illustrated by the area between M_{upper}^d and M_{lower}^d in Figure 4-3. So if M_t^* is the target value of M_t, there is a

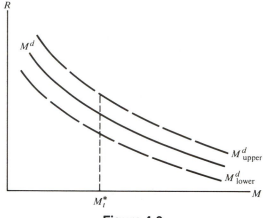

Figure 4-3

range of possible R_t values that would correspond to M_t^* on the actual realized M^d function.

Furthermore, there are sources of unpredictability in bank behavior that suggest that there is actually a stochastic disturbance term in the money supply relationship, similar to the one afflicting money demand. Thus equation (11) should actually be written as

$$M_t = \bar{\mu}(R_t)H_t + \zeta_t, \tag{16}$$

where ζ_t is the random disturbance to money supply behavior. The M^s curve should consequently be viewed as the midpoint in a range of possible locations, as shown in Figure 4-4.

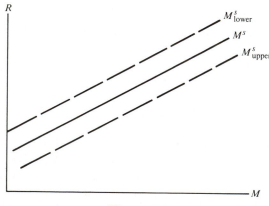

Figure 4-4

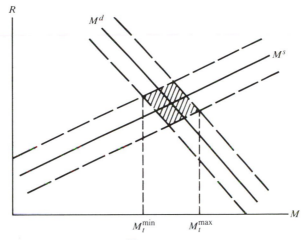

Figure 4-5

Redoing the money control exercise, then, we see that the Fed selects a value for H_t that it *expects* to be appropriate to induce the value of M_t to turn out to equal M_t^*. But because of the various sources of randomness,[4] the actual intersection of the money demand and supply curves can be anywhere in the shaded region in Figure 4-5. The resulting value of M_t, then, will lie somewhere between M_t^{min} and M_t^{max}, as drawn. Values close to M_t^* are more likely to result when the Fed sets H_t as described than if H_t were chosen differently, but *exact* control of M_t cannot be achieved.

4.4   Alternative Control Procedures

Having described a procedure by which the Fed could try to achieve money stock targets, it must now be recognized that this procedure has *not*, in actual practice, been used by the Fed to any significant extent.[5] There are two distinct reasons for that statement. First, during most of its history the Fed has simply not attempted to achieve money stock targets, but has instead tried to obtain desired values of other macroeconomic variables. Second, even when the Fed has attempted to hit money stock targets, as was arguably the case during 1979–1982, it has

---

[4] Including some that we have not yet mentioned.
[5] That procedure, it should be said, is the one studied in most textbooks on money and banking.

used operating procedures that differ from the one outlined in Section 4.3. To illustrate that different procedures could be used if M_t control is desired, and also to introduce considerations involved in choosing among them, consider the following scheme. Suppose that at the start of period t, instead of committing itself to provide a value of H_t that is expected to induce a money stock outcome of M_t^*, the Fed commits itself to maintaining a value of the interest rate R_t that is expected to result in a money stock outcome of M_t^*. For example, R_t could be set at the value R_t^* depicted in Figure 4-6. The outcome would then be somewhere on the line segment between points B and C, so the possible range of M_t values would be from $M_t^{\min}$ to $M_t^{\max}$. Given that value and R_t^*, the "money supply" relation (16) would then determine H_t. Under this type of procedure there is little or no randomness affecting R_t once period t begins, and the extent of randomness affecting M_t is different than when H_t is set and maintained by the Fed. Terminologically, the procedure in Figure 4-6 is said to be one in which the Fed uses an interest rate *instrument*, whereas the instrument in the procedure of Section 4.3 is high-powered money.

An instrument (or "operating instrument"), to elaborate, is a variable that the policy authority manipulates more-or-less directly in an attempt to exert indirect control over some other "target" variable. In light of that definition, it might be asked how the Fed can directly control the interest rate R_t. The answer is that the Fed maintains a huge portfolio of marketable U.S. government securities, including Treasury

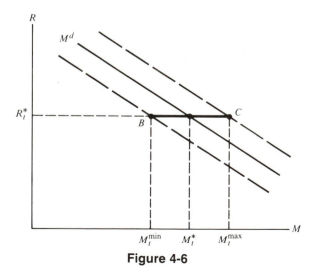

Figure 4-6

bills and bonds.[6] It can then keep the interest rate on (say) 90-day Treasury bills at the value it chooses by standing ready to buy or sell these bills at a price that implies that chosen interest rate.[7] In actual practice, the Fed focuses its attention on the *federal funds rate*, which is the rate on one-day loans among banks, but that does not alter the situation significantly as the federal funds and Treasury bill rates move together very closely.

Having found that there are at least two distinct procedures for attempting to achieve M_t target values, the next step is to consider which of the two is superior. Can the Fed, in other words, exert more accurate M_t control by using an H_t instrument or an R_t instrument? In response to this question, we shall first illustrate the relevant considerations by means of a graphical device and then, in Section 4.6, develop a more formal algebraic analysis.

To proceed graphically, let us temporarily make the (unsatisfactory) assumption that the relevant measure of *inaccuracy* of money stock control is provided by the distance between M_t^{min} and M_t^{max} in diagrams such as Figures 4-5 and 4-6. In that case, the preferred instrument (and associated operating procedure) is the one that gives rise to the smaller M_t *range*, where we use that term to refer to $M_t^{max} - M_t^{min}$. For given specifications of M^s and M^d curves, and given randomness bands around those curves, we can then determine which procedure implies the smaller M_t range.

As a first illustration, consider the situation depicted in Figure 4-7. There it can be seen that the M_t range with the H_t instrument is $M^4 - M^1$ while that with the R_t instrument is $M^3 - M^2$. In that particular case, then, the procedure using R_t as the instrument would be better—would permit more accurate M_t control.[8] If the situation were as depicted in Figure 4-8, by contrast, H_t would be the better instrument.

From experimentation with diagrams like these, it can be determined that the better instrument will be H_t or R_t (respectively), depending on whether M^s or M^d has the narrower bands—measured along the M axis—and also that the margin of superiority will depend on the relative slopes of the M^s and M^d curves.

---

[6] In May 1985 it held about $164 billion of U.S. government securities, of which $73 billion was in the form of Treasury bills.

[7] The reader will recall that the interest rate on a security with a given maturity value varies inversely with the current price of that security. Consider, as an illustration, a security that pays its owner $1000 on maturity and provides no "coupon" interest payments along the way. If that security is purchased for $900 one period before it matures, the implied rate of interest is $(1000 - 900)/900 = 0.1111$, or 11.11 percent per period.

[8] In the sense of minimum M_t range.

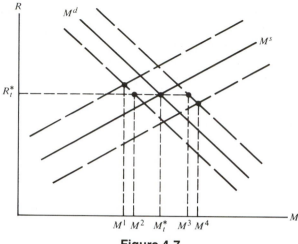

Figure 4-7

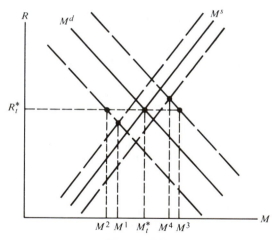

Figure 4-8

Reflection upon these diagrams will indicate, however, that the graphical technique tends to put the comparison in a way that is inappropriately biased against the H_t instrument. That is so because the quadrilateral area pertaining to the H_t instrument actually implies a greater clustering of outcomes near the center of the M_t range than does the line pertaining to the R_t instrument. Consequently, for an unbiased analysis we need to utilize a more powerful analytical technique. Such a technique is developed in the next section.

4.5 **Algebraic Analysis**

To proceed algebraically, it will be useful to adopt specific functional forms for the money supply and demand equations. In keeping with the discussion in Chapter 3, we assume that these relationships are linear in the logarithms of all variables, except that they are linear in R_t itself. In particular, we assume that the M^d and M^s functions are as follows:

$$\log \frac{M_t}{P_t} = a_0 + a_1 \log y_t - a_2 R_t + \varepsilon_t, \tag{17}$$

$$\log M_t = b_0 + b_1 \log H_t + b_2 R_t + \zeta_t. \tag{18}$$

Here we have put a minus sign before $a_2 R_t$ so that the coefficients a_1, a_2, b_1, and b_2 will all be positive. The disturbances ε_t and ζ_t are assumed to be purely random, in the sense that for each t (i.e., in each period) the probability distribution of ε_t has mean zero and variance σ_ε^2, while the distribution of ζ_t has mean zero and variance σ_ζ^2. These distributions are unaffected by past events; the disturbances are serially independent. For notational convenience let us use the definitions $p_t = \log P_t$, $m_t = \log M_t$, and $h_t = \log H_t$. Then we can write the demand–supply system as[9]

$$m_t = p_t + a_0 + a_1 \log y_t - a_2 R_t + \varepsilon_t, \tag{19}$$

$$m_t = b_0 + b_1 h_t + b_2 R_t + \zeta_t. \tag{20}$$

We begin the analysis by considering the procedure with the high-powered money instrument. Thus we assume that at the start of period t the Fed uses its knowledge of the system (19)–(20) to set h_t so as to make the expected value of m_t equal to the target value m_t^*.[10] To do that the Fed in effect replaces ε_t, ζ_t, $\log y_t$, and p_t in (19) and (20) with their expected values, sets $m_t = m_t^*$, and (by eliminating R_t) solves for the appropriate value of h_t. Thus we write

$$m_t^* = p_t^e + a_0 + a_1 \log y_t^e - a_2 R_t + 0, \tag{21}$$

$$m_t^* = b_0 + b_1 h_t + b_2 R_t + 0. \tag{22}$$

Then, by solving these two equations, we find that h_t should be set as

$$h_t = \frac{(a_2 + b_2)m_t^* - b_2(p_t^e + a_1 \log y_t^e) - (a_0 b_2 + a_2 b_0)}{a_2 b_1}, \tag{23}$$

given the objective of making $m_t = m_t^*$ using h_t as the instrument.

---

[9] Note that m_t has a different meaning than in Chapter 3, where it stands for M_t/P_t.
[10] The target is, then, being formulated in terms of $\log M_t$ rather than M_t itself.

But as we know from Section 4.4, this target will typically not be attained precisely. That is because, when the events of period t occur, ε_t and ζ_t will usually not be exactly equal to their mean values of zero, and p_t and log y_t will not be exactly equal to their expected values p_t^e and log y_t^e. Consequently, the actually realized value of m_t will usually not be m_t^*, even though h_t has been set appropriately. What will the value of m_t be? That can be determined from equations (19) and (20), which describe the system, with h_t specified as in (23). Thus we solve (19) and (20) for

$$m_t = \frac{a_2 b_1 h_t + b_2(p_t + a_1 \log y_t) + a_0 b_2 + a_2 b_0 + b_2 \varepsilon_t + a_2 \zeta_t}{a_2 + b_2}. \quad (24)$$

Then we substitute the value of h_t given in (23) into (24) and obtain

$$m_t = m_t^* + \frac{b_2(p_t - p_t^e) + b_2 a_1(\log y_t - \log y_t^e) + b_2 \varepsilon_t + a_2 \zeta_t}{a_2 + b_2}. \quad (25)$$

From this we see that the *control error* $m_t - m_t^*$ is a linear combination of the random disturbances, ε_t and ζ_t, and the expectational errors, $p_t - p_t^e$ and log $y_t - $ log y_t^e. For any period t the control error will be given by the long term on the right of equation (25).

Now to compare the merits of the control procedure being analyzed with others, we need a measure of the extent to which control errors will result from this procedure *on average*, over a large number of periods. From the study of statistics we know that the most appropriate such measure is the *mean-squared error* *(MSE)* for m_t, defined as

$$\text{MSE for } m_t = E(m_t - m_t^*)^2. \quad (26)$$

In this expression the error $m_t - m_t^*$ is squared so that both positive and negative errors will count toward the total, rather than canceling out each other, and so that large errors will be weighted more heavily than small errors. The symbol E indicates that the expected value of $(m_t - m_t^*)^2$ is being computed; that is, our measure is the mean (or expected value or mathematical expectation) of the probability distribution of the random variable $(m_t - m_t^*)^2$.[11] (A brief review of relevant concepts from probability theory is provided in the appendix to Chapter 8.)

In calculating the magnitude of the MSE, it will be helpful to introduce a new composite variable z_t defined as

$$z_t = p_t - p_t^e + a_1(\log y_t - \log y_t^e) + \varepsilon_t. \quad (27)$$

---

[11] This error is a random variable, since ε_t, η_t, and the expectational errors are random variables.

Then using this definition, it is clear from (25) that the control error can be expressed as

$$m_t - m_t^* = \frac{a_2 \zeta_t + b_2 z_t}{a_2 + b_2}. \tag{28}$$

Thus we have expressed the m_t control error as a weighted average of the money supply disturbance ζ_t and the composite money demand disturbance z_t. The latter is a composite random variable in that it includes expectational errors as well as ε_t. Inclusion of these errors implies that the variance of z_t, denoted σ_z^2, will be different from σ_ε^2. But since rational formation of expectations implies that $p_t - p_t^e$ and $\log y_t - \log y_t^e$ will have mean values of zero and will be uncorrelated with events of the past,[12] the composite variable z_t will also have those properties. Formally, then, we know that $E(z_t) = 0$, $E(z_t^2) = \sigma_z^2$, and $E(z_t z_{t-i}) = 0$ for $i = 1, 2, \ldots$.

Finally, we are ready to compute the MSE value $E(m_t - m_t^*)^2$. To do so, first note that since $m_t - m_t^*$ is a weighted average of random variables with zero means, its mean is zero. Therefore, $E(m_t - m_t^*)^2$ equals the variance of $m_t - m_t^*$, as well as the mean-squared value of that expression. But we know, from basic probability theory, how to compute the variance of a random variable that is a linear combination (linear function with fixed coefficients) of other variables. In particular, if X_1 and X_2 are random variables while α_1 and α_2 are constants, the variance of $\alpha_1 X_1 + \alpha_2 X_2$ is given by the formula

$$\begin{aligned} \operatorname{var}(\alpha_1 X_1 + \alpha_2 X_2) = {} & \alpha_1^2 \operatorname{var}(X_1) + \alpha_2^2 \operatorname{var}(X_2) \\ & + 2\alpha_1 \alpha_2 \operatorname{cov}(X_1, X_2), \end{aligned} \tag{29}$$

where $\operatorname{cov}(X_1, X_2)$ is the covariance of those variables. Applying this formula to the problem at hand, we find that

$$\begin{aligned} E(m_t - m_t^*)^2 = {} & \left(\frac{a_2}{a_2 + b_2}\right)^2 \sigma_\zeta^2 + \left(\frac{b_2}{a_2 + b_2}\right)^2 \sigma_z^2 \\ & + \frac{2a_2 b_2}{(a_2 + b_2)^2} \operatorname{cov}(\zeta_t, z_t). \end{aligned} \tag{30}$$

The usefulness of this expression will become apparent shortly. But before continuing, let us note that if ζ_t and z_t are independent, the covariance term will equal zero and the expression can be simplified to

$$E(m_t - m_t^*)^2 = \frac{a_2^2 \sigma_\zeta^2 + b_2^2 \sigma_z^2}{(a_2 + b_2)^2}. \tag{31}$$

---

[12] These statements are substantiated in Chapter 8, where we turn our attention to expectational considerations. The appendix to that chapter reviews probability concepts used in the present section.

And since ζ_t refers to disturbances to money supply, which mainly involves bank behavior, while z_t refers to the behavior of (nonbank) money holders, it is probably reasonable to assume that these variables are nearly independent, in which case (31) will be good approximation to the more complete (30). In what follows, consequently, we will use the simplified version (31).

We now shift our attention to another money stock control procedure discussed above, the one with R_t used as the Fed's operating instrument. Our objective is to compute a MSE expression comparable to (31) but which pertains to this other operating procedure. As it happens, the calculations are much simpler in this second case. That is so because, as Figure 4-6 suggests, the money supply equation (20) is not involved in the determination of m_t. Instead, the Fed simply sets R_t so as to make m_t in (19) equal to the target value m_t^*, taking as given the anticipated values for ε_t, p_t, and $\log y_t$. That is, it solves (21) for the appropriate value of R_t. But the actual outcome will be governed by (19), given that value of R_t. The resulting control error can then be found by subtracting (21) from (19). It is

$$m_t - m_t^* = p_t - p_t^e + a_1(\log y_t - \log y_t^e) + \varepsilon_t. \tag{32}$$

But the right-hand side of the latter will be recognized as precisely equal to our composite variable z_t. Thus $m_t - m_t^* = z_t$ in this case, and the relevant MSE value is simply

$$E(m_t - m_t^*)^2 = \sigma_z^2. \tag{33}$$

Our remaining task is to compare the MSE expressions (31) and (33) pertaining to the two alternative operating procedures under discussion. Doing so, the main conclusion that we reach is that if $\sigma_\zeta^2 \le \sigma_z^2$ (i.e., if the money supply disturbance variance is relatively small), the procedure based on the h_t instrument will be superior. To see that, suppose first that $\sigma_\zeta^2 = \sigma_z^2$. Then (31) reduces to

$$\frac{a_2^2 \sigma_z^2 + b_2^2 \sigma_z^2}{(a_2 + b_2)^2} = \frac{a_2^2 + b_2^2}{a_2^2 + 2a_2 b_2 + b_2^2} \sigma_z^2, \tag{34}$$

which is smaller than σ_z^2 since the denominator is larger than the numerator. (Recall that a_2 and b_2 are positive.) But making σ_ζ^2 smaller than σ_z^2 (holding the latter fixed) can only reduce the value of (31), so it follows that (31) must be smaller than (33) provided that $\sigma_\zeta^2 \le \sigma_z^2$. The last inequality is, then, a *sufficient* condition for high-powered money to be a better instrument than the interest rate. As z_t is composed of three distinct sources of error, this condition seems quite likely to prevail in actuality.

If $\sigma_\zeta^2 > \sigma_z^2$, however, it is possible that R_t will be the better instrument. That result will be more likely, it can be seen from (31), the larger is a_2 in relation to b_2 (i.e., the steeper the money demand curve is relative to the money supply curve).[13]

4.6 Conclusions

The two conclusions that we have just obtained are of the "if then" type, with the "if then" phrase referring to relative parameter values. It would be somewhat more satisfying, of course, to be able to reach unconditional conclusions.[14] In that regard it is important to recognize that there are other possible money stock control procedures besides the two that we have considered, one procedure corresponding to each possible instrument variable. For example, the Fed could use total reserves (TR_t) instead of H_t or R_t as its instrument. In fact, during the much-discussed period of October 1979–September 1982, the Fed used nonborrowed reserves, $TR_t - BR_t$, as its instrument. Now the model described above is not quite adequate for study of that procedure, because of a complication present during 1979–1982 that we have not yet discussed.[15] For that reason, as well as others, we delay analysis of the 1979–1982 procedure to Chapter 11. But when that analysis is conducted, it will be possible to reach some rather strong conclusions.

The present chapter has emphasized that in the United States the money stock is not under the direct control of the monetary authority and indeed is not *precisely* controllable even indirectly. That emphasis should *not* be permitted to obscure the fact that the monetary authority can, under arrangements like those of the United States, strongly influence the behavior of the money stock and exert a considerable degree of control. Over the period of a year, the Fed can probably determine the money stock growth rate to within two percentage points. For example, if it were seriously to try for 4 percent growth one year, actual growth would almost certainly (despite random shocks) turn out to be between 3 and 5 percent. Thus it is reasonable, in the

---

[13] The general type of analysis utilized in this section was developed by Poole (1970). It was first applied to the money stock control problem by Pierce and Thomson (1972), whose analysis was extended to a dynamic model with rational expectations by McCallum and Hoehn (1983).

[14] All conclusions are based on some model specification, of course.

[15] The complication in question is the existence of lagged reserve requirements, that is, regulations that made required reserves depend on past (rather than current) deposit magnitudes.

context of many monetary and macroeconomic issues, to think of the money stock as being accurately controllable by the monetary authority. Indeed, the standard practice in much of macroeconomic analysis is to assume that the monetary authority directly controls the money stock. The discussion of this chapter does not show that practice to be useless; it points to a refinement that can be made to standard analyses. The next several chapters of this book, in fact, will consist of analysis of precisely that type—the money stock will be treated as directly controllable by the monetary authority.[16]

Problems

1. Suppose that at a certain point in time 10 percent of all bank reserves has been obtained from the Fed's discount window. Also, suppose that the public holds four times as much in deposits as in currency and that the banking system's nonborrowed reserves are $40 billion. What are the amounts of high-powered (base) money and M1 money in existence?

2. Imagine an economy in which banks hold borrowed reserves according to the relation

$$\frac{BR_t}{TR_t} = 5(R_t - d_t),$$

where R_t and d_t are the interest rate and discount rate (measured in fractional units) in period t. In a particular period, required reserves are $88 billion, nonborrowed reserves are $81 billion, and the discount rate is 10 percent. What will be the amount of excess reserves if the interest rate is 12 percent?

3. Consider an economy with money demand and money supply relations as follows:

$$m_t = p_t + \alpha_0 + 0.8 \log y_t - 2R_t + \varepsilon_t,$$
$$m_t = b_0 + h_t + 0.5R_t + \zeta_t.$$

Here p_t, m_t, and h_t are logs of the price level, the money stock, and high-powered money, respectively.

---

[16] One more point should be added. Our emphasis on control of the money stock does not necessarily imply that such control *should* be exercised by the monetary authority. Whether such control is desirable is a subject that will be touched upon in Part III. The material of this chapter would be important, however, even if it were concluded that money stock control is not a desirable objective for the Fed, because discussions of monetary policy invariably focus heavily on the topic.

Suppose that $\sigma_\varepsilon^2 = 0.04$ and $\sigma_\zeta^2 = 0.05$. Also, suppose that prediction errors for p_t and $\log y_t$ are negligible and that $\text{Cov}(\varepsilon_t, \zeta_t) = 0$. Calculate the value of the mean-squared control error $E(m_t - m_t^*)^2$ under the assumption that R_t is used as the instrument variable. Then repeat assuming that h_t is the instrument.

References

Barro, Robert J., *Macroeconomics*. (New York: John Wiley & Sons, Inc., 1984), Chap. 16.

Broaddus, Alfred, *A Primer on the Fed*. (Richmond, Va.: Federal Reserve Bank of Richmond, 1988).

Campbell, Colin D., and Rosemary G. Campbell, *An Introduction to Money and Banking*, 5th ed. (Hinsdale, Ill.: Dryden Press, 1984).

Dornbusch, Rudiger, and Stanley Fischer, *Macroeconomics*, 3rd ed. (New York: McGraw-Hill Book Company, 1984), Chap. 8.

McCallum, Bennett T., and James G. Hoehn, "Instrument Choice for Money Stock Control with Contemporaneous and Lagged Reserve Requirements," *Journal of Money, Credit, and Banking* 15 (February 1983), 96–101.

Pierce, James L., and Thomas D. Thomson, "Some Issues in Controlling the Stock of Money," in *Controlling Monetary Aggregates II: The Implementation*. Federal Reserve Bank of Boston Conference Series No. 9, 1972.

Poole, William, "Optimal Choice of Monetary Policy Instruments in a Simple Stochastic Macro Model," *Quarterly Journal of Economics* 84 (May 1970), 197–216.

Monetary Macroeconomics

5

The Static Classical
and Keynesian
Models

5.1 Introduction

In Chapter 4, our analysis was of the partial equilibrium type in the sense that it considered money demand and supply relationships in isolation (i.e., ignoring interactions with the rest of the economy). In particular, values of the price level P_t and real output y_t were treated as exogenous to the variables under study. But that is not the case in reality; values of P_t and y_t depend in part on the prevailing magnitudes of the interest rate and the stock of money. It is important, therefore, to consider a more complete macroeconomic system, one that provides endogenous determination of P_t, y_t, and other variables in a general equilibrium context.

We begin our efforts toward that objective in the present chapter with a brief summary of two well-known models that have been prominent ever since macroeconomics emerged as a distinct topic in the 1930s: the "classical" and "Keynesian" models. These are aggregative representations of the entire economy that are designed to facilitate analysis of the interaction between monetary and real variables, a feature that is extremely desirable. The versions with which we begin also have an undesirable feature, however, in being *static* in specification. One way in which these models are static is that they treat the economy's capital stock—its collection of productive machines, plants, highways, and so on—as *fixed* in quantity. As a result of that simplification, the models are not well designed for the analysis of policy actions or other events that would tend to induce substantial changes in the stock of capital within the relevant time frame. They are capable, however, of describing the effects of an exogenously generated change in the capital stock—one caused, for example, by an earthquake. The other way in which the models are static is that they treat *expectations* concerning future events as exogenous (i.e., determined outside of the system under study). But whereas these are significant weaknesses, they are ones that can be remedied. Ways of doing so will be considered in subsequent chapters.

In describing the basic classical and Keynesian models, it will be helpful to distinguish between components pertaining to aggregate supply, on the one hand, and aggregate demand, on the other. Since the two models utilize the same theory of aggregate demand, we shall describe that part first.

5.2 The *IS* Function

Our discussion of aggregate demand begins with the national income identity, which simply divides total output or production into the portion used for current consumption by households, the portion invested in productive capital by firms, and the portion purchased and disposed of by the government.[1] Letting y be total output, c consumption, i investment, and g government purchases, the identity is

$$y = c + i + g \qquad (1)$$

for the time period in question.

Our second relationship is not an identity, but a behavioral specification that is intended to describe households' choices concerning consumption—as opposed to saving—out of disposable income. With the latter represented as $y - \tau$, where τ denotes net[2] taxes collected by the government, the *consumption function* may be written as

$$c = C(y - \tau), \qquad 0 < C' < 1. \qquad (2)$$

Here we are using the symbol C to denote the name of a function whose argument is $y - \tau$. Thus the requirement that the derivative $C'(y - \tau)$ be positive but less than 1.0 implies that an increment to

---

[1] For the present we ignore foreign trade with other economies. That neglect is remedied in Chapter 14.

[2] By net taxes we mean taxes minus transfer payments (such as unemployment compensation or social security benefits) by the government to households.

disposable income will increase consumption c but by an amount smaller than the magnitude of the increment to $y - \tau$. The derivative C' is often termed the "marginal propensity to consume."

To understand the basic idea expressed by (2), recall that saving s is by definition that part of disposable income that is not spent on current consumption, $s = y - \tau - c$. Then it becomes clear that (2) suggests that households' decisions regarding consumption versus saving are determined entirely by the magnitude of their disposable income. Now it is certainly plausible that $y - \tau$ would be the *main* determinant of c and s, at least if we ignore situations in which these variables are changing rapidly through time, but it seems likely that the rate of interest, denoted r, would also be an important determinant. The purpose of saving, after all, is to acquire assets that can be used to increase future consumption. And the higher is the rate of interest, the more will be returned to the saver in the future for a given quantity of saving in the present. Thus it seems likely that a better specification than (2) would be

$$c = C(y - \tau, r), \qquad 0 < C_1 < 1. \tag{2'}$$

With this specification the marginal propensity to consume becomes the partial derivative of C, which is now a function of two variables, with respect to $y - \tau$. This partial derivative, $\partial C / \partial (y - \tau)$, is denoted C_1. The partial derivative with respect to the interest rate, C_2, is probably negative, since higher interest rates make the reward to saving greater. That presumption is not fully justified by standard microeconomic analysis, however, since the "income effect" of an increase in r works the other direction.[3] In any event, we begin by using the simpler consumption function (2) and then show that use of (2') would not seriously alter our conclusions.

The third relationship in the model is also a behavioral relationship, but one that describes business firms' investment behavior. It indicates that investment spending is positively related to the current level of output and negatively related to the rate of interest, r. Letting I denote the function, with I_1 and I_2 its partial derivatives with respect to y and r, we express the investment relationship as

$$i = I(y, r), \qquad I_1 > 0, \quad I_2 < 0. \tag{3}$$

To understand the reason why I is an increasing function of y and a decreasing function of r, it is helpful to consider a more fundamental relationship. The more fundamental idea is that it will be profitable for firms to invest when the marginal product of capital—which reflects the increment to output for a given amount of labor that is made possible by a unit increment to the capital stock—exceeds the rate of

---

[3] On this subject, see Henderson and Quandt (1980, pp. 331–33).

interest. The latter measures the cost to a firm of borrowing (or the opportunity cost of not lending), so when the marginal product of capital exceeds r, it will pay for firms to borrow and invest. Thus the more fundamental relationship is of the form

$$i = \tilde{I}\left(\frac{\text{MPK}}{r}\right), \qquad \tilde{I}' > 0,$$

where MPK is the marginal product of capital.[4] Now suppose that $y = F(n, k)$ is the production function, which has the properties $F_1 > 0$, $F_2 > 0$, $F_{11} < 0$, $F_{22} < 0$, and $F_{12} > 0$, where F_1 and F_{11} are the first and second derivatives with respect to n, and so on. Then MPK is $F_2(n, k)$ and our basic relationship becomes

$$i = \tilde{I}\left[\frac{F_2(n, k)}{r}\right].$$

Now the marginal product of capital is itself positively related to n, the quantity of labor employed. (That is the meaning of the assumption $F_{12} > 0$.) So when n is high, $F_2 = \text{MPK}$ will be high. But for given k, n will be high precisely when y is high, so we can think of our last equation as saying that i is positively influenced by y. Also, since $\tilde{I}$ is an increasing function of MPK/r, it is a decreasing function of r. This explains why I is increasing in y and decreasing in r. What remains to be answered is why k does not appear as an argument. The answer is that it does, actually, but since we are carrying out static analysis with a *fixed* capital stock, k is not treated as a variable. Thus its value can be suppressed.

Relationships (1), (2), and (3) can be combined by substituting the last two into the first. That step yields

$$y = C(y - \tau) + I(y, r) + g. \tag{4}$$

Now g and τ are variables that are under the government's control and are therefore taken as exogenous. There are, therefore, only two endogenous variables in (4). Accordingly, the combinations of r and y that satisfy the composite relationship (4) for given values of g and τ can be plotted on a two-dimensional graph. This is done in Figure 5-1: the curve labeled *IS* depicts the combinations of r and y values that are consistent with relationships (1), (2), and (3)—and so with relationship (4). The curve is termed the "*IS* curve" because it is concerned with the *investment* and *saving* behavior of the private sector.

An alternative way of thinking of the *IS* curve is to solve equation (4)

---

[4] Here $\tilde{I}$ is the name of a function that is different than, though related to, I.

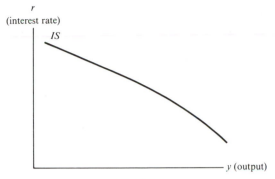

Figure 5-1

for y in terms of r, g, and τ. Suppose, for example, that the consumption function $c = C(y - \tau)$ is of the linear form

$$c = \gamma_0 + \gamma_1(y - \tau),$$

where γ_0 and γ_1 are constants, with $0 < \gamma_1 < 1$. Suppose also that the investment function $i = I(y, r)$ is linear, so that

$$i = \delta_0 + \delta_1 y + \delta_2 r, \qquad \delta_1 > 0 > \delta_2.$$

Then in this case (4) would be written as

$$y = \gamma_0 + \gamma_1(y - \tau) + \delta_0 + \delta_1 y + \delta_2 r + g.$$

Then terms involving y can be collected on the left-hand side,

$$(1 - \gamma_1 - \delta_1)y = \gamma_0 - \gamma_1 \tau + \delta_0 + \delta_2 r + g,$$

and the latter written as

$$y = \frac{1}{1 - \gamma_1 - \delta_1} (\gamma_0 + \delta_0 + \delta_2 r + g - \gamma_1 \tau). \tag{5}$$

Then Figure 5-1 is simply a plot of the relationship between y and r described by equation (5).

In Figure 5-1 the *IS* curve is drawn with a negative slope. Is that simply an accident or is it justified by our basic assumptions? Since $\delta_2 < 0$, it is justified if $1 - \gamma_1 - \delta_1$ is positive. Now our assumption that $0 < \gamma_1 < 1$ implies that $1 - \gamma_1 > 0$, but since $\delta_1 > 0$ we cannot be certain that $1 - \gamma_1 - \delta_1 > 0$. It is, however, generally agreed by macroeconomists that this is the case, that the actual value of $1 - \gamma_1 - \delta_1$ is positive. Consequently, the negative slope of *IS* is taken to be an essential feature of the model.

Given the condition $1 - \gamma_1 - \delta_1 > 0$, then, we can easily evaluate the direction of effect of g and τ on the IS curve. Since the coefficient on g in equation (5) is $1/(1 - \gamma_1 - \delta_1)$, it is clear that an increase in g will shift the IS curve to the right (i.e., will imply a higher y value for any given value of r). Similarly, the coefficient on τ is $-\gamma_1/(1 - \gamma_1 - \delta_1)$, which implies that the IS curve shifts to the left if τ increases. Those features of the relationship are depicted in Figure 5-2. The solid line shows the position of the IS function for certain hypothetical values of g and τ, values denoted g^0 and τ^0. The two dashed lines show what the positions would be for other values of g and τ such that $g^1 > g^0$ and $\tau^1 > \tau^0$.

In general, we do not presume that the consumption and investment functions (2) and (3) are linear. So in general the expression of the IS curve given by (5) is not applicable. But a more general function with the same qualitative properties will be. Let us designate this function as

$$y = \sigma(r, g, \tau), \tag{6}$$

where the partial derivatives have the signs $\sigma_1 < 0$, $\sigma_2 > 0$, $\sigma_3 < 0$.

To conclude this section, let us note that the foregoing would be affected very little if we adopted the more adequate consumption specification (2′). In the linear case we might then write $c = \gamma_0 + \gamma_1(y - \tau) + \gamma_2 r$ and the counterpart of equation (5) would have a co-efficient of $(\delta_2 + \gamma_2)/(1 - \gamma_1 - \delta_1)$ on r. As long as $\delta_2 + \gamma_2$ is negative, the qualitative properties of the counterpart would, however, be unchanged. Thus we can use the general representation (6) and think of it as applying even if the consumption versus saving decision is affected by the rate of interest.

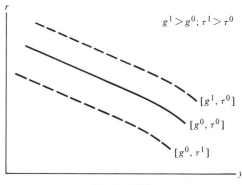

Figure 5-2

5.3 The *LM* Function

We now turn our attention to another type of behavior that is important in determining aggregate demand for output, namely, "money demand" behavior. Having treated that subject at length in Chapter 3, we shall at this point simply provide a brief review. For the purposes of the present discussion, imagine an economy in which households can hold their financial wealth in only two forms, currency or bonds. Bonds are assets that reflect loans from households to either the government or to firms. They are interest-bearing assets; indeed, it is the promise of earning interest that induces households to make these loans (i.e., to hold these assets). We assume that households are indifferent as to whether they make loans to the government or to businesses, so the same interest rate will pertain to both types of bonds. Again we will use r to denote this rate of interest.[5]

The other asset that households can hold is currency, which is this economy's medium of exchange (i.e., its *money*). This asset pays no interest. The reason that households[6] hold currency is that it *is* the medium of exchange, something that is generally acceptable in payment for any kind of purchase. This general acceptability, which is not possessed by bonds, facilitates a household's transactions and makes it willing to hold currency (money) even though it pays no interest. But the higher the rate of interest, the more costly it will be to a household to hold any given amount of money because it is forgoing more interest earnings from holding bonds. Accordingly, the quantity of money that households wish to hold is smaller, other things equal, the higher is the rate of interest.

What are the "other things" in the previous sentence? Clearly, one is the volume of transactions—the volume of purchases—that the household plans to make per unit of time. There are various plausible measures of this volume, but the one that we shall use is y, which is one measure of all *final* transactions. Thus we assume that the quantity of money that households choose to hold at a point of time is positively related to y and negatively related to r. But it is crucial to recognize that these are determinants of the *real* quantity of money. Thus if M is the stock of money in nominal (e.g., dollar) terms and P is the price level—that is, the money price (e.g., dollar price) of a typical bundle

---

[5] The alert reader will wonder why we have not distinguished between "real" and "nominal" rates of interest. That distinction will be introduced and emphasized in Chapter 6.

[6] Firms also hold money, of course, but for simplicity their holdings will be ignored in this discussion.

of output—the demand function for money balances will be of the form

$$\frac{M^d}{P} = L(y,r), \qquad L_1 > 0 > L_2. \tag{7}$$

Hence $M^d = PL(y,r)$ is the quantity of money demanded in nominal terms when the price level is P, real income is y, and the rate of interest on bonds is r.

Although each household chooses the quantity of money that it holds, the economy's total stock of money M^s is controlled by the government. (Here we neglect the complications discussed in Chapter 4.) Since it does not take long to alter the amount of currency that one holds, either by purchasing interest-bearing bonds or consumption goods, it is reasonable to assume that actual holdings correspond very closely to desired (demanded) holdings for each household. Thus in the aggregate we have

$$M^d = M^s; \tag{8}$$

that is, the quantity of money demand equals the quantity supplied. The assumption that M^s is controlled by the government does not make this equality any more unusual than the ordinary "supply equals demand" condition.

Given (8), there should be no loss in content if we simply use the symbol M to denote both M^d and M^s. Relationship (7) and (8) can then be combined to yield

$$\frac{M}{P} = L(y,r). \tag{9}$$

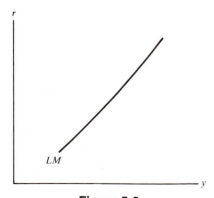

Figure 5-3

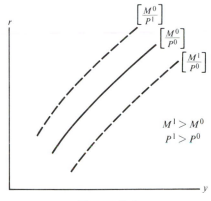

Figure 5-4

Now for any given value of M/P, (9) defines a relationship between y and r. Since $L_1 > 0$ and $L_2 < 0$, this relationship is upward sloping when we plot it on a graph such as that of Figure 5-3. This sort of plot is referred to as an "*LM* curve" and constitutes a building block of our aggregate demand theory that is comparable to the *IS* curve. The position of an economy's *LM* curve clearly depends on the value of M/P that prevails. Since $L_1 > 0$, it is easy to verify that the position of *LM* will shift to the right if M/P increases. If M is unchanged and P increases, then, *LM* must shift to the left. These properties are summarized in Figure 5-4.

5.4 The Aggregate Demand Function

We have seen how to summarize an economy's saving–investment behavior in terms of an *IS* function and its money demand (or asset holding) behavior in terms of an *LM* function. Clearly, at any point in time the same values of r and y must pertain to both aspects of behavior. Thus the relations

$$y = \sigma(r, g, \tau) \tag{6}$$

and

$$\frac{M}{P} = L(y, r) \tag{9}$$

must hold simultaneously. It is then possible to use one of these equations to eliminate r from the other. The result will be a function relating y to M/P, g, and τ:

$$y = \psi\left(\frac{M}{P}, g, \tau\right).$$ (10)

Because of the assumed properties of (6) and (9), furthermore, it can be shown that in (10) y is an increasing function of M/P and g, and a decreasing function of τ. Now M, g, and τ are exogenous policy variables, controlled by the government. So it is natural to focus on the relationship implied by (10) between y and P. But since y is positively related to M/P, it must be negatively related to P for given values of M, g, and τ. This relationship is depicted in Figure 5-5. Since it is a downward-sloping relationship in a price–quantity diagram, it is often referred to as an "aggregate demand" curve or function. That is the type of usage that is implied by our distinction between aggregate demand and supply. From what has been said, it should be clear that the positional properties of the aggregate demand or AD curve are as indicated in Figure 5-6.

Since the AD function is derived from the IS and LM curves, there is a logical relationship between them that can be expressed graphically. In particular, for given IS and LM curves, the combinations of y and P values that the AD curve describes can be derived by considering—for given values of M, g, and τ—alternative hypothetical values of P. These imply different positions of the LM function (recall Figure 5-1) such as those depicted for $P^1 > P^2 > P^3$ in the top part of Figure 5-7. By considering "all" possible values of P, a curve such as that shown in the bottom part of Figure 5-7 is obtained.

With this graphical apparatus, shifts in AD resulting from changes in M, g, or τ can be related to the underlying IS and LM functions. In

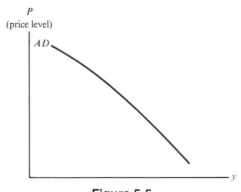

Figure 5-5

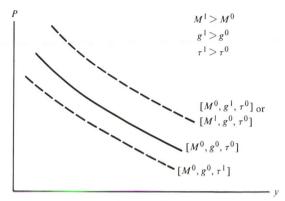

Figure 5-6

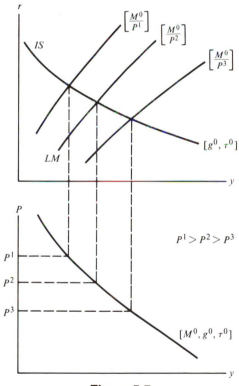

Figure 5-7

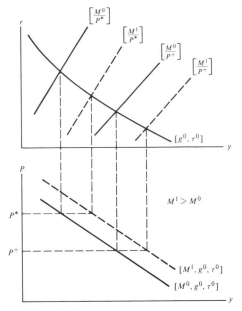

Figure 5-8

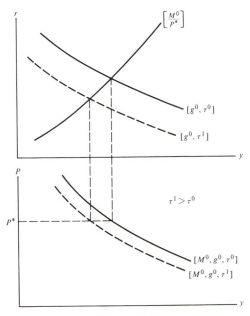

Figure 5-9

Figure 5-8, for example, the effect of an increase in the money supply from M^0 to M^1 is depicted. Note that P^* and P^+ are arbitrarily chosen reference prices.

Figure 5-9 illustrates, in a similar way, the effect of an increase in taxes from τ^0 to τ^1. To check their understanding of this material, readers are encouraged to prepare a similar diagram showing the effect of an increase (or decrease) in government purchases, g.

5.5 The Classical Aggregate Supply Function

We now turn our attention to aggregate supply. As indicated briefly in Section 5.1, there are two different versions of the aggregate supply function that need to be considered, versions that give rise to two different macroeconomic models, "classical" and "Keynesian" models. The basic difference between the two supply theories is that the classical version assumes that wages adjust promptly to equate the quantities of labor supplied and demanded within each period, while the Keynesian version assumes that nominal wages are "sticky" (i.e., do not adjust promptly). In this section we develop the classical version.

Let us begin with the demand for labor on the part of firms, which produce the economy's output. Each firm's production possibilities are characterized by a production function such as

$$y = F(n,k), \qquad (10')$$

where n is the quantity of labor employed per period, k the quantity of capital utilized, and y the resulting output. As indicated earlier, the production function has the properties $F_1 > 0$, $F_2 > 0$, $F_{11} < 0$, $F_{22} < 0$, and $F_{12} > 0$. That is, the marginal product is positive but decreasing for each input, while an increase in the quantity of one input enhances the marginal product of the other input.

It was mentioned in Section 5.1 that the models under discussion are ones in which the stock of capital is treated as fixed. Thus for each firm we are concerned with its "short-run" behavior, in the sense in which that term is used in microeconomics. Accordingly, we can represent the firm's production function by

$$y = f(n), \qquad (11)$$

where $f(n) \equiv F(n,k)$ for the relevant fixed value of k. The properties of F then imply that $f' > 0$ and $f'' < 0$, where f' is the marginal product of labor (MPL). In this notation, $f'' < 0$ indicates that the MPL diminishes with increasing quantities of labor, as shown in Figure 5-10.

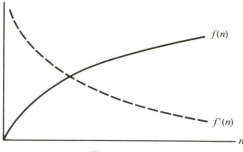

Figure 5-10

As in standard microeconomic analysis, we assume that the typical firm acts so as to maximize its profit or net revenue. In addition, we assume that this typical firm both buys and sells (inputs and output, respectively) in competitive markets. The prices in these markets are W and P, the nominal wage rate (per unit of labor) and the price of output (per unit). From a short-run perspective, then, the firm's object is to maximize

$$NR = Py - Wn - \text{fixed costs.} \qquad (12)$$

Here NR denotes net revenue per period, which consists of sales receipts Py less expenditures on labor (Wn) and fixed inputs. To find the value of the firm's choice variable n that maximizes (12), we insert $y = f(n)$ in the receipts term and find the derivative of expression (12) with respect to N:

$$\frac{d(NR)}{dn} = Pf'(n) - W. \qquad (13)$$

For a maximum, this must equal zero, so we have[7]

$$0 = Pf'(n) - W, \qquad (14)$$

or equivalently,

$$f'(n) = \frac{W}{P}. \qquad (15)$$

Thus, for a given capital stock, the firm maximizes its net revenue by producing output at the rate corresponding to an employment of labor such that the MPL $f'(n)$ is equal to W/P, the *real* wage. This condition

---

[7] Since $f'' < 0$ for all n, it is the case that $d^2(NR)/dn^2 < 0$, which assures us that (15) describes a maximum (rather than a minimum) for NR.

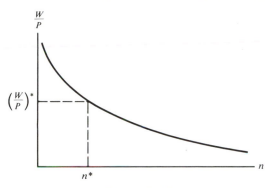

Figure 5-11

can usefully be thought of as defining the quantity of labor demanded. Graphically, we can represent the labor demand curve by plotting $f'(n)$ against n, with n on the horizontal axis. Then if the real wage is measured along the vertical axis, the $f'(n)$ curve becomes a labor demand curve: for any given value of W/P, the $f'(n)$ curve shows what value of n will satisfy the profit-maximization condition (15). That value of n will then be the quantity of labor demanded by the firm at the real wage in question. If W/P equals $(W/P)^*$, for example, n^* will be the quantity of labor demanded (see Figure 5-11).

The foregoing description is for a single firm. But for any given real wage it is possible conceptually to determine the labor demand for each firm and then add up these quantities to obtain a labor demand function for all firms together. Under certain conditions the resulting aggregate labor demand function will correspond to the marginal product of labor for an aggregate economy-wide production function.[8] In what follows we assume that these conditions are satisfied. In fact, we will interpret the equations $y = f(n)$ and $f'(n) = W/P$ as representing the short-run production function and labor demand function for the economy as a whole.

To determine total employment, it is natural to combine the labor demand function with one representing labor supply. For the latter, we shall simply write

$$n = h\left(\frac{W}{P}\right), \qquad h' \geq 0, \qquad \textbf{(16)}$$

assuming that the aggregate quantity of labor supplied is an increasing function of the real wage: the higher is the real payment per hour for

---

[8] See Sargent (1979, pp. 6–10).

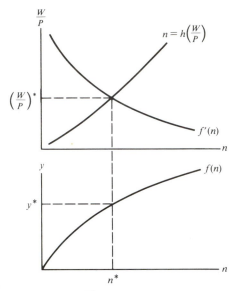

Figure 5-12

working, the greater will be the extent to which individuals will sacrifice leisure for the earnings to be had from employment.[9]

The top panel of Figure 5-12 brings together labor supply and demand. With the curves as drawn, the equilibrium quantity of employment will be n^* and the real wage will be $(W/P)^*$. An important feature of Figure 5-12 is that it also includes a plot of the production function, $y = f(n)$. Specifically, the horizontal axis in the bottom panel measures the same quantity of labor as in the top panel, and the function f is the same in both panels. Thus if n^* is the quantity of employment, y^* must be the corresponding quantity of output. Figure 5-12 depicts, then, the determination of three variables: n, W/P, and y.

Now define the real wage as $w = W/P$. Then from an algebraic perspective, what the last statement amounts to is the proposition that the three equations

$$y = f(n), \tag{11}$$

$$f'(n) = w, \tag{15}$$

$$n = h(w), \tag{16}$$

---

[9] The alert reader will note that there is a slight inconsistency here with our labor supply assumption in Chapter 3. To eliminate the inconsistency would complicate the money demand analysis in a manner that seems unwarranted.

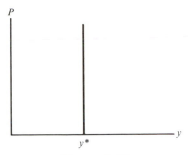

Figure 5-13

completely determine the values of the only three variables involved: n, w, and y. In this model, there is no interaction with other variables. Thus total output y is determined independently of the price level, P. Since y is the quantity of output chosen by producers, it is reasonable to view it as the quantity supplied. The *aggregate supply function* under our current classical assumptions is then of the form depicted in Figure 5-13: it is simply a vertical line at the particular value (say, y^*) determined by the solution to equations (11), (15), and (16). The nature and significance of this rather special relationship—or lack of a relationship!—will become clearer as we progress.

5.6 The Classical Model

Let us now bring together the aggregate demand theory of Section 5.4 with the aggregate supply model of Section 5.5. Mathematically, we can express the resulting *classical model* by means of the following equations:

$$y = C(y - \tau, r) + I(y, r) + g, \tag{4}$$

$$\frac{M}{P} = L(y, r), \tag{9}$$

$$y = f(n), \tag{11}$$

$$f'(n) = \frac{W}{P}, \tag{15}$$

$$n = h\left(\frac{W}{P}\right). \tag{16}$$

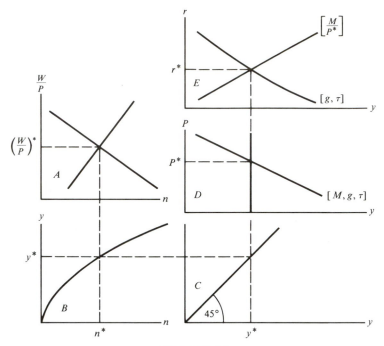

Figure 5-14

Since the variables M, g, and τ are regarded as being *exogenously*[10] set by the monetary and fiscal authorities, these five equations are just adequate in number to determine the system's five *endogenous* variables, which are y, r, n, P, and W. Given these five values, then, the identity $w = W/P$ determines the real wage. (Alternatively, we could think of W/P as the fifth variable in the system with the identity determining W.) Furthermore, the consumption and investment functions (2') and (3) determine c and i, given y, r, n, P, and W. For many purposes, however, it will be convenient and sufficient to neglect these last two variables and focus attention on the basic five-equation system and its five variables.

A graphical presentation of this model may be helpful. One convenient way of representing the system is exhibited in Figure 5-14. There part A includes the labor demand and supply functions (15) and (16), which together determine $(W/P)^*$ and n^*. The production function (11), shown in part B, then determines y^*. The value of the latter is

---

[10] An exogenous variable is one that is determined exogenously (i.e., *outside* the system at hand). By contrast, an endogenous variable is determined inside the system at hand—by the relationships that constitute the model.

transferred over to part C, where the 45° line permits y^* to be read off onto the horizontal axis (in the same value as on the vertical axis of part B). That value of y^* is then transferred upward to parts D and E. The latter includes IS and LM functions that intersect at y^*, thereby determining r^*.[11] Finally, the aggregate demand (AD) curve implied by IS and LM is shown in part D, which indicates the same value P^* of P as that associated with the LM curve. The AD curve is not explicitly included among the five equations of the model, but is present implicitly.[12]

To illustrate how the graphical version of the system can be used to analyze the effects of a change in some exogenous variable, let us first suppose that taxes are increased from τ^0 to τ^1. The resulting responses are illustrated in Figure 5-15. Readers should be certain that they can explain every aspect of that figure's construction.

The other experiment that we consider at present is that of an exogenous, policy-induced increase in the stock of money from M^0 to M^1. In this case the increase in M leads the AD curve to shift rightward as shown in Figure 5-16, with the new position indicated by point A. That point is defined by the original price level P^0 and the y value that corresponds to the intersection of the unshifted IS curve and the LM curve located by M^1/P^0. This value of y cannot be an equilibrium value, of course, for the quantity of output supplied remains at y^0. Thus the price level must rise to P^1 to equate AS and AD. As the increase in P shifts the LM curve to the left and does not affect IS, it follows that the final position of the LM curve must be same as its initial position, since that is the only position that will agree with the unchanged value of $y = y^0$ and the unchanged position of IS. This conclusion implies that $M^1/P^1 = M^0/P^0$.

In the new equilibrium, then, the values of $y, r, n, W/P$, and M/P are all the same as before the increase in M. It follows that the values of P and W must have risen in proportion to M, for otherwise either W/P or M/P would have changed. In short, the increase in the money stock changes all nominal variables in the same proportion and results in no change in any of the real variables. This property of the system is referred to as monetary neutrality. In the classical model, in other words, we have a case of the *neutrality of money*.[13]

---

[11] A more precise statement is as follows. For the already determined value of y^*, the IS function determines r^*. Then for equilibrium to obtain, the LM function must pass through the point y^*, r^*. So P^* is determined as the value of P that locates LM so as to pass through y^*, r^*, given the exogenous value of M.

[12] Readers should test their understanding of Section 5.4 by trying to explain this last statement.

[13] Note that, by contrast, the change in τ leads to changes in r and M/P. The change in r, moreover, implies that the (unchanged) value of y in Figure 5-15 will be split differently among c, i, and g.

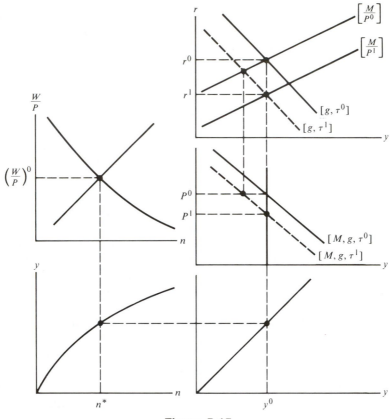

Figure 5-15

5.7   The Keynesian Aggregate Supply Function

Our next task is to specify a second and alternative theory of aggregate supply—one that is commonly termed "Keynesian." The crucial characteristic of this theory is that it does *not* utilize the assumption that the wage rate adjusts promptly to equate labor supply and demand. Instead, the Keynesian theory treats the nominal wage almost as if it were an exogenous variable, determined outside the system under study. The theory is not quite that radical, however. The idea is not actually that W is unaffected by labor supply and demand, but rather that W adjusts *slowly*—slowly enough that it is appropriate to treat W as a given magnitude in any single period. Thus the theory views W as a predetermined variable, not as one that is strictly exogenous.

Nevertheless, if the wage rate is predetermined, it cannot adjust to

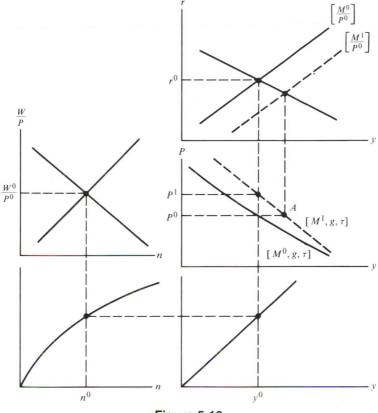

Figure 5-16

bring labor supply and demand into equality. Thus we need to distinguish between n^s and n^d, the quantities supplied and demanded, and to recognize that their values may differ. When we do so, the labor market subsystem becomes

$$f'(n^d) = \frac{W}{P}, \tag{15'}$$

$$n^s = h\left(\frac{W}{P}\right), \tag{16'}$$

$$W = \bar{W}, \tag{17}$$

where $\bar{W}$ denotes the relevant predetermined value of W. Since in this system n^s and n^d are distinct variables, we need now to specify which (if either) of these will be the quantity of labor actually employed, n. For reasons that will be briefly described below, the assumption of the

Keynesian model is that

$$n = n^d. \tag{18}$$

That is, the quantity of employment is assumed to be determined by labor demand—by firms' profit-maximizing choices.

Now, by using (17) and (18) in (15'), we can summarize the main aspects of the labor market subsystem in the single equation

$$f'(n) = \frac{\overline{W}}{P}. \tag{15''}$$

But this indicates that, with a given value of $\overline{W}$, the value of n will be related to the price level P. Furthermore, the production function $y = f(n)$ and (15'') together imply that y is functionally related to P. Indeed, (11) and (15'') imply that, since $f'(n)$ decreases with n, y is an increasing function of P. To demonstrate this implication graphically, let P^1, P^2, and P^3 be different possible values of the price level such that $P^1 < P^2 < P^3$. Then we know that $\overline{W}/P^1 > \overline{W}/P^2 > \overline{W}/P^3$. Plotting those three values of W/P in Figure 5-17, we are then able to read off the associated employment values (n^1, n^2, and n^3) and then the

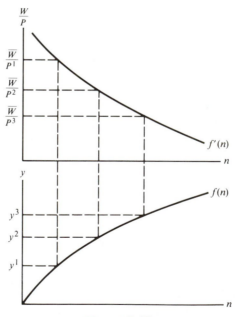

Figure 5-17

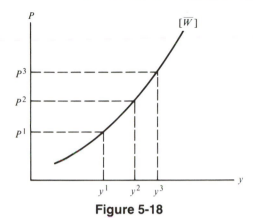

Figure 5-18

output values (y^1, y^2, and y^3) implied by the production function. From Figure 5-17 we see that $y^1 < y^2 < y^3$, just as suggested.

Furthermore, for a given $\bar{W}$ we can plot on a diagram such as Figure 5-18 the y values associated with all possible values of P. Such a plot gives us the Keynesian version of the aggregate supply (AS) function. This function, unlike the classical version, is upward sloping: the quantity of output supplied is an increasing function of the price level.

It should be mentioned in passing that some discussions of the Keynesian AS theory assume that while W does not promptly adjust downward when $n^s > n^d$, it does promptly adjust upward when $n^d > n^s$. In that case, $n = n^d$ cannot exceed the value of n at which $n^d = n^s$. There are a few advantages to that version of the Keynesian theory, but we will not embark on a discussion of it here, simply to avoid being distracted from the topics that are central to our objectives.

One point that should be emphasized regarding the Keynesian AS function is that, as indicated in Figure 5-18, its position depends on $\bar{W}$. The reader should try to explain carefully why it is that an increase in $\bar{W}$ would shift the AS curve to the left.

The motivating idea behind the Keynesian model of supply is that, for a variety of institutional and sociological reasons, wages in actual industrialized economies do not fluctuate from day to day or month to month in response to shifts in labor supply or demand. Many workers, it is presumed, are involved in long-lasting employment agreements that specify their wage rates for a year (or even three years) in advance. The quantity of work that they perform in any given month is then determined, within limits, by the employers.

5.8   The Keynesian Model

We now combine the AD theory of Section 5.4 with the Keynesian AS theory of Section 5.7. The resulting system, which constitutes the *Keynesian model*, can be written as follows:

$$y = C(y - \tau, r) + I(y, r) + g, \qquad (4)$$

$$\frac{M}{P} = L(y, r), \qquad (9)$$

$$y = f(n), \qquad (11)$$

$$f'(n) = \frac{\bar{W}}{P}. \qquad (15'')$$

Here $\bar{W}$ is, as explained above, a predetermined variable. Furthermore, the policy variables M, g, and τ are again set exogenously. Consequently, the system includes as endogenous variables just y, r, n, and P. The four equations (4), (9), (11), and (15'') are then adequate in number to determine the values of the endogenous variables.

It will be noted that this system does not include the labor supply function (16'). The system has been written that way to emphasize the point that labor supply plays no role in determining the value of n.[14] We can add (16') to the system, however, in which case it will determine the value of n^s resulting from the real wage as determined in the main part of the system. Then n^s can be compared with the value of n that prevails to determine something akin to an "unemployment" magnitude.

Graphically, the Keynesian model can be represented as in Figure 5-19. There it will be seen that there are two prominent differences from the classical model. First, as just mentioned, the labor supply function is not involved in the determination of n. Second, the AS curve is not vertical. That means, of course, that output is not determined solely in a subsystem (involving only production considerations) as it is in the classical model as presented above.[15] In other words, the Keynesian model does not "dichotomize" (i.e., split into two segments).

---

[14] That statement is true in our present static context, but would not be true in a dynamic version of the Keynesian model in which labor demand–supply imbalances affect future values of W.

[15] Our version features one simplification—the absence of a "real-balance effect"— that is necessary for that property. A more properly specified classical model would *not* dichotomize (yet would feature monetary neutrality). On this subject, see Patinkin (1965).

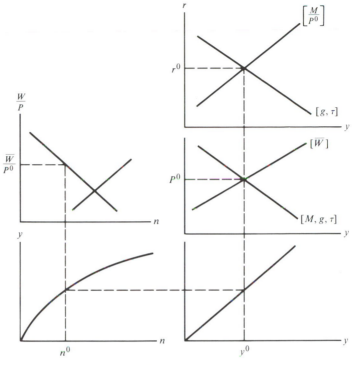

Figure 5-19

To illustrate the workings of this model—and one of its most important properties—consider the effects of an increase in the stock of money. In Figure 5-20 we trace out the effects of an increase from M^0 to M^1. It will readily be observed that the results are dramatically different from those of Figure 5-16, which examined the same policy action in the context of the classical model. In particular, the Keynesian model is one in which the neutrality of money does *not* obtain; an increase in M lowers r and raises n and y. Also, P rises by a smaller proportion than M, so M/P rises. The increase in n reflects a movement along the labor demand curve to a lower value of the real wage.

The fact that the classical and Keynesian models have such sharply different characteristics leads one naturally to wonder which of the two is better, that is, is more useful in understanding actual macroeconomic phenomena. As it happens, however, that question is not one that can be answered in a few sentences. Indeed, it is in a sense the central question of all macroeconomics. Consequently, we will not try to provide a brief answer here. Instead, we attempt to develop some appreciation of the merits and demerits of each of the two models—or, rather, extensions of these models—as the course proceeds.

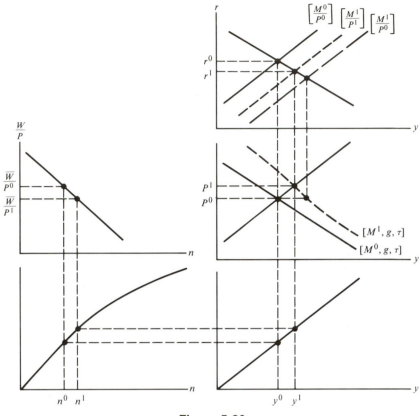

Figure 5-20

Appendix: *IS–LM* and Maximizing Analysis

In recent years, use of the *IS–LM* apparatus summarized above has attracted considerable criticism on various grounds. One strand of criticism identifies the *IS–LM* approach with Keynesian analysis and contrasts it with an alternative "market clearing" approach.[16] A second strand suggests that more assets need to be included[17] while a third features the purely methodological argument that useful models need to be based on explicit maximization analysis of the choice problems of individual agents.[18] In partial response to these three strands of criti-

---

[16] In the textbook by Barro (1984), the *IS–LM* formulation appears only within a chapter entitled "The Keynesian Theory of Business Fluctuations."

[17] A recent expression of this position is provided by Brunner and Meltzer (1988).

[18] An accessible statement of this position is provided by Sargent (1982).

cism, it is argued in the following paragraphs that the first is basically misdirected, that the second suffers from imprecision, and that the third has merit in principle but does not discredit *IS–LM* analysis in practice for issues of the type considered in this book.

Critics who take the first of the three strands of argument probably have in mind an undesirable practice, common in the 1950s and 1960s, of using the aggregate demand function of Section 5.4 as if it were itself a complete model by treating the price level as a constant. Under that assumption, the system's behavior is indeed even more anticlassical than in the Keynesian model of Section 5.8. For example, an increase in the money stock brings about no price-level response and so implies an even larger increase in output than suggested by Figure 5-20. There is, however, no need to use the *IS–LM* apparatus in that way. If it is viewed instead as a model of aggregate demand, it can be combined with the classical supply function of Section 5.5 to yield a model that is rather similar to the "market-clearing" model emphasized by Barro (1984).[19] That point will be developed below.

The second strand of argument, which suggests that additional assets need to be recognized, is imprecise in the following sense: it does not specify *for what issues* such recognition is necessary. Certainly, it is true that for some purposes—to answer some questions—the analyst would want to include another type of asset besides money and the security that yields interest at the rate r. But for other purposes, the limited *IS–LM* menu of assets may nevertheless be entirely adequate. For issues relating to sustained inflation, for example, there is no need to distinguish between real yields on long-term bonds, commercial paper, bank loans, and physical capital. Indeed, it would appear that recognition of more assets is inessential for most issues of monetary macroeconomics.[20]

The third strand of criticism, which postulates the desirability of models derived from explicit maximization analysis of agents' choice problems, requires a more lengthy discussion. In principle, the basic postulate seems quite unassailable; explicit maximization analysis is helpful in isolating crucial variables and eliminating internal inconsistencies. But it is not necessary that the analysis be conducted anew each time a model is to be used; if the behavioral relations of the *IS–LM* framework are sensible, then there is no need for them to be freshly derived each time they are used. The actual issue, then, is whether these relations are well specified, that is, internally consistent and congruent with the data.

---

[19] That strategy is utilized extensively by Bailey (1972).

[20] Brunner and Meltzer (1988) list, however, a number of issues that cannot be addressed within a two-asset *IS–LM* framework.

To check on internal consistency, it will be useful to look for possible discrepancies between *IS–LM* behavioral relations and ones derived from explicit maximization analysis conducted in a closely related framework. In developing such an analysis, we shall, as in Barro (1984), ignore the existence of firms. We assume, in other words, that production is carried out by household units otherwise similar to those of Section 3.2. This step facilitates the analysis considerably, without affecting the principal conclusions.[21]

Formally, we now assume (as in Chapter 3) that the typical household seeks at time t to maximize the multiperiod utility function

$$u(c_t, l_t) + \beta u(c_{t+1}, l_{t+1}) + \beta^2 u(c_{t+2}, l_{t+2}) + \cdots . \tag{A1}$$

Here c_t and l_t are consumption and leisure in period t, while β is a discount factor $(0 < \beta < 1)$ reflecting positive time preference. The household's choices are constrained by a relationship

$$l_t = \psi(c_t, m_t), \qquad \psi_1 < 0, \ \psi_2 > 0 \tag{A2}$$

that specifies the amount of time left for leisure after a variable amount is devoted to shopping and a fixed amount (say, $\bar{n}$) to productive labor. For any given amount of consumption, shopping time is reduced and leisure increased by larger real money holdings m_t.

In Chapter 3 each household's current income was treated as independent of its behavior. Here, by contrast, we assume that each household operates a productive facility, producing output from labor and capital inputs according to the production function

$$y_t = F(n_t, k_{t-1}), \tag{A3}$$

where $F(\ )$ has the properties mentioned in Section 5.2. Here n_t and k_{t-1} are the quantities of labor and capital employed by the typical household in period t. There are competitive rental markets for both factors so each household has the option of using greater or smaller amounts in production than its own supplies (i.e., than $\bar{n}$ and the amount of capital held over from the previous period). But since households are assumed to be alike, the quantities chosen will in equilibrium be the same as those supplied for each household. Consequently, we can proceed by treating n_t in (A3) as a constant and k_{t-1} as a predetermined variable.

Let us then use $f(k_{t-1})$ to denote the typical household's production and write its budget constraint for period t as

$$f(k_{t-1}) + v_t = c_t + k_t - k_{t-1} + m_t - (1 + \pi_{t-1})^{-1} m_{t-1}. \tag{A4}$$

---

[21] That this is so is shown by Barro (1984, pp. 220–30).

Here v_t represents lump-sum transfers to the household from government (measured net of taxes) while $m_t = M_t/P_t$ and $\pi_{t-1} = (P_t - P_{t-1})/P_{t-1}$. This constraint says that current output plus transfers can be used to purchase consumption goods or to make additions to the household's holding of assets (capital and real money balances).

The household's problem at t is to choose values for c_t, m_t, l_t, and k_t so as to maximize (A1) subject to (A2) and (A4), with similar constraints holding for each period in the future. The mathematical steps involved are analogous to those described in Section 3.2, and result after some work in the following necessary first-order conditions:

$$\frac{u_2(c_t, l_t)\psi_2(c_t, m_t)}{u_1(c_t, l_t) + u_2(c_t, l_t)\psi_1(c_t, m_t)} = -\frac{1}{[f'(k_t) + 1](1 + \pi_t)}, \quad \text{(A5)}$$

$$\frac{u_1(c_t, l_t) + u_2(c_t, l_t)\psi_1(c_t, m_t)}{u_1(c_{t+1}, l_{t+1}) + u_2(c_{t+1}, l_{t+1})\psi_1(c_{t+1}, m_{t+1})} = \beta[f'(k_t) + 1]. \quad \text{(A6)}$$

These, together with (A2) and (A4), determine the household's choices at t of c_t, m_t, l_t, and k_t.

Now we wish to compare the behavioral equations resulting from this maximization analysis with those that appear in the *IS–LM* framework. To facilitate that comparison, imagine that (A2) is substituted into both (A5) and (A6). Then l_t is eliminated and the left-hand sides of both become functions involving only the variables c_t and $m_t = M_t/P_t$, with values for period $t + 1$ also appearing in (A6). The point to be emphasized is that these modified versions of (A5) and (A6) are closely related to the *LM* and *IS* functions derived in Sections 5.3 and 5.2.

The similarity is greatest in the case of the *LM* function, for the left-hand side of our modified version of (A5) is precisely the same as that of equation (11) in Chapter 3,[22] while the right-hand side of (A5) differs only by its inclusion of $[f'(k_t) + 1](1 + \pi_t)$ in place of $(1 + R_t)$. But the former product is approximately equal to $1 + f'(k_t) + \pi_t$ in which $f'(k_t)$ is the real rate of return on capital in the household maximization model. Thus the two equations would coincide exactly if this real rate of return were equal to $R_t - \pi_t$. But precisely that equality is justified by the discussion in Chapter 6. So our modified (A5) is fully equivalent to the money demand function derived in Section 3.2, and the latter forms the basis for the *LM* specification in Section 5.3.

Turning next to condition (A6) with (A2) inserted, what we have is a relationship between the marginal product of capital, $f'(k_t)$, and the ratio of the marginal utilities of consumption in periods t and $t + 1$. But

---

[22] Actually, equation (11) of Chapter 3 must be rearranged for this statement to be true, but the rearrangement requires only division by the term in curly brackets.

that ratio involves the household's preferences regarding consumption in the present as compared with consumption in the future, which is what the "consumption function" of Section 5.2 is designed to reflect. Furthermore, the properties of the two relationships are fairly similar, since diminishing marginal utility of consumption (i.e., $u_{11} < 0$) implies that higher interest rates are associated in (A6) with smaller levels of current consumption demand,[23] as with the *IS* relation (4) of Section 5.2.

Because of this similarity, it turns out that for many important policy experiments the workings of a classical (flexible price) model are virtually the same whether aggregate demand behavior is represented by equations like (A5) and (A6) or by *IS* and *LM* relations.[24] Monetary neutrality, for example, is a property of the model under both specifications. Also, in both cases an increased rate of government purchases will tend to drive up the rate of interest.

There are other policy experiments, to be sure, which give rise to different outcomes in the two models. One relevant example concerns the effects of different money growth rates (and different anticipated inflation rates) on the real rate of return to capital. There is no problem in modifying the *IS–LM* apparatus so as to reflect a dependence of this rate of return. But the construction of the *IS* function presumes a fixed stock of capital, as a careful reading of Section 5.2 will disclose. Thus the *IS–LM* apparatus tends to lead the analyst astray when the experiment under investigation implies outcomes that would induce an adjustment in the capital stock. Such implications are more common in response to fiscal policy changes, however, than ones involving monetary policy. Consequently, the *IS–LM* framework is more satisfactory for issues of the type emphasized in this book than it is for general macroeconomic analysis. For many monetary policy actions, the response of the capital stock is small enough in a full maximizing model that *IS–LM* predictions will be approximately the same.

We have discussed only classical models, but if the aggregate demand portion of the *IS–LM* model is satisfactory with flexible prices, it should also be satisfactory when combined with an aggregate supply specification featuring sticky prices. So our conclusions apply also in the case of Keynesian models.

In sum, the properties of a macroeconomic model with aggregate demand relations of the *IS–LM* type are fairly similar to those of a comparable model derived via explicit maximization analysis. Indeed,

---

[23] This statement presumes, however, an elaboration of the *IS–LM* demand analysis that is designed to take account of anticipated inflation. Such an elaboration is developed and emphasized in Chapter 6.

[24] This argument presumes that changes in the left-hand side of (A6) are quantitatively dominated by changes in the term $u_1(c_t, l_t)$.

the *LM* portion of the *IS–LM* setup is identical to a money demand relation obtained with the maximization approach. For many issues, accordingly, the properties of the two types of model are similar— especially for issues that depend primarily on money demand behavior. We conclude, then, that judicious use of *IS–LM* relations can be fruitful in monetary economics, since these relations are comparatively simple in specification and are therefore easy to use. That conclusion presumes, however, that the analysis in question does not ignore price-level changes or the effects of inflation on interest rates. Such effects form the main topic of Chapter 6.

Problems

1. What is the relationship (if any) between equation (15) and the familiar condition, marginal cost = marginal revenue?
2. In the classical model, equations (11) and (15) could be expressed more completely as $y = f(n, k)$ and $f_1(n, k) = W/P$. Using this model, analyze the effects on all endogenous variables of an earthquake that destroys a portion of the economy's capital stock (without harming the population).
3. The discussion following equation (3) suggests a flaw in the analysis called for in Problem 2. Discuss the source of this flaw, explaining which of the model's relationships would be likely to break down.
4. Compare the levels of employment determined in the Keynesian model for two different values of the predetermined money wage, $\bar{W}^0$ and $\bar{W}^1 < \bar{W}^0$.
5. In the development of economic thought, an important role was played by a modified version of the classical model in which the consumption function becomes $c = C(y, \tau, M/P)$ with $C_3 > 0$. The idea is that greater real wealth, of which M/P is one component, leads to more consumption relative to saving from any income level. With this modification, does the classical model continue to have the property called "neutrality of money"? Does it continue to "dichotomize"?
6. Does the property called "neutrality of money" imply that a monetary economy would have the same output if it were a barter economy with no money?
7. Analysis that compares static equilibrium positions before and after some postulated change is termed comparative-static analysis. One type of comparative-static experiment that is of great importance concerns the effects of technological change, a process that alters the quantity of output produced from given amounts of labor (and capital). To illustrate such a change, suppose that an economy's

production function is initially $y = 2n^{0.5}$, but then a technological innovation shifts it to $y = 3n^{0.5}$. For concreteness, also suppose that labor supply behavior is described by $n = 100 \, W/P$. Determine algebraically the equilibrium values of n^* and y^* before and after the technological improvement. Also, represent the change graphically, using diagrams like those of Figure 5-14. What would be the qualitative effects on r^*, P^*, and $(W/P)^*$ according to the classical model?

References

Bailey, Martin J., *National Income and the Price Level*, 2nd ed. (New York: McGraw-Hill Book Company, 1971) Chaps. 2, 3.

Barro, Robert J., *Macroeconomics*. (New York: John Wiley & Sons, Inc., 1984) Chaps. 6–8, 19.

Brunner, Karl, and Allan H. Meltzer, "Money and Credit in the Monetary Transmission Process," *American Economic Review Papers and Proceedings* 78 (May 1988), 446–51.

Dornbusch, Rudiger, and Stanley Fischer, *Macroeconomics*, 3rd ed. (New York: McGraw-Hill Book Company, 1984) Chaps. 11, 12.

Henderson, James M., and Richard E. Quandt, *Microeconomic Theory*, 3rd ed. (New York: McGraw-Hill Book Company, 1980).

Keynes, John M., *The General Theory of Employment, Interest and Money*. (London: Macmillan Publishing Company, 1936).

Patinkin, Don, *Money, Interest, and Prices*, 2nd ed. (New York: Harper & Row, Publishers, 1965), Chaps. 9–15.

Sargent, Thomas J., "Beyond Demand and Supply Curves in Macroeconomics," *American Economic Review Papers and Proceedings* 72 (May 1982), 382–89.

Sargent, Thomas J., *Macroeconomic Theory*. (New York: Academic Press, Inc. 1979), Chaps. 1, 2.

6

Steady Inflation

6.1 Introduction

At this point we begin the transition from static to dynamic analysis. In Chapter 5 the analytical method was to compare static equilibrium positions of the economy prevailing before and after some postulated change in an exogenous variable (or some postulated shift in a behavioral relation). The dynamic behavior of the variables in the time interval after the postulated change, but before the attainment of the new equilibrium position, was not considered. In effect, then, this analysis was timeless; we simply did not keep track of the passage of time. But it would clearly be extremely desirable to be able to describe the behavior of an economy functioning in real time—to explain movements in variables from quarter to quarter, for example. Full-fledged dynamic analysis is much more difficult than comparative statics, however, so we shall have to proceed slowly. The first step, accordingly, will be to develop the concept of a *steady-state* equilibrium, in which some of the system's variables change over time but in a restrictive manner. In particular, in steady-state analysis all variables are required to be growing at a constant rate—at a rate that is unchanging as time passes. For some of the variables that rate will be zero; that is, the values of the variables themselves will be constant. The values of the other variables, by contrast, will be changing through time, but will be doing so at a rate that is constant. This rate may in principle differ from variable to variable; all that the steady-state concept requires is that each variable be growing at *some* constant rate. In many cases, however, the same rate will apply to all variables that are growing at nonzero rates.

By a "growth rate" what is meant here is the *relative* rate of change (through time) of a variable. Thus in terms of variables that change continuously through time, the measure of the growth rate is not the time derivative, but that derivative divided by the value of the variable itself. For the variable x, the growth rate would be $(1/x)\,dx/dt$, not dx/dt, for instance. The amount of the change per unit time is measured *relative* to the magnitude prevailing.

In our discussion we shall not, however, treat our variables as changing continuously through time. Instead, we will work with discrete periods of time—*periods* such as months or quarters or years—pretending that the value of any variable is the same throughout each period but liable to change "between" periods. From this perspective, the growth rate of x between periods $t - 1$ and t might possibly be defined as $(x_t - x_{t-1})/x_{t-1}$, where x_t is the value of x in period t and x_{t-1} its value in period $t - 1$. It would be just as logical, however, to define the growth rate of x as $(x_t - x_{t-1})/x_t$, or as $(x_t - x_{t-1})/0.5(x_t + x_{t-1})$, instead of the expression in the preceding sentence. Indeed, reference to the continuous-time concept $(1/x)\,dx/dt$ suggests that a definition preferable to all of the foregoing would be

$$
\begin{aligned}
\text{growth rate of } x \text{ between } t - 1 \text{ and } t &= \Delta \log x_t \\
&= \log x_t - \log x_{t-1} \\
&= \log \frac{x_t}{x_{t-1}}.
\end{aligned}
\tag{1}
$$

Here $\log x_t$ means the natural logarithm, that is, the logarithm to the base $e = 2.713$, of the variable x_t. The symbol Δ attached to any dated variable indicates the difference between the dated value and that of the previous period, so that (for example) Δz_t means $z_t - z_{t-1}$. In the present case, then, $\Delta \log x_t$ means $\log x_t - \log x_{t-1}$. Finally, the last equality in (1) obtains as a result of the properties of logarithms: for any number A and B, $\log (A/B) = \log A - \log B$.

That the definition of the growth rate given by expression (1) is consistent with the continuous-time concept may be seen by recalling that the derivative (w.r.t. x) of $\log x$ is $1/x$. Thus in continuous time the concept $(1/x)\,dx/dt$ is equivalent to $d \log x/dt$, while the latter has $\Delta \log x_t$ as its discrete-time analog.

The main advantage of working with expression (1) rather than the other discrete-time possibilities stems from the following fact: because of the properties of logarithms, the growth rate of a product such as YZ is equal to the sum of the growth rates of Y and Z. To prove that, note that if $X_t \equiv Y_t Z_t$, then

$$
\begin{aligned}
\Delta \log X_t = \log X_t - \log X_{t-1} &= \log (Y_t Z_t) - \log (Y_{t-1} Z_{t-1}) \\
&= \log Y_t + \log Z_t - \log Y_{t-1} - \log Z_{t-1} = \log Y_t - \log Y_{t-1} \\
&\quad + \log Z_t - \log Z_{t-1} = \Delta \log Y_t + \Delta \log Z_t.
\end{aligned}
\tag{2}
$$

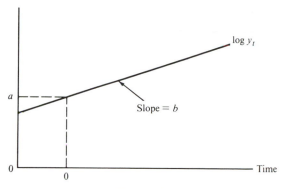

Figure 6-1

Similarly, it is true that if $X_t \equiv Y_t/Z_t$, then $\Delta \log X_t = \Delta \log Y_t - \Delta \log Z_t$. That is, the growth rate of a ratio of two variables is the difference in the growth rates of these variables. These identities, which would *not* hold under other definitions, are highly useful.

Given our definition of growth rates, the concept of a steady-state equilibrium implies that the steady-state time path of a variable y_t must conform to an equation of the form

$$\Delta \log y_t = b, \tag{3}$$

where b is some constant. This in turn implies that the steady-state values of y_t are describable by an expression of the form

$$\log y_t = a + bt, \tag{4}$$

where b is the same constant as in (3) and where a is a constant that equals the logarithm of the value of y_t in period $t = 0$. (That is, $a = \log y_0$.) Consequently, any steady-state time path can be represented graphically as in Figure 6-1. The *slope* of the line representing $\log y_t$ gives the growth rate of y_t.[1]

The logarithmic definition of growth rates (or rates of change) that we have adopted for discrete-time variables may seem strange to some readers, who are familiar with some alternative concept such as $(x_t - x_{t-1})/x_{t-1}$. The main reason for our choice is that algebraic manipulations with the $\Delta \log x_t$ definition are simpler and clearer. Also, our concept accords well with the continuous-time measure $(1/x)\,dx/dt$. These reasons seem adequate to justify our convention, especially since

---

[1] Strictly speaking, we should plot values of $\log y_t$ only at discrete points for $t = 0, 1, 2, \ldots$ when the discrete-time representation is being used. For convenience, however, we will use continuous graphs to depict discrete-time variables.

$\Delta \log x_t$ is *numerically* close to $(x_t - x_{t-1})/x_{t-1}$ whenever the latter number is reasonably small relative to 1.0. That is, for growth rates of the order of magnitude of 0.05, 0.10, or 0.15 (in *percentage* terms these are growth rates of 5, 10, and 15 percent), the values of $(x_t - x_{t-1})/x_{t-1}$ and $\Delta \log x_t$ are approximately the same. That this must be true can be verified by noting that our concept $\Delta \log x_t$ equals

$$\log \frac{x_t}{x_{t-1}} = \log\left(\frac{x_t}{x_{t-1}} - \frac{x_{t-1}}{x_{t-1}} + 1\right) = \log\left(1 + \frac{x_t - x_{t-1}}{x_{t-1}}\right) \quad (5)$$

and recalling that, for small values of the number z, $\log(1 + z)$ is approximately equal to z.[2] Thus $\Delta \log x_t$ is approximately equal to $(x_t - x_{t-1})/x_{t-1}$ when the latter is small.

6.2   Real Versus Nominal Interest Rates

At this point it will be convenient to introduce the heretofore ignored distinction between real and nominal interest rates. This distinction is important in the context of steady-state analysis because a steady-state equilibrium may feature a constant but nonzero rate of change of the price level, that is, a nonzero inflation rate. Since this nonzero inflation rate will be constant over time in a steady state, it is implausible to believe that the economy's individuals will not recognize the existence of inflation and correctly anticipate that it will continue to prevail in the future. Indeed, the requirement that inflation (and other variables) be correctly anticipated is a natural assumption for steady-state analysis, and is one that we shall henceforth utilize.[3]

But with the price level changing over time, the economically relevant rate of interest on a loan with provisions specified in monetary terms depends on the anticipated inflation rate. Imagine, for example, a loan of $1000 for a period of one year, with the provision that the borrower must pay the lender $1100 at the end of the year. In monetary terms, the rate of interest on this loan is 0.10 (or 10 percent). But if the lender expects the price level to be 10 percent higher at the end of the year than at the time of the loan, he expects to be repaid an amount that is worth in real terms only just as much as the amount lent. Thus to him the (expected) real rate of interest on the loan is zero. If, however, he expected the price level to be only 4 percent higher, he would

---

[2] Technically, for z close to zero the first-order Taylor series approximation to $\log (1 + z)$ is z.

[3] In effect, then, our definition of a steady state is an ongoing situation in which every variable is growing at some constant rate and in which expectations are correct.

anticipate receiving a payment worth in real terms 106 percent of his loan. In this case, the real interest rate as viewed by the lender would be $0.10 - 0.04 = 0.06$ or 6 percent.

From this type of reasoning we see that in general the real rate of interest on a loan specified in monetary terms is the *nominal* (monetary) rate of interest minus the expected inflation rate for the life of the loan. In particular, if R_t is the nominal rate of interest on one-period loans made in t, and π_t is the inflation rate expected between t and $t + 1$, the real rate r_t will be given by

$$r_t = R_t - \pi_t. \tag{6}$$

The distinction represented in this equation reflects one of the most important ideas in monetary economics. It will be utilized extensively in the discussion that follows. For other discussions of this distinction, and the material of this chapter more generally, the reader is referred to Bailey (1971, Chap. 4) and Barro (1984, Chap. 8).

6.3 Inflation in the Classical Model

Having introduced some necessary tools, we are now in a position to develop the analysis of a steady, ongoing inflation. This analysis will be conducted in the context of the classical model. We begin with this model, rather than the Keynesian version, for two reasons. First, it is clear that, because of its assumption of a given money wage rate, the Keynesian model would have to be seriously modified to permit a sensible analysis of ongoing inflation.[4] Second, since steady-state comparisons represent a type of "long-run" analysis, designed for the elucidation of policies maintained over a long span of time,[5] the assumption of wage flexibility is not at all inappropriate—as many economists believe it would be for "short-run" issues.

Let us begin the analysis by assuming that the monetary authority, in a classical economy with no growth of population and no technical progress, causes the money stock to increase period after period at the rate μ. Thus we assume that

$$\Delta \log M_t = \mu, \tag{7}$$

where M_t is the money stock in period t. From the discussion in Section 6.1 we know that the path of M_t can then be depicted as in Figure 6-2, which is drawn under the assumption that μ is positive. Now,

---

[4] Which would presumably be accompanied by ongoing increases in the nominal wage rate.

[5] That this is so will become apparent subsequently.

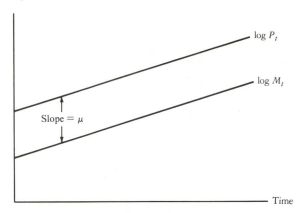

Figure 6-2

in a situation such as this, it seems natural to guess—on the basis of our knowledge of the comparative static properties of the classical model—that the price level P_t will also grow over time at the rate μ. In that case, the path of P_t would be as shown in Figure 6-2, where the slope of the path of log P_t is the same as that of log M_t.[6]

To verify that P_t would in fact behave in this conjectured manner, we must consider the complete model. In Section 5.6 the latter was summarized with the five following equations:

$$y = C(y - \tau, r) + I(y, r) + g,$$

$$\frac{M}{P} = L(y, r),$$

$$y = f(n),$$

$$f'(n) = \frac{W}{P},$$

$$n = h\left(\frac{W}{P}\right).$$

Since we are now assuming that there is no change in population or technology as time passes, we can use the final three of these to determine the values of y_t, n_t, and W_t/P_t that will prevail in our steady state. Note that in doing this, however, we are implicitly assuming that

---

[6] Note that it is unimportant whether the log P_t path is drawn above or below log M_t in Figure 6-2; the relative vertical locations depend on the units of measurement of the economy's single commodity and are therefore arbitrary.

the capital stock is constant over time, an assumption that we will want to relax subsequently.

With y_t equal to the constant value y^*, determined in the manner just described, it remains to determine the behavior of P_t and r_t. But from the discussion in Section 6.2, we know that we must consider whether it is the real or nominal interest rate that appears in the *IS* and *LM* equations. As it happens, the answer is that both appear—or, more precisely, that R_t appears in one equation and r_t in the other. In particular, the analysis of Chapter 3 indicates that it is R_t that belongs in the *LM* equation,[7] which we therefore rewrite as

$$\frac{M_t}{P_t} = L(y_t, R_t). \tag{8}$$

Reflection on the nature of the *IS* function as discussed in Section 5.2 indicates, however, that it is the real rate r_t that is relevant for saving and investment decisions, basically because people care about real magnitudes. The *IS* curve can then be represented as

$$y_t = C(y_t - \tau, r_t) + I(y_t, r_t) + g.$$

Here we have written the tax and government spending variables as constants, which they must be (with no growth in population) for a steady state. Solving this last equation for r_t, we then obtain

$$r_t = \Omega(y_t), \tag{9}$$

where the g and τ values are suppressed for notational simplicity.

Our next task is to bring the *IS* and *LM* equations together as in the various diagrams of Chapter 5. That task is rendered more difficult by the appearance of R_t in (8) and r_t in (9), but this problem can be overcome by means of expression (6). From (6) we know that $R_t = r_t + \pi_t$, so we can substitute (9) into the latter and obtain

$$R_t = \Omega(y_t) + \pi_t. \tag{10}$$

For a given value of π_t, then, equations (8) and (10) may be solved for R_t and P_t since M_t is exogenously set by the policy authorities and y_t is given as y^*.

Graphically, we proceed as shown in Figure 6-3. There the vertical axis measures R_t, so the *LM* curve is plotted as usual. Then the function

---

[7] This is demonstrated formally in the analysis of Section 3.3. The basic idea can, however, be expressed very simply as follows: since the nominal interest rate paid on money is zero and that on "bonds" is R_t, the difference between these is R_t. Similarly, the real interest rate on money is $0 - \pi_t = -\pi_t$ while the real rate on bonds is $R_t - \pi_t$, so the difference between these is also R_t. It is R_t, therefore, that measures the marginal opportunity cost of holding wealth in the form of money, which is the relevant determinant.

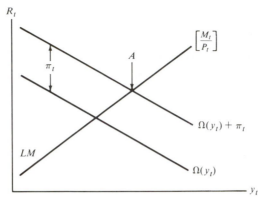

Figure 6-3

$\Omega(y_t)$ is drawn in place; it shows where the *IS* curve would be if π_t were equal to zero. Finally, the actual *IS* curve is obtained by adding vertically the quantity π_t to this last curve at each point, as suggested by (10). The relevant intersection occurs at point A.

To depict a steady-state equilibrium we modify the analysis of Figure 6-3 in three ways. First, we recognize that steady-state output will be given as y^*, so the relevant intersection (like point A) must lie on a vertical line through y^*. Second, the value of y, R, π, and M/P are recognized to be constant over time.[8] Third, the value of π must be the same as $\Delta \log P_t$, and for M/P to be constant $\Delta \log P_t$ must be the same as μ. Consequently, $\pi = \mu$ in the steady state with no output growth.[9] Recognizing these modifications, we can depict a situation of steady-state equilibrium with an inflation rate of $\pi = \mu$ as shown in Figure 6-4. Here the value of R is determined by the intersection of the *IS* curve $R = \Omega(y) + \pi$ and the vertical line $y = y^*$. The *LM* curve must of course pass through that same point. So the role of the *LM* relation is—just as in the static analysis of Section 5.6—only to determine the value of real money balances M/P, given y and R. With M exogenous, that value determines the price level.

The main conclusion of the foregoing is that we have been able to assemble the components of our model in a way that is internally consistent. This verifies, then, that P_t does indeed grow at the rate μ in the steady state, as conjectured above. Figure 6-4 provides, conse-

---

[8] We have already discussed why y and π will be constant. That R must be constant is a consequence of the fact that r_t must be constant—which will be explained in Section 6.6—and that $R_t = r_t + \pi_t$. Then with y and R constant, M/P will be constant by equation (8).

[9] If y is growing because of technical progress or population growth, then P_t will grow less rapidly than M_t. This will be explained in Section 6.6.

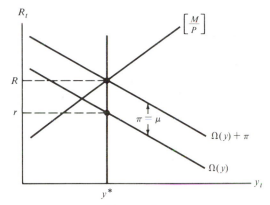

Figure 6-4

quently, a representation of a steady-state equilibrium. The latter differs from a static equilibrium in that the values of M and P are continually changing from period to period. In particular, they are growing at the rate μ, that is, $\Delta \log P_t = \Delta \log M_t = \mu$. This fact can be emphasized by appending to Figure 6-4 a companion diagram that would look exactly the same as Figure 6-2.

6.4   Comparative Steady States

The main purpose of a diagram like Figure 6-4 is to facilitate the *comparison* of different steady states, just as the main purpose of a static equilibrium diagram like Figure 5-14 is to serve as a prelude to static equilibria comparisons such as that of Figure 5-15. Accordingly, we shall now carry out, as an example, a graphical analysis of a comparison of two steady states.

This is done in Figure 6-5. There the initial steady-state equilibrium is one in which the money stock growth rate is μ^0, while the second (steady-state) equilibrium is with a higher money growth rate, μ^1. The value of y^* is not affected by the change of μ from μ^0 to μ^1, nor is the position of the $\Omega(y)$ curve. Thus the relevant IS curve in terms of the nominal interest rate is higher in the second steady state: $\Omega(u) + \pi^1$ lies above $\Omega(y) + \pi^0$. The equilibrium value of the nominal interest rate is therefore higher also; $R^1 > R^0$. Indeed, since the real interest rate r is determined by the intersection of $r = \Omega(y)$ and $y = y^*$, it is the same in the two steady-state equilibria; consequently, R^1 exceeds R^0 by the same amount as π^1 exceeds π^0, which is in turn the amount by

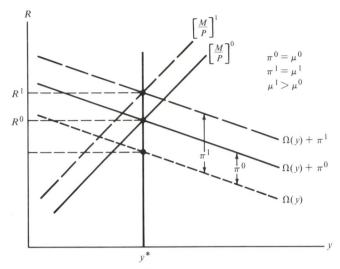

Figure 6-5

which μ^1 exceeds μ^0. The higher is the money growth rate, therefore, the higher is the nominal interest rate—and by the same amount.

One of the main implications of the analysis in Figure 6-5 is that the value of real money balances in the second steady-state equilibrium is smaller than in the first; that is, $(M/P)^1 < (M/P)^0$. That this must be so is clear from consideration of the diagram—where $\Omega(y^*) + \pi^1$ is above $\Omega(y^*) + \pi^0$—since the position of the LM curve is farther to the right the higher the M/P. Thus in a comparison of steady states, the one with the *higher* growth rate of the nominal money stock will feature a *smaller* quantity of real money balances held by the economy's individuals! This somewhat paradoxical conclusion is one of the key propositions of neoclassical monetary analysis.

The comparison of steady-state equilibria in Figure 6-5 may be further investigated by means of a companion diagram that plots time paths of $\log M_t$ and $\log P_t$. In Figure 6-6 it is assumed that the initial steady state (with $\mu = \mu^0$) prevails for time periods up to $t = t^+$. Then at time t^+ the growth rate of M_t changes to μ^1. This is represented in Figure 6-6 by the increased slope of the $\log M_t$ path for periods after t^+.[10] The time paths for $\log P_t$ in the initial and final steady states are also shown in Figure 6-6. Since M/P is constant in each of these

---

[10] While the growth rate changes abruptly at $t = t^+$, the value of the money stock M_t itself does not jump upward or downward at that instant in the example depicted.

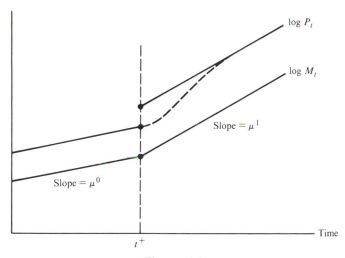

Figure 6-6

steady-state equilibria, the slope of log P_t is the same as the slope of log M_t in both cases. But since the value of M/P is smaller in the final equilibrium (as emphasized in the preceding paragraph) the height of the log P_t path must be higher, relative to the height of the log M_t path, reflecting an increased value of P/M.

From the way in which the log P_t path is drawn in Figure 6-6, it appears that the price level jumps upward in a discontinuous fashion at time t^+. This aspect of the diagram should not be taken literally, however, for the diagram is intended only to describe the comparison of steady-state positions. Although our analytical apparatus tells us a good deal about this comparison, it does not tell us enough to permit any reliable description of the transition between the initial and final steady states. In this respect, comparative steady-state analysis is similar to comparative statics: we do not know how the system behaves dynamically during the transition from one equilibrium to another.

In particular, it is possible that the time path of P_t would move toward the new steady-state path only gradually, as indicated by the dashed curve in Figure 6-6 rather than by jumping upward at t^*. But notice that if this is the case, then during the transition P_t *must grow faster* than M_t for some time. An increase in the money growth rate will, therefore, require either a jump in the price level or an inflation rate that temporarily exceeds the new (higher) money growth rate. Analogously, a sustained decrease in an economy's money growth rate requires either an abrupt fall in the price level or an interval of time during which the inflation rate is lower than the new (lowered) money growth rate.

These last statements depend, it should be said, on the assumption that there is no upward or downward jump in the level of the money stock—no discontinuity in the M_t path. For if there were an appropriate downward jump in M_t, then P_t would not have to jump upward for M_t/P_t to fall as required.

In addition, it should be pointed out that our analysis assumes that the change in the money growth rate that takes place at t^+ comes as a complete surprise to the economy's private individuals. In each period before t^+ they confidently believe that the money growth rate will continue to equal μ^0 indefinitely. If the change from μ^0 to μ^1 at t^+ were foreseen, the price level would begin to rise toward its new steady-state path before the change in $\Delta \log M_t$ actually occurs.

To conclude this section, it may be useful to emphasize the importance of distinguishing clearly between statements pertaining to the properties of one steady state and statements comparing alternative steady states. In particular, while growth rates of all variables in a given steady state are constant over time, these may change if the economy moves to a different steady state. In the first steady state of Figures 6-5 and 6-6, for example, $\Delta \log P_t$ is constant at the value μ^0. In the second steady state it is again constant, but at a different value, namely μ^1. If one wants to say that some variable will have the same value in different steady states, the proper terminology is not "constant" but "invariant across steady states."

6.5   Analysis with Real-Balance Effects

In footnote 15 and Problem 5 of Chapter 5, the possibility was mentioned that households' consumption choices depend positively on their real *wealth*, in addition to the y and r determinants. In particular, the consumption function $c = C(y - \tau, r, M/P)$ was introduced, with M/P reflecting the monetary component of real wealth held by households. That change in specification gives rise, by way of analysis paralleling that of Section 5.2 and 6.3, to an *IS* function of the form

$$r_t = \Omega\left(y_t, \frac{M_t}{P_t}\right) + \pi_t, \qquad \Omega_1 < 0, \Omega_2 > 0, \qquad (11)$$

where now Ω is a function of two variables. With the classical model thus modified, it ceases to be true that the real interest rate r will be the same in steady-state equilibria with different inflation rates (i.e.,

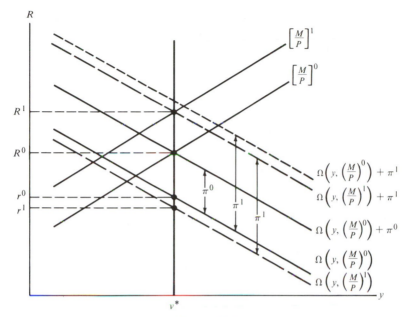

Figure 6-7

different values of $\mu = \pi$). That is, the classical model ceases to have the property of "superneutrality," to use a term that is often employed to describe a model in which all real variables except M/P are independent of the inflation rate.

To demonstrate graphically that superneutrality does not prevail when the "real-balance effect" is important,[11] consider Figure 6-7. There each of the IS functions includes M/P as an argument, as required by (11). Thus when an increase in the money growth rate increases π from π^0 to π^1, the resulting decrease in M/P itself tends to cause the IS curve to shift to the left. This type of shift also pertains to $\Omega(y, M/P)$, which locates the position of the IS curve in the absence of inflation.[12] Thus the decrease in M/P to $(M/P)^1$ shifts the $\Omega(y, M/P)$ curve leftward and drives its intersection with $y = y^*$ downward. This implies that the real interest rate r^1 is lower than r^0, as suggested

---

[11] A model is said to feature a "real-balance effect" when the consumption function includes M/P as an argument. This term was used extensively by Patinkin (1965).

[12] Note that $\Omega[y^*, (M/P)^0]$ in Figure 6-7 does not, however, refer to the zero inflation equilibrium, for $(M/P)^0$ corresponds to the value of real balances that obtains with $\mu = \mu^0 > 0$.

above.[13] The nominal rate increases, but by less than the difference between μ^0 and μ^1. Whether this type of effect is of major importance empirically is unclear, but the reader should be aware of the theoretical possibility.

6.6 Analysis with Output Growth

All of the foregoing discussion in this chapter has been conducted under the assumption that real output is constant over time. In most actual economies, by contrast, output tends to grow as time passes. We need, then, to consider how the analysis must be modified to reflect that fact.[14]

In this context it is useful to distinguish three possible reasons for growth in aggregate output. They are

(i) Growth of population (and, therefore, labor supply).
(ii) Growth of the capital stock.
(iii) Technical progress (i.e., an increase in the amount of output possible from given inputs of labor and capital).

By far the simplest case to analyze is the one in which only (i) applies—all growth is due to increased population. In this case we can proceed by simply *reinterpreting* all the equations and diagrams above so that the quantity measures (i.e., y, n, c, M, etc.) are understood to refer to *per capita* values rather than aggregates. Then, with μ being understood as referring to the growth rate of the money stock per person, the equations and diagrams continue to be applicable. For example, if the population (and output) growth rate were 0.02, and the *total* money stock growth rate were 0.10, the per capita value for μ would be 0.08. This would be the steady-state value of π and R would exceed r in the steady state by 0.08 (i.e., by 8 percent).

If growth in the capital stock occurs, however, matters become somewhat more complicated. Within a single steady state there is no need for modification of the analysis in the absence of technical progress, for in that case the steady-state condition requires that total

---

[13] If we were permitting the capital stock to change across steady states, the lower value of r would induce a greater value of k. This would, in turn, permit a greater quantity of output for any given input of labor.

[14] For a useful discussion, see Barro and Fischer (1976).

capital and labor must grow at the same rate.[15] Thus the quantity of capital can be thought of in per capita terms and the argument of the preceding paragraph can be repeated. But for comparisons *across* steady states, this type of argument will be valid only if the values of the capital/labor ratio are not different in the two steady-state equilibria. If the model is of the simpler type discussed in Section 6.4, that condition may be satisfied. But if real-balance effects are important, as discussed in Section 6.5, the different steady states may feature different real interest rates, and these will correspond to different values of the capital stock per person (or per unit of labor). Consequently, valid comparative steady-state analysis cannot be conducted by means of the per capita reinterpretation device. A more extensive overhaul of the analysis is needed.

When technical progress is recognized, full-fledged steady-state analysis is still more complex. Indeed, unless the technical progress is of a special type known as Harrod-neutral (or "labor augmenting"), steady-state growth is not possible. For an excellent discussion of this and related topics, the reader is referred to Solow (1970).

There is a useful result that can easily be obtained, however, without going into the complexities of steady-state analysis that recognizes capital accumulation and technical progress. In particular, suppose that the aggregate (not per capita) money demand function is of the form

$$\frac{M_t}{P_t} = L(y_t, R_t), \tag{12}$$

where M_t and y_t refer to aggregate magnitudes, and suppose that aggregate output grows steadily (for whatever reason) at the rate ν. Then we can show that if a steady-state equilibrium prevails, the inflation rate will be $\mu - \gamma_1\nu$, where γ_1 is the elasticity of L with respect to y_t. The best way to see that is to consider an *approximation* to $L(y_t, R_t)$ of the Cobb–Douglas form $e^{\gamma_0}y_t^{\gamma_1}R_t^{\gamma_2}$, where γ_1 is the elasticity in question.[16] Then taking logs, we have

$$\log M_t - \log P_t = \gamma_0 + \gamma_1 \log y_t + \gamma_2 \log R_t \tag{13}$$

or, equivalently,

$$\Delta \log M_t - \Delta \log P_t = \gamma_1 \, \Delta \log y_t + \gamma_2 \, \Delta \log R_t. \tag{14}$$

---

[15] Output is given by $y_t = F(n_t, k_t)$, and the function F is typically assumed to be homogeneous of degree 1. That property implies that the rate of output growth is a weighted average of the growth rates of n_t and k_t. But it is shown in footnote 17 that k_t must grow at the same rate as output—so n_t must do the same.

[16] This is, of course, the form suggested by equation (20) of Chapter 3. We could just as well use instead the form given by equation (26) of Chapter 3, which corresponds more closely to the analysis in Chapters 7 and 8.

Now in our steady state it is true that $\Delta \log R_t = 0,$[17] $\Delta \log y_t = \nu$, and $\Delta \log M_t = \mu$ by assumption. Equation (14) then shows that

$$\Delta \log P_t = \mu - \gamma_1 \nu, \tag{15}$$

which is the result stated above.

6.7   The Welfare Cost of Inflation

The analysis of the preceding sections suggests that the pace of a steady, anticipated inflation has little effect on the values of most real variables including per capita income, consumption, and the real rate of interest. To help bring out the main points, let us ignore growth and suppose that there is no significant real-balance effect, in which case the above-mentioned variables are entirely unaffected by the rate at which steady inflation proceeds. A natural question to ask, then, is whether the rate of inflation is of any consequence in terms of the welfare of the society's individuals. After all, these individuals care—as we have emphasized in several places—only about real magnitudes. So why should inflation be of any concern whatsoever, provided that it is steady and anticipated?

From a practical perspective, actual inflation is of importance largely because it is usually irregular in pace and largely unanticipated. But in response to the foregoing question, which is of considerable theoretical interest, we note that there is one real variable that is not invariant to the inflation rate but, instead, takes on different values across alternative steady states with different rates of money creation and inflation. In particular, the level of real money balances depends negatively, as Figure 6-5 illustrates, on the prevailing inflation rate. But that suggests that there are welfare effects of inflation, for a relatively small level of real balances implies that a relatively large amount of time and energy must be devoted to "shopping" for any given level of spending. Since leisure is desired by individuals, it follows that higher steady inflation rates lead to lower utility levels for society's individuals.

---

[17] It was promised above that we would explain why the real rate of interest must be constant in a steady state (thereby implying that R_t will also be constant). Roughly speaking, the idea is that consumption and investment must grow at the same rate for their sum (and thus output) to grow at a constant rate. (Why? If one grew at a faster rate, its share in output would increase, so output growth would increase). Also, investment and capital must grow at the same rate, because of their relationship. Thus capital must grow at the same rate as output—the capital/output ratio must be constant. But this implies a constant marginal product of capital, and the latter is in equilibrium equal to the real rate of interest. For more details, see Solow (1970).

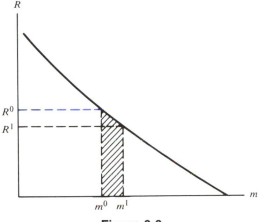

Figure 6-8

In light of the foregoing conclusion, it is of considerable interest to develop a technique for measuring the magnitude of the welfare cost of a steady, anticipated inflation. The approach that we shall take, which was introduced by Bailey (1956), utilizes a type of reasoning that is associated with "consumer surplus" analysis in the areas of public finance and applied microeconomics.[18] For our purposes, the crucial point is that the height of any demand curve indicates the value to buyers of incremental units of the commodity in question. In the context of money demand, the relevant demand curve plots real balances demanded, $m = M/P$, on the horizontal axis and the nominal interest rate, R, on the vertical axis, as in Figure 6-8. The nominal interest rate is relevant because it represents the opportunity cost to the holder of an incremental unit of money. If the prevailing interest rate is R^0 and real money holdings are m^0, for example, a one-unit increase in m will require money holders to sacrifice R^0 units per period in the form of forgone interest.[19]

Rational individuals would not be holding money, thereby sacrificing interest, unless they were receiving some benefits from the money balances held. But our analysis in Chapter 3 tells us what these benefits are; they are the time and energy that do not need to be devoted to

[18] For a textbook exposition of consumer surplus analysis, see Varian (1987, Chap. 15). An extension and correction of Bailey's analysis is provided by Tower (1971).
[19] If the price level has the units of dollars per bushel, then $m = M/P$ has the units of bushels. If the interest rate R is expressed as an annual rate, then R bushels per year must be given up for a one-bushel increase in m. Alternatively, R dollars per year must be given up for a $1 increase in m.

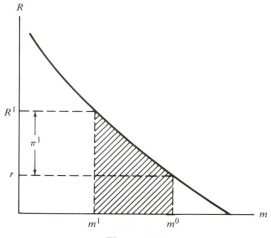

Figure 6-9

shopping because of the transaction-facilitating services provided by money. For any particular change in the level of money holdings, moreover, the change in these benefits (the volume of these services) can be calculated by summing the incremental benefits. Since those incremental benefits are represented by the height of the demand curve, the relevant sum for any change is represented by the *area* under the demand curve between the initial and final positions.[20] If, for example, money holdings increased from m^0 to m^1 in Figure 6-8, the additional transaction-facilitating services to money holders would be quantitatively represented by the shaded area under the curve between m^0 and m^1. Conversely, if money holdings were reduced from m^1 to m^0, that area would measure the reduction in money services (or the increase in time and energy devoted to shopping).

Now consider an economy experiencing a steady inflation at the rate π^1, as depicted in Figure 6-9, and suppose that this economy is one in which superneutrality prevails. The quantity of real money balances is m^1, which is smaller than the quantity m^0 that would be held if the inflation rate were zero. The transaction-facilitating services are accordingly less—more time and energy are devoted to shopping—and the reduced magnitude of these services is measured by the shaded area.

---

[20] For a smooth demand curve, the argument is like that employed in the definition of a definite *integral*. Thus we visualize many narrow rectangles (under the curve) of common width, and consider the sum of their areas in the limit as the width of each rectangle approaches zero and the area enclosed by the rectangles approaches that under the smooth curve.

Thus this area represents the social cost of steady, anticipated inflation at the rate π^1 in the economy under consideration.

One aspect of this result needs a bit of discussion. It is fairly easy to see that anticipated inflation reduces the volume of monetary services and decreases the welfare of money holders. But are there no other effects that need to be considered? In answer, it is necessary to recognize that the foregoing analysis assumes that newly created money is turned over by the monetary authority to the government, which then distributes it to households as transfer payments (i.e., negative taxes). In addition, the analysis assumes that these transfers are paid in a lump-sum fashion, that is, in such a way that any household's behavior has no influence on the amount that it receives. An alternative assumption regarding the way that money enters the economy will be considered toward the end of this section.

For the present, let us retain the assumption that money enters via lump-sum transfers and carry out a numerical calculation designed to illustrate the general magnitude of welfare losses arising from steady inflation according to the analysis illustrated in Figure 6-9. For the purpose of this example, again suppose that the aggregate money demand function has the form

$$\log m = \gamma_0 + \gamma_1 \log y + \gamma_2 \log R \tag{16}$$

and that the values of the elasticities are $\gamma_1 = 1$ and $\gamma_2 = -0.2$. Then we have, equivalently, that

$$m = e^{\gamma_0} y R^{-0.2}, \tag{17}$$

which can be solved for R:

$$R = \left(e^{\gamma_0} \frac{y}{m} \right)^5. \tag{18}$$

Now suppose that in the absence of inflation the rate of interest is $R = r = 0.03$ and the ratio y/m is 6.[21] Then to satisfy (18), the value of e^{γ_0} must be 0.08266.

With this demand function, let us calculate the welfare loss from a steady inflation rate of 10 percent per year, which makes $R = 0.03 + 0.10 = 0.13$. First, we find that y/m would rise to 8.04. Then we arbitrarily set $y = 1$, which means that our calculated loss will be expressed as a fraction of one year's GNP. With this convention we have a value of $m^0 = 0.1667$ with zero inflation and $m^1 = 0.1244$ with 10 percent inflation. The problem, then, is to evaluate the definite

---

[21] For the United States, the ratio of nominal GNP to nominal M1 was about 5.96 in 1987.

integral

$$\int_{0.1244}^{0.1667} \left(\frac{0.08266}{m}\right)^5 dm. \tag{19}$$

The steps are as follows:

$$0.08266^5 \int_{0.1244}^{0.01667} m^{-5} dm = 0.0000039 \left[\frac{0.1667^{-4} - 0.1244^{-4}}{-4}\right]$$

$$= 0.0000039 \left[\frac{1295 - 4176}{-4}\right] = 0.0028. \tag{20}$$

The answer, therefore, is that a 10 percent inflation rate leads to a social cost equivalent to just under three-tenths of 1 percent of GNP. If, instead, we considered an inflation rate of 100 percent per year, the result would turn out to be 2.0 percent of GNP.

Clearly, the magnitude of the cost that we have calculated is very small for inflation rates of the magnitude experienced in most developed countries in recent years.[22] We shall return to that point later, but first we need to consider two other topics.

The first of these is the assumption, implicit in the discussion to this point, that "money" is a homogeneous entity that pays no interest to its holders. In fact, of course, the M1 money stock in the United States is composed of three types of assets: currency, demand deposits, and OCDs (i.e., other checkable deposits). The last of these, moreover, pays interest to its holders. Accordingly, a more realistic quantitative analysis of the cost of a steady inflation would have to take account of that heterogeneity.[23]

The other topic concerns the way in which money enters the economy or, to express the matter differently, the interaction of money creation with fiscal policy. Instead of our previous assumption, let us now suppose that the government uses money creation as a source of revenue. Thus we imagine that the government uses newly printed currency not to make lump-sum transfer payments, but to finance part of its purchases of goods and services.[24] In this case, the creation of

---

[22] It should be kept in mind, however, that Argentina, Bolivia, Brazil, and Israel have recently experienced much higher inflation rates (but not steadily).

[23] Since OCDs do not pay as much interest as safe short-term assets such as Treasury bills, the difference in these rates is the relevant opportunity cost for this component. Taking account of such complications would probably yield even smaller estimates of the cost of steady inflation.

[24] This way of describing the process presumes that the monetary authority turns newly printed currency over to the government. In actuality, the process is a little less blatant. But the effects would be the same if the government were to sell bonds to banks and the monetary authority were then to create high-powered money to keep bank reserves from falling.

money (and the associated inflation) yields some benefit to household (or firms) since the extra revenue enables the government to reduce its tax collections without reducing government purchases. Inflation still imposes a cost by bringing about a reduced level of real money holdings, but also provides a benefit in the form of reduced tax collections.

In this situation the appropriate way to formulate the cost-of-inflation question is as follows. Suppose that the rate of government purchases is given. These purchases must be financed in some way, either by an explicit tax of some type or by money creation (i.e., revenue from inflation).[25] Each type of tax has some distorting effect that imposes a cost on society, just as money creation does. The problem is to design a package of revenue sources so as to minimize the cost to society of raising the total revenue needed to finance government purchases. Basic marginal reasoning indicates that a necessary condition for this minimization to occur is that, at the margin, the cost to society per dollar of revenue be the same for each revenue source that is utilized to any positive extent. If a possible source has a high cost per dollar of revenue even when used to a small extent, it will be optimal not to make use of that source.

It is possible to show that, for revenue from inflation (money creation), the marginal cost per dollar of revenue is given by the following expression:[26]

$$\frac{d \text{ cost}}{d \text{ rev}} = \frac{\eta}{1 - \eta(\pi/R)} \tag{21}$$

Here η stands for the absolute value of the elasticity of money demand with respect to the interest rate: $\eta = -\gamma_2 = -(dm/dR)R/m$. Since $\pi/R = 0$ when the inflation ratio is zero, but becomes positive and rises toward 1.0 as higher inflation rates are considered, expression (21) equals η for a zero inflation rate and exceeds η for higher values of π. Accordingly, if the actual value of η is about 0.2, as assumed in our numerical example, then the cost per dollar of revenue raised by inflation is rather high. If the cost of raising government revenue is less than 20 cents per dollar for taxes such as the income tax, the property tax, or any specific excise tax, then it would be efficient not to use inflation (money creation) as a source of revenue.

---

[25] We abstract from the possibility of government borrowing, which amounts to finance by means of taxes to be collected in the future.

[26] This formula was described by Marty (1976). To show that it is valid, note that since the cost of inflation is $\int R \, dm$, the marginal value is $-R \, dm = -(r + \pi) \, dm$. The marginal revenue from a change in the steady rate is $d(m\pi) = m\,d\pi + \pi\,dm$. Thus the ratio, which gives the marginal cost per unit of revenue, is $-(r + \pi) \, dm/d\pi$ divided by $m + \pi\,dm/d\pi$. Inserting $-m\eta/R$ for $dm/d\pi = dm/dR$ and rearranging, one can obtain expression (21).

6.8   Concluding Comments

In this chapter we have introduced tools appropriate for the analysis of a steady, ongoing (and hence anticipated) inflation and have developed several key results of such analysis. Although actual inflations are usually unsteady in their pace and not completely anticipated, most of the points developed can be extremely useful in thinking about actual experiences. One good example is provided by the result of Section 6.4 that a sustained decrease in an economy's inflation rate requires either an abrupt fall in the price level or an interval of time during which the inflation rate is lower than the new money growth rate. The result is highly pertinent to the experience of the United States during the years 1984–1986, when inflation was unusually low in relation to money growth.

In conclusion, something should be said regarding the numerical results of Section 6.7, as they suggest that a moderate amount of steady inflation imposes extremely small costs on society. Do these results imply that it is rather foolish for people to dislike inflation intensely, as many seem to do? A full response to that question would require a book of its own, but three brief comments can be made. First, some of the popular dislike of inflation probably does involve a lack of understanding, as when a worker blames inflation for rising prices of things that he purchases but attributes increases in his nominal wages to his own diligence and skill. This type of illusion may affect attitudes without having any impact on economic behavior. Second, in actual economies substantial inflation is (as mentioned before) almost never steady or accurately anticipated. Consequently, there may be major distributional effects, involving wealth losses for creditors and wealth gains for debtors, whenever debts are specified in nominal units. Such redistributions do not affect aggregate wealth or income yet may reasonably be regarded as socially undesirable. Third, the possibility of achieving substantial private rewards from inflation may induce both households and firms to devote valuable human resources to the task of predicting future inflation rates. Also, because tax schedules are often specified in terms of nominal magnitudes, resources may be devoted to activities designed to minimize tax payments, activities that would be unnecessary in the absence of inflation.[27] In both cases, these resources are being allocated to activities that are socially wasteful as they yield neither goods nor services that give utility to the economy's individuals. For the reasons mentioned in these last two comments, and others

---

[27] The specification of tax schedules in nominal terms can lead to resource misallocations even when inflation is anticipated, as Feldstein (1983) emphasizes.

discussed by Fischer and Modigliani (1978), it is likely that even mild inflations are highly undesirable in terms of the welfare of individuals in actual economies.

Problems

1. Consider a classical economy in which the full employment rate of output is $y_t = 200$, the money demand function is $M_t/P_t = 0.3\, y_t/R_t$, and saving–investment behavior satisfies $y_t = 250 - 1000\, r_t$. (Here r_t and R_t are real and nominal interest rates, measured in fractional units.) If the central bank creates money at a rate of 10 percent per period, what will be the steady-state values of the nominal interest rate and the real quantity of money?
2. Explain the meaning of the aphorism "the faster money is created, the less there is." It will be helpful to utilize a plot of R versus y and an associated diagram with time on the horizontal axis.
3. Verify the calculated welfare cost of a 100 percent inflation rate in the numerical example of Section 6.7.
4. Consider the economy represented in Figure 6-9. Suppose that a slight *deflation* is created by the monetary authority, so that the nominal rate of interest R falls below the real rate, r. Will this deflation improve welfare, under the assumptions made for Figure 6-9, relative to the zero-inflation steady state? What is the *optimum rate of inflation*? Compare your answer with that given by Milton Friedman, as described by Barro and Fischer (1976, p. 144).

References

Bailey, Martin J., "The Welfare Cost of Inflationary Finance," *Journal of Political Economy* 64 (April 1956), 93–110.

Bailey, Martin J., *National Income and the Price Level*, 2nd ed. (New York: McGraw-Hill Book Company, 1971).

Barro, Robert J., *Macroeconomics*. (New York: John Wiley & Sons, Inc., 1984).

Barro, Robert J., and Stanley Fischer, "Recent Developments in Monetary Theory," *Journal of Monetary Economics* 2 (April 1976), 133–67.

Feldstein, Martin, *Inflation, Tax Rules, and Capital Formation*. (Chicago: University of Chicago Press, 1983).

Fischer, Stanley, and Franco Modigliani, "Towards an Understanding of the Real Effects and Costs of Inflation," *Weltwirtschaftsliches Archiv* 114 (1978), 810–33.

Marty, Alvin L., "A Note on the Welfare Cost of Money Creation," *Journal of Monetary Economics* 2 (January 1976), 121–24.

Mundell, Robert J., "Inflation and Real Interest," *Journal of Political Economy* 55 (June 1963), 280–82.

Patinkin, Don, *Money, Interest, and Prices*, 2nd ed. (New York: Harper & Row, Publishers, 1965).

Solow, Robert M., *Growth Theory*. (Oxford: Oxford University Press, 1970).

Tower, Edward, "More on the Welfare Cost of Inflationary Finance," *Journal of Money, Credit, and Banking* 3 (November 1971), 850–60).

Varian, Hal R., *Intermediate Microeconomics: A Modern Approach*. (New York: W. W. Norton & Company, Inc., 1987).

Inflationary Dynamics

7.1 The Cagan Model

We are now prepared to advance from steady-state analysis to genuine dynamics, that is, the study of period-to-period variations in the values of a system's exogenous and endogenous variables. As the step is not a trivial one, we shall try to keep matters as simple as possible by initially working with a model in which there are very few variables. Fortunately, it will be possible to study a system that includes only *two* variables, yet which is useful for the analysis of some actual historical experiences that are themselves of great interest. The example that provides this fortuitous combination of features is Phillip Cagan's (1956) famous study of hyperinflations (i.e., extremely severe inflationary episodes).[1] Most of this chapter will accordingly be devoted to a discussion and interpretation of the model developed by Cagan, and some of the analysis that he carried out using this model.

Given that the Cagan model is a model of inflation, it will come as no surprise to the reader to learn that its two central variables are the price level and the money stock. What may come as a surprise is the implied suggestion that satisfactory analysis can be conducted using only these two variables. The reason this is possible is that the model is intended only for the analysis of truly severe inflations; precisely because of their severity, these episodes are ones during which movements in the price level and money stock are so large as to swamp movements in real

---

[1] Cagan's definition of a hyperinflation requires the inflation rate to exceed 50 percent *per month* for at least a few months. That definition is rather arbitrary, but was certainly satisfactory for his purposes.

variables such as output or the real rate of interest. In such circumstances, consequently, movements in the real variables can be neglected.

To be more specific, suppose that an economy's aggregate money demand function is of the form described toward the end of Section 3.4. In particular, suppose that this demand function can be expressed as

$$\log \frac{M_t}{P_t} = \alpha_0 + \alpha_1 \log y_t + \alpha_2 R_t + u_t, \tag{1}$$

where M_t is the money stock, P_t is the price level, y_t is real income, $R_t = r_t + \Pi_t = $ nominal interest rate, and u_t is a stochastic disturbance. Then if movements in y_t and r_t (the real interest rate) can be neglected, the equation can be written as

$$\log \frac{M_t}{P_t} = (\alpha_0 + \alpha_1 \log y + \alpha_2 r) + \alpha_2 \Pi_t + u_t \tag{2}$$

or equivalently as

$$\log \frac{M_t}{P_t} = \gamma + \alpha \Pi_t + u_t, \tag{3}$$

where Π_t is the expected inflation rate and where we have defined the parameters $\alpha \equiv \alpha_2$ and $\gamma \equiv \alpha_0 + \alpha_1 \log y + \alpha_2 r$. Furthermore, if we let m_t and p_t denote logarithms of the money stock and the price level, respectively, so that $\log (M_t/P_t) = \log M_t - \log P_t = m_t - p_t$, then (3) can be rewritten once more to give

$$m_t - p_t = \gamma + \alpha \Pi_t + u_t. \tag{4}$$

This simplified version of a money demand equation is then the central ingredient of the Cagan model. It is a relation involving only two variables in the sense that the expected inflation rate Π_t is the expected value of $\Delta p_{t+1} = p_{t+1} - p_t$, that is, the value of $p_{t+1} - p_t$ anticipated by the economy's individuals as of period t. Thus m_t and p_t are, in a sense, the only variables involved.

To complete the specification of the model, one must also adopt some hypothesis concerning money supply behavior. In his study, Cagan typically assumed that m_t was determined exogenously by the monetary authority of the economy in question. Under that assumption, (4) can be thought of as a relationship that describes the behavior of the price level—or its log—given exogenous values for m_t. We shall very briefly consider below whether that assumption of Cagan's is an appropriate one of hyperinflation analysis.

Table 7-1

Country	Dates	Avg. Inflation Rate[a] (percent per month)	Real Money Balances,[a] Minimum/Initial
Austria	Oct. 1921–Aug. 1922	47.1	0.35
Germany	Aug. 1922–Nov. 1923	322	0.030
Greece	Nov. 1943–Nov. 1944	365	0.007
Hungary	Mar. 1923–Feb. 1924	46.0	0.39
Hungary	Aug. 1945–July 1946	19,800	0.003
Poland	Jan. 1923–Jan. 1924	81.1	0.34
Russia	Dec. 1921–Jan. 1924	57.0	0.27

[a] Data from Cagan (1956).

7.2 Hyperinflation Episodes

In the study in which he developed the model just described, Cagan examined seven hyperinflations experienced by European countries during this century. The countries involved were Austria, Germany, Greece, Hungary (two occasions), Poland, and Russia. The dates of the experiences are shown in Table 7-1, where the months indicated are the initial and concluding months in which the inflation rate exceeded 50 percent. For each month included in the periods indicated, Cagan was able to compile, from various records kept at the time, reasonably good estimates of the economy's money stock and price level.[2] The next-to-last column in Table 7-1 reports the average inflation rate over each of the seven periods. As the reported numbers are average inflation rates expressed as percentage points per *month*,[3] it can be seen that the episodes under discussion were indeed quite severe!

An informative statistic relating to these inflationary experiences is reported in the final column of Table 7-1. It will be recalled that our theory of money demand implies that, other things equal, individuals will hold smaller quantities of real money balances when the nominal interest rate is high—the reason, of course, being that the nominal

---

[2] The money stock figures included currency and, except for Greece and Russia, bank deposits. Various price indices were used to represent the price level. The data used by Cagan were far from perfect, as he recognized, but most scholars have viewed it as entirely serviceable. For more details, see Cagan (1956, pp. 96–117).

[3] In this chapter we shall (following Cagan) report numerical inflation rates in percentage, rather than fractional form. The values in Table 7-1 are, accordingly, measured as 100 times $(P_t - P_{t-1})/P_{t-1}$, rather than as Δp_t.

interest rate measures the cost of holding wealth in the form of money instead of some interest-bearing asset. During the hyperinflations under discussion, however, financial markets were disrupted so badly that there was no possibility for ordinary individuals to purchase and hold securities that paid market-determined interest rates. Under such circumstances, the cost of holding money is measured—as equation (2) implicitly indicates—by the expected inflation rate, as it reflects the rate at which money is expected to decrease in value. Accordingly, our money demand theory suggests that the level of real money holdings should decline over the course of a hyperinflation as the inflation rate increases and individuals come to anticipate further increases. If the theory is correct, then, real balances should fall during the hyperinflation episodes to values below those prevailing at the start. In the final column of Table 7-1, measured values for the minimum value of M_t/P_t are reported as fractions of the initial M_t/P_t values. It will readily be seen that this theoretical implication is strongly supported by the data; in all seven cases the minimum M_t/P_t value attained was well below the value prevailing at the start of the episode. Individuals, apparently, did react to the increased cost of holding money balances by reducing their money holdings in real terms, even though this required them to expend greater amounts of time and energy in conducting their transactions.

7.3 Cagan's Estimates

One of the main objectives of Cagan's study was to present evidence bearing on the proposition that money demand behavior is orderly and well behaved, rather than erratic or irrational. One way of doing this was to estimate, statistically, a money demand function of the form (4). If it fit the data well even under the extreme conditions of a hyperinflation and exhibited the type of properties implied by a discussion such as ours—which is just an application of standard money demand considerations—this would be evidence supporting the notion that money demand is well behaved. In particular, the theory would receive support if month-to-month variations in real money balances were well explained by the holding-cost variable Π_t, as suggested by equation (4).[4]

A major difficulty in conducting this type of study was provided by the nonexistence of data on Π_t. Since the latter is the *expected* inflation

---

[4] For a statement roughly to this effect, see Cagan (1956, p. 27).

rate, not the actual rate, Cagan had no observations or official data pertaining to this variable. Accordingly, he was forced to devise a model of expectation formation to represent Π_t in terms of variables that could be observed and measured.

The expectational model that Cagan developed, while working under the guidance of Milton Friedman, eventually became well known as the model of "adaptive expectations." In terms of our notation for the problem at hand, the adaptive expectations formula for the unobserved Π_t can be expressed as

$$\Pi_t - \Pi_{t-1} = \lambda(\Delta p_t - \Pi_{t-1}), \qquad 0 \le \lambda \le 1. \tag{5}$$

Here the idea is that the expected inflation rate is adjusted upward, relative to its previous value, when the most recent actual inflation rate (Δp_t) exceeds its own previously expected value (Π_{t-1}).[5] Correspondingly, if Δp_t were smaller than Π_{t-1}, the value of Π_t would be lowered relative to Π_{t-1}. The extent of the adjustment is indicated by λ: if the parameter λ is close to 1.0, the adjustment is relatively strong (and weak if λ is close to 0.0).

In addition, the value of λ can be thought of as reflecting the *speed* of adjustment of expectations. To understand this interpretation, let us rewrite (5) as follows:

$$\Pi_t = \lambda \, \Delta p_t + (1 - \lambda)\Pi_{t-1}. \tag{6}$$

But that form of the relation implies that $\Pi_{t-1} = \lambda \, \Delta p_{t-1} + (1 - \lambda)\Pi_{t-2}$, which can be substituted back into (6) to give

$$\Pi_t = \lambda \, \Delta p_t + (1 - \lambda)[\lambda \, \Delta p_{t-1} + (1 - \lambda)\Pi_{t-2}]. \tag{7}$$

Similarly, $\Pi_{t-2} = \lambda \, \Delta p_{t-2} + (1 - \lambda)\Pi_{t-3}$ could be used in (7), and so on. Repeating such substitutions indefinitely leads to an expression of the form

$$\Pi_t = \lambda \, \Delta p_t + \lambda(1 - \lambda) \, \Delta p_{t-1} + \lambda(1 - \lambda)^2 \, \Delta p_{t-2} + \cdots, \tag{8}$$

since the term $(1 - \lambda)^n$ approaches zero as $n \to \infty$. From equation (8), then, we see that the expected inflation rate Π_t can be expressed (under the adaptive expectations formula) as a weighted average[6] of all current and past actual inflation rates Δp_{t-j} (for $j = 0, 1, 2, \ldots$). More

---

[5] This type of formula may be applied to any variable. In the present example the dating of the variables may appear more natural if it is recalled that Π_t is the anticipated value of $\Delta p_{t+1} = p_{t+1} - p_t$.

[6] That the coefficients in (8) sum to 1.0, which makes Π_t a weighted average rather than just a linear combination of Δp_{t-j} values, can be seen as follows. The sum is $\lambda[1 + (1 - \lambda) + (1 - \lambda)^2 + \cdots]$, but since $1 - \lambda$ is a fraction, the formula for a geometric series can be used to write $1 + (1 - \lambda) + (1 - \lambda)^2 + \cdots = 1/[1 - (1 - \lambda)] = 1/\lambda$. Thus we have $\lambda(1/\lambda) = 1$.

weight is attached to recent as opposed to distant values, it can be seen, the larger is λ. In this sense, λ measures the speed of expectational adjustment.

We now see how to use the adaptive expectations formula in the context of Cagan's problem. By means of the formula, it is possible to eliminate Π_t from equation (4), thereby obtaining an expression involving only observable variables (plus the disturbance term). To do this, substitute version (6) of the expectational formula into (4) to obtain

$$m_t - p_t = \gamma + \alpha[\lambda\,\Delta p_t + (1 - \lambda)\Pi_{t-1}] + u_t. \qquad (9)$$

Then write (4) for period $t - 1$ and solve it for $\Pi_{t-1} = (m_{t-1} - p_{t-1} - \gamma - u_{t-1})/\alpha$. Putting the latter into (9) and rearranging then gives

$$m_t - p_t = \gamma\lambda + \alpha\lambda\,\Delta p_t + (1 - \lambda)(m_{t-1} - p_{t-1}) + v_t, \qquad (10)$$

where the composite disturbance is

$$v_t = u_t - (1 - \lambda)u_{t-1}. \qquad (11)$$

Clearly, equation (10) no longer includes terms involving the unobserved Π_t variable. It can, therefore, be estimated empirically, although there may be some difficulties created by the nature of the composite disturbance.

In effect,[7] Cagan estimated an equation like (10) by ordinary least-squares regression for each of the episodes listed in Table 7-1. That is, he (in effect) regressed the dependent variable $m_t - p_t$ on the explanatory variables Δp_t and $m_{t-1} - p_{t-1}$. The coefficients attached to these two variables then provided estimates of $\alpha\lambda$ and $1 - \lambda$, respectively. Using the estimate of λ implied by the latter, the former could then be made to yield an estimate of α. Some of the main facts concerning Cagan's estimates are provided in Table 7-2.

From Table 7-2 it will be seen that in two respects Cagan's results appeared highly favorable to his theory. First, the estimated values of the slope coefficient α are all negative, as the theory implies. Second, the extent to which fluctuations in $m_t - p_t$ values are "explained" by the model, as measured by the R^2 values in the final column, is quite high. In Cagan's words, "The regression fits the data for most months

---

[7] Actually, Cagan carried out his computations in a less straightforward way, but the procedures are in principle approximately equivalent. In general, our description of Cagan's work makes it appear more simple and streamlined than it actually was. In 1954–1956, econometric theory was much less well developed than it is today and, even more important, computations had to be carried out on mechanical desk calculators (for which "long division" was something of a strain!).

Table 7-2

Episode	Cagan's Estimates of:		
	α	λ	R^2
Austria	−8.55	0.05	0.978
Germany	−5.46	0.20	0.984
Greece	−4.09	0.15	0.960
Hungary	−8.70	0.10	0.857
Hungary	−3.63	0.15	0.996
Poland	−2.30	0.30	0.945
Russia	−3.06	0.35	0.942

of the seven hyperinflations with a high degree of accuracy, and thus the statistical results strongly support the hypothesis" (p. 87).[8]

In fact, while Cagan's study was an ingenious and pathbreaking piece of work, the statistical procedures that he utilized were inappropriate. In particular, under the hypothesis that m_t is exogenous, p_t is the model's main endogenous variable. Therefore, Δp_t is not exogenous or predetermined, and so does not belong on the right-hand side of a least-squares regression. Furthermore, with the lagged dependent variable $m_{t-1} - p_{t-1}$ used as a regressor, estimates will be inappropriate (i.e., inconsistent) if the equation's residuals are serially correlated [as subsequent analysis by Kahn (1975) and others have shown them to be]. Thus the numerical results presented by Cagan cannot be considered reliable. Nevertheless, because the concepts involved are of great interest and importance, we shall continue in the next section to discuss Cagan's results.

7.4 Stability Analysis

Another major objective of Cagan's study was to determine whether the dramatic price-level increases during the hyperinflation episodes were simply consequences of the enormous money stock increases that

[8] The phrase "for most months" appears because Cagan's sample periods used in the regressions omitted the final few observations in three of the episodes. His justification for the omission of these observations, which were not well explained by the model, was that "in hyperinflation rumors of currency reform encourage the belief that prices will not continue to rise rapidly for more than a certain number of months. This leads individuals to hold higher real cash balances than they would ordinarily desire in view of the rate at which prices are expected to rise in the current month" (1956, p. 55). A sophisticated analysis of this idea was undertaken, with impressive results, by Flood and Garber (1980).

the monetary authorities were engineering, or whether the price-level increases were in some sense "self-generating." The way that Cagan approached this issue was to determine whether his estimated models formally possessed the property of *dynamic stability*. Stability in this sense[9] is possessed by a system if, when displaced from an equilibrium position, it tends to return to that position as time passes. An unstable system, by contrast, is one in which any departure from equilibrium is self-reinforcing (i.e., leads to even greater departures).

An illustration of these concepts can be provided by the simple stochastic system

$$y_t = a + by_{t-1} + \epsilon_t, \qquad a > 0, \tag{12}$$

where y_t is the system's only endogenous variable and ϵ_t is a purely random disturbance with mean zero. If the absolute value of b in (12) is less than 1.0, any departure of y_t from its equilibrium value—which is $\bar{y} = a/(1 - b)$—will tend to disappear as time passes.[10] If $b > 1.0$, however, the succeeding values of $y_t - \bar{y}$ will explode, getting larger and larger in absolute value in each succeeding period. And if $b < -1.0$, explosive oscillations will result. Thus for a stochastic first-order difference equation of the form (12), the necessary and sufficient condition for dynamic stability is $|b| < 1.0$.[11]

To prove that these assertions are true, consider the system's evolution starting in period $t = 1$ with an arbitrary initial condition y_0. Then the values of y_t in the succeeding periods will be

$$y_1 = a + by_0 + \varepsilon_1$$
$$y_2 = a + b(a + by_0 + \varepsilon_1) + \varepsilon_2$$
$$y_3 = a + b[a + b(a + by_0 + \varepsilon_1) + \varepsilon_2] + \varepsilon_3$$
$$\vdots$$
$$y_t = a(1 + b + b^2 + \cdots + b^{t-1}) + b^t y_0 + \varepsilon_t$$
$$+ b\varepsilon_{t-1} + b^2\varepsilon_{t-2} + \cdots + b^{t-1}\varepsilon_1.$$

Since $1 + b + \cdots + b^{t-1} = (1 - b^t)/(1 - b)$, the latter can be rewrit-

---

[9] The term "stability" is often used in an entirely different way: a behavioral relation is said to be "stable" if it does not shift erratically as time passes.

[10] To see that the equilibrium value is as stated, note that if $y_{t-1} = a/(1 - b)$ and $\epsilon_t = 0$, then y_t will be $a + b[a/(1 - b)] = a[1 + b/(1 - b)] = a/(1 - b)$.

[11] If by chance b equals 1.0 exactly, explosions will not occur, but there will be no tendency for y_t to return to any equilibrium value.

ten as

$$y_t = \frac{a(1 - b^t)}{1 - b} + b^t y_0 + \text{random terms}$$

$$= \frac{a}{1 - b} + b^t\left(y_0 - \frac{a}{1 - b}\right) + \text{random terms}.$$

Then, neglecting random terms and recalling that $\bar{y} = a/(1 - b)$, we have $y_t - \bar{y} = b^t(y_0 - \bar{y})$. But that expression shows that $y_t \rightarrow \bar{y}$ as $t \rightarrow \infty$ if and only if $|b| < 1.0$.

The foregoing argument can be extended, furthermore, to a system of the form

$$y_t = a + by_{t-1} + cx_t + \varepsilon_t, \tag{13}$$

where x_t is an exogenous variable. Indeed, the only difference in this case is that the equilibrium value is not constant over time, but changes with changes in the value of x_t. In particular, the expression $a + cx_t + b(a + cx_{t-1}) + b^2(a + cx_{t-2}) + \cdots$ defines a moving equilibrium *path*, one toward which the system tends to gravitate if it is dynamically stable. It is not difficult to determine that in this case stability will again prevail if and only if $|b| < 1.0$.

These concepts can be applied to the Cagan model by solving (10) for p_t, rather than $m_t - p_t$. Doing so, we obtain

$$p_t = \frac{-\lambda\gamma + (\alpha\lambda + 1 - \lambda)p_{t-1} + m_t - (1 - \lambda)m_{t-1} - v_t}{1 + \alpha\lambda} \tag{14}$$

Then with m_t taken to be exogenous, $m_t - (1 - \lambda)m_{t-1}$ plays the role of x_t in equation (13). Accordingly, we see that the stability condition analogous to $|b| < 1.0$ is that

$$\left|\frac{\alpha\lambda + 1 - \lambda}{1 + \alpha\lambda}\right| < 1.0, \tag{15}$$

since p_{t-1} is the system's lagged endogenous variable. The way to determine whether the hyperinflation model possesses dynamic stability for a given episode is then to use the parameter estimates in Table 7-2 to compute the left-hand expression in (15) and compare its absolute value with 1.0.

To illustrate this type of analysis, Table 7-3 reports relevant values for each of Cagan's episodes based on the estimates of α and λ in Table 7-2. It will be seen that the resulting values for the coefficient of p_{t-1} suggest that the estimated system would be unstable in two of the seven cases, those for Germany and Russia, and stable in the other

Table 7-3

Episode	Estimates of:		
	$\alpha\lambda + 1 - \lambda$	$1 + \alpha\lambda$	$\dfrac{\alpha\lambda + 1 - \lambda}{1 + \alpha\lambda}$
Austria	0.516	0.556	0.928
Germany	-0.292	-0.092	3.17
Greece	0.236	0.386	0.611
Hungary	0.030	0.130	0.230
Hungary	0.305	0.455	0.670
Poland	0.010	0.310	0.032
Russia	-0.421	-0.070	5.92

five. This conclusion does not fully agree with Cagan's, because of a small error that led him to consider a slightly different composite parameter.[12] We will not here attempt to reach any substantive conclusion concerning stability in the European hyperinflations, in part because of the econometric problems mentioned at the end of Section 7.3 and in part for a reason to be developed in Section 7.5.[13] Our object in this discussion has been to introduce the *concept* of dynamic stability and indicate how it can in principle be investigated, not to generate conclusions concerning the example at hand.

7.5 Weakness of Adaptive Expectations

From the foregoing discussion of Cagan's study, it should be apparent that his results and conclusions depend not only on his specification of money demand behavior, but also on the assumption that expectations are formed in the manner implied by the adaptive expectations formula

---

[12] This discrepancy arose because Cagan referred to the stability condition for a continuous-time model, while his empirical estimates were for a discrete-time formulation. On this point, see Benjamin Friedman (1978).

[13] Still another reason is that the assumption that m_t is exogenous, on which the foregoing stability analysis depends, is highly implausible. While the monetary authorities in each country *could* have generaged m_t values totally "from outside" the economic system, in practice they certainly must have responded to what they saw happening to the price level—which would make their actions partly endogenous.

(5).[14] If people's expectations did not actually conform to this formula, the statistical estimates of α will be unreliable and the stability analysis will be inapplicable.

In that regard it needs to be emphasized that while the sort of "error correction" behavior expressed in (5) has some intuitive appeal, it is nevertheless open to very serious objections. In particular, the formula implies the possibility of *systematic* expectational errors—that is, errors that are systematically related to information available to individuals at the time at which their expectations are formed. To see that this possibility exists, consider a hypothetical case in which, because of constantly increasing money growth rates, inflation regularly increases each period, always exceeding (except when by chance v_t is large and negative) its previous values. From (8) we know that the value of Π_t given by the adaptve expectations formula is a weighted average of current and past Δp_t values, so Π_t will in all periods be smaller[15] than Δp_t. Thus the expected inflation rate Π_t will in all periods be smaller than the actual inflation rate Δp_{t+1} that it is intended to forecast. There will be, period after period, repeated expectational errors of the same kind.

But since economic actions are in part based on expectations, expectational errors are *costly* to the individuals who make them—for when these errors occur, actions arc based on incorrect beliefs about future conditions. Consequently, purposeful economic agents—utility-maximizing individuals and profit-maximizing firms—will seek to avoid expectational errors. They cannot be entirely successful in this endeavor, of course, because no one can foresee the future. But they can reduce and virtually eliminate *systematic* sources of error by appropriate reactions. In the example of ever-increasing inflation, for instance, they could use—instead of the adaptive expectations formula—a forecasting rule for Δp_{t+1} that adds some positive amount to the most recently observed inflation rate Δp_t. That the adaptive expectations formula can be suboptimal in such an obvious (and easily improved upon) manner is a very telling criticism of that formula. For that reason, few macroeconomic researchers rely on it today.[16] Consequently, in Chapter 8 we introduce the idea of "rational expectations," which provides the preeminent expectational hypothesis as of 1985—the one that most researchers use in their work.

---

[14] And on the assumption discussed in footnote 13.

[15] In the assumed case at hand.

[16] During the period 1956–1975, however, the adaptive expectations formula (together with some close relations) was very popular.

Problems

1. In Section 7.3 it was stated that Cagan's econometric estimates of α and λ are inappropriate. Describe a procedure for consistent estimation of α and λ under Cagan's assumptions about expectations and exogeneity of m_t. In doing this, you may (unrealistically) assume that the composite disturbance v_t is white noise.

2. How would you estimate α if you knew that the correct expectational formula was not adaptive expectations, but instead $\Pi_t = \delta \Delta p_t + (1 - \delta) \Delta p_{t-1}$ with $0 < \delta < 1$?

3. Imagine an isolated market in which the demand and supply relations are as follows:

Demand: $\quad q_t = a_0 + a_1 p_t + v_t, \qquad a_1 < 0.$

Supply: $\quad q_t = b_0 + b_1 p_t^e + u_t, \qquad b_1 > 0.$

Suppose, furthermore, that u_t and v_t are purely random and that expectations are formed according to $p_t^e = p_{t-1}$. Under what conditions will this system be dynamically stable?

4. Suppose that Cagan had assumed that expectations were described by $\Pi_t = \Delta p_t$, so that the expected value of Δp_{t+1} was equal to the most recent actual value. What would he have concluded with regard to dynamic stability?

References[17]

Barro, Robert J., *Macroeconomics*. (New York: John Wiley & Sons, Inc., 1984), pp. 192–97.

Cagan, Phillip, "The Monetary Dynamics of Hyperinflation," in *Studies in the Quantity Theory of Money*, ed. Milton Friedman. (Chicago: University of Chicago Press, 1956).

Flood, Robert P., and Peter M. Garber, "An Economic Theory of Monetary Reform," *Journal of Political Economy* 88 (February 1980), 24–58.

Friedman, Benjamin M., "Stability and Rationality in Models of Hyperinflation," *International Economic Review* 19 (February 1978), 45–64.

Kahn, Moshin S., "The Monetary Dynamics of Hyperinflation," *Journal of Monetary Economics* 1 (July 1975), 355–62.

Poole, William, *Money and the Economy: A Monetarist View*. (Reading, Mass.: Addison-Wesley Publishing Company, Inc., 1978).

---

[17] The items by Barro (1984) and Poole (1978) provide alternative nontechnical discussions of Cagan's study.

Rational Expectations

8.1 Basic Properties

We concluded Chapter 7 by arguing that because expectational errors are costly to those who make them, purposeful agents will try to form expectations in a manner that eliminates avoidable errors. Furthermore, systematic errors—that is, errors that occur predictably under certain conditions—are avoidable; by observing the particular conditions that lead to errors, agents can take action to offset any systematic tendency to err. An attractive hypothesis for economic analysis of expectational behavior, consequently, is that agents are successful in avoiding regular sources of error. Because they are purposeful, agents manage their affairs in such a way that there is very little systematic component to their expectational error process. Errors are committed, of course, but they occur at random.

But how is the absence of systematic expectational error expressed analytically? Is there some formula, perhaps more complex than that for adaptive expectations, that will yield this condition? In this regard it is important to recognize that the absence of systematic expectational error cannot generally be represented by *any* algebraic formula comparable to the adaptive expectations formula (8) of Chapter 7. It might be possible to write a formula expressing Π_t in terms of Δp_t, Δp_{t-1}, ... that would avoid errors in the particular case of ever-increasing inflation,[1] but the coefficients in this formula would then be wrong if a different inflationary pattern—say, repeating cycles—was generated by the monetary authority. In fact, *whatever* the coefficients attached to past Δp_t values in an expression such as $\Pi_t = \gamma_1 \Delta p_{t-1} + \cdots$, there will

---

[1] Reference here is to the example of Section 7.5.

always be *some* inflation path that will make Π_t systematically different from Δp_{t+1} (i.e., systematically in error).[2]

The message of the foregoing is that to express analytically the hypothesis that agents avoid systematic expectational errors, we want not a formula but instead an analytic *condition* that rules out such errors. To see what the appropriate condition is, let us consider an agent forming her expectation at time t of p_{t+1}—next period's (log) price level—and let us denote that expectation by p_{t+1}^e. Then the expectational error that will occur, when period $t + 1$ comes to pass, is $p_{t+1} - p_{t+1}^e$. And the condition that we want to adopt is that this error, $p_{t+1} - p_{t+1}^e$, not be systematically related to any information possessed by the agent in period t (when the expectation was formed).

The way to achieve this condition, it turns out, is to assume that expectations subjectively held (i.e., believed) by agents are equal to the mean of the probabilty distribution of the variable being forecast, given available information. For example, p_{t+1} is from the vantage point of period t a random variable. Its mean from that vantage point is $E(p_{t+1}|\Omega_t)$, the mathematical expectation (i.e., mean) of the probability distribution of p_{t+1}, *given* the information Ω_t—where this last symbol denotes the set of information available to the agent at time t. Thus the expectational hypothesis that we are seeking can be adopted by assuming that, for any variable p_{t+j} and any period t,

$$p_{t+j}^e = E(p_{t+j}|\Omega_t). \tag{1}$$

In words, this condition requires that the *subjective* expectation (forecast) of p_{t+1} held by agents in t be equal to the *objective* (mathematical) expectation of p_{t+1} conditional on Ω_t (i.e., the mean of the actual conditional probability distribution of p_{t+1} given information available in t).

But where, the reader may well ask, does the *actual* probability distribution of p_{t+1} come from? In a literal sense, it is of course unknown. But the economist who wishes to use this expectational hypothesis in the context of a model, has in the course of constructing that model adopted his own view of how p_t is actually generated. Thus the only logically coherent way for him to proceed is to use the probability distribution of p_{t+1} *as expressed in his model* as the basis for computing $E(p_{t+1}|\Omega_t)$; his model *is* his view of the actual economy.

To this point we have argued in favor of an expectational hypothesis that rules out systematic errors and have asserted that condition (1) will do so. Let us now prove that this assertion is true. First, we calculate

---

[2] For example, if the coefficients are $\gamma_1, \gamma_2, \ldots$, an inflationary path satisfying $\Delta p_{t+1} = \delta + \gamma_1 \Delta p_{t-1} + \gamma_2 \Delta p_{t-1} + \cdots$ will result in Δp_{t+1} values that always exceed their forecasts Π_t by the amount δ.

what the *average* expectational error will be over a large number of periods if (1) is utilized. To do that, we find the mean of the distribution of $p_{t+1} - p_{t+1}^e$ values.[3] That is, we compute

$$E(p_{t+1} - p_{t+1}^e) = E[p_{t+1} - E(p_{t+1}|\Omega_t)] = E(p_{t+1}) - E[E(p_{t+1}|\Omega_t)]$$

$$= E(p_{t+1}) - E(p_{t+1}) = 0,$$

(2)

showing that the average error is zero. In this calculation the only tricky step is the next-to-last one, where the fact that $E[E(p_{t+1}|\Omega_t)]$ equals $E(p_{t+1})$ is used. The validity of that fact, which is special case of the "law of iterated expectations," is demonstrated in the appendix to this chapter. This "law" reflects the commonsense idea that the expectation of an expectation that will be based on more information than is currently available will simply be the expectation given the lesser available information.

Thus we see that the average expectational error under hypothesis (1) will be zero. To complete the demonstration that there will be no systematic relation between $p_{t+1} - p_{t+1}^e$ and any information available in t, let x_t denote *any* variable whose value is known to agents at t. Thus x_t is an element of Ω_t. Then consider the covariance of $p_{t+1} - p_{t+1}^e$ and x_t. Since $E(p_{t+1} - p_{t+1}^e)$ is zero, this covariance will be the mean of the distribution of the product $(p_{t+1} - p_{t+1}^e)x_t$. We evaluate this covariance as follows:

$$E[(p_{t+1} - p_{t+1}^e)x_t] = E[(p_{t+1} - E(p_{t+1}|\Omega_t))x_t]$$

$$= E(p_{t+1}x_t) - E[E(p_{t+1}|\Omega_t)x_t].$$

(3)

But because x_t is an element of Ω_t, it is true that $x_t E(p_{t+t}|\Omega_t) = E(x_t p_{t+1}|\Omega_t)$. Then using the law of iterated expectations, we see that the final term in (3) equals $E(x_t p_{t+1})$. That shows, then, that the covariance is zero:

$$E[(p_{t+1} - p_{t+1}^e)x_t] = 0.$$

(4)

This implies that the expectational error is, in a statistical sense, unrelated to any element of Ω_t (i.e., to any available information).[4] Thus we have shown that the adoption of assumption (1) will, in fact, imply that systematic expectational errors will be absent.

This conclusion accords well, it might be added, with the commonsense idea that the "best" forecast of a value to be realized by a random

---

[3] The mean of the distribution of a random variable is, of course, one measure of what the average value of the variable will be when many observations on that variable are taken.

[4] Actually, our proof shows only that $p_{t+1} - p_{t+1}^e$ is uncorrelated with x_t, not that it is statistically independent (a somewhat stronger condition).

variable is the mean of the probability distribution of that random variable.[5] The tricky aspect of our current application is that the relevant distribution is a conditional distribution—one that reflects the information available to the agent at the time she forms her expectation.

The hypothesis concerning expectations that we have outlined was first put forth by John F. Muth (1961). Because the type of expectational behavior postulated is purposeful, and the absence of avoidable errors is necessary for optimality on the part of the agents in the modeled economy, Muth chose the term *rational expectations* to describe his hypothesis. As it happens, Muth's ideas were not immediately embraced by the economics profession, in part because his paper was difficult to understand and some aspects were not clearly spelled out. The profession's appreciation of the theory was greatly enhanced in the early 1970s by a number of path-breaking papers by Robert E. Lucas, Jr., in which the rational expectations notion was extended and also applied to important issues in macroeconomics. These papers have been collectively republished in Lucas (1981). Writings by Thomas J. Sargent (1973) and Robert J. Barro (1977) were also important in developing the widespread support for rational expectations that exists today.

8.2 Application to the Cagan Model

We have concluded that agents will be forming expectations in a rational manner if they use, as their subjective expectation (forecast) of some future variable, the mean of that variable's objective conditional probability distribution as depicted by the analyst's model. Let us now illustrate the use of this approach by studying a familiar example, the Cagan model of inflation, under the assumption that expectations are formed rationally.

The main ingredient of the Cagan model is the demand function for real money balances, which we now write as

$$m_t - p_t = \gamma + \alpha \Delta p_{t+1}^e + u_t, \qquad \alpha < 0. \tag{5}$$

Here m_t and p_t are logs of the money stock and the price level, respectively, while γ and α are parameters. The stochastic disturbance u_t

---

[5] This commonsense criterion breaks down if the model at hand is nonlinear. In general, the discussion of this chapter is fully appropriate only for linear systems. Rational expectations analysis of nonlinear models is quite difficult and, consequently, is not considered in this book.

is assumed to be purely random, that is, to be drawn in each period from an unchanging distribution with mean zero and variance σ_u^2. As the distribution is at each date unaffected by previous drawings, u_t will be free of serial correlation. As a convenient abbreviation for this specification, which will be used frequently, we say that u_t is a "white noise" disturbance.

In (5), Δp_{t+1}^e denotes the subjective expectation formed in period t of Δp_{t+1}, the inflation rate between t and $t + 1$. To impose the rational expectations assumption, we follow the example of equation (1) and specify that

$$\Delta p_{t+1}^e = E(\Delta p_{t+1}|\Omega_t). \tag{6}$$

In addition, let us adopt a simplified notation by which $E_t x_{t+j}$ means, for any variable x_{t+j}, the same as $E(x_{t+j}|\Omega_t)$, that is, the mean of that variable's distribution conditional upon information available in period t. Then we can use this notation to write (5) and (6) together as

$$m_t - p_t = \gamma + \alpha E_t \Delta p_{t+1} + u_t. \tag{7}$$

This last expression will not be fully defined, however, until we specify the content of Ω_t, that is, specify precisely what information is available to agents in period t. In a subsequent chapter, we explore alternative informational specifications, but for now it will be assumed that Ω_t includes values from period t, and all previous periods, of *all* of the model's variables. Thus for the example at hand we assume that in period t agents know $p_t, p_{t-1}, \ldots, m_t, m_{t-1}, \ldots$. Also, the concept of rationality implies that they understand the workings of the economy; this they need to do to avoid systematic errors. In the context of our model, this implies that these agents are aware of equation (7), so they can infer the values of $u_t, u_{t-1}, \ldots$. Thus these, too, are included in Ω_t.

Continuing, we note next that since p_t is known to agents at t, the expectation $E_t p_t$ is equal to p_t itself. Consequently, the expected inflation rate $E_t(p_{t+1} - p_t)$ is equal to $E_t p_{t+1} - p_t$ and (7) can thus be rewritten once more as

$$m_t - p_t = \gamma + \alpha(E_t p_{t+1} - p_t) + u_t. \tag{8}$$

It is this version that we shall work with in what follows.

Beginning with equation (8), we might try to develop a solution for p_t in the following way. First, the terms in p_t can be collected to give

$$m_t = \gamma + \alpha E_t p_{t+1} + (1 - \alpha)p_t + u_t \tag{9}$$

Then the latter can be rearranged thus:

$$p_t = \frac{m_t - \gamma - \alpha E_t p_{t+1} - u_t}{1 - \alpha}. \tag{10}$$

But even with m_t exogenous the latter is *not* a solution, as it contains the expectational variable $E_t p_{t+1}$.

One way to proceed, given that difficulty, is to update (10) to get an expression for p_{t+1} and then apply E_t, yielding

$$
\begin{aligned}
E_t p_{t+1} &= \frac{E_t(m_{t+1} - \gamma - \alpha E_{t+1} p_{t+2} - u_{t+1})}{1 - \alpha} \\
&= \frac{E_t m_{t+1} - \gamma - \alpha E_t p_{t+2}}{1 - \alpha}.
\end{aligned}
\tag{11}
$$

[Here $E_t u_{t+1} = 0$ because u_t is white noise, while $E_t(E_{t+1} p_{t+2}) = E_t p_{t+2}$ by the law of iterated expectations.] Expression (11) can then be substituted into (10) and the latter rearranged to give the following:

$$
p_t = \frac{m_t - \dfrac{\alpha}{1-\alpha} E_t m_{t+1} - \gamma + \dfrac{\alpha}{1-\alpha}\gamma + \dfrac{\alpha^2}{1-\alpha} E_t p_{t+2} - u_t.}{1-\alpha}.
\tag{12}
$$

Next, (10) could be rewritten for p_{t+2}, E_t applied, and the result substituted for $E_t p_{t+2}$. That would bring in $E_t p_{t+3}$, but the process could again be repeated. Indeed, by repeating the process indefinitely, all expected future p_t terms could ultimately be eliminated,[6] giving a solution for p_t in terms of the current disturbance u_t, the current money stock m_t, and the expectations of all future m_t values $E_t m_{t+1}$, $E_t m_{t+2}$, ... To be exact, the expression is

$$
\frac{m_t - \gamma(1-\alpha) - u_t + \left(\dfrac{\alpha}{\alpha-1}\right) E_t m_{t+1} + \left(\dfrac{\alpha}{\alpha-1}\right)^2 E_t m_{t+2} + \cdots}{1-\alpha}.
\tag{13}
$$

Now this type of solution to the Cagan model with RE is instructive, as it emphasizes that the value of the price level in period t depends on the values of the money stock that are expected for each period in the entire infinite future. But that fact implies that to determine p_t, the analyst must also know these expectations of future m_t values. Thus he must know something about the ongoing nature of the money supply *behavior* of the monetary authority—or, in other words, the policy *process* that is in place.

For an example of what is meant by a policy process, consider the

---

[6] This statement assumes that $[\alpha/(\alpha-1)]^j E_t p_{t+j} \to 0$ as $j \to \infty$, which will happen (unless p_{t+j} explodes) since $|\alpha/(\alpha-1)| < 1$.

following specification of money supply behavior:

$$m_t = \mu_0 + \mu_1 m_{t-1} + e_t. \tag{14}$$

Here the (log of the) money stock in period t depends on its previous value, m_{t-1}, and also on a purely random component e_t. The latter, which is formally a white noise disturbance, represents the unsystematic component of policy behavior (the systematic part of which is $\mu_0 + \mu_1 m_{t-1}$).

Armed with this specification, it is then possible to determine the expectations at t of future m_t values. For m_{t+1}, the expectation is simply $E_t m_{t+1} = \mu_0 + \mu_1 m_t$, which follows because $E_t e_{t+1} = 0$. Next, for m_{t+2} we have

$$
\begin{aligned}
E_t m_{t+2} &= E_t(\mu_0 + \mu_1 m_{t+1} + e_{t+2}) \\
&= \mu_0 + \mu_1 E_t m_{t+1} = \mu_0 + \mu_1(\mu_0 + \mu_1 m_t).
\end{aligned}
\tag{15}
$$

This type of calculation can in principle be repeated for every future period, ultimately yielding upon substitution into (13) a proper solution for p_t.

Futhermore, analogous calculations could be carried out if the m_t process were different. But there must be a m_t process specified. With rational expectations, the value of p_t depends on time t expectations of m_t values into the entire future, and to determine these, some specification of the process must be made as part of the model.

8.3 Solution Procedure

When a particular policy process for m_t has been specified, however, there is another way of solving the model that is simpler than the one just outlined. It works as follows. By combining (9) and (14), the model at hand may be written as

$$\gamma + \alpha E_t p_{t+1} + (1 - \alpha)p_t + u_t = \mu_0 + \mu_1 m_{t-1} + e_t. \tag{16}$$

This shows p_t to be dependent on the values of m_{t-1}, u_t, e_t, and $E_t p_{t+1}$. But what does the latter depend on? Well, from (11) we know that $E_t p_{t+1}$ depends on $E_t m_{t+1}$ and $E_t p_{t+2}$, since $E_t u_{t+1}$ equals zero. But $E_t m_{t+1}$ is itself determined by m_t which depends only on m_{t-1} and e_t, so $E_t m_{t+1}$ brings in no additional variables. Also, by extension of the foregoing $E_t p_{t+2}$ depends on $E_t m_{t+2}$ and $E_t p_{t+3}$, and the former brings in no new variables while the latter leads to $E_t p_{t+4}$—and so on.

The upshot of this line of reasoning is that p_t evidently depends only on m_{t-1}, u_t, and e_t; the presence of $E_t p_{t+1}$ does not itself bring in any additional determinants. Consequently, since the model is linear, we conjecture that there is a solution of the form

$$p_t = \phi_0 + \phi_1 m_{t-1} + \phi_2 u_t + \phi_3 e_t, \tag{17}$$

for some constants $\phi_0, \ldots, \phi_3$—if we can just find what they are. But if that conjecture is true, then $p_{t+1} = \phi_0 + \phi_1 m_t + \phi_2 u_{t+1} + \phi_3 e_{t+1}$ and it follows that

$$E_t p_{t+1} = \phi_0 + \phi_1 m_t = \phi_0 + \phi_1(\mu_0 + \mu_1 m_{t-1} + e_t). \tag{18}$$

Now suppose that (17) and (18) are substituted into (16). The result is, clearly,

$$\gamma + \alpha[\phi_0 + \phi_1(\mu_0 + \mu_1 m_{t-1} + e_t)]$$
$$+ (1 - \alpha)(\phi_0 + \phi_1 m_{t-1} + \phi_2 u_t + \phi_3 e_t) + u_t \tag{19}$$
$$= \mu_0 + \mu_1 m_{t-1} + e_t.$$

But for (17) to be a valid solution, as conjectured, it must hold whatever values of u_t and e_t are generated by chance and whatever m_{t-1} happens to be. Therefore, (19) must also be a legitimate equality *whatever* the values are of m_{t-1}, u_t, and e_t. But that requirement is extremely useful, for it implies that the following conditions must pertain to the ϕ's:

$$\alpha\phi_1\mu_1 + (1 - \alpha)\phi_1 = \mu_1, \tag{20a}$$

$$(1 - \alpha)\phi_2 + 1 = 0, \tag{20b}$$

$$\alpha\phi_1 + (1 - \alpha)\phi_3 = 1, \tag{20c}$$

$$\gamma + \alpha\phi_0 + \alpha\phi_1\mu_0 + (1 - \alpha)\phi_0 = \mu_0. \tag{20d}$$

Now these four conditions—obtained by equating coefficients on both sides of (19) for m_{t-1}, u_t, e_t, and 1—are just what is needed, for they permit us to solve for the four unknown ("undetermined") coefficients—the ϕ's. In particular, from (20a) and (20b) we find that

$$\phi_1 = \frac{\mu_1}{1 - \alpha + \alpha\mu_1} \tag{21}$$

and

$$\phi_2 = \frac{-1}{1 - \alpha}. \tag{22}$$

Furthermore, using (21) we find from (20c) and (20d) that

$$\phi_3 = \frac{1 - \alpha\phi_1}{1 - \alpha} = \frac{1 - \alpha\mu_1/(1 - \alpha + \alpha\mu_1)}{1 - \alpha} = \frac{1}{1 - \alpha + \alpha\mu_1} \tag{23}$$

and

$$\phi_0 = \frac{\mu_0(1 - \alpha)}{1 - \alpha + \alpha\mu_1} - \gamma. \tag{24}$$

By putting (21)–(24) in (17), then, we obtain

$$\begin{aligned} p_t = {} & \frac{\mu_0(1 - \alpha)}{1 - \alpha + \alpha\mu_1} - \gamma + \frac{\mu_1}{1 - \alpha + \alpha\mu_1} m_{t-1} \\ & - \frac{1}{1 - \alpha} u_t + \frac{1}{1 - \alpha + \alpha\mu_1} e_t. \end{aligned} \tag{25}$$

The latter is our sought-after *solution* for p_t. That is, it describes the evolution over time of the endogenous variable p_t in terms of the exogenous shocks u_t and e_t and the predetermined variable m_{t-1}. It defines a time path for p_t.

There are other forms, it should be said, in which this solution can be expressed. A prominent one can be obtained by noting that $\mu_0 + \mu_1 m_{t-1} + e_t$ can be replaced by m_t giving

$$p_t = \frac{-\alpha\mu_0}{1 - \alpha + \alpha\mu_1} - \gamma + \frac{1}{1 - \alpha + \alpha\mu_1} m_t - \frac{1}{1 - \alpha} u_t. \tag{26}$$

In addition, (14) can be solved for m_t in terms of $e_t, e_{t-1}, \ldots$ [7] and put into (26). The result is

$$\begin{aligned} p_t = {} & \frac{-\alpha\mu_0}{1 - \alpha + \alpha\mu_1} - \gamma - \frac{1}{1 - \alpha} u_t \\ & + \frac{\mu_0/(1 - \mu_1) + e_t + \mu_1 e_{t-1} + \cdots}{1 - \alpha + \alpha\mu_1}. \end{aligned} \tag{27}$$

While (26) and (27) are valid solutions, they are just different ways of writing the solution (25). That is, for any set of values for $u_t, u_{t-1}, \ldots$ and $e_t, e_{t-1}, \ldots$, each of them implies the same path of p_t values as does (25).

8.4 Properties of the Solution

Let us now briefly consider the way in which the price level behaves in the present model, that is, the way in which p_t responds to exogenous shocks. By inspection of (25) it is easily seen that a positive u_t disturbance will, since $\alpha < 0$, lower p_t relative to what it would have been if

---

[7] Repeated elimination of past m_t values, in a manner like that of Section 7.3, indicates that $m_t = \mu_0/(1 - \mu_1) + e_t + \mu_1 e_{t-1} + \cdots$.

the value of u_t had been zero. That direction of effect is entirely in keeping with intuition, as a positive u_t represents a higher-than-normal level of money demand—a circumstance that naturally leads to a high value of money in terms of goods (i.e., a low price level).

Similarly, it is not surprising that a positive e_t serves—other things equal—to increase p_t, for $e_t > 0$ represents a higher-than-normal money supply. It will be noticed, however, that the magnitude of the effect of e_t on p_t is less than one for one, and therefore less than proportionate in terms of the raw variables M_t and P_t. Specifically, the coefficient on e_t in (25), (26), or (27) is $1/[1 - \alpha(1 - \mu_1)]$ and with $|\mu_1| < 1.0$, as one would normally presume to be the case, $1 - \alpha(1 - \mu_1)$ will be strictly greater than 1.0. That the effect is not one for one may seem to reflect a failure of the "quantity-theory" property to hold, that is, the property of price-level responses being proportionate to money stock changes. But let us investigate this matter more carefully before concluding that the present model conflicts with quantity-theory propositions.

As a first step in this investigation, note that the postulated nature of the money supply process is such that the effect of a nonzero e_t disturbance on the money stock itself is only temporary. That this is so can be seen by examination of the expression for m_t given in footnote 7: if e_t is increased by one unit, m_t will be one unit higher, but $m_{t+1}, m_{t+2}, \ldots$ will be higher by only $\mu_1, \mu_1^2, \ldots$ units, with these values getting smaller and smaller as elapsed time is greater. Thus the policy "experiment" in question is not the same as that in the usual quantity-theory comparison, as the latter implicitly assumes a *permanent* change in the money stock.

To focus on something closer to the usual comparison, there are two ways to proceed. One is to consider e_t disturbances to m_t that *are* permanent. This case may be obtained by letting μ_1 in the m_t process equal 1.0. To see that this makes the e_t effect on m_t permanent, suppose that $\mu_0 = 0$ in (14) so that we have $m_t = m_{t-1} + e_t$. Then each e_t affects m_t one for one *and* remains fully present in the initial condition for m_{t+1}. If there were never any more disturbances, the values of m_{t+2}, m_{t+3}, and so on, would all fully reflect the shock to e_t.[8] And when $\mu_1 = 1$, equation (25) shows that p_t does in fact respond one for one to e_t.

The second way to represent a permanent change is to consider how the system would be different if μ_0 in (14) were changed. Suppose, for

---

[8] If μ_0 were nonzero, the same would be true but relative to a different path. It will be noted that the m_t process under discussion is of the type often referred to as a "random walk" process. (When $\mu_0 \neq 0$, the process is a "random walk with drift.")

example, that μ_0 was one unit higher than in a reference case. Then the *average* value of m_t would be $1/(1 - \mu_1)$ units higher, as can be seen from the expression in footnote 7. Now from (27) we can find that in this case the average value of p_t would be greater by the following amount:

$$
\begin{aligned}
\frac{-\alpha}{1 - \alpha + \alpha\mu_1} + \frac{1/(1 - \mu_1)}{1 - \alpha + \alpha\mu_1} &= \frac{1/(1 - \mu_1) - \alpha}{1 - \alpha + \alpha\mu_1} \\
&= \frac{1/(1 - \mu_1) - \alpha(1 - \mu_1)/(1 - \mu_1)}{1 - \alpha + \alpha\mu_1} \\
&= \frac{1}{1 - \mu_1}.
\end{aligned}
$$

(28)

Thus a change in the average value of m_t does, in fact, have a one-for-one effect on p_t in this RE version of the Cagan model. In other words, when the question is posed properly, it is found that the model does have the quantity-theory property. A lesson of this illustration is that in dynamic, stochastic models with rational expectations, it is necessary to be very careful when posing questions about the magnitude of effects of exogenous on endogenous variables.

8.5 Examples of Rational Expectation Solutions

As the main purpose of the present chapter is to learn about RE analysis, let us now consider some examples other than the Cagan model. These examples will be so simple as to be without obvious economic meaning, the objective being to make the relevant technical points as clearly as possible.

First, let us illustrate the basic solution strategy recommended above by means of a model that is somewhat like the Cagan model but expressed in terms of a variable y_t that has no particular economic interpretation. Thus we assume that the behavior of y_t is governed by

$$ y_t = \alpha_0 + \alpha_1 E_t y_{t+1} + u_t, \tag{29} $$

where u_t is white noise. Then the relevant determinants of y_t include only u_t and a constant, and we conjecture that the solution is of the form

$$ y_t = \phi_0 + \phi_1 u_t. \tag{30} $$

To find ϕ_0 and ϕ_1, we note that if (30) is true, then $E_t y_{t+1} = \phi_0$,[9] so substitution into (29) yields

$$\phi_0 + \phi_1 u_t = \alpha_0 + \alpha_1 \phi_0 + u_t. \tag{31}$$

But for this to hold for all possible u_t values, it must be the case that $\phi_0 = \alpha_0 + \alpha_1 \phi_0$ and $\phi_1 = 1$, which are conditions analogous to (20a)–(20d) above. The solution, then, is

$$y_t = \frac{\alpha_0}{1 - \alpha_1} + u_t. \tag{32}$$

For a second example, let us retain (29) but now assume that the disturbance u_t is not white noise but instead obeys

$$u_t = \rho u_{t-1} + \xi_t, \qquad |\rho| < 1, \tag{33}$$

where ξ_t is white noise. That is, u_t is a first-order autoregressive disturbance. Now in this case, we can think of u_{t-1} and ε_t as the determinants of y_t. That being the case, it is natural to conjecture that

$$y_t = \phi_0 + \phi_1 u_{t-1} + \phi_2 \xi_t. \tag{34}$$

Then $E_t y_{t+1}$ is given by

$$\begin{aligned} E_t y_{t+1} &= \phi_0 + \phi_1 u_t + \phi_2 E_t \xi_{t+1} \\ &= \phi_0 + \phi_1 (\rho u_{t+1} + \xi_t). \end{aligned} \tag{35}$$

Substituting (33)–(35) into (29) then yields

$$\phi_0 + \phi_1 u_{t-1} + \phi_2 \xi_t = \alpha_0 + \alpha_1 [\phi_0 + \phi_1 (\rho u_{t-1} + \xi_t)] + \rho u_{t-1} + \xi_t. \tag{36}$$

The implied conditions on the ϕ's are $\phi_0 = \alpha_0 + \alpha_1 \phi_0$, $\phi_1 = \alpha_1 \phi_1 \rho + \rho$, and $\phi_2 = \alpha_1 \phi_1 + 1$. From these we find that

$$y_t = \frac{\alpha_0}{1 - \alpha_1} + \frac{\rho}{1 - \alpha_1 \rho} u_{t-1} + \frac{1}{1 - \alpha_1 \rho} \xi_t \tag{37}$$

or, using (33),

$$y_t = \frac{\alpha_0}{1 - \alpha_1} + \frac{1}{1 - \alpha_1 \rho} u_t. \tag{38}$$

A third example retains the autoregressive disturbance (33) but assumes that the expectation relevant to the determination of y_t is not

---

[9] Here $E_t y_{t+1} = E_t(\phi_0 + \phi_1 u_{t+1}) = \phi_0$ because u_t is white noise (implying that $E_t u_{t+1} = 0$).

$E_t y_{t+1}$ but $E_{t-1} y_t$—the value of y_t anticipated one period earlier. Thus the system consists of

$$y_t = \alpha_0 + \alpha_1 E_{t-1} y_t + u_t \tag{39}$$

plus (33). Again we conjecture a solution of form (34), so for $E_{t-1} y_t$ we have

$$E_{t-1} y_t = \phi_0 + \phi_1 u_{t-1} \tag{40}$$

as $E_{t-1} \xi_t = 0$. Putting (33), (34), and (40) into (39) yields

$$\phi_0 + \phi_1 u_{t-1} + \phi_2 \xi_t = \alpha_0 + \alpha_1(\phi_0 + \phi_1 u_{t-1}) + \rho u_{t-1} + \xi_t, \tag{41}$$

which implies the conditions $\phi_0 = \alpha_0 + \alpha_1 \phi_0$, $\phi_1 = \alpha_1 \phi_1 + \rho$, and $\phi_2 = 1$. The solution, then, is

$$y_t = \frac{\alpha_0}{1 - \alpha_1} + \frac{\rho}{1 - \alpha_1} u_{t-1} + \xi_t. \tag{42}$$

8.6 Models with Lagged Variables

A fourth example is one that appears at first glance to be similar to the three of Section 8.5, but which turns out to involve a new type of difficulty. The example is provided by

$$y_t = \alpha_0 + \alpha_1 E_t y_{t+1} + \alpha_2 y_{t-1} + u_t, \tag{43}$$

with u_t white noise, which is like (29) except that the previous period's value of the endogenous variable is included in the equation. Because of its appearance in (43), y_{t-1} must certainly be added to the list of relevant determinants. Accordingly, we now conjecture a solution of the form

$$y_t = \phi_0 + \phi_1 y_{t-1} + \phi_2 u_t. \tag{44}$$

In that case, we will have

$$\begin{aligned} E_t y_{t+1} &= \phi_0 + \phi_1 y_t \\ &= \phi_0 + \phi_1(\phi_0 + \phi_1 y_{t-1} + \phi_2 u_t), \end{aligned} \tag{45}$$

where (44) has been used for y_t. Putting (44) and (45) into (43) yields

$$\phi_0 + \phi_1 y_{t-1} + \phi_2 u_t = \alpha_0 + \alpha_1[\phi_0 + \phi_1(\phi_0 + \phi_1 y_{t-1} + \phi_2 u_t)]$$
$$+ \alpha_2 y_{t-1} + u_t \tag{46}$$

and this implies the conditions

$$\phi_0 = \alpha_0 + \alpha_1\phi_0 + \alpha_1\phi_1\phi_0,$$
$$\phi_1 = \alpha_1\phi_1^2 + \alpha_2, \qquad\qquad\qquad (47)$$
$$\phi_2 = \alpha_1\phi_1\phi_2 + 1.$$

The new difficulty in this example shows up clearly in the second of these conditions, as it is a quadratic equation in ϕ_1. Thus it is implied that

$$\phi_1 = \frac{1 + \sqrt{1 - 4\alpha_1\alpha_2}}{2\alpha_1} \quad \text{or that} \quad \phi_1 = \frac{1 - \sqrt{1 - 4\alpha_1\alpha_2}}{2\alpha_1}. \quad (48)$$

So the issue arises: which of the two values for ϕ_1 in (48) is appropriate for the solution expression (44)?

The answer to this question is found by noting that if $\alpha_2 = 0$, the present model reduces to the same model as in the first example of Section 8.5, for which we already know the solution to be $y_t = [\alpha_0/(1 - \alpha_1)] + u_t$. But with $\alpha_2 = 0$, equation (48) gives two different values, $(1 + 1)/2\alpha_1 = 1/\alpha_1$ and $(1 - 1)/2\alpha_1 = 0$. Now the first of these implies that $\phi_1 = 1/\alpha_1$, so that y_{t-1} appears in the solution when $\alpha_2 = 0$, whereas the second implies that $\phi_1 = 0$, so that y_{t-1} does not appear. Therefore, since we know that with $\alpha_2 = 0$ the solution is $y_t = [\alpha_0/(1 - \alpha_1)] + u_t$, in which y_{t-1} does not appear, we conclude that the second expression in (48)—the one with the "minus sign" attached to the square root—is appropriate. We have found which value in (48) is appropriate by seeing which of them gives the answer that we already know to be correct in a special case of the model.

As it happens, the type of difficulty faced in this example frequently arises when the model at hand includes a lagged endogenous variable, like y_{t-1}. Fortunately, it also happens that the approach just exemplified will almost always enable the analyst to decide which of the coefficient values [analogous to the ϕ_1 values in (48)] will be appropriate for the model at hand. That is, the analyst considers a special case of the model for which a variable falls out, permitting him to find a solution by the standard procedure of Section 8.5. He then chooses the coefficient value that agrees with the "known" solution in the special case.[10]

8.7   Multiple Solutions

Unfortunately, it must be reported that some economists do not agree with the approach recommended in Section 8.6. Instead, they favor the

[10] This procedure is described in more detail in McCallum (1983).

utilization of solution forms that include a larger number of determinants—in technical terms, a larger set of "state variables." This step leads them to find not a unique solution, as in our examples above, but an infinite multiplicity of solutions. Most of these solutions will imply rather peculiar behavior of the model's endogenous variables, often leading to price explosions.

To illustrate the effects of including "extra" determinants or state variables in the conjectured solution, consider the following example. It consists of the Cagan model in the case in which (only for simplicity) the money stock is held constant over time (i.e., $m_t = m$). Then the model can be written as

$$m - p_t = \gamma + \alpha(E_t p_{t+1} - p_t) + u_t, \tag{49}$$

where we assume that u_t is white noise. In this case, our recommended procedure would suggest that the solution is of the form

$$p_t = \phi_0 + \phi_1 u_t, \tag{50}$$

which implies that $E_t p_{t+1} = \phi_0$. Putting these into (49), we get

$$m = \gamma + \alpha\phi_0 + (1 - \alpha)(\phi_0 + \phi_1 u_t) + u_t, \tag{51}$$

which leads to the solution

$$p_t = \frac{m - \gamma - u_t}{1 - \alpha}. \tag{52}$$

This agrees, as it should, with (25). But if we try a solution of the form

$$p_t = \phi_0 + \phi_1 u_t + \phi_2 p_{t-1} + \phi_3 u_{t-1}, \tag{53}$$

even though p_{t-1} and u_{t-1} do not appear in (49), we will calculate that

$$E_t p_{t+1} = \phi_0 + \phi_2(\phi_0 + \phi_1 u_t + \phi_2 p_{t-1} + \phi_3 u_{t-1}) + \phi_3 u_t. \tag{54}$$

Substitution of (53) and (54) into (49) then results in

$$m = \gamma + \alpha[\phi_0 + \phi_2(\phi_0 + \phi_1 u_t + \phi_2 p_{t-1} + \phi_3 u_{t-1}) + \phi_3 u_t]$$
$$+ (1 - \alpha)(\phi_0 + \phi_1 u_t + \phi_2 p_{t-1} + \phi_3 u_{t-1}) + u_t,$$

which gives rise to the conditions

$$m = \gamma + \alpha\phi_2\phi_0 + \phi_0,$$
$$0 = \alpha\phi_2\phi_1 + \alpha\phi_3 + (1 - \alpha)\phi_1 + 1, \tag{55}$$
$$0 = \alpha\phi_2^2 + (1 - \alpha)\phi_2,$$
$$0 = \alpha\phi_2\phi_3 + (1 - \alpha)\phi_3.$$

Now the third of these implies that ϕ_2 equals zero or $(\alpha - 1)/\alpha$. If zero is chosen, as the procedure of Section 8.6 would suggest, the solution described in (52) will be obtained. But if instead the value $\phi_2 = (\alpha - 1)/\alpha$ is used, two peculiarities will occur. First, putting that value into the fourth of conditions (55) gives

$$0 = \alpha\left(\frac{\alpha - 1}{\alpha}\right)\phi_3 + (1 - \alpha)\phi_3,$$

which is satisfied for *any* value of ϕ_3. Indeed, the model fails to determine ϕ_3, so (53) will be a solution no matter what value is arbitrarily used for ϕ_3. Thus there is an infinite multiplicity of solutions when one chooses $\phi_2 = (\alpha - 1)/\alpha$. Second, since $\alpha < 0$ this choice implies that $\phi_2 > 1$ and that implies that p_t is dynamically unstable. As time passes, p_t gets larger and larger even though m_t is constant!

These two aberrations take place when extra state variables are included in the conjectured solution essentially because that step includes in expectational expressions like (54) terms that appear only because they are arbitrarily expected (by the model's individuals) to appear. The resulting effects are therefore properly considered to be "bubble" or "bootstrap" effects.

For some special types of investigation it may make sense to admit the possibility of bootstrap effects. But as a basic strategy for working with RE models for typical purposes, it is here recommended that these effects be ruled out. To do so, the procedure outlined in Sections 8.5 and 8.6 may be used. That procedure involves—to recapitulate—using only the minimal necessary number of determinants (or state variables) in the conjectured solution forms for the model's endogenous variable or variables. Then, also, in models in which nonlinearities arise in the conditions determining the ϕ_j coefficients, special cases of the model are considered as in Section 8.6 to choose among the possible values. This strategy will result in a unique RE solution and that solution will be free of bootstrap effects.

Appendix: Mathematical Expectation—A Review

The object in this appendix is to provide a brief and nontechnical review of some basic concepts of probability theory that are frequently utilized in Chapter 8 and elsewhere in the book. The discussion is fairly self-contained, but proceeds at a pace that presumes some previous study of the material.

Let X denote a *random variable*, that is, a variable pertaining to some actual or conceptual experiment whose outcome is random—is determined (at least in part) by chance. The possible outcomes are represented by specific numerical values $x_1, x_2, x_3, \ldots$ in the discrete case or by all values x within some interval (possibly from $-\infty$ to $+\infty$) in the continuous case. The probabilities of the different possible outcomes are given by a discrete or continuous *density function*, $f(x)$. Let us first consider the nature of $f(x)$ in the discrete case, and also introduce the concept of mathematical expectation, before turning to the more relevant continuous case.

Suppose the *discrete* random variable X has a finite number J of possible outcomes, $x_1, x_2, \ldots, x_J$. Then for each $j = 1, 2, \ldots, J$, the density function specifies a value $f(x_j)$ that is the probability of occurrence of that value: $f(x_j) = \text{Prob}\{X = x_j\}$. For each number except $x_1, \ldots, x_J$ the probability of occurrence is zero, so $f(x) = 0$ for all other values of x. Thus the probability distribution for X is in this discrete and finite case is fully characterized by the density function $f(x)$. The same would be true, furthermore, if there were a countable infinity of possible values $x_1, x_2, \ldots$. Note that we are using uppercase letters to name random variables and lowercase letters to refer to specific values that may be realized.

Probabilities are by design analogous to relative frequencies. Consequently, any probability is a nonnegative number less than or equal to 1.0, and the probabilities of all possible outcomes sum to 1.0. The density function f, therefore, has the properties $f(x) \geq 0$ and $f(x) \leq 1$ for all x, and also $\sum_{j=1}^{J} f(x_j) = 1$. Furthermore, since $f(x) = 0$ for values except $x_1, \ldots, x_J$, the third property can be written as $\Sigma f(x) = 1$, where the unspecified summation is understood as applying to all x values from $-\infty$ to $+\infty$. That notational convention will be utilized extensively in what follows.

If X is a discrete random with density $f(x)$, then the *mean* of the distribution of X is the probability-weighted average given by the sum $\sum_{j=1}^{J} x_j f(x_j)$, which can also be denoted $\Sigma x f(x)$. Often the symbol μ_x is used to denote the mean of X:

$$\mu_x = \sum x f(x). \tag{A1}$$

This concept is entirely analogous, it will be observed, to the simple mean of a collection of numbers if $f(x)$ is viewed as the fraction of all numbers of the collection that have the value x. Thus the mean of a random variable X is a measure of the "central tendency" of its probability distribution, just as the mean of a collection of numbers is a measure of their central tendency (or "average").

Also of great importance is a measure of the "spread," or "dispersion" of the probability distribution of X known as its *variance*. If we let σ_x^2 denote the variance of X, it is defined in the discrete case by

$$\sigma_x^2 = \sum (x - \mu_x)^2 f(x). \tag{A2}$$

Again, there is a correspondence with the variance of a collection of numbers. For some purposes the square root of the variance of X is used instead of the variance itself, often because it has the same units of measurement as X and μ_x. This measure, σ_x, is termed the *standard deviation*.

One extremely simple example of a discrete probability distribution is provided by the following density function:

j	x_j	$f(x_j)$
1	0	0.1
2	1	0.4
3	2	0.3
4	3	0.1
5	4	0.1

Here, there are five possible outcomes, $0, 1, 2, 3,$ and 4, with associated probabilities as shown. For all x values except these five, Prob $\{X = x\}$ is zero. Note that $\Sigma f(x) = 0.1 + 0.4 + 0.3 + 0.1 + 0.1 = 1.0$. With this probability distribution, the random variable X has a mean value of $\mu_x = 0(0.1) + 1(0.4) + 2(0.3) + 3(0.1) + 4(0.1) = 1.7$. Its variance is $\sigma_x^2 = (0 - 1.7)^2(0.1) + (1 - 1.7)^2(0.4) + (2 - 1.7)^2(0.3) + (3 - 1.7)^2$ $(0.1) + (4 - 1.7)^2(0.1) = 1.21$, and the standard deviation is therefore $\sigma_x = 1.1$.

Now consider the case in which X is a *continuous* random variable. Again there is a density function $f(x)$ that describes probabilities pertaining to the outcome of the relevant random experiment. And again the property $f(x) \geq 0$ applies. But now there are an uncountable infinity of different possible values for x, so the probability of any single particular value is zero. But the probability of X assuming some value on the interval between a and b, for example, can be obtained by integrating $f(x)$ over that interval:

$$\text{Prob}\{a < X < b\} = \int_a^b f(x)\,dx. \tag{A3}$$

This is analogous to the discrete case, since integration is analogous to summation. Since the probability of occurrence of some value $-\infty \leq x \leq +\infty$ is 1, we have $\int f(x)\,dx = 1$. Here and in what follows, any integration sign without explicitly stated limits should be understood as denoting integration over all values from $-\infty$ to $+\infty$.

If X is a continuous random variable with density $f(x)$, its mean is defined as

$$\mu_x = \int xf(x)\,dx, \tag{A4}$$

and its variance as

$$\sigma_x^2 = \int (x - \mu_x)^2 f(x)\,dx. \tag{A5}$$

Thus the concepts are entirely analogous to the discrete case, the only difference being that integration takes the place of summation.

For a simple example of a continuous random variable, suppose that X can only occur on the interval of values between 0 and 5, and that the chances of occurrence in any smaller interval within that span depend only on its length. (Thus, for example, the probability of $1.5 \le X \le 2.5$ is the same as $2.3 \le X \le 3.3$.) Then the density function would be $f(x) = 0.2$ for $0 \le x \le 5$, with $f(x) = 0$ elsewhere (i.e., for all x values outside the interval from 0 to 5). The mean value would be

$$\mu_x = \int_0^5 0.2x\,dx = 0.2\,\frac{x^2}{2}\,\bigg|_0^5 = (0.1)(25 - 0) = 2.5.$$

To check his or her understanding, the reader should verify that in this example the standard deviation of X is 1.44.

We are now prepared to define the most important concept of this review. That concept is the *mathematical expectation* of a random variable. From one perspective the mathematical expectation is simply the mean of the distribution of a random variable; if X is a continuous random variable, then its mathematical expectation $E(X)$ equals $\int xf(x)\,dx = \mu_x$. But there is a reason for introducing the new term, for it permits a generalization that is extremely useful. Suppose X is a discrete *or* continuous random variable with density $f(x)$. Then let $\phi(X)$ be a function that pertains to the various possible outcomes x. This function defines a new (related) random variable $\phi(X)$. It would be possible to determine its density function and from it the mean of $\phi(X)$. But we can shortcut that process by utilizing the following definition: the mathematical expectation of $\phi(X)$ is denoted $E[\phi(X)]$ and is given by[11]

$$E[\phi(X)] = \int \phi(x)f(x)\,dx \tag{A6}$$

---

[11] It is assumed throughout this appendix that all integrals and summations are absolutely convergent.

in the continuous case and by

$$E[\phi(X)] = \sum \phi(x)f(x) \tag{A7}$$

in the discrete case. Thus the mathematical expectation of $\phi(X)$ is simply the probabilistic average of $\phi(X)$ computed relative to the density function for X. It is identical to the mean of the distribution of the implied random variable $\phi(X)$, but can be determined without ever explicitly deriving the density function for that random variable itself.

The usefulness of the concept of mathematical expectation as defined in (A6) and (A7) stems from the flexibility and generality provided by the function $\phi(X)$, and also from a fact of considerable notational convenience: many formulas expressed in terms of the "expectation operator" $E(\cdot)$ are precisely the same for discrete *and* continuous random variables. Whenever using such formulas, consequently, there is no need to specify which type is involved. For example, consider two special cases in which $\phi(X) = X$ and $\phi(X) = (X - \mu_x)^2$, respectively. Then it is almost immediately apparent from (A6) and (A7) that we have $E(X) = \mu_x$ and $E[(X - \mu_x)^2] = \sigma_x^2$, whether X is discrete or continuous. The first of those special cases shows clearly that the mathematical expectation or *expected value* of X is the same entity as the mean of the distribution of X.

There are a few relationships involving expected values that are so useful and simple that commitment to memory is recommended. Three of these are as follows. Let X be any random variable with mean $E(X)$, let c_0 and c_1 be arbitrary constants, and let $\phi_1(X)$ and $\phi_2(X)$ be functions with means $E[\phi_1(X)]$ and $E[\phi_2(X)]$. Then

$$E(c_0) = c_0, \tag{A8}$$

$$E(c_0 + c_1 X) = c_0 + c_1 E(X), \tag{A9}$$

$$E[c_1\phi_1(X) + c_2\phi_2(X)] = c_1 E[\phi_1(X)] + c_2 E[\phi_2(X)]. \tag{A10}$$

These relationships are straightforward implications of the linearity properties of summation and integration operations. Thus a proof of (A10) for the continuous case is as follows:

$$
\begin{aligned}
E[c_1\phi_1(X) + c_2\phi_2(X)] &= \int [c_1\phi_1(x) + c_2\phi_2(x)]f(x)\,dx \\
&= c_1 \int \phi_1(x)f(x)\,dx + c_2 \int \phi_2(x)f(x)\,dx \\
&= c_1 E[\phi_1(X)] + c_2 E[\phi_2(X)].
\end{aligned}
$$

For the discrete case, the steps would be similar but with summations used instead of integrals. Note that (A8) and (A9) are simply special cases of (A10) and so do not require separate proofs.

At this point we need to extend the discussion of expected values to a *multivariate* setting, that is, one in which the experiment at hand involves two or more jointly distributed random variables. For simplicity, we shall limit our treatment to the *bivariate* (i.e., two-variable) case. Assume, then, that X and Y are jointly distributed random variables with bivariate density function $f(x,y)$. In this case, there are two variables whose outcomes are jointly determined by some random experiment. The probabilities of different values are described by the density $f(x,y)$. In the discrete case, the relevant specification is

$$\text{Prob}\{X = x \text{ and } Y = y\} = f(x, y), \qquad \textbf{(A11)}$$

and in the continuous case it is

$$\text{Prob}\{a < X < b \text{ and } c < Y < d\} = \int_c^d \int_a^b f(x,y) \, dxdy. \quad \textbf{(A12)}$$

In both cases $f(x, y) \geq 0$.

To illustrate the nature of bivariate distributions, it will be useful to consider a discrete example. In this example there are only three possible values for X (namely, $-1, 0$, and 1) and two for Y (2 and 3). The probabilities of the various bivariate outcomes are as indicated in the following tabulation:

	$y = 2$	$y = 3$
$x = -1$	0.10	0.30
$x =\ \ 0$	0.02	0.06
$x =\ \ 1$	0.13	0.39

Thus, for example, $\text{Prob}\{X = -1 \text{ and } Y = 2\} = 0.10$ while $\text{Prob}\{x = 1 \text{ and } Y = 3\} = 0.39$. It can easily be verified that the probabilities sum to unity: $\sum_x \sum_y f(x,y) = 1$.

Now even in the context of a bivariate distribution, the analyst may for some reason be concerned with the probability of X-values or Y-values *alone*, that is, considered without reference to the other variable. In the example at hand, these univariate distributions are clearly as follows:

x	$f(x)$	y	$f(y)$
-1	0.40	2	0.25
0	0.08	3	0.75
1	0.52		

Note how these values are obtained: $f(x)$ is found, for each x, by adding the $f(x, y)$ entries over both y values. Similarly, $f(y)$ is found by adding $f(x, y)$ over all three x values. Such procedures are applicable generally, so we have the formulas

$$f(x) = \sum_y f(x, y), \tag{A13}$$

$$f(y) = \sum_x f(x, y). \tag{A14}$$

The resulting univariate density functions $f(x)$ and $f(y)$ are referred to as "marginal" or "unconditional" density functions, pertaining to marginal or unconditional univariate probability distributions that are relevant in the bivariate context.

Closely analogous formulas are available, moreover, in the continuous case. Suppose that X and Y are jointly distributed continuous random variables with bivariate density $f(x, y)$. Then, since integration is the counterpart of summation (or addition), the formulas for univariate marginal densities for X and Y are as follows:

$$f(x) = \int f(x, y)\, dy, \tag{A15}$$

$$f(y) = \int f(x, y)\, dx. \tag{A16}$$

Furthermore, for summation over *both* variables we have $\iint f(x, y)\, dx\, dy = 1$.

Notation can be confusing in the bivariate (or multivariate) context. Indeed, it will be noted that we have already used the symbol f to stand for three different functions—one bivariate and two univariate density functions—in the context of a single random experiment. Consequently, the meaning of the symbol $f(2)$ is (for example) ambiguous. One remedy is to use different letters to refer to the different density functions. We could, for example, use $f(x, y)$, $g(x)$, and $h(y)$ for the three densities. More common, however, is the practice of using f to refer to all density functions but with subscripts attached to denote the relevant variables. In the case at hand, we would then have $f_{XY}(x, y)$, $f_X(x)$, and $f_Y(y)$. This practice eliminates ambiguity; it is clear that $f_Y(2)$ refers to the marginal density of Y. When there is little chance of confusion, however, most authors use the imprecise notation exemplified by $f(x, y)$, $f(x)$, and $f(y)$. In what follows we shall, for the sake of simplicity and neatness, follow that strategy.

The next concept to be introduced is a different type of univariate distribution that is relevant in the bivariate context. The nature of this distribution can be illustrated by reference to the discrete example used previously. Suppose that, for example, the analyst is concerned with the probability distribution of X *given that* Y takes on the value 3. This distribution is termed the *conditional* distribution of X given $y = 3$, and the relevant probabilities are described by the conditional density function $f(x|3)$. It should be clear that the probabilities for $x = -1$, $x = 0$, and $x = 1$ are, in our numerical example, proportional to the entries 0.30, 0.06, and 0.39. But these numbers do not sum to 1, so they do not qualify as probabilities. Thus we need to divide each of them by 0.75, the relevant value $f_Y(3)$. This step yields the conditional density, $f(x|3)$, as follows:

x	$f(x \mid 3)$
-1	0.40
0	0.08
1	0.52

Now, for the case at hand, the conditional density $f(x|3)$ happens to coincide with $f(x)$. That is a coincidence, however, about which more will be said later.

Consideration of the foregoing example suggests that, in general, conditional distributions can be obtained from a bivariate density such as $f(x, y)$ by way of the formulas

$$f(x|y) = \frac{f(x, y)}{f(y)}, \tag{A17}$$

$$f(x|y) = \frac{f(x, y)}{f(x)}. \tag{A18}$$

Indeed, the suggestion is warranted, provided that $f(y)$ is nonzero in (A17) and $f(x)$ nonzero in (A18).[12] Furthermore, these formulas are valid in both the discrete and continuous cases.

As it happens, the particular numerical example used above illustrates the important concept of probabilistic *independence*. The general idea is that the probabilities of various values for one variable are "independent of" (i.e., unaffected by) the value of the other variable. In our numerical example it is indeed the case that conditional probabilities for X, given some value of y, are independent of the y value. For example, it can easily be verified that the function $f(x|2)$ is exactly the same as that tabulated above for $f(x|3)$. And that sameness implies

---

[12] For y such that $f(y) = 0$, $f(x|y)$ is not defined. Similarly, for x such that $f(x) = 0$, $f(y|x)$ is not defined.

that $f(x)$ coincides with each of these conditional densities. The question then arises: is it also true that the conditional distributions for Y are independent of the given values of x? In the numerical example a mere glance will show that they are. But what is important is that this phenomenon occurs generally; if X is independent of Y in a bivariate distribution, then Y will be independent of X. Let us then quickly develop a proof of that proposition.

With X independent of Y by assumption, we have $f(x) = f(x|y)$. But for all values such that $f(x|y)$ is defined, we can then multiply by $f(y)$ and obtain $f(x) f(y) = f(x|y) f(y)$. But by equation (A17), the right-hand side equals $f(x, y)$, so we have that $f(x) f(y) = f(x, y)$ if X is independent of Y. But equation (A18) then implies that $f(x) f(y) = f(x) f(y|x)$ if $f(y|x)$ is defined. But that implies that $f(y) = f(y|x)$ whenever the latter is defined, and completes the proof.

We are now prepared to consider mathematical expectations or expected values in the bivariate context. Accordingly, let us assume that X and Y are jointly distributed random variables with bivariate density $f(x, y)$. Also, let $\phi(x, y)$ be a single-valued function of two variables. Then the mathematical expectation of $\phi(X, Y)$ is defined as

$$E[\phi(X, Y)] = \sum_x \sum_y \phi(x, y) f(x, y) \tag{A19}$$

in the discrete case and as

$$E[\phi(X, Y)] = \iint \phi(x, y) f(x, y) \, dx \, dy \tag{A20}$$

in the continuous case. Thus the mathematical expectation is, as in the univariate context, the mean of an implied random variable. Evidently, equations (A19) and (A20) constitute generalizations of (A6) and (A7).

Before continuing, let us dispose of a possible source of ambiguity. Suppose, as a special case, that we take $\phi(X, Y) = X$ and use (A20) to find $E(X)$. (Thus we are assuming that X and Y are continuous.) The result is

$$E(X) = \iint x f(x, y) \, dx \, dy. \tag{A21}$$

It will be recalled, however, that it is possible to obtain an unconditional univariate density for X, its marginal density, by means of equation (A15). If we let $f_X(x)$ denote this density, we have

$$f_X(x) = \int f(x, y) \, dy. \tag{A22}$$

Then since f_X is a univariate density for the random variable X, we can find the latter's expectation as

$$E(X) = \int x f_X(x) \ dx. \tag{A23}$$

Thus we have a second way, different from (A21), of evaluating $E(X)$. Fortunately, they yield the same result, as we can see by inserting (A22) into (A23):

$$\int x f_X(x) \ dx = \int x \int f(x,y) \ dy \ dx = \int \int x f(x,y) \ dx \ dy.$$

Therefore, the mathematical expectation of X can be found either from the definition (A20) or as the mean of the marginal distribution $f(x)$. Similarly, $E(Y)$ can be found from (A20) or as the mean of $f(y)$.

The mathematical expectations $E(X)$ and $E(Y)$ are unconditional expected values. For some purposes, however, the analyst may be concerned with expectations conditional upon some occurrence, that is, with expectations relative to some conditional distribution. Indeed, conditional means of this type play an important role in dynamic economic analysis with rational expectations. Let us denote the conditional expectation of X given y as $E(X|y)$ and similarly denote the conditional expectation of Y given x as $E(Y|x)$. Since these expectations are the means of conditional distributions, they may be obtained from the formulas

$$E(X|y) = \int x f(x|y) \ dx, \tag{A24}$$

$$E(Y|x) = \int y f(y|x) \ dy. \tag{A25}$$

One might also be interested in the variances or other properties of these conditional distributions, of course, but we will not consider them here.

Previously we mentioned the concept of statistical independence, which implies that conditional distributions for one variable are not dependent on given values of the other variable. Whenever X and Y are independent, it will be true that

$$f(x,y) = f(x)f(y), \tag{A26}$$

as examination of the proof concerning independence will reveal. Also we noted that our numerical example of a bivariate distribution has the property of independence. Cases in which statistical independence obtain are, however, exceptional. More typically, jointly distributed random variables will be related to some extent—the conditional distributions $f(x|y)$, for example, will depend on y. It is possible to devise measures of the strength of the association between random variables such as X and Y. The most important measure of this type is the *covariance*, defined as

$$\sigma_{XY} = \text{Cov}(X, Y) = E[(X - EX)(Y - EY)]. \qquad \text{(A27)}$$

A related measure of considerable usefulness is the correlation, which results when σ_{XY} is divided by σ_X and σ_Y (the standard deviations of the marginal distributions of X and Y):

$$\text{Corr}(X, Y) = \frac{\sigma_{XY}}{\sigma_X \sigma_Y}. \qquad \text{(A28)}$$

The principal attractions of the correlation measure are that it is unit-free and in all cases lies between -1 and $+1$ in value. Both the covariance and correlation measures of association equal zero, as one would hope, for random variables that are independent. This fact follows readily from definition (A20) and the property (A19):

$$
\begin{aligned}
\sigma_{XY} &= E[(X - EX)(Y - EY)] \\
&= E[XY - XEY - YEX + (EX)(EY)] \\
&= E(XY) - EX(EY) - EY(EX) + (EX)(EY) \\
&= E(X)E(Y) - EX(EY) = 0.
\end{aligned}
\qquad \text{(A29)}
$$

It is not the case, however, that zero covariance implies independence.

To conclude this review of probabilistic concepts, it will be useful to provide a statement and proof of the "law of iterated expectations," introduced in Section 8.1. For simplicity we shall continue to assume that only two random variables are involved. As with many of the concepts of this appendix, however, the basic logic of the argument is applicable to multivariate cases with three or more jointly distributed random variables.

Let the two variables at hand be denoted X and Y and suppose that they are continuous random variables with a bivariate probability density function $f(x, y)$. Suppose also that the conditional density of Y given X is denoted $f(y|x)$ and that the marginal (univariate) densities for Y and X are $f(y)$ and $f(x)$. From the results above, it will be recalled that $f(y|x) = f(x, y)/f(x)$, that $f(y) = \int f(x, y)\, dx$, and that $f(x) = \int f(x, y)\, dy$.

In this context, the law of iterated expectations asserts that the (unconditional) mean of the conditional mean of Y given X, which is random in any context in which X is random, equals the (unconditional) mean of Y itself. In symbols, the mean of $E(Y|X)$, which is $E[E(Y|X)]$, is equal to $E(Y)$. To prove this, we first note that $E(Y|X) = \int yf(y|x)\, dy$.

Then the mean of *that* is

$$E\left[\int yf(y|x)\, dy\right] = \int\int\left[\int yf(y|x)\, dy\right]f(x,y)\, dy\, dx.$$

But $\int yf(y|x)\, dy$ is not a function of y, so the last expression above can be written as

$$\int\left\{\left[\int yf(y|x)\, dy\right]\int f(x,y)\, dy\right\} dx.$$

Then, since $\int f(x,y)\, dy = f(x)$, we have

$$\int\left[\int yf(y|x)\, dy\right]f(x)\, dx = \int\int y\frac{f(x,y)}{f(x)}\, dy\, f(x)\, dx = \int\int yf(x,y)\, dy\, dx$$

$$= \int y\left[\int f(x,y)\, dx\right] dy = \int yf(y)\, dy.$$

But the final expression *is* the mean of the unconditional distribution of Y. Thus we have shown that

$$E[E(Y|X)] = E(Y).$$

If X and Y had a discrete, rather than continuous, bivariate distribution, all of the foregoing could be redone by interpreting the density functions as discrete probability (mass) functions and using summations rather than integrals. In that case the proof would be

$$E\left[\sum_y yf(y|x)\right] = \sum_x\sum_y\left[\sum_y yf(y|x)\right]f(x,y)$$

$$= \sum_x\left\{\left[\sum_y yf(y|x)\right]\sum_y f(x,y)\right\}$$

$$= \sum_x\left[\sum_y yf(y|x)\right]f(x) = \sum_x\sum_y y\frac{f(x,y)}{f(x)}f(x)$$

$$= \sum_x\sum_y yf(x,y) = \sum_y y\left[\sum_x f(x,y)\right]$$

$$= \sum_y yf(y) = E(Y).$$

Problems

1. Another example of the type considered in Section 8.5 uses equation (29),

$$y_t = \alpha_0 + \alpha_1 E_t y_{t+1} + u_t ,$$

and assumes that u_t is autocorrelated but now in a different fashion than specified by (33). Instead, in this example, u_t has the *moving-average* form

$$u_t = \xi_t + \theta \xi_{t-1},$$

where ξ_t is white noise. Find a solution for y_t in this case.

2. Consider again the market described in Problem 3 of Chapter 7 but now assume that expectations are formed rationally, that is, $p_t^e = E_{t-1} p_t$. [Here $E_{t-1} p_t \equiv E(p_t | \Omega_{t-1})$ with Ω_{t-1} including $p_{t-1}, p_{t-2}, \ldots,$ $q_{t-1}, q_{t-2}, \ldots$.] Derive a solution for p_t and then give a new answer to that problem.

3. Consider a market in which supply depends on current price

$$q_t = b_0 + b_1 p_t + u_t, \qquad b_1 > 0$$

while demand depends not only on the current price, but also on the price rationally expected to prevail in the near future:

$$q_t = a_0 + a_1 p_t + a_2 E_t p_{t+1} + v_t.$$

Here $a_1 < 0$ and $a_2 > 0$ while u_t and v_t are white-noise disturbances. Find the solution for p_t.

4. Suppose that money demand in an economy is characterized by the Cagan demand function (8) with u_t white noise. Cagan's assumption regarding money supply behavior does not prevail, however. Instead the central bank creates money according to the relation

$$m_t = \beta_0 + \beta_1 p_{t-1} + e_t,$$

with e_t white noise. Show that in this case the solution procedure of Section 8.3 leads, as in Section 8.6, to two possible values for the coefficient attached to p_{t-1} in the conjectured solution. Determine which of the two corresponds to the solution recommended in Section 8.7 by considering a special case in which $\beta_1 = 0$.

5. Consider an economy in which the *LM* and *IS* functions are given by equations (1) and (2) of Chapter 10. Suppose the economy is purely classical so that $y_t = \bar{y}$. Then these equations can be condensed to

$$LM \qquad m_t - p_t = \gamma + c_2 R_t + \varepsilon_t, \qquad c_2 < 0$$

$$IS \qquad R_t = r + E_t(p_{t+1} - p_t) + \eta_t.$$

For simplicity, delete ε_t. Then assume that the monetary authority creates money according to

$$MP \qquad m_t = \mu_0 + \mu_1 t + e_t.$$

Assume that e_t and η_t are white noise and find the solution for p_t and then for R_t.

References

Barro, Robert J., "Unanticipated Money Growth and Unemployment in the United States," *American Economic Review* 67 (March 1977), 101–15.

Lucas, Robert E., Jr., *Studies in Business-Cycle Theory.* (Cambridge: Mass.: The MIT Press, 1981).

McCallum, Bennett T., "On Non-Uniqueness in Rational Expectations Models: An Attempt at Perspective," *Journal of Monetary Economics* 11 (March 1983), 139–68.

Muth, John F., "Rational Expectations and the Theory of Price Movements," *Econometrica* 29 (June 1961), 315–35.

Sargent, Thomas J., "Rational Expectations, the Real Rate of Interest, and the Natural Rate of Unemployment," *Brookings Papers on Economic Activity*, (No. 2, 1973), 429–72.

Inflation and Unemployment: Alternative Theories

9.1 Dynamics and the Keynesian Model

In our discussion of steady inflation and dynamics we have thus far used versions of only one of the two static models introduced in Chapter 5: namely, the classical model. Within the classical framework there is, because of its property of monetary neutrality, almost no connection between real variables (such as employment or output) and nominal variables (money, prices, etc.). Consequently, changes in monetary variables may occur without exerting any influence on real variables, with the exception of real money balances. Here we wish to consider the possibility of utilizing some version of the other model of Chapter 5, the one termed Keynesian, which by contrast does feature a strong connection between real and monetary variables. We wish to do so because there is reason to believe that such connections may be important in actual economies. Because this topic is a difficult and controversial one, there are a number of different hypotheses that need to be considered. To provide some perspective on these hypotheses, our discussion will proceed in a historical fashion. That is, we shall review some of the ideas and arguments that have been influential during the postwar period in order to develop a well-rounded understanding of the basic issues involved.

To begin, let us recall that there is only one significant difference between the basic classical and Keynesian models as presented in Chapter 5. Specifically, while the former assumes that prices (including wages) adjust promptly so as to equate supply and demand quantities on all markets, the latter assumes that nominal wages do not adjust within the relevant period. In the Keynesian model, consequently, it is possible for labor demand and supply quantities to be unequal. In particular, it is possible that an excess supply of labor will prevail for some appreciable span of time.

Now, as all readers of these pages well know, the economist's stock in trade is an approach to the analysis of market phenomena that relies upon the equality of supply and demand. Relevant aspects of behavior are classified as affecting one (or the other) side of the market, in standard economic analysis, and the outcome of the various forces is represented by the price–quantity combination that makes supply equal to demand. A natural question, then, is as follows: *Why* is it that John Maynard Keynes departed from tradition—by letting labor supply and demand quantities differ—in developing the analytical framework of his famous book, *The General Theory of Employment, Interest, and Money* (1936)?[1]

The answer has to do, of course, with the experiences of actual economies that Keynes had observed. As most introductory textbooks explain, the U.S. economy experienced during the 1930s a period that has been subsequently labeled the Great Depression.[2] From 1930 until the outbreak of World War II, total U.S. output was below its 1929 level and unemployment rates were exceptionally high—indeed, over 14 percent from 1931 through 1940 and over 20 percent for 1932–1935. A brief look back at Table 1-2 will quickly suggest just how unusual and unfortunate this period was for the United States.

Nevertheless, the experience in Keynes's own country, the United Kingdom, had arguably been even more striking. While the United Kingdom's peak annual unemployment rate of 22.5 percent (in 1932) was not as high as that of the United States (25.2 percent in 1933), the depression period had begun for the United Kingdom in 1921 rather than 1930—and it lasted continuously until World War II.[3] The United

---

[1] It should be mentioned that it is an interesting and debatable question whether the "Keynesian model" of Chapter 5 is a fair representation of the analytical framework actually put forth in Keynes's *General Theory*. But for the purposes at hand—which concern macroeconomic analysis of the connection between monetary policy and output fluctuations—it will be appropriate simply to proceed as if the Keynesian model did represent Keynes's thought. The next few paragraphs constitute a parable, not a study in the history of thought.

[2] For a brief review, see Dornbusch and Fischer (1984, Chap. 10).

[3] The unemployment rates can be read from Figure 9-2. Their magnitude is made even more striking by a comparison with Figure 9-1, which gives values for 1861–1913 (i.e., from the first year for which unemployment figures are available until the start of World War I). In Figure 9-1 it will be seen that unemployment did not exceed 11 percent in any year prior to 1921. In fact, the period 1861–1913 had seen $6\frac{1}{2}$ trade cycles in the United Kingdom, during most of which the unemployment rate varied between 2 and 8 or 9 percent.

Kingdom unemployment rate, which had only once before exceeded 10 percent, stayed above that value (except for 1927) from 1921 until 1940!

The point of all this is that the U.K. and U.S. experiences led Keynes, writing in 1934–1935, to conclude that a useful macroeconomic model should *not* require that labor supply equal labor demand ($n^s = n^d$) at all times. To him it seemed clear that the British economy of 1921–1935 was one in which n^s was for many years greater than n^d. Thus he thought it desirable—indeed, imperative—to devise a framework in which $n^s > n^d$ could exist for an extended period, not just as a transient phenomenon.[4]

But as a framework intended to be helpful in analyzing actual economics and designing macroeconomic policies, the basic Keynesian model had—even on its own grounds—one extremely serious defect. This defect can be readily identified by a reminder of *how* the model works. In particular, as emphasized in Sections 5.7 and 5.8, the model gets its distinctive properties by treating the nominal wage rate W as something that is not explained by the model but is simply *given*. Thus the question quickly arises: How can one conduct analysis of an actual economy with a model that treats W as coming out of the blue?

To some followers of Keynes—and perhaps to Keynes himself—this feature of the Keynesian model did not at first seem to present any great problem. Analysis at any point of time (say t) would simply treat the current value of W_t as given and would ignore future values of that variable and most others. Policy decisions (or diagnosis) would be made just for the current period. Then when the next period ($t + 1$) arrived, the new value W_{t+1} would be treated as given and decisions regarding $t + 1$ would be made taking that new value as given. In this way it is, in fact, possible to proceed without ever providing any explanation of the economy's W_t values.

But a moment's thought will convince today's readers, more accustomed than economists of the 1930s to dynamic analysis, that this method of proceeding is highly undesirable. For even if W_t is given in t as a residue of the past, the particular value of W_t that prevails must certainly depend on what the economic conditions were in the past. The nominal wage in the Keynesian model is properly viewed as *predetermined* variable, not an exogenous variable. And this implies that policy actions taken today will (by affecting today's conditions) have an effect on *future* values of W_t—on W_{t+1}, W_{t+2}, and so on. The procedure

---

[4] It should be emphasized that this conclusion did not rest on a belief that $n^s = n^d$ would correspond to zero measured unemployment. Rather, the 1861–1913 experience suggested that a "full employment" state, in which $n^s = n^d$ analytically, would appear empirically as one with 4 to 5 percent measured unemployment, the average figure in each of several cycles.

of the preceding paragraph fails, however, to recognize such a dependence. Consequently, it can lead to policy actions that are undesirable because of reliance on analysis that fails to take account of some relevant effects—ones that will show up in the future.

By the 1950s various economists had recognized this problem and had begun the attempt to overcome it. Even if one takes W_t as given in t, they noted, it is not necessary to take it to be given in an inexplicable way. A natural way to proceed, instead, would be to add to the Keynesian model another equation (or set of equations) that *explains* values of W_t, period by period, as a function of conditions prevailing in the past. By adding such an equation to explain W_t, and then using the Keynesian model to explain the period-t values of the other variables on the basis of that given W_t, one could construct a complete macroeconomic model that might be used sensibly—that is, avoiding the inconsistency mentioned above. This completed model would work like the Keynesian static model within each period, but would also explain movements of W_t between periods and would thereby permit a dynamic analysis of an ongoing economy in which n_t^s can differ from n_t^d.

9.2 The Original Phillips Curve

Numerous attempts to carry out the agenda just described, by devising a submodel to explain W_t, have been made. The first of these to become truly important was that of A. W. Phillips. In his famous paper of 1958, Phillips suggested essentially that the (nominal) wage rate in any period could be explained by recent values of the unemployment rate. The idea was very simple; it was expressed in the opening sentences of his paper as follows.

> When the demand for a commodity or service is high relatively to the supply of it we expect the price to rise, the rate of rise being greater the greater the excess demand. Conversely when the demand is low relatively to the supply, we expect the price to fall, the rate of fall being greater the greater the deficiency of demand. It seems plausible that this principle should operate as one of the factors determining the rate of change of money wage rates, which are the price of labour services. When the demand for labour is high and there are very few unemployed we should expect employers to bid wage rates up quite rapidly, each firm and each industry being continually tempted to offer a little above the prevailing rates to attract the most suitable labour from other firms and industries (Phillips, 1958, p. 283).

In support of this hypothesis, that the rate of change of W_t depends negatively on the unemployment rate, Phillips presented evidence relating to the U.K. economy over the period 1861–1957. Two of his

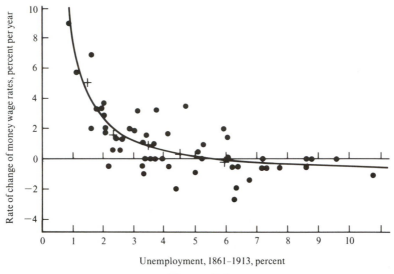

Figure 9-1

diagrams are reproduced as Figures 9-1 and 9-2. The former shows a rather impressive relationship of the type hypothesized for the years 1861–1913.[5] For 1913–1948 the relationship did not hold up so well, as can be seen from Figure 9-2, but that period included two world wars—when wage and price controls would tend to destroy normal patterns—and the abnormal years of the depression. After 1948, the old relationship reappeared: in Phillips's Figures 10 and 11 (not shown here) the points for 1948–1957 lay remarkably close to the curve fitted in Figure 9-1.

Thus the original Phillips curve can be represented algebraically as follows, where $w_t = \log W_t$ and UN_t = unemployment rate (in fractions) for period t:

$$\Delta w_t = f(UN_{t-1}). \tag{1}$$

Here f is a function with a negative slope: $f' < 0$. Now, by adding an equation like (1) to a Keynesian model like that of Section 5.8, we would obtain a system that could be used to depict the dynamic move-

---

[5] The extent to which this evidence was supportive of his argument was enhanced by recognition that Phillips posited an influence also from the rate of change of the unemployment rate: "It seems possible that a second factor influencing the rate of change of money wage rates might be the rate of change of the demand for labour, and so of unemployment" (Phillips, 1958, p. 283). Here we are neglecting this second aspect of Phillips's hypothesis for simplicity. To the extent that we focus on steady states, nothing is thereby lost.

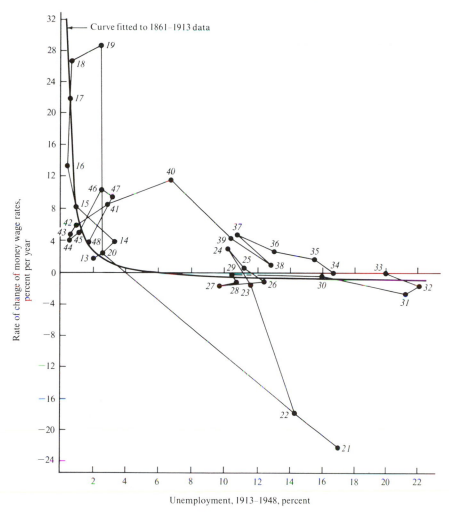

Figure 9-2

ments over time of the economy's main macroeconomic variables, provided that time paths or generating processes are specified for the exogenous policy variables. Such, in effect, was the approach to macroeconomic analysis that was adopted by many leading researchers in the late 1950s and throughout the 1960s.

One reason why the Phillips hypothesis attracted widespread support is that it completed the Keynesian model in the manner just described. But another reason, most likely, is that it focused attention in a simple and rather direct manner on two of the most prominent measures of macroeconomic performance: the unemployment rate and the inflation

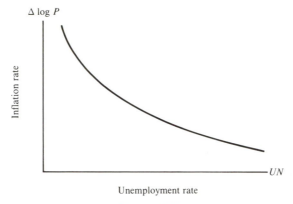

Figure 9-3

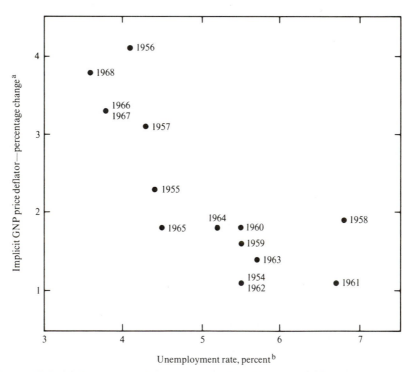

Figure 9-4.   [a] Change during year, calculated from end of year
deflators (derived by averaging the fourth quarter of a given year and the
first quarter of the subsequent year).[b] Average for the year.
SOURCES: Department of Commerce, Department of Labor, and
Council of Economic Advisors.

rate. To see how the latter is involved, imagine a steady-state situation of the type discussed in Chapter 6. In the absence of technical progress, the price level and the money wage rate will each grow (in a steady state) at the same rate as does the money stock. With technical progress, moreover, the money wage will grow at a rate that exceeds the price-level growth rate by the fixed amount λ, where λ is the appropriate measure of the rate of technical progress. Across different steady states, then, the growth rate of W_t will (for any given rate of technical progress) exceed the inflation rate by the same amount, λ. The inflation rate will therefore be high if and only if the rate of growth of W_t is high. Consequently, $\Delta \log P_t$ and $\Delta \log W_t$ will be perfectly correlated across steady states. But that means that a relation between $\Delta \log W_t$ and unemployment implies a similar relation between $\Delta \log P_t$, the inflation rate, and unemployment. So there is, according to the original Phillips hypothesis, a *tradeoff* between steady-state values of the unemployment rate and the inflation rate. Qualitatively, this tradeoff might appear as in Figure 9-3.

Now, if such a tradeoff were known to exist, it is likely that macroeconomic policy making would tend to emphasize its existence and nature, for the tradeoff *means* that an economy cannot permanently reduce its inflation rate without creating additional unemployment. Since these two variables are ones that policymakers and the public tend to emphasize, the existence of a Phillips-type tradeoff would be of enormous political significance. That, it is being suggested, is a second reason why the Phillips hypothesis attracted support.[6] (See Figure 9-4.)

9.3 The Augmented Phillips Curve

As early as 1966–1967, however, it was being argued by Milton Friedman and Edmund Phelps that the original Phillips formulation contains a serious flaw.[7] In particular, in the third sentence of the passage quoted in Section 9.2, the word "real" should be inserted in place of the word "money." Since both firms and workers care about the latter's

---

[6] That inflation–unemployment tradeoff considerations have been important in policy deliberations is nicely evidenced by the role of a Phillips-curve plot in the 1969 *Economic Report of the President* (p. 95). The same diagram shows that the U.S. postwar data did, at that time, seem to support the existence of such a tradeoff. To emphasize that point, a copy of the diagram appears in the text as Figure 9-4.

[7] The most frequently cited article is Friedman (1968). The ideas were presented earlier, however, by Phelps (1967) and Friedman (1966). The latter is a beautifully insightful yet informal discussion of only a few pages.

real wages, not their nominal wages, it is the real wage that should rise when there is excess demand for labor (or fall when there is excess supply).

According to the Friedman–Phelps argument, in other words, the left-hand side of (1) should represent the rate of change of the real wage, W_t/P_t. But that rate of change is $\Delta \log (W_t/P_t)$, which equals $\Delta \log W_t - \Delta \log P_t$. So using $p_t = \log P_t$, we should under this argument rewrite (1) as

$$\Delta w_t - \Delta p_t = f(UN_{t-1}). \tag{2}$$

The purpose of the relation under discussion is, however, to explain nominal wage rate changes settled upon by firms and workers on the basis of conditions prevailing in the recent past. But the actual value of Δp_t could not be known in the past (e.g., in period $t - 1$) but could only be anticipated. If, then, we use Δp_t^e to denote the value of Δp_t expected in period $t - 1$ to be realized in t, we would have $\Delta w_t - \Delta p_t^e = f(UN_{t-1})$, which when rearranged can be written as

$$\Delta w_t = f(UN_{t-1}) + \Delta p_t^e. \tag{3}$$

The latter describes the determination, according to the Friedman–Phelps hypothesis, of the wage rate in period t: its logarithm, w_t, is equal to w_{t-1} plus $f(UN_{t-1}) + \Delta p_t^e$. All three of those variables are ones that obtained in period $t - 1$,[8] it will be noted, so the general type of analysis described in Section 9.1 can be conducted using (3) instead of (1).

Because of the appearance of the expected inflation rate as an additional variable on the right-hand side of (3), this revised formulation is often referred to as an *expectations-augmented* Phillips curve. As that phrase is rather awkward, we shall henceforth refer to (3) simply as an *augmented* Phillips relationship.[9]

Whatever terminology is adopted, the most important feature of the Friedman–Phelps relation (3) is that it does *not* imply the existence of a steady-state tradeoff between inflation and unemployment. To see that, note that steady-state conditions would again entail $\Delta w_t = \Delta p_t + \lambda$. Thus the steady-state relation between inflation and UN would be

$$\Delta p + \lambda = f(UN) + \Delta p^e. \tag{4}$$

But steady-state conditions also imply that expected and actual inflation rates are the same (i.e., that $\Delta p^e = \Delta p$). Those two terms fall out

---

[8] Equivalently, we could think of (3) as describing the determination in period t of the wage to rule in period $t + 1$. In that case we would write the equation as $w_{t+1} = w_t + f(UN_t) + \Delta p_{t+1}^e$.

[9] There are other terms for relations like (3); some of these will be mentioned below.

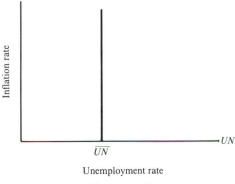

Figure 9-5

of (4), then, leaving us with

$$\lambda = f(UN). \tag{5}$$

But this expression shows clearly that the steady-state unemployment rate is not related to the steady-state inflation rate when the Phillips relationship governing wages is of the augmented type posited by Friedman and Phelps. Under their hypothesis, that is, the relevant steady-state diagram appears as in Figure 9-5, where $\overline{UN}$ is the value of UN determined by (5)—the latter being a single equation involving a single variable.

When Friedman and Phelps first put forth their argument for the augmented version of the Phillips curve, its validity was not imme-diately accepted by all economists. The idea that expected inflation would to some extent influence money wage settlements was conceded, but many economists believed that its effect would be only *partial*. They believed, that is, that the true relationship was of the following form, with α *between* the extreme values of 0 and 1 posited by the Phillips and Friedman–Phelps hypotheses:

$$\Delta w_t = f(UN_{t-1}) + \alpha \, \Delta p_t^e, \qquad (0 \le \alpha \le 1). \tag{6}$$

Given this disagreement, various economists attempted to estimate the value of α econometrically, using postwar data for the U.S. and other economies. The first few attempts of this type resulted in esti-mates of α around 0.5, far below the value hypothesized by Friedman and Phelps.[10] These attempts relied, however, upon the assumption

---

[10] Two prominent studies of this type were conducted by Solow (1969) and Gordon (1970).

that expectations were formed adaptively. It was soon pointed out by Sargent (1971) that if expectations are actually rational, tests that assume them to be adaptive will lead to erroneous estimates of α. New econometric procedures were therefore developed and subsequent tests assuming rational expectations led to estimates of α that were quite close to the 1.0 value suggested by Friedman and Phelps.[11] Because of that evidence and other types developed subsequently,[12] as well as the a priori theoretical strength of the Friedman–Phelps position, this point of view has gradually come to be very widely accepted by macroeconomists of almost all persuasions.[13]

The last statement pertains, however, only to the specific issue concerning the existence of a "long-run" tradeoff of the type implied by steady-state comparisons. The precise features of the wage adjustment equation (3) have not been generally accepted. In fact, the basic approach implicit in both the Phillips and Friedman–Phelps formulations has been strongly challenged, as we shall see in the remaining sections of this chapter. Furthermore, some analysts have favored models that imply the existence of a long-run tradeoff in a different sense than that pertaining to alternative steady states.

Before turning to the discussion of these more recent aggregate supply theories, it will be useful to include a brief digression. The purpose of this digression is to emphasize that there is a very tight relationship between unemployment rates and aggregate output measures. In particular, since output is high and unemployment is low whenever employment is high, there is a strong negative relationship between unemployment rates and detrended output levels. That such is the case is illustrated by the statistics plotted in Figure 9-6, which pertains to real GNP and unemployment for the U.S. economy for the years 1950–1984. Because this type of relationship was emphasized in a well-known article by Arthur Okun (1962), it has come to be known as "Okun's law." In the remaining sections of this chapter we shall make use of Okun's law by proceeding as if high (low) unemployment rates were essentially the same phenomena as low (high) values of output measured relative to trend or "normal" values. These normal values, moreover, will be interpreted as reflecting market-clearing conditions.

---

[11] Such findings were reported by Sargent (1973) and McCallum (1976).

[12] A notable study was provided by Barro (1977).

[13] To be more specific, the absence of a steady-state tradeoff between Δp and UN has come to be accepted. In other words, the Friedman–Phelps model has come to be viewed as more accurate—or less misleading—than the original Phillips formulation.

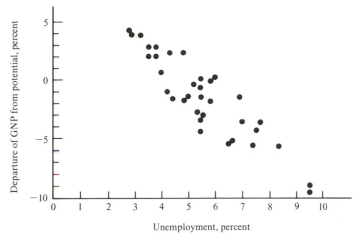

Figure 9-6.   Okun's law. Rates of unemployment are closely related to percentage departures of real GNP from normal GNP.
Source: Hall and Taylor (1986).

9.4   Lucas's Monetary Misperceptions Theory

An important alternative approach to the inflation–unemployment re-lation was developed in the 1970s by Robert E. Lucas, Jr. In a series of ingenious and influential articles (1972a, b, 1973), Lucas worked out a theory of Phillips-type correlations that result not from slow wage or price adjustments, but from individuals' mistaken beliefs about current macroeconomic conditions, *misperceptions* that arise because indi-viduals have incomplete information concerning the state of the eco-nomy. The idea is that individual sellers who observe changes in the market price of their own product may not know whether any particu-lar price change is caused by a change in the economy-wide average state of aggregate demand or by a change in relative product demands that is significant for their own product. Thus an individual seller of product *z* who observes an increase in *its* price does not know whether or not to increase her output, for that is a response that would be optimal if the cause were a relative demand increase but not if it were an increase in aggregate demand (which would lead with complete information to proportionate increases in all prices and no output effects). Accordingly, each individual supplier responds to any unex-pected[14] price change in an intermediate manner, changing output in

---

[14] The same is not true for expected or anticipated price changes because their cause arose in the past, according to Lucas's model, and is therefore known to individuals who then understand whether or not an output response is appropriate.

the same direction but by less than if she *knew* the source to be a relative demand shift.

Some symbols will be necessary to provide a more precise explanation of Lucas's theory. Let $p_t(z)$ be the (log of the) price in period t of product z and let p_t be (the log of) the economy-wide average price level. Then the supply of product z in t would be positively related to $p_t(z) - p_t$ if individual suppliers knew the current value p_t; suppliers want to produce and sell more when relative-price conditions are favorable. But Lucas assumes that suppliers do not know p_t. Instead, they can only form a current perception of p_t, denoted $E_z p_t$ in market z, based on incomplete information. This information in z consists of the current price of the seller's own product, $p_t(z)$, and information available from the past, which is for simplicity assumed to be complete. Then the rational perception of p_t in z is $E_z p_t = E(p_t | p_t(z), \Omega_{t-1})$, the conditional expectation of p_t given available information. And Lucas showed that this perception would be equal, under fairly general conditions, to a weighted average of $p_t(z)$ and $E_{t-1} p_t$, where the latter denotes the expectation of p_t based on information available in $t - 1$. Thus, if θ and $1 - \theta$ are the weights, $E_z p_t = \theta p_t(z) + (1 - \theta)E_{t-1} p_t$.

Combining the two relations just described, we see that the period-t supply of product z would be

$$
\begin{aligned}
y_t(z) &= \bar{y}(z) + \gamma[p_t(z) - \theta p_t(z) - (1 - \theta)E_{t-1}p_t] \\
&= \bar{y}(z) + \gamma(1 - \theta)[p_t(z) - E_{t-1}p_t],
\end{aligned}
\tag{7}
$$

where $\bar{y}(z)$ is "normal" supply in z and where γ is a positive constant. But this relation pertains only to product z. Suppose that we average similar equations over all products in order to get a measure of aggregate supply, y_t. Then if γ is the same in all markets—a simplifying assumption designed to abstract from distributional matters—this summation yields

$$
y_t = \bar{y} + \gamma(1 - \theta)[p_t - E_{t-1}p_t],
\tag{8}
$$

where $\bar{y}(z)$ is the economy-wide average of normal output, because p_t is an average of the various individual product prices.

This last relation, equation (8), provides one representation of Lucas's misperception theory of aggregate supply. It suggests that y_t is high relative to normal output when p_t exceeds $E_{t-1}p_t$, that is, when the price level is greater than the value previously expected. Since $E_{t-1}p_{t-1} = p_{t-1}$, it follows that

$$
\begin{aligned}
p_t - E_{t-1}p_t &= p_t - p_{t-1} - E_{t-1}p_t + p_{t-1} \\
&= p_t - p_{t-1} - (E_{t-1}p_t - E_{t-1}p_{t-1}) = \Delta p_t - E_{t-1}\Delta p_t.
\end{aligned}
\tag{9}
$$

Thus the model also implies that output is high when actual inflation is greater than the value expected, a relation that is similar—since by Okun's law $y_t - \bar{y}_t$ will be high whenever UN_t is low—to the Friedman–Phelps relation (4). In terms of aggregative variables, then, the Lucas model seems to be much the same as a version of the Friedman–Phelps argument modified to pertain on a period-by-period basis. Equation (9) could be combined with the aggregate demand portion of the models of Chapter 5 (i.e., the *IS* and *LM* functions) to produce a model that would describe the dynamic behavior of y_t, p_t, and r_t for given paths of policy variables and with rational expectations. This model would imply behavior of the variables that is quite similar to that implied by the Keynesian model together with the Friedman–Phelps equation (3), plus rational expectations.

But despite similarities there is an important difference. The rationale for the Friedman–Phelps equation stresses time lags between expectation formation and inflation realization; $\Delta p_t - \Delta p_t^e$ is relevant however expectations are formed and even if agents in t know the current value of p_t (and Δp_t). In the Lucas model, by contrast, the basic driving variable is the average discrepancy between each local price $p_t(z)$ and the local perception of the aggregate price level. If each agent *knew* the average price level, each supplier would base his decision on $p_t(z) - p_t$, not $p_t(z) - E_z p_t$. Averaging over all products would then give a value of zero in the aggregate; the average value across markets of $p_t(z) - p_t$ is $p_t - p_t = 0$. The Lucas theory is based on the presumption that local *misperceptions* of the average price level are important.

This feature of the Lucas model has been important in shaping economists' attitude toward the theory. Initially, it gave a strong impetus to its acceptance, for the model seemed more consistent with the traditional supply-equals-demand approach mentioned in Section 9.1.[15] And the idea that imperfect information could be the source of the Phillips relation seemed highly appealing, as information imperfections surely exist in reality. But more recently this feature has worked against the Lucas model. For it became understood that the model implies that there will be no Phillips relation, even temporarily, if individuals know current values of the aggregate money stock—even if these values reflect imperfect measurement of that variable.[16] Consequently, since the Fed publishes statistics pertaining to the U.S. money

---

[15] Indeed, supply and demand *are* equal in each period and in each market, if one takes the point of view that these magnitudes should be measured *conditional* upon agents' available information.

[16] To be more precise, the point is as follows. If reported measurements of the aggregate money supply are randomly different from the "true" values that agents actually respond to, then Lucas's theory implies that there will be no relation between output or employment variables and the measured money stock magnitudes. This result was developed in a significant paper by King (1981).

stock *weekly*, it seems implausible that absence of price level or money stock data—monetary misperceptions—could be an important source of output movements noted in data for (say) quarter-year periods. Most economists today, then, doubt the relevance of the Lucas model to current business cycle fluctuations. Monetary misperceptions may have been important in the prewar U.S. or U.K. economies, but they probably are not in the 1980s.

9.5   Taylor's Relative-Prices Theory

Another influential model of the inflation–unemployment relation, very different from Lucas's, has been developed and implemented empirically in a number of papers by John B. Taylor (1979, 1980). The emphasis in Taylor's model is on the price charged by a seller *relative* to the prices of other sellers,[17] in a setting in which prices are set and held fixed for a number of periods. To exemplify the mechanism at work, suppose that prices when set stay in force for two periods. Furthermore, suppose that the price-setting decisions are staggered in the sense that half of the sellers change their prices each period. Within any period, consequently, half of the prices in force will have been set at the start of that period and the other half will have been set at the start of the previous period. Thus, if each of the sellers setting a price at the start of t chooses the same price, x_t, the average price p_t in effect during t will be

$$p_t = 0.5(x_t + x_{t-1}). \tag{10}$$

But the heart of the theory lies in the manner in which x_t is chosen. As mentioned above, Taylor emphasizes relative prices. Now a price set at the first of period t will be in effect during periods t and $t + 1$, so the basis for comparison for a price set at t will be the average of x_{t-1} and x_{t+1}, for these are the prices that will prevail for the other group of sellers in periods t and $t + 1$. But as of t, x_{t+1} is not known, so its expectation must be used. Thus at the start of t the seller is concerned with his price *relative to* the magnitude

$$0.5(x_{t-1} + E_{t-1}x_{t+1}). \tag{11}$$

The latter provides the starting point for his decisions. But it is plausible that the seller would set his own price somewhat above or below the value given by (11), depending on whether he expects demand to be

---

[17] Most of Taylor's writings have emphasized nominal wages rather than product prices. But the same logic is applicable in either case. For a recent textbook exposition of Taylor's approach, see Hall and Taylor (1986, Chap. 14).

high or low relative to normal during the time that his price will prevail. To express that idea, together with the notion of staggered price setting, Taylor assumes that the new price chosen (by half of the sellers) at the start of t is

$$x_t = 0.5(x_{t-1} + E_{t-1}x_{t+1}) + \delta E_{t-1}[(y_t - \bar{y}) + (y_{t+1} - \bar{y})], \quad (12)$$

where y_t is real demand at t and $\bar{y}$ reflects the "normal" magnitude of that variable. The slope parameter δ in this equation is presumably positive.

Together, equations (10) and (12) constitute Taylor's model of aggregate-supply or Phillips curve phenomena. It is clear that they can be generalized to reflect price setting for a larger number of periods—say, four instead of two—with a correspondingly smaller fraction of all prices being changed in each period. The resulting equations can be combined with relations depicting aggregate demand to obtain a dynamic macroeconomic model that is intended to explain time paths of the important aggregative variables.

Taylor's theory is also open to certain objections. The most important of these is that the model implies the existence of a permanent tradeoff between unemployment and purely monetary values. There is no simple tradeoff between steady-state inflation and unemployment, as in the original Phillips curve analysis, but there is a more subtle tradeoff that can remain in force indefinitely. To see that, let us replace expectations with realized values in equation (12), obtaining

$$0.5(x_t - x_{t-1}) - 0.5(x_{t+1} - x_t) = \delta(y_t - \bar{y}_t) + \delta(y_{t+1} - \bar{y}_{t+1}). \quad (13)$$

Now the left-hand side of the latter is -0.5 times $\Delta x_{t+1} - \Delta x_t$, and the latter is the change in the inflation rate measured in terms of newly set prices. So Taylor's model implies that a monetary policy that makes $\Delta x_{t+1} - \Delta x_t$ positive—one that increases the inflation rate (thus measured) period after period—will have an effect on the value of $y_t = \bar{y}_t$, which is tightly linked to the unemployment rate. Thus the model implies that the unemployment rate can be permanently affected by monetary policy. But this is a notion that many economists find inherently implausible. It amounts to a denial of the *natural-rate hypothesis*, which, as formulated by Lucas (1972b), asserts that there is *no* path of prices (or inflation rates) that will keep output permanently above or below its normal (market-clearing) value.

9.6 Fischer's Sticky-Wage Theory

A theory that is often classified together with Taylor's was put forth by Stanley Fischer (1977). The principal element of similarity is that Fischer's model, like Taylor's, splits sellers into two (or more) groups that set nominal prices which stay in effect for two (or more) periods. The prices that are in this sense preset are for labor (i.e., wages) in Fischer's model but that is not the main thing that distinguishes it from Taylor's.[18] Instead, the distinction stems from the precise way in which these wages are set, which differs from Taylor's scheme in two ways. First, while wages are set (for half of the work force) at the start of t to prevail in periods t and $t + 1$, the values for those two periods are typically not the same. Second, the value set for each period equals the expected market-clearing level.

To express this assumption algebraically, let's us use z_t to denote the log of the real wage for some group in period t. Then $z_t = w_t - p_t$, where w_t is the log of the nominal wage rate. Also, let $\bar{z}_t$ be the market-clearing value of z_t. At the start of t, then, the expected market-clearing value of the real wage for t is $E_{t-1}\bar{z}_t + E_{t-1}p_t$. That wage will prevail during period t for half of the workers, according to Fischer's theory, while the other half of the workers will have had their period-t wage set at the start of $t - 1$ at the level $E_{t-2}\bar{z}_t + E_{t-2}p_t$, which was then expected to clear the market.

The other crucial ingredient in Fischer's model is a specification of how employment—and hence output—is determined. In this regard, Fischer adheres to the assumption that firms choose employment levels so that the marginal product of labor will be brought into equality with the prevailing real wage. Since the marginal product of labor decreases with the quantity of employment, this implies that output for each group of firms is negatively related to $w_t - p_t$. For each group, then, $y_t - \bar{y}_t$ is negatively related to $w_t - p_t$. Using the expressions given above for the two groups, Fischer postulates a log-linear aggregate relationship of the form

$$
\begin{aligned}
y_t - \bar{y}_t = \gamma_0 + \gamma_1[0.5(E_{t-1}\bar{z}_t + E_{t-1}p_t - p_t) \\
+ 0.5(E_{t-2}\bar{z}_t + E_{t-2}p_t - p_t)],
\end{aligned}
\tag{14}
$$

where γ_1 is negative. This expression summarizes Fischer's aggregate supply theory. It could be used—instead of the Phillips relation (1), or the Friedman–Phelps modification (6), or Lucas's model (9), or Taylor's (10) and (12)—to complete a macroeconomic model whose aggregate demand sector is given by some version of *IS* and *LM* relations.

It should be noted that, with γ_1 negative, the Fischer model postulates that employment and output are increasing functions of the

---

[18] As mentioned above, Taylor's model is often expressed in terms of wages.

price surprise term $p_t - E_{t-1}p_t$. In that regard, the Fischer model is like Lucas's and the Friedman–Phelps type of Phillips relation. However, Fischer's also implies a separate effect due to the two-period surprise $p_t - E_{t-2}p_t$, as can be seen from (14), and is in that way unlike these other two. Despite this second channel of price-level effects on output, however, the Fischer model satisfies the natural-rate hypothesis. That conclusion follows directly from the basic assumption that wages are set at expected market-clearing levels, together with the postulate of rational expectations, for the latter implies that expectational errors are purely random.

Does the Fischer formulation have any significant weaknesses? Obviously, the answer to this query must be "yes," for otherwise there would not be various theories still in competition for the status of a generally accepted aggregate supply theory. As it happens, the main trouble with the Fischer model concerns its real wage behavior. In particular, to the extent that the model itself explains fluctuations in output and employment, these should be inversely related to real wage movements: output should be high, according to the model, when real wages are low.[19] But in the actual U.S. economy, there is no strong empirical relationship of that type. In fact, there seems to be a weak relationship of precisely the opposite type—real wages have a slight tendency to be above normal when output and employment are above normal. This fact is illustrated in Figure 9-7, which plots detrended real wages for U.S. industry against detrended output for that sector (using quarterly data for 1954–1985).

That cyclical fluctuations in U.S. output are not closely related to fluctuations in real wages should come as no surprise, when one stops to think about the nature of typical American jobs. As emphasized by Robert Hall (1980), a majority of the employed workers at any point of time are in a job that they have held for several years and intend to hold for several more. In that sense, the typical employment relation is one of long duration. But if an employee is attached to a particular firm for (say) 15 years, why should the number of man-hours that he works in one month be related to the wage rate at which he is paid during that month? As Hall says, each month's wage bill is in the nature of an "installment payment" for a quasi-permanent arrangement. For this reason, it is probably wrong to expect employment fluctuations to bear any close relation one way or the other to real wage movements.

---

[19] If fluctuations are principally due to cyclical movements in $\bar{y}_t$ and $\bar{z}_t$, which are treated as exogenous throughout this chapter, then the existing data would not be inconsistent with Fischer's model. But in this case the latter would not itself be providing an explanation for the relationship at hand.

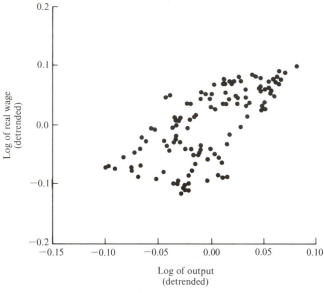

Figure 9-7

9.7   Real Business Cycle Theory

More recently, a great deal of professional attention has been devoted to an approach that is quite different from those of Taylor and Fischer. Whereas those theories seek to explain Phillips-type correlations as resulting from the response of output and employment to monetary shocks, the *real business cycle* (RBC) approach turns the causal pattern around. It supposes, in other words, that real responses to monetary stimuli are nonexistent or negligible and that the observed correlations reflect instead the response of monetary variables to real output and employment movements that result from random disturbances to the economy's production function. Emphasis has not been given to correlations of real and normal variables, however, but to the time-series behavior of key real variables and to correlations between pairs of real variables.[20]

One way to view the RBC approach is as a sophisticated version of the classical model of Section 5.6. This version recognizes changes over time in the capital stock, unlike its simpler predecessor, and emphasizes the importance of random shocks (such as weather or technological innovations) to the production function. Instead of $y_t = F(n_t)$, that

---

[20] In the development of this approach, the most influential papers have been Kydland and Prescott (1982), King and Plosser (1984), and Prescott (1986).

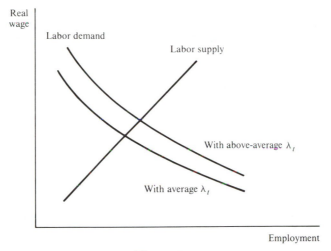

Figure 9-8

is, it features a production function of the form

$$y_t = \lambda_t F(n_t, k_t), \tag{15}$$

where λ_t is a random productivity shock whose realizations affect the amount of output (y_t) that can be produced with given amounts of labor and capital inputs (n_t and k_t).[21] Also, $F(n_t, k_t)$ has constant returns to scale and the other usual properties: $F_1 > 0$, $F_2 > 0$, $F_{11} < 0$, $F_{22} < 0$, and $F_{12} > 0$. With this specification, the marginal product of labor in period t is $\lambda_t F_1(n_t, k_t)$, so that an above-average value for λ_t implies a greater-than-normal demand for labor. The labor demand function relating n_t to the real wage rate lies, in other words, above the position that would be normal given the existing stock of capital. If the labor supply function is upward sloping and is itself unaffected by λ_t, then the above-average outcome will lead to above-average values for both n_t and the real wage z_t. This is illustrated in Figure 9-8. Output responds positively to the technological shock both because n_t is high and because the amount produced with given input quantities is high. Similarly, employment, output, and the real wage will all be abnormally low (relative to the existing stock of capital) when λ_t takes on a value that is below its average.

Realized values of λ_t are also important for saving and investment (capital accumulation) decisions, which interact with current labor

---

[21] In this section lowercase letters do *not* denote logarithms.

supply–demand choices and help to determine future productive capacities. The extent to which investment responds to a λ_t shock depends on the degree of permanence of such shocks. If they are typically long lasting—if a high value of λ_t tends to be followed by high values of λ_{t+1}, λ_{t+2}, and so on—there will be more of an incentive to invest than if the λ_t shocks are usually transitory. In the RBC analysis it is assumed that technology shocks possess a high degree of permanence. In particular, it is typically assumed that the stochastic process generating the $\lambda_t s$ is of the form

$$\lambda_t = \alpha_0 + \alpha_1 \lambda_{t-1} + \varepsilon_t, \tag{16}$$

with ε_t white noise and with a value of α_1 that is close to unity (e.g., 0.9 or 0.95). This seems to be a fairly realistic assumption, since the effects of technological innovations do not dissipate quickly.[22] New engineering knowledge, for instance, does not disappear after the period in which it is developed. Weather shocks are more transitory, but are of fairly minor importance in highly industrialized economies with small agricultural sectors.

Taking these important dynamic considerations into account, Kydland and Prescott (1982) demonstrate that a *quantitative* version of the RBC model, one that incorporates realistic specifications for production and utility functions, will generate cyclical fluctuations (in response to simulated λ_t shocks) that are surprisingly similar to those of the U.S. economy.[23] In other words, several important cyclical properties of the model's simulations are similar to the actual cyclical properties of the U.S. economy as reflected in quarterly (seasonally adjusted) data for the postwar era. Partly for this reason, and partly because of the various weaknesses of other theories mentioned above, the RBC approach has attracted a considerable amount of interest on the part of macroeconomic researchers.[24]

It is noteworthy that there exists a close relationship between the RBC approach and Lucas's monetary-misperceptions theory of the Phillips relationship. In particular, both theories utilize the traditional supply-equals-demand approach to macroeconomic analysis, in contrast with the more Keynesian theories that emphasize temporary rigid-

---

[22] It is difficult to verify empirically whether assumptions about the λ_t process are realistic because λ_t is not a directly observable variable. A notable attempt to justify the usual RBC assumptions is provided by Prescott (1986).

[23] Labor supply and saving specifications are not simply posited in RBC analysis, as our exposition seems to suggest. Instead, they are rigorously derived from explicit maximization analysis of agents' choice problems and brought together in a general-equilibrium context. Thus RBC analysis conforms to the methodological position mentioned in the appendix to Chapter 5.

[24] The entire March/May 1988 issue of the *Journal of Monetary Economics* is devoted to RBC analysis.

ity of nominal wages and/or prices. In fact, the basic RBC model can be viewed as a more fully worked-out version of Lucas's model together with two crucial assumptions: that production function shocks are important and that individuals do possess information concerning current money stock magnitudes.[25]

It was mentioned above that the RBC approach rationalizes observed correlations between monetary and real variables as resulting from monetary sector responses to real fluctuations generated by the λ_t shocks. In this regard it is stressed that actual monetary authorities do not exert direct control over the money stock, but influence it indirectly via interest rate or bank reserve instruments. Furthermore, in many countries the monetary authorities do not strenuously attempt to hit predetermined money stock targets. Instead, they focus attention on interest rates and often take actions designed to smooth movements in certain rates. It is then plausible that such actions would tend to result in money stock expansions during periods with positive productivity shocks and higher-than-normal output levels, so positive correlations between output (or employment) and money stock magnitudes would be observed in the detrended data. No fully satisfactory account of this part of the story has yet been developed, however.

The most serious shortcoming of the RBC approach is, however, the absence of any very convincing description of the postulated but unobservable technology shocks. A significant problem is that economy-wide fluctuations are generated, in RBC models such as Kydland and Prescott (1982), in response to economy-wide technology shocks. The same λ_t realization, in other words, is taken to apply to all producers. But, in actuality, any particular technological change would affect the production function for only a few of the economy's thousands of distinct commodities. And, if the random shocks in different sectors are stochastically independent, their effects will tend to average out, yielding a relatively small variance in the aggregate.

For this reason, as well as others,[26] most economists are unconvinced that the RBC approach offers a satisfactory way of modeling aggregate supply behavior in actual economies. Many would agree, nevertheless, that the RBC proponents have performed a valuable service by emphasizing that a substantial component of the cyclical variability that we

---

[25] As explained above, this last assumption nullifies the monetary misperceptions source of output fluctuations.

[26] Many of the objections involve detailed analysis that would be inappropriate in this introductory discussion. Two points can be explained easily, however. First, most RBC models imply that real wages and labor productivity are too strongly correlated with output; the correlations implied by the model are much greater than those in the actual U.S. data. Second, another objection is provided by the U.S. experience of 1981–1985: as mentioned in Chapter 1, as substantial monetary policy tightening in 1981 was soon followed by a sharp recession.

observe may be explained by real shocks of a technological nature. Fluctuations stemming from that source do not imply any failure of markets to clear; they would be observed even in a perfectly functioning competitive economy. Thus there is no obvious reason to believe that society would benefit from attempts by the monetary or fiscal policy authorities to counteract these fluctuations.[27] What portion of all observed variability should be attributed to shocks of that type is a current research issue of great interest and importance.

9.8 Conclusions

In this chapter we have described several different models that are intended to describe the connection, in terms of cyclical fluctuations, between nominal and real variables. Understanding this connection is extremely important, as it governs the effect of monetary policy on employment, output, and other crucial real magnitudes. An understanding of the link seems essential in the design of an optimal monetary policy.

The first of the alternative hypotheses considered was that put forth by Phillips, who suggested that the rate of change of nominal wages is governed primarily by recent unemployment—a proxy for the excess supply of labor. That idea was challenged by Friedman and Phelps, who argued that the hypothesized relationship should be between unemployment and the rate of change of real—not nominal—wages. It was suggested, moreover, that both economic theory and econometric evidence provide support for the Friedman–Phelps viewpoint. An important implication is that there is no "long-run" tradeoff between unemployment and inflation rates, in the following sense: maintaining a higher inflation rate over a long span of time will not tend to induce a lower average rate of unemployment.

Following a brief digression on "Okun's law," we then described four recently developed models of the connection between employment and monetary magnitudes. The first of these is the monetary misperceptions theory developed by Lucas. It is an ingenious theory that builds upon the fact that individual sellers do not have complete information concerning the state of the economy. It seems to assume too much ignorance on their part, however, to be highly relevant to current-day industrial economies. Taylor's model, by contrast, emphasizes the idea that nominal wages or other prices are often preset, in a

---

[27] The situation is somewhat analogous to that posed by weather-induced seasonal fluctuations. It would not be sensible for the monetary authority to try to stimulate increased economic activity in January and February or to discourage production during the harvest season.

staggered fashion, for several periods (i.e., months or quarters) at a time. Quantities are then determined, at the preset prices, by demand. The model injects some nominal price "stickiness" into the discussion, which is probably a realistic step. But a technical detail of Taylor's model makes it inconsistent with the theoretically attractive natural rate hypothesis, that is, the notion that monetary policy cannot *permanently* affect the rate of unemployment. The third of these models, due to Fischer, is like Taylor's in that it features preset nominal wages and employment determined by labor demand. But the wages are preset at levels that are expected to clear markets, so with rational expectations the Fischer model satisfies the natural rate hypothesis. Its main weakness is the counter-factual implication that employment fluctuations are strongly related, in an inverse manner, to real wage fluctuations. Fourth is the real business cycle model, which emphasizes that fluctuations can result from shocks to production functions and that money-output correlations may be due to monetary responses to exogenous output movements. The main problem with this theory is the absence of any convincing description of the initiating shocks. On the basis of these considerations, it would seem that a satisfactory model might reflect the desirable features of Fischer's—that is, prices that are preset at expected market-clearing levels—but without building in the notion that employment fluctuations are driven by real wages and with recognition of the influence of real supply shocks. In the next chapter, we shall develop a model of precisely that type.

Problems

1. For the United Kingdom, wage change and unemployment figures for the years 1948–1957 are as follows:

	Wage Change (percent)	**UN (percent)**
1948	3.7	2.7
1949	1.9	1.7
1950	4.5	1.7
1951	10.5	1.3
1952	6.4	2.1
1953	2.9	1.7
1954	4.3	1.4
1955	6.9	1.2
1956	7.7	1.3
1957	5.4	1.5

Compare these with the curve in Figure 9-1 fitted to points for 1861–1913.

2. For the United States, inflation and unemployment figures for the years 1972–1981 are as follows:

	Inflation (percent)	UN (percent)
1972	3.4	5.5
1973	8.3	4.8
1974	12.2	5.5
1975	7.0	8.3
1976	4.8	7.6
1977	6.8	6.9
1978	9.0	6.0
1979	13.3	5.8
1980	12.4	7.0
1981	8.9	7.5

Compare these with the points for 1954–1968 plotted in Figure 9-4. What does this comparison suggest regarding the original and Fried-man–Phelps versions of the Phillips curve?

3. Consider an economy in which aggregate demand and supply relations are as follows:

$$y_t = \beta_0 + \beta_1(m_t - p_t) + v_t, \tag{AD}$$

$$y_t = \bar{y} + \alpha(p_t - E_{t-1}p_t). \tag{AS}$$

The random demand disturbance v_t is autocorrelated:

$$v_t = \rho v_{t-1} + \xi_t,$$

where ξ_t is white noise.

Now suppose the monetary authority conducts policy according to

$$m_t = \mu_0 + \mu_1 v_{t-1} + e_t, \tag{MP}$$

where e_t is white noise unrelated to the v_t process.

Derive a solution for p_t. Then use it to obtain an expression for $p_t - E_{t-1}p_t$ and substitute into (AS) to find a solution for y_t.

4. A complete model that incorporates Taylor's theory can be constructed by adding, to equations (10) and (12), an aggregate demand relation and a policy rule for m_t. Suppose that aggregate demand is as in Problem 3 (but with v_t white noise) and that policy is $m_t = \mu + e_t$, with e_t white noise.

To solve this model for x_t and y_t, substitute (10) and the policy rule into the demand relation. Then conjecture that x_t and y_t solutions are of the form

$$x_t = \phi_{10} + \phi_{11}x_{t-1} + \phi_{12}e_t + \phi_{13}v_t,$$

$$y_t = \phi_{20} + \phi_{21}x_{t-1} + \phi_{22}e_t + \phi_{23}v_t.$$

Finally, find values implied for the undetermined coefficients $\phi_{10}, \ldots, \phi_{23}$. Note that this procedure amounts to a generalization of that described in Section 8.3.

References

Barro, Robert J., "Unanticipated Money Growth and Unemployment in the United States," *American Economic Review* 67 (March 1977), 101–15.

Dornbusch, Rudiger, and Stanley Fischer, *Macroeconomics*, 3rd ed. (New York: McGraw-Hill Book Company, 1984).

Fischer, Stanley, "Long-Term Contracts, Rational Expectations, and the Optimal Money Supply Rule," *Journal of Political Economy* 85 (February 1977), 191–205.

Friedman, Milton, "Comments," in *Guidelines, Informal Controls and the Market Place*, G. P. Shultz and R. Z. Aliber, eds. (Chicago: University of Chicago Press, 1966).

Friedman, Milton, "The Role of Monetary Policy," *American Economic Review* 58 (March 1968), 1–17.

Gordon, Robert J., "The Recent Acceleration of Inflation and Its Lessons for the Future," *Brookings Papers on Economic Activity*, (No. 1, 1970), 8–41.

Hall, Robert E., "Employment Fluctuations and Wage Rigidity," *Brookings Papers on Economic Activity*, (No. 1, 1980), 91–123.

Hall, Robert E., and John B. Taylor, *Macroeconomics: Theory, Performance, and Policy*. (New York: W. W. Norton & Company, Inc., 1986).

Keynes, John M., *The General Theory of Employment, Interest, and Money*. (London: Macmillan Press, 1936).

King, Robert G., "Monetary Information and Monetary Neutrality," *Journal of Monetary Economics* 7 (March 1981), 195–206.

King, Robert G., and Charles I. Plosser, "Money, Credit, and Prices in a Real Business Cycle," *American Economic Review* 74 (June 1984), 363–80.

Kydland, Finn E., and Edward C. Prescott, "Time to Build and Aggregate Fluctuations," *Econometrica* 50 (November 1982), 1345–70.

Lucas, Robert E., Jr., "Expectations and the Neutrality of Money," *Journal of Economic Theory* 4 (April 1972), 103–24, (a).

Lucas, Robert E., Jr., "Econometric Testing of the Natural Rate Hypothesis," in *The Econometrics of Price Determination*, O. Eckstein, ed. Washington: Board of Governors of the Federal Reserve System, 1972, (b).

Lucas, Robert E., Jr., "Some International Evidence on Output-Inflation Tradeoffs," *American Economic Review* 63 (June 1973), 326–34.

McCallum, Bennett T., "Rational Expectations and the Natural Rate Hypothesis: Some Consistent Estimates," *Econometrica* 44 (January 1976), 43–52.

Okun, Arthur, "Potential GNP: Its Measurement and Significance," *Proceedings of the Business and Economic Statistics Section of the American Statistical Association* (1962).

Phelps, Edmund S., "Phillips Curves, Expectations of Inflation, and Optimal Unemployment over Time," *Economica* 34 (August 1967), 254–81.

Phillips, A. W., "The Relation Between Unemployment and the Rate of Change of Money Wage Rates in the United Kingdom, 1861–1957," *Economica* 25 (August 1958), 283–300.

Prescott, Edward C., "Theory Ahead of Business Cycle Measurement," *Carnegie-Rochester Conference Series on Public Policy* 25 (Autumn 1986), 11–44.

Sargent, Thomas J., "A Note on the Accelerationist Controversy," *Journal of Money, Credit, and Banking* 3 (August 1971), 50–60.

Sargent, Thomas J., "Rational Expectations, the Real Rate of Interest, and the Natural Rate of Unemployment," *Brookings Papers on Economic Activity*, (No. 2, 1973), 429–72.

Solow, Robert M., *Price Expectations and the Behavior of the Price Level.* (Manchester, England: Manchester University Press, 1969).

Taylor, John B., "Staggered Wage Setting in a Macro Model," *American Economic Review Papers and Proceedings* 69 (May 1979), 108–13.

Taylor, John B., "Aggregate Dynamics and Staggered Contracts, *Journal of Political Economy* 88 (February 1980), 1–23.

10

Money and Output: An Analytical Framework

10.1 Introduction

Having surveyed various theories of aggregate supply or Phillips-curve relations between monetary and real variables, our objective now is to set forth one particular model to be used in subsequent analyses of macroeconomic issues involving nominal–real interactions. Ideally, for such a model to be most fruitful it should satisfy several requirements. In particular, it should be

(i) Reasonably simple to work with.
(ii) Generally compatible with the basic principles of economic theory.
(iii) Adequately consistent with essential empirical regularities concerning macroeconomic fluctuations in actual economies.[1]

In an attempt to develop such a model, our strategy will be to begin with a relatively streamlined version. Then various elaborations will be introduced to take account of significant aspects of reality ignored in the basic version, a step directed toward the satisfaction of criterion (iii). Finally, compatibility of the approach with theoretical principles

---

[1] The set of empirical regularities regarded as "essential" may depend on the questions under investigation.

will be discussed and some qualifications concerning its usefulness will be mentioned.

In implementing this strategy, it will be extremely convenient to have at hand a specific representation of the modeled economy's aggregate *demand* relations. Accordingly, let us now assume that this economy's saving–investment and money demand behavior can be well represented by *IS* and *LM* functions of the general type discussed in Chapters 5 and 6. More specifically, let us assume that the money demand function is of the special form introduced as equation (26) of Chapter 3 and later emphasized in Chapter 6. Letting

m_t = log of normal money stock
p_t = log of price level
y_t = log of real output
R_t = nominal interest rate
ε_t = stochastic disturbance term

we then have

$$m_t - p_t = c_0 + c_1 y_t + c_2 R_t + \varepsilon_t. \tag{1}$$

Here the parameter signs are $c_0 > 0$, $c_1 > 0$, and $c_2 < 0$. This *LM* function summarizes behavior pertaining to money demand and supply. For simplicity, we pretend (as we have since Chapter 4) that the money stock m_t is directly manipulated by the government's monetary authority.

Next for the *IS* relation summarizing saving and investment behavior, we adopt a specific parametric version of equation (10) of Chapter 6, namely:

$$R_t = b_0 + b_1 y_t + E_{t-1}(p_{t+1} - p_t) + \eta_t. \tag{2}$$

Here we have parameter signs $b_0 > 0$ and $b_1 < 0$, the latter reflecting the negative relation between output demand and the real rate of interest, which is $r_t = R_t - E_{t-1}(p_{t+1} - p_t)$, of the type depicted in Figure 5-7. The term η_t reflects a stochastic shock to saving or investment behavior. It may possibly be correlated with the *LM* shock ε_t, but they are distinct variables.

In equation (2) the term $E_{t-1}(p_{t+1} - p_t)$ reflects the expected inflation rate between periods t and $t + 1$. The use of the conditional expectation operator E_{t-1} indicated that rational expectations is being assumed in the analysis and that these expectations are based on information that includes all data from the past (periods $t - 1$ and before) but none pertaining to the present (period t). The latter part of this assumption is questionable; it might be more realistic to assume that individuals know some period-t values when forming expectations relevant for demand and supply in period t. But the route we have taken in assuming that $E_{t-1}(p_{t+1} - p_t)$ to be relevant is analytically simpler than the alternative and does not critically affect most of the conclusions.[2]

On the basis of equations (1) and (2) it is possible to derive an "aggregate demand" function, analogous to the concept discussed for a static model in Section 5.4, that reflects properties of both. In particular, we can substitute (2) into (1) to obtain

$$m_t - p_t = c_0 + c_1 y_t + c_2[b_0 + b_1 y_t + E_{t-1}(p_{t+1} - p_t) + \eta_t] + \varepsilon_t. \quad \text{(3)}$$

By combining terms and solving for y_t, we then have

$$y_t = \beta_0 + \beta_1(m_t - p_t) + \beta_2 E_{t-1}(p_{t+1} - p_t) + v_t, \quad \text{(4)}$$

where the β's are composite parameters related to those in (1) and (2) as follows:

$$\beta_0 = -\frac{c_0 + c_2 b_0}{c_1 + c_2 b_1},$$

$$\beta_1 = \frac{1}{c_1 + c_2 b_1},$$

$$\beta_2 = \frac{-c_2}{c_1 + c_2 b_1}.$$

Here, since c_2 and b_1 are negative, we have $\beta_1 > 0$ and $\beta_2 > 0$. Also, v_t is a composite stochastic disturbance: $v_t \equiv -(\varepsilon_t + c_2\eta_t) / (c_1 + c_2 b_1)$.

What equation (4) indicates is that the quantity of output demanded in period t, for consumption and investment purposes combined, is positively related to the current magnitude of real money balances and to the current magnitude of expected inflation. In the formulation that we have used there are no fiscal variables included, but that is an omission that has been made only for simplicity. In general, government spending would appear in an *IS* function such as (2) and would therefore show up in the derived aggregate demand relation. Tax collections may appear, also, although that is a more questionable matter. In the remainder of this chapter, we make extensive use of relation (4).

10.2   Aggregate Supply: Basic Model

We now begin with the primary task of this chapter, the development of a model of aggregate supply. The general approach to be utilized presumes that product prices are set at the start of each period at

---

[2] That it does affect one important conclusion is explained in Section 11.2.

expected market-clearing levels. These prices do not change within the period, however, so unexpected shocks to demand or supply conditions will usually make the actual market-clearing values turn out to be different than had been expected. In such instances the quantity produced and sold will be that specified at the prevailing price by the demand function. The idea behind this assumption is that individual suppliers find it advantageous to preset their prices and then satisfy whatever demands materialize at those prices, even if they exceed the quantities they would normally wish to supply.[3]

At the aggregate level, then, the quantity of output that is exchanged in any period will be determined, once the price level p_t is given,[4] by the aggregate demand function (4). The way in which "supply-side" considerations enter the picture is via the determination of p_t. As stated in the preceding paragraph, the principle governing this determination is that p_t is preset at the expected value of the market-clearing price, which is denoted $\bar{p}_t$. Thus in symbols we have

$$p_t = E_{t-1}\bar{p}_t. \tag{5}$$

But for this last relation to be useful, we must spell out the nature of $\bar{p}_t$.

In order to do so, let us use $\bar{y}_t$ to denote the value of y_t that corresponds to a situation of market clearing (i.e., demand equals supply) in the labor market. In other words, $\bar{y}_t$ is the quantity that would be produced if the economy functioned according to the classical model of Chapter 5 or the real business cycle model of Chapter 9. For the moment it will be further assumed that the value $\bar{y}_t$ grows smoothly as time passes. Thus we specify that

$$\bar{y}_t = \delta_0 + \delta_1 t, \tag{6}$$

where δ_1 measures the rate of growth of market-clearing output. (More realistic specifications for $\bar{y}_t$ are considered in Section 10.3.)

Now by definition the market-clearing price $\bar{p}_t$ is the value that would equate the aggregate demand quantity, as given by (4), to $\bar{y}$. In the present setup, then, $\bar{p}_t$ is the value of p_t that satisfies the equality

$$\beta_0 + \beta_1(m_t - p_t) + \beta_2 E_{t-1}(p_{t+1} - p_t) + v_t = \bar{y}_t.$$

By rearranging the latter, moreover, that value can be written explicitly as

$$\bar{p}_t = \frac{\beta_0 - \bar{y}_t + \beta_1 m_t + \beta_2 E_{t-1}p_{t+1} + v_t}{\beta_1 + \beta_2}. \tag{7}$$

---

[3] The task of rationalizing this idea is discussed in Section 10.5.
[4] The following discussion will occasionally refer to variables such as the "price level" when the symbol at hand actually pertains to its logarithm.

At this point we have specified a system consisting of the equations (4), (5), (6), and (7). Aggregate demand is given by (4), so in one sense equations (5)–(7) together might be thought of as describing aggregate supply. The variable $\bar{p}_t$ reflects both supply and demand influences,[5] however, so that terminology could certainly be questioned. It is not necessary, however, for us to be concerned with terminological issues. What matters is how the model functions.

In that regard it should be noted that to complete the model another relation must be added, one that describes monetary policy behavior. For a simple but nontrivial example, let us now suppose that the monetary policy process is the same as that discussed in Sections 8.2 and 8.3. Thus for the moment we assume that m_t is generated according to

$$m_t = \mu_0 + \mu_1 m_{t-1} + e_t \qquad |\mu_1| < 1, \tag{8}$$

where e_t is a white noise disturbance representing the nonsystematic or purely random component of policy behavior. With this addition, our system becomes (4)–(8), a set of equations sufficient in number to determine the behavior of the model's five endogenous variables, $\bar{y}_t$, $\bar{y}$, p_t, $\bar{p}_t$, and m_t.

To gain an understanding of the workings of this model, it will be useful to derive solution expressions for p_t and y_t. In some respects it would be natural to do this first for p_t. In this particular model, however, it so happens that it is an easier task to solve for y_t. We begin, accordingly, with that variable.

Because of the special features of the model that make it relatively easy to solve for y_t, the procedure used in this solution is different from that developed in Chapter 8. In particular, we begin by rewriting, for convenient reference, the demand function (4):

$$y_t = \beta_0 + \beta_1(m_t - p_t) + \beta_2 E_{t-1}(p_{t+1} - p_t) + v_t. \tag{4}$$

Next we note that our definition of $\bar{p}_t$ implies that

$$\bar{y}_t = \beta_0 + \beta_1(m_t - \bar{p}_t) + \beta_2 E_{t-1}(p_{t+1} - \bar{p}_t) + v_t. \tag{9}$$

Then we calculate the conditional expectation (given Ω_{t-1}) of each side of (9), obtaining

$$E_{t-1}\bar{y}_t = \beta_0 + \beta_1 E_{t-1}(m_t - \bar{p}_t) + \beta_2 E_{t-1}(p_{t+1} - \bar{p}_t). \tag{10}$$

But with equation (6) generating $\bar{y}_t$, its value will be known in advance, so $E_{t-1}\bar{y}_t = \bar{y}_t$. Also, from (5) we have that $p_t = E_{t-1}\bar{p}_t$. Consequently,

---

[5] That demand influences are involved is revealed by the presence on the right-hand side of (7) of the parameters β_0, β_1, and β_2.

(10) can be rewritten as

$$\bar{y}_t = \beta_0 + \beta_1(E_{t-1}m_t - p_t) + \beta_2(E_{t-1}p_{t+1} - p_t). \tag{11}$$

Then (11) can be subtracted term by term from (4), a step that yields

$$y_t - \bar{y}_t = \beta_1(m_t - E_{t-1}m_t) + v_t. \tag{12}$$

Finally, since (8) implies that $m_t - E_{t-1}m_t = e_t$, equation (12) can equivalently be expressed as

$$y_t = \bar{y}_t + \beta_1 e_t + v_t. \tag{13}$$

The latter is our sought-for solution for y_t—it expresses y_t in terms of variables (or shocks), all of which are exogenous.

Inspection of either equation (13) or (12) readily indicates how output behaves in the model at hand. In particular, output deviates from its market-clearing value $\bar{y}_t$ whenever a nonzero shock affects aggregate demand (i.e., $v_t \neq 0$) or a monetary policy shock occurs (i.e., $m_t \neq E_{t-1}m_t$). Furthermore, since the parameter β_1 is positive, it is clear that a positive monetary surprise ($m_t > E_{t-1}m_t$) will give rise to an output level that is greater than $\bar{y}_t$ and in that sense higher than normal. This happens because, with p_t temporarily fixed, an unexpectedly large money stock makes the demand for output unexpectedly high, and suppliers meet that demand by producing more than they would normally choose to produce.[6]

Over any large number of periods, however, the average value of y_t and the average value of $\bar{y}_t$ will be equal. More precisely, the mean of the distribution of the random variable $y_t - \bar{y}_t$ will be zero. This result can easily be obtained by calculating the unconditional expectation $E(y_t - \bar{y}_t)$ from equation (12): since $Ev_t = 0$ and

$$E(m_t - E_{t-1}m_t) = E(e_t) = 0, \tag{14}$$

we immediately conclude that $E(y_t - \bar{y}_t) = 0$. Furthermore, that result holds not only with (8) but with *any* policy rule. For (12) does not depend on (8) and whatever the systematic part of the policy process for m_t is like, it remains true that $E(e_t) = 0$. Thus the present model is one that satisfies the *natural-rate hypothesis*, mentioned in Section 9.5. In other words, there is no monetary policy that will keep y_t permanently high or low in relation to $\bar{y}_t$.

---

[6] For simplicity our model abstracts from inventories. If these were recognized, a monetary shock would lead to some inventory drawdown but also some above-normal production.

Let us now turn our attention to the price level. To study the behavior of p_t we begin by substituting expression (7) into (5) and calculating the expectation $E_{t-1}\bar{p}_t$. This step gives

$$p_t = \frac{\beta_0 - \bar{y}_t + \beta_1 E_{t-1} m_t + \beta_2 E_{t-1} p_{t+1}}{\beta_1 + \beta_2}. \tag{15}$$

Next from the policy specification (8) we see that $E_{t-1} m_t = \mu_0 + \mu_1 m_{t-1}$. Substitution of the latter into (15) yields

$$p_t = \frac{\beta_0 - \bar{y}_t + \beta_1(\mu_0 + \mu_1 m_{t-1}) + \beta_2 E_{t-1} p_{t+1}}{\beta_1 + \beta_2}. \tag{16}$$

Equation (16) is not a solution for p_t, however, because the expectation $E_{t-1} p_{t+1}$ appears on the right-hand side. To obtain a solution it will be necessary to use a procedure like that of Chapter 8.

Consider, accordingly, the system consisting of equations (16) and (8):

$$m_t = \mu_0 + \mu_1 m_{t-1} + e_t. \tag{8}$$

Inspection of these equations suggests that m_{t-1} and $\bar{y}_t$ are the only variables that are relevant determinants of p_t. The indicated conjecture then is that p_t has a solution of the form

$$p_t = \phi_0 + \phi_1 \bar{y}_t + \phi_2 m_{t-1}. \tag{17}$$

Proceeding under that supposition, we infer that[7]

$$
\begin{aligned}
E_{t-1} p_{t+1} &= \phi_0 + \phi_1 E_{t-1} y_{t+1} + \phi_2 E_{t-1} m_t \\
&= \phi_0 + \phi_1(\bar{y}_t + \delta_1) + \phi_2(\mu_0 + \mu_1 m_{t-1}).
\end{aligned} \tag{18}
$$

Next, substitution into (16) gives

$$
\begin{aligned}
&\phi_0 + \phi_1 \bar{y}_t + \phi_2 m_{t-1} \\
&= \frac{\beta_0 - \bar{y}_t + \beta_1 \mu_0 + \beta_1 \mu_1 m_{t-1} + \beta_2 \phi_1(\bar{y}_t + \delta_1) + \beta_2 \phi_2(\mu_0 + \mu_1 m_{t-1})}{(\beta_1 + \beta_2)}.
\end{aligned} \tag{19}
$$

Since the latter must hold as a equality for all possible values of $\bar{y}_t$ and

----

[7] Note that $E_{t-1}\bar{y}_{t+1} = \bar{y}_{t+1} = \delta_0 + \delta_1(t+1) = \delta_0 + \delta_1 t + \delta_1 = \bar{y}_t + \delta_1$.

m_{t-1}, the following three conditions are implied:

$$\phi_0 = \frac{\beta_0 + \beta_1 \mu_0 + \beta_2 \phi_0 + \beta_2 \phi_1 \delta_1 + \beta_2 \phi_2 \mu_0}{\beta_1 + \beta_2},$$

$$\phi_1 = \frac{-1 + \beta_2 \phi_1}{\beta_1 + \beta_2}, \tag{20}$$

$$\phi_2 = \frac{\beta_1 \mu_1 + \beta_2 \phi_2 \mu_1}{\beta_1 + \beta_2}.$$

Solving these for ϕ_2, ϕ_1, and ϕ_0 finally yields the desired results:

$$\phi_2 = \frac{\mu_1 \beta_1}{\beta_1 + \beta_2(1 - \mu_1)},$$

$$\phi_1 = \frac{-1}{\beta_1}, \tag{21}$$

$$\phi_0 = \mu_0 + \frac{\beta_0}{\beta_1} - \frac{\delta_1 \beta_2}{\beta_1} + \frac{\beta_2 \mu_0 \mu_1}{\beta_1 + \beta_2(1 - \mu_1)}.$$

The conclusion is that the price level evolves, in our basic model, according to (17) with coefficients as indicated in (21).[8] As we have already found that y_t evolves according to (13), this completes the solution to the basic model.

10.3 Normal Output

There are various ways in which the model of the preceding section can be enriched, without alteration of its essential characteristics, by the addition of features that offer an increase in realism. One of the more important modifications pertains to the assumed time-series behavior of $\bar{y}_t$, the economy's market-clearing rate of output. While equation (6) does recognize that this magnitude typically grows over time, as is the case in actual economies, that equation unrealistically depicts such growth as deterministic (i.e., without stochastic ingredients). In reality, however, the productive capacity of actual economics is affected from period to period (e.g., from quarter to quarter) by variations in weather, by changes in people's desires concerning work versus leisure,

---

[8] One characteristic of the p_t solution that is worthy of note is the negative coefficient ϕ_1 attached to $\bar{y}_t$. If $\delta_1 > 0$, so that $\bar{y}_t$ grows over time, $\phi_1 < 0$ implies that p_t will fall over time, given that the money supply rule (8) features no growth in m_t.

and by shifts in those technological relations that economists summarize in terms of a production function. All of these changes occur, moreover, in a fashion that is primarily random from the perspective of an economic analyst. Consequently, our model can be improved by adding stochastic ingredients to the process determining $\bar{y}_t$.

The simplest way of doing so would be merely to add a mean-zero random disturbance term, u_t, to equation (6), thereby obtaining

$$\bar{y}_t = \delta_0 + \delta_1 t + u_t. \tag{22}$$

In this formulation the average growth rate of market-clearing output is δ_1, but the exact value would fluctuate randomly from period to period. If the u_t process is purely random white noise, the model of Section 10.2 would be affected very little by this change. In terms of the solution for output, the main difference would be that the expectation $E_{t-1}\bar{y}_t$ would not equal $\bar{y}_t$ itself, but would equal $\bar{y}_t - u_t$. That last expression would appear on the left-hand side of equation (11), and (13) would therefore become

$$y_t = \bar{y}_t - u_t + \beta_1 e_t + v_t. \tag{23}$$

Thus y_t would, according to the model, deviate from its market-clearing value $\bar{y}_t$ whenever the latter was affected by a current disturbance, as well as in response to monetary policy and demand shocks. It would perhaps be sensible to regard $\bar{y}_t - u_t$ as reflecting "normal" output, however, since the effect of u_t is merely transitory. In that sense, (23) would continue to imply that output differs from its normal value only in response to nonzero realizations of the shocks e_t and v_t.

It is almost certainly unrealistic, however, to think of shocks to $\bar{y}_t$ as having only transitory, one-period effects. Although that might be true of weather-related phenomena, it seems highly probable that technology shocks would be more long-lasting in their impact. Improvements in engineering knowledge, for instance, are essentially permanent in their effects. Taste changes pertaining to work versus leisure choices are also unlikely to be reversed quickly.

A specification regarding $\bar{y}_t$ which goes to the other extreme from (22), by treating all shocks as fully permanent, is as follows:

$$\bar{y}_t - \bar{y}_{t-1} = \delta + u_t. \tag{24}$$

Here again u_t is assumed to be white noise, but now it affects the *change* in $\bar{y}_t$, $\bar{y}_t - \bar{y}_{t-1}$, rather than the departure of $\bar{y}_t$ from a linear trend. Thus the effects of a nonzero u_t are not erased in period $t + 1$ but remain embedded in the system via the altered level of y_t. On the other hand, specification (24) is like (22) in permitting growth since δ can be positive. Indeed, the average change in $\bar{y}_t$ (and thus the average growth rate for market-clearing output, whose log equals $\bar{y}_t$) is δ. A value of

0.01 for δ in (24) would imply a 1 percent average growth rate for market-clearing output in (24), as would a value of 0.01 for δ_1 in (22).

The different stochastic specification in (24) gives rise, however, to a significantly different *operational* solution for y_t in our model. The point in this regard is that $\bar{y}_t$ is a variable on which empirical data are not collected. Whatever its imperfections, real GNP is an empirical measure that is intended to correspond to aggregate output (i.e., our variable y_t). But there is no such counterpart in the official statistics for $\bar{y}_t$. To render a solution equation such as (13) operational therefore requires some type of substitution to eliminate the unobservable $\bar{y}_t$. If (22) is the specification for $\bar{y}_t$, then $\delta_0 + \delta_1 t$ can be used in (23) in place of $\bar{y}_t - u_t$: the operational equation is

$$y_t = \delta_0 + \delta_1 t + \beta_1 e_t + v_t. \tag{25}$$

But if (24) is the relevant process for $\bar{y}_t$, the necessary substitution requires that (13) be first-differenced. That is, the first step is to express (13) as

$$\Delta y_t = \Delta \bar{y}_t + \beta_1 \Delta e_t + \Delta v_t. \tag{26}$$

Then (24) can be used to replace $\Delta \bar{y}_t$ with $\delta + u_t$, giving

$$\Delta y_t = \delta + u_t + \beta_1 \Delta e_t + \Delta v_t, \tag{27}$$

or equivalently,

$$y_t = y_{t-1} + \delta + u_t + \beta_1 \Delta e_t + \Delta v_t. \tag{27'}$$

Clearly, this relation has different stochastic properties than (25).

It should be mentioned that the specification (24) for $\bar{y}_t$ tends to undermine the concept of "normal" output. Precisely because the effect of u_t shocks is permanent in (24), the "normal" value itself must be viewed as changing with each shock, as well as with the passage of time. Thus the normal value of $\bar{y}_t$ in period $t = 18$, for example, will be different from the perspective of period 17 than it was in period 16, unless by chance u_{17} turns out to be precisely zero.

In recent years considerable interest has been expressed in the hypothesis that in actual economies the effects on $\bar{y}_t$ of shocks are entirely permanent, as implied by formulation (24). That hypothesis has been suggested, for example, by Nelson and Plosser (1982) and Campbell and Mankiw (1987) on the basis of time-series studies of actual data for U.S. real GNP.[9] In this regard it is important to recognize that there is another way to formalize the idea that shocks to

---

[9] The present discussion simplifies, for the sake of expositional clarity, the argument of these writers, who claim not that y_t is a "random walk" as in (24), but more generally that the process for y_t has an autoregressive "unit root." The point developed in the present paragraph remains valid and relevant under that generalization.

$\bar{y}_t$ have long-lasting effects, indeed, a way that relies on a generalized version of specification (22) rather than (24). In particular, consider the following equation:

$$\bar{y}_t = \delta_0 + \delta_1 t + \delta_2 \bar{y}_{t-1} + u_t. \tag{28}$$

Here u_t is again white noise. This formulation generalizes (22) by adding an additional term, $\delta_2 y_{t-1}$, in which δ_2 is assumed to satisfy $|\delta_2| \le 1$. The average growth rate under this specification is $\delta_1/(1 - \delta_2)$, so if (for example) $\delta_2 = 0.9$, a value of 0.001 for δ_1 would correspond to 1 percent per period.

That the effect of shocks in (28) is long-lived is easy to see: a positive u_t raises $\bar{y}_t$ by the same amount. Then the enhanced $\bar{y}_t$ raises $\bar{y}_{t+1}$ by that amount multiplied by δ_2—and *that* effect enhances $\bar{y}_{t+2}$, and so on. In fact, if δ_2 has a value close to 1.0, formulation (28) becomes very similar to (24) provided that δ in the latter is approximately equal to $\delta_1/(1 - \delta_2)$ in the former. Econometric studies have suggested that δ_2 in (28) is in fact rather close to 1.0 in actual economies. This has led some analysts to work with the simpler formulation (22), in which shock effects are fully permanent. This step amounts to assuming that shocks, which are long-lasting, are fully permanent. But the econometric studies do not actually show that to be the case. They show that δ_2 values are close to 1.0—say, over 0.95—but that is not quite the same as showing that the value is *precisely* 1.000. Indeed, statistical studies are generally incapable of establishing *precise* parameter values. The conclusion that shock effects are fully permanent is therefore not warranted. For many purposes it does not matter whether one's model implies fully permanent, or only nearly permanent, shocks. But for some purposes this distinction does matter, and in such cases it should be recognized that the answer—whether shocks are fully permanent— is unknown.

10.4 Multiperiod Pricing

Another significant modification to the basic model of Section 10.2 involves the idea that prices may be preset not for one period but, as in the models of Taylor and Fischer described in Chapter 9, for two or more periods. To illustrate the consequences of this idea, let us consider the case of two periods. In particular, we suppose that at the start of period t, prices for half of the economy's products are set for periods t and $t + 1$. Further, in the spirit of Fischer's approach, we also assume that the values for t and $t + 1$ do not need to be the same and that the price for each period is set equal to the expected market-clearing level.

At the start of t, then, half of the sellers set prices for t at the level $E_{t-1}\bar{p}_t$ and for $t + 1$ at the level $E_{t-1}\bar{p}_{t+1}$. In such an economy, half of the prices *prevailing in period t* will be equal to $E_{t-1}\bar{p}_t$, while the other half will have been set one period earlier at the level $E_{t-2}\bar{p}_t$. In place of equation (5), then, the present model specifies that the (average) price level in period t is

$$p_t = 0.5(E_{t-1}\bar{p}_t + E_{t-2}\bar{p}_t). \tag{29}$$

The other assumptions of Section 10.2 are unchanged, however. Thus the model consists of (4), (29), and (6)–(8).

With this modification, the special features of the basic model that permit a simple derivation of the solution for y_t are lost. Indeed, the derivation becomes rather complicated even with the specification (6) for $\bar{y}_t$. To illustrate some of the features of this model without excessive complexity, our approach will be to simplify by taking a special case of the aggregate demand function in which $\beta_2 = 0$ (so that expected inflation does not affect current demand). In this case it can fairly easily be verified that a sequence of steps analogous to (9)–(11) lead to the following replacement for (12):

$$y_t - 0.5(E_{t-1}\bar{y}_t + E_{t-2}\bar{y}_t) = 0.5\,\beta_1(m_t - E_{t-1}m_t) \\ + 0.5\,\beta_1(m_t - E_{t-2}m_t) + v_t. \tag{30}$$

To translate the latter into a more easily interpreted expression, we first note that $E_{t-1}\bar{y}_t = E_{t-2}\bar{y}_t = \bar{y}_t$ according to equation (6). Also, we quickly note that $m_t - E_{t-1}m_t = e_t$. But to evaluate $m_t - E_{t-2}m_t$ takes a bit more effort. Given the policy process (8), we see that

$$E_{t-2}m_t = E_{t-2}(\mu_0 + \mu_1 m_{t-1} + e_t) = \mu_0 + \mu_1 E_{t-2}m_{t-1}. \tag{31}$$

But $m_{t-1} - E_{t-2}m_{t-1} = e_{t-1}$,   so $E_{t-2}m_t = \mu_0 + \mu_1(m_{t-1} - e_{t-1})$. Therefore,

$$m_t - E_{t-2}m_t = \mu_0 + \mu_1 m_{t-1} + e_t - (\mu_0 + \mu_1 m_{t-1} - \mu_1 e_{t-1}) \\ = e_t + \mu_1 e_{t-1}. \tag{32}$$

Putting all of these derived expressions back into (30), we then conclude that in the present model output obeys

$$y_t = \bar{y}_t + \beta_1 e_t + 0.5\beta_1\mu_1 e_{t-1} + v_t. \tag{33}$$

From this result, the main conclusion is that the previous period's monetary policy shock, e_{t-1}, as well as that for the current period, affects output in the case in which prices are set for two periods.

Otherwise, the results are much as in Section 10.2, provided that (6) and the simplified version of (4) are used.[10]

From the way in which the foregoing derivation has proceeded, it is clear that more lagged values of e_t would affect y_t if prices were preset for more than two periods at a time. If, for example, periods corresponds to quarters and sellers revised their price schedules for the next four quarters only once a year, then e_t, e_{t-1}, e_{t-2}, and e_{t-3} would all appear in a relation analogous to (33) that pertained to quarterly data.

There exists some econometric evidence indicating that current and lagged values of monetary policy shocks (or "surprises") do in fact have effects on output in the U.S. economy. In a series of influential studies, Robert Barro found important explanatory effects for empirical estimates of e_t, e_{t-1}, ... in regression equations designed to explain fluctuations in output and unemployment rates.[11] For example, one of the estimated equations reported by Barro and Rush (1980), pertaining to quarterly U.S. data for the period 1947.3–1978.1, is as follows:

$$
\begin{aligned}
y_t = 5.6 &\quad + 0.0083t + 0.067g_t + 1.03e_t \\
(0.03) &\quad (0.00006) \quad (0.0007) \quad (0.36) \\
\\
+ 1.40e_{t-1} &+ 1.36e_{t-2} + 1.94e_{t-3} + 1.67e_{t-4} \\
(0.36) &\quad (0.35) \quad\quad (0.33) \quad\quad (0.32) \\
\\
+ 1.43e_{t-5} &+ 1.27e_{t-6} + 0.88e_{t-7} + 0.54e_{t-8}. \\
(0.32) &\quad (0.32) \quad\quad (0.32) \quad\quad (0.32)
\end{aligned}
\tag{34}
$$

Here the figures in parentheses are standard errors; some relevant statistics are $R^2 = 0.997$, $\hat{\sigma} = 0.0817$, and DW = 0.3. The time trend (t) and government spending (g_t) variables enter as proxies for the normal rate of output ($\bar{y}_t$), while the e_t measures are as explained in footnote 11. It is evident that the strongest indicated effect on y_t comes from e_{t-3}, the money growth "surprise" of three quarters earlier, but that e_{t-j} variables provide significant explanatory power back through e_{t-7}.[12] The 0.3 value of the Durbin–Watson statistic indicates very

---

[10] Additional complexities would arise if these provisions were not met.

[11] The original papers are Barro (1977, 1978), and Barro and Rush (1980). The first two used annual data in the study of unemployment and output fluctuations, respectively, while the third also investigated quarterly data. In all these studies, the empirical measures used for e_t are *residuals* from regression equations that explain fluctuations in Δm_t, the growth rate of the (M1) money stock. A number of critics have disputed the specifications used by Barro for both the Δm_t and the y_t (or unemployment rate) equations, and it is fairly widely agreed that some of his conclusions are dubious. [On this, see Gordon (1982) and Mishkin (1982).] But the conclusion that residuals from money growth equations have important explanatory power for y_t movements is reasonably robust to specificational alterations.

[12] That is, the ratio of the coefficient estimate to its associated standard error exceeds 2.0, implying that a test of the hypothesis that the coefficient is zero could be rejected at conventional significance levels.

strong autocorrelation of the equation's residuals, but the main results are nearly unaltered when a correction for autoregressive disturbances is applied.

10.5   Rationale for Price Stickiness

In this section the purpose is to provide some discussion of a critical assumption relied on in the models of this chapter, namely, that product prices are preset and subsequent demands satisfied. Our reason for needing to adopt *some* assumption involving sticky prices has been developed in Chapter 9 and reinforced in Section 10.4. It may be summarized in two points, as follows. First, evidence suggests that in fact money growth surprises (i.e., unusually rapid money growth rates) lead to increased levels of output and employment. Second, the main theory attempting to explain such effects under flexible-price assumptions—namely, the "misperceptions" theory of Lucas—is inapplicable to modern developed economies (because it assumes an implausible degree of ignorance on the part of individuals). Also, the reason for treating product prices, rather than wages, as sticky was explained in Chapter 9 on both empirical and theoretical grounds.[13]

But providing reasons why economists "need" to have a model with sticky prices does not serve to explain why firms choose to behave in the postulated fashion. In that regard, the most prominent and perhaps the most successful attempt is one due to Okun (1981). Basically, his argument is that frequent price changes are avoided by individual sellers because each change tends to upset the informal but significant relationship that the firm has with its regular, repeat-purchase customers: the firm does not want such a customer to abandon that status and become one who actively searches among competing sellers for the best deal. The same line of thought helps to explain why firms produce enough to satisfy demand, in cases in which demand quantities exceed market-clearing levels: sending a customer away empty-handed will almost certainly induce him to join the group of active searchers.

An important difficulty with the foregoing argument for price stickiness, or temporary inflexibility, is that whereas the justification provided logically applies to *real* prices, it is *nominal* price stickiness that is relevant for the model of Section 10.2. In fact, this same problem pertains quite generally to most existing attempts to explain price stickiness. The problem may be expressed as a question. If prices are

---

[13] These are the absence of countercyclical real wage fluctuations and the long-duration nature of many employment relations.

to be preset (for whatever reason), why are they not preset in real terms by means of indexation (or "linkage") arrangements? The actual cost of including a standard indexation clause in explicit contracts would be trivial, and retail prices could be stated as subject to adjustment whenever a designated index number changed. Why does this typically not happen? Why do so many actual transactions fail to conform to the economists' principle that individuals and firms are concerned only with real magnitudes?

In an attempt to surmount the foregoing difficulty, McCallum (1986) has recently put forth an argument intended to justify possible reinterpretation of the relevant models in terms of nominal prices. The basic idea is disarmingly simple; it is that, for many products, the benefits to an individual *buyer* provided by indexation are exceedingly small. Such benefits consist, since expected inflation is reflected in prices even when unindexed, of nothing more than insurance against the risk of the effect of unanticipated inflation on the product price in question.[14] But the amount of unanticipated inflation that could occur over the next quarter is *very* small, so the value of insurance against its effect on any single product price is tiny. Therefore, for most products the computational costs of having prices expressed in unfamiliar indexed form will outweigh the benefits. So buyers will prefer nonindexed prices and sellers will respond by providing them. Thus for such products any stickiness that exists will pertain to nominal prices.

It would be foolish to claim that the position developed in the foregoing paragraphs is truly satisfactory, for it does not seem so even to the writer. Instead, what these paragraphs constitute is an attempt to provide as good a rationalization as is possible for a model featuring nominal price stickiness with quantities determined by demand. In turn, the motivation for such a model is the belief that prices do not, in reality, adjust promptly to shocks and that it may be better to use a poorly understood but empirically reasonable price adjustment relation than to pretend—counterfactually—that nominal adjustments take place promptly.

10.6 Conclusion

The main purpose of this chapter has been to present the basic model of Section 10.2 and to demonstrate—in Sections 10.3 and 10.4—how it can be extended to incorporate various alternative hypotheses concerning market-clearing output and the duration of temporary price rigidity. The possibility of adopting various combinations of these two types

---

[14] Note that the risk of changes in *relative* prices is not avoided by indexation.

of extensions gives the analyst a great deal of flexibility within the general framework proposed. Consequently, there is a good possibility that the analyst will be able to find a version of the model that will be consistent with the specific empirical regularities that are critically important in the context of the problem at hand.

Yet despite this flexibility, it is true that any model of the type described will have the property that deviations of y_t from market-clearing values $\bar{y}_t$ will arise only in response to demand shocks and expectational errors. Therefore, if expectations are formed rationally, the average value of $y_t - \bar{y}_t$ deviations will be zero, since the average value (unconditional expectation) of shocks and expectational errors must be zero. As this remains true regardless of the monetary policy process in effect, any model of the type will have the property that the average deviation is independent of monetary policy. This is a desirable feature of the proposed framework for, as mentioned in Section 9.5, most macroeconomists accept as a theoretical principle the hypothesis that deviations like $y_t - \bar{y}_t$ (or the unemployment rate) cannot be affected permanently by monetary policy.

The primary suggestion of the chapter, then, is that an attractive specification of aggregate supply is provided by the summary equation (12), perhaps modified as in Section 10.3 or 10.4. This specification satisfies the criteria of simplicity, empirical accuracy, and theoretical plausibility well enough to be useful in the construction of dynamic macroeconomic models in which the interaction of monetary and real variables is important. Several examples of analyses of this type are provided in Chapter 11.

But while it is argued here that equation (12) or some variant can be useful in the construction of models that provide insight regarding important macroeconomic and monetary phenomena, it is *not* suggested that (12) or any variant provides a quantitatively *accurate* description of the period-by-period dynamics of aggregate supply behavior. If it were the case that (12) did literally provide an accurate model, that would be recognized by macroeconomic specialists, and this model would be widely accepted by such specialists. In fact, however, there is no single model or framework that is widely accepted. Instead, as Chapter 9 emphasized, there are a substantial number of competing theories, each of which has attracted a significant amount of support.[15] Thus it must be concluded that the economics profession has not yet succeeded in developing a theory that explains accurately the period-by-period dynamics of aggregate supply.

---

[15] A recent review of competing theories is provided by Dotsey and King (1987).

Problems

1. Consider an economy in which $\bar{y}_t$ and m_t are constant over time ($\bar{y}_t = \bar{y}$, $m_t = m$), but a fiscal variable z_t affects aggregate demand as follows:

$$y_t = \beta_0 + \beta_1(m - p_t) + \beta_2 E_{t-1}(p_{t+1} - p_t) + \beta_3 z_t + v_t.$$

Here $\beta_3 > 0$. Suppose that fiscal policy is conducted according to

$$z_t = \gamma_0 + \gamma_1 z_{t-1} + f_t.$$

By means of a procedure like that of Section 10.2, find a solution for y_t. (Here f_t is a white noise disturbance.)

2. The model of Section 10.2 can be modified by replacing equation (5) with the following adjustment relation:

$$p_t - p_{t-1} = \theta(y_{t-1} - \bar{y}_{t-1}) + E_{t-1}(\bar{p}_t - \bar{p}_{t-1}).$$

Here $\theta > 0$ so the hypothesis is similar to an augmented Phillips relation for prices, but with the expected change in $\bar{p}_t$ included in the last term (instead of the expected change in p_t).

Using the demand function (4), the policy rule (8), and the assumption that $\bar{y}_t = \bar{y}$, find a solution expression for y_t.

3. Does the model outlined in Problem 2 satisfy the "natural rate" hypothesis as defined in Section 9.5? To develop an answer, determine whether $E(y_t - \bar{y}_t)$, the unconditional mean of $y_t - \bar{y}_t$, is independent of monetary policy behavior.

References

Barro, Robert J., "Unanticipated Money Growth and Unemployment in the United States," *American Economic Review* 67 (March 1977), 101–15.

Barro, Robert J., "Unanticipated Money, Output, and the Price Level in the United States," *Journal of Political Economy* 86 (August 1978), 549–80.

Barro, Robert J., and Mark Rush, "Unanticipated Money and Economic Activity," in *Rational Expectations and Economic Policy*, ed. Stanley Fischer. (Chicago: University of Chicago Press for National Bureau of Economic Research, 1980).

Campbell, John V., and N. Gregory Mankiw, "Are Output Fluctuations Transitory?" *Quarterly Journal of Economics* 102 (1987), 857–880.

Dotsey, Michael, and Robert G. King, "Business Cycles," in *The New Palgrave: A Dictionary of Economics*, John Eatwell, Murray Milgate, and Peter Newman, eds. (London: Macmillan Press, Limited, 1987).

Gordon, Robert J., "Price Inertia and Policy Ineffectiveness in the United

States 1890–1980," *Journal of Political Economy* 90 (December 1982), 1087–1117.

Hall, Robert E., and John B. Taylor, *Macroeconomics: Theory, Performance, and Policy*. (New York: W. W. Norton Company, Inc., 1986).

Lucas, Robert E., Jr., "Expectations and the Neutrality of Money," *Journal of Economic Theory* 4 (April 1972), 103–24.

McCallum, Bennett T. "On 'Real' and 'Sticky Price' Theories of the Business Cycle," *Journal of Money, Credit, and Banking* 18 (November 1986), 397–414.

Mishkin, Frederick S., "Does Anticipated Monetary Policy Matter? An Econometric Investigation," *Journal of Political Economy* 90 (February 1982), 22–51.

Nelson, Charles R., and Charles I. Plosser, "Trends and Random Walks in Macroeconomic Time Series," *Journal of Monetary Economics* 10 (September 1982), 139–62.

Okun, Arthur M., *Prices and Quantities: A Macroeconomic Analysis*. (Washington, D.C.: The Brookings Institution, 1981).

Monetary Policy

11

Analysis of Alternative Policy Rules

11.1 Introduction

Although the understanding of monetary and macroeconomic phenomena is an interesting and worthwhile objective in its own right, the importance of dynamic macroeconomic models is strongly enhanced by their potential usefulness in the formulation of monetary and macroeconomic policy. In the present chapter we shall discuss some important and interesting topics pertaining to the use of dynamic macroeconomic models in policy formulation: In particular, three topics that have been prominent in the research literature during the past 10–15 years will be considered in Sections 11.2, 11.3, and 11.4. Throughout, variants of the model of Section 10.2 are utilized.

11.2 Monetary Policy Ineffectiveness?

An issue that attracted much attention in the late 1970s concerns the extent to which monetary policy can in principle be used to smooth out business cycles, that is, fluctuations in aggregate measures of employment and production. The words "in principle" appear in the preceding sentence to emphasize that the issue under investigation is not whether actual policymakers are motivated to behave in a way that would mitigate fluctuations or whether they possess accurate econometric models of the economy to be used in such attempts. Instead, the issue is whether attempts, if made and based on an accurate model, would be successful.

This issue warrants discussion because the model of Section 10.2, which represents an important class of models, suggests that such attempts at countercyclical policy would be entirely unsuccessful. To demonstrate that point explicitly, let us recall that the model as developed in Section 10.2 can be summarized with the following three equations, in which y_t, p_t, and m_t denote logarithms of real output, the price level, and the money stock:

$$y_t = \beta_0 + \beta_1(m_t - p_t) + \beta_2 E_{t-1}(p_{t+1} - p_t) + v_t, \tag{1}$$

$$y_t - \bar{y}_t = \beta_1(m_t - E_{t-1}m_t) + v_t, \tag{2}$$

$$m_t = \mu_0 + \mu_1 m_{t-1} + e_t. \tag{3}$$

Here equation (1) is an aggregate demand function, describing expenditure behavior for consumption and investment purposes, that results from solving out the nominal interest rate from saving–investment (*IS*) and money demand (*LM*) relations. Equation (2) summarizes the behavior of output relative to its market-clearing level—whose log is $\bar{y}_t$—which may be generated by any of the various processes discussed in Section 10.3. Finally, equation (3) is one possible formulation describing monetary policy behavior. It does not explicitly depict the type of policy with which we are concerned here, that is, policy designed to mitigate fluctuations in y_t. We begin with it here nevertheless, mainly because it was the example used in Section 10.2. Its specification will be generalized in the following discussion.

As a preliminary matter, it is useful to recall that in equations (1)–(3), the variables v_t and e_t represent purely random (white noise) disturbance terms. In particular, v_t reflects shocks to the preferences of consumers and investors, while e_t reflects any erratic or unsystematic component of monetary policy behavior that might exist for whatever reason. Being purely random, these disturbances are exogenous in the system (1)–(3).

Turning now to the matter of fluctuations in y_t, we note that these may arise because of fluctuations in market-clearing output, $\bar{y}_t$, or because of fluctuations in the discrepancy between output and its market-clearing value, represented (in logs) by $y_t - \bar{y}_t$. Of these two sources, it is the latter with which stabilization policy is concerned. The proper objective of policy, that is, is to keep y_t close to its market-clearing value $\bar{y}_t$ and thereby minimize the economic inefficiencies that arise whenever markets fail to bring supply and demand into equality. A highly relevant summary measure of the extent to which deviations of y_t

from $\bar{y}_t$ do occur is the average value of the squared deviation, that is, the average value of $(y_t - \bar{y}_t)^2$. From a probabilistic viewpoint, this average is represented by the mean of its unconditional distribution. In symbols, the relevant measure is written as $E(y_t - \bar{y}_t)^2$, where $E(X)$ denotes (as in Chapter 8) the mathematical expectation or mean of the distribution of the random variable X. Note that $E(y_t - \bar{y}_t)^2$ is being used to designate $E[(y_t - \bar{y}_t)^2]$, *not* $[E(y_t - \bar{y}_t)]^2$.

In the context of the model (1)–(3), it is extremely easy to see that monetary policy is ineffective in influencing $E(y_t - \bar{y}_t)^2$, in the sense that the latter measure does not depend on the monetary authority's choice of the parameters μ_0 and μ_1. (These parameters are considered because in (3) they reflect the systematic component of policy behavior.) All that is necessary for the analysis is to compute the expectation of the square of the left-hand side of equation (2). This is accomplished by squaring the right-hand side and then determining its unconditional mean. For the first step we have

$$(y_t - \bar{y}_t)^2 = \beta_1^2 e_t^2 + v_t^2 + 2\beta_1 e_t v_t. \tag{4}$$

Then it remains only to determine the mean, or mathematical expectation, of each of the three terms on the right-hand side. For the first term we have $E(\beta_1^2 e_t^2) = \beta_1^2 E e_t^2$, since β_1 is a nonstochastic parameter. But since e_t is a random variable with mean zero, it follows that $E e_t^2$ is simply equal to the variance of the distribution of e_t, which we denote σ_e^2. Thus the (mathematical) expectation of the first term on the right-hand side of (4) is

$$E(\beta_1^2 e_t^2) = \beta_1^2 \sigma_e^2.$$

Similar but simpler reasoning indicates that the expectation of the second term equals σ_v^2, the variance of the distribution of v_t. Finally, for the third term we have $E(2\beta_1 e_t v_t) = 2\beta_1 E(e_t v_t)$, since $2\beta_1$ is a parameter. Now since e_t and v_t are random variables with means equal to zero, $E(e_t v_t)$ is the *covariance* of these two variables. But our assumption that e_t is the purely unsystematic component of policy implies that it is not systematically related to v_t (i.e., that it is independent of v_t). And as we have reviewed in the appendix to Chapter 8, independence of two random variables implies a zero covariance. Thus it follows that $E(2\beta_1 e_t v_t) = 0$.

Bringing together the three expressions just derived, we are able to evaluate the mean of the right-hand side of (4). In particular, we have

$$E(y_t - \bar{y}_t)^2 = \beta_1^2 \sigma_e^2 + \sigma_v^2. \tag{5}$$

From the last expression, the ineffectiveness result follows immediately. The parameters μ_0 and μ_1 are not involved in the expression for $E(y_t - \bar{y}_t)^2$, so different values for those parameters would have no effect on its magnitude. Our measure of the relevant aspect of fluctuations in y_t is therefore unaffected by policy choices of μ_0 and μ_1. In that specific and carefully defined sense, monetary policy is ineffective for stabilizing output in the basic model of Section 10.2.

A more striking and important conclusion, however, is that this same type of policy-ineffectiveness result would continue to hold if the monetary policy rule (3) were of a much more general form. Specifically, let us replace (3) with

$$m_t = \mu(\Omega_{t-1}) + e_t, \tag{6}$$

where $\mu(\Omega_{t-1})$ is *any* function of the variables appearing in the set Ω_{t-1}. The latter, in turn, is (as in Chapter 8) a symbol referring to *all* relevant variables occurring in period $t-1$ and in previous periods. Thus for the model at hand, we would have

$$\Omega_{t-1} = \{y_{t-1}, y_{t-2}, \ldots; p_{t-1}, p_{t-2}, \ldots; m_{t-1}, m_{t-2}, \ldots\}.$$

In (6), e_t again reflects the unsystematic part of policy while $\mu(\Omega_{t-1})$ reflects the systematic part. The latter now is specified to depend on past values of all relevant variables, possibly including past values of $y_t - \bar{y}_t$. But because this part is systematic, its effects on m_t will be correctly anticipated by optimizing agents forming rational expectations. Therefore, formulation (6) has the implication that

$$m_t - E_{t-1}m_t = e_t, \tag{7}$$

just as in (4). Consequently, the analysis of the previous paragraphs applies if the policy rule is of the highly general form (6). For *any* policy rule falling into that class, the policy-ineffectiveness result will obtain in the model at hand.

This result, incidentally, offers a dramatic example of the importance of dynamic methods in the context of policy analysis. Specifically, the model just examined is one in which p_t has a predetermined or "given" value *within* each period. Consequently, comparative static analysis that treats p_t as fixed will suggest that the larger is m_t, the larger will be $m_t - p_t$ and therefore $y_t - \bar{y}_t$ [according to (1)]. From the perspective of any single period, therefore, output is enhanced by an expanded money stock. But from a dynamic perspective, it is recognized that the value *at which* p_t is fixed in any period will depend on expectations that depend on the policy rule in force. In the present model, the net outcome is as described by the policy-ineffectiveness result. From the perspective of average behavior over a large number of periods, therefore, the suggestion of single-period comparative static analysis is highly misleading.

Results similar to the foregoing were developed in several prominent articles published in the 1970s, the most famous of which was authored by Sargent and Wallace (1975). Although inspired by the work of Lucas (1972), the Sargent–Wallace analysis was conducted in a model that was similar in structure to augmented Phillips curve specifications that were being used at the time by most macroeconomic researchers. The difference between the Sargent–Wallace analysis and that common at the time was only that, instead of the then-standard adaptive expectations formula, Sargent and Wallace assumed rational expectations. In their model this change led to a policy-ineffectiveness conclusion like that developed above. As a consequence, many economists acquired the impression that the hypothesis of rational expectations *itself* implied that monetary policy is ineffective in stabilizing output. This impression was mistaken, however; the result that holds in the Sargent–Wallace (1975) model—and in our basic model!—does not hold generally.

To demonstrate the claim just made, our approach will be to modify some feature of the model (1), (2), and (6) and show that, despite continued adherence to the assumption of rational expectations, the implied value of $E(y_t - \bar{y}_t)^2$ turns out to depend in magnitude on parameters pertaining to the systematic part of the policy rule. Although there are other examples that have attracted more attention in the literature,[1] the one to be explored here makes only one essential change to the system underlying equations (1), (2), and (6). That change is to specify that the expected inflation rate that appears in the aggregate demand function (1) is $E_t(p_{t+1} - p_t)$ rather that $E_{t-1}(p_{t+1} - p_t)$. This altered specification will be appropriate if knowledge of current variables is available to individuals at the time at which they express their demand–supply decisions for the bonds (or other securities) that bear the nominal interest rate R_t referred to in equation (1) of Chapter 10.[2] In addition to this essential change, we also adopt— but only for convenience in exposition—an inessential simplifying assumption to the effect that $\bar{y}_t$ is constant over time: $\bar{y}_t = \bar{y}$. Finally, as it will suffice for making the relevant point, we revert to the specific policy equation (3) in place of the more general (6).

Even though our altered model involves only one essential change, in comparison to the specification of Section 10.2, that change shows up in a second way in the system (1)–(3). That is because equation (2) is itself a derived expression pertaining to the implications for output of demand–supply interactions; it is not a pure "structural" supply function. Thus,

---

[1] The best known example, due to Fischer (1977), involves a specification in which some nominal prices—in his case, wages—are set for two periods at a time. In that example it is also necessary (for the result) to specify that shocks to aggregate demand are serially correlated.

[2] Note that this altered assumption is more similar than that of Chapter 10 to the one used in the discussion of the Cagan model of Chapter 8.

by referring back to the procedure used to derive equation (12) of Chapter 10, it is easily determined that the change in informational specification that we have adopted will lead to the following equation instead of (2):[3]

$$y_t - \bar{y}_t = \beta_1(m_t - E_{t-1}m_t) + \beta_2(E_t p_{t+1} - E_{t-1}p_{t+1}) + v_t. \quad (8)$$

Thus we see that output depends not only on e_t and v_t, but also on the revision in expectations regarding p_{t+1} that occurs with the arrival of new information in period t.

According to (8), the policy-ineffectiveness result will *not* pertain to our modified system if the revision term $E_t p_{t+1} - E_{t-1}p_{t+1}$ depends on one of the policy parameters μ_0 or μ_1. To see that this is in fact the case, let us begin by substituting (8) and (3) into the modified version of (1):

$$\bar{y}_t + \beta_1 e_t + \beta_2(E_t p_{t+1} - E_{t-1}p_{t+1}) + v_t$$
$$= \beta_0 + \beta_1[(\mu_0 + \mu_1 m_{t-1} + e_t) - p_t] + \beta_2(E_t p_{t+1} - p_t) + v_t. \quad (9)$$

Here the terms involving e_t, v_t, and $E_t p_{t+1}$ cancel out, leaving

$$\bar{y}_t - \beta_2 E_{t-1}p_{t+1} = \beta_0\mu_0 + \beta_1\mu_1 m_{t-1} - \beta_1 p_t - \beta_2 p_t. \quad (10)$$

Since m_{t-1} and $\bar{y}_t$ are the only determinants of p_t involved and since $\bar{y}_t$ has for simplicity been assumed to equal a constant, we conjecture that

$$p_t = \phi_0 + \phi_1 m_{t-1}. \quad (11)$$

In light of the latter, we have that

$$E_{t-1}p_{t+1} = \phi_0 + \phi_1 E_{t-1}m_t = \phi_0 + \phi_1(\mu_0 + \mu_1 m_{t-1}). \quad (12)$$

Furthermore, we note for future reference that

$$E_t p_{t+1} - E_{t-1}p_{t+1} = \phi_1(E_t m_t - E_{t-1}m_t) = \phi_1 e_t, \quad (13)$$

since $E_t m_t = m_t$. Now, substitution of (11) and (12) into (10) yields

$$\bar{y} - \beta_2[\phi_0 + \phi_1(\mu_0 + \mu_1 m_{t-1})]$$
$$= \beta_0 + \beta_1\mu_0 + \beta_1\mu_1 m_{t-1} - (\beta_1 + \beta_2)(\phi_0 + \phi_1 m_{t-1}). \quad (14)$$

In the manner familiar from Chapter 8, the latter implies the conditions

$$\bar{y} - \beta_2\phi_1\mu_0 = \beta_0 + \beta_1\mu_0 - \beta_1\phi_0$$
$$- \beta_2\phi_1\mu_1 = \beta_1\mu_1 - (\beta_1 + \beta_2)\phi_1. \quad (15)$$

---

[3] In Problem 2 at the end of the present chapter, the reader is asked to verify this claim.

Clearly, the second of these can be solved for ϕ_1, as follows:

$$\phi_1 = \frac{\beta_1 \mu_1}{\beta_1 + \beta_2(1 - \mu_1)}. \tag{16}$$

Now (16) plus the first of equations (15) can be used in (11) to yield a solution for p_t. But of more importance for the issue at hand, (16) and expression (13) together imply that the revision term in (8) is

$$E_t p_{t+1} - E_{t-1} p_{t+1} = \frac{\beta_1 \mu_1}{\beta_1 + \beta_2(1 - \mu_1)} e_t. \tag{17}$$

Accordingly, the solution for output in the present model can be written, from (8) and (17), as

$$y_t - \bar{y} = \beta_1 e_t + \frac{\beta_2 \beta_1 \mu_1}{\beta_1 + \beta_2(1 - \mu_1)} e_t + v_t. \tag{18}$$

This last expression indicates that the model has the property indicated above, namely, that $E(y_t - \bar{y}_t)^2$ depends on a policy parameter. That this is true is obvious from the presence of μ_1 in the second term on the right-hand side. Different values of μ_1 give rise to different values of the output variability measure, $E(y_t - \bar{y})^2$.

In fact, it is an easy matter to determine what value of μ_1 will, in the model at hand, lead to the smallest value of $E(y_t - \bar{y})^2$. Rearranging the right-hand side of (18) yields

$$\frac{\beta_1^2 + \beta_1 \beta_2}{\beta_1 + \beta_2(1 - \mu_1)} e_t + v_t, \tag{19}$$

so the variability measure will be smallest for the μ_1 measure that minimizes the square of $1/[\beta_1 + \beta_2(1 - \mu_1)]$. In other words, we want the value of μ_1 that maximizes $[\beta_1 + \beta_2(1 - \mu_1)]^2$, subject to the constraint that $|\mu_1| \leq 1$.[4] But with β_1 and β_2 both positive, that criterion is met with $\mu_1 = -1$, so that $[\beta_1 + \beta_2(1 - \mu_1)^2] = (\beta_1 + 2\beta_2)^2$. In sum, we have found that in the model consisting of (3), (8), and (1) with $E_t(p_{t+1} - p_t)$, the variability measure $E(y_t - \bar{y})^2$ depends on the policy parameter μ_1, and the choice $\mu_1 = -1$ leads to the smallest extend of output variability.

Before leaving the subject, it should be said explicitly that there are other minor and plausible modifications to the model which will also invalidate the policy-ineffectiveness result. The existence of multiperiod price setting has already been mentioned. Another prominent

---

[4] That constraint is necessary, as readers will recall from Chapter 8, to avoid dynamic instability of m_t.

possibility is that when choosing m_t, the monetary authority has available some information pertaining to conditions in period t. If the policy choice of m_t is based on information that was not available (to private agents or to the monetary authority) when p_t was set, then parameters of the policy rule may be relevant for $E(y_t - \bar{y}_t)^2$.

11.3 The Lucas Critique

The material in Section 11.2 has illustrated the manner in which policy analysis is properly conducted in dynamic and stochastic macroeconomic models. In such models it is obviously not possible to compare "the outcome" of a change in some policy variable, as is done in static models such as those of Chapter 5. Instead, the appropriate comparison pertains to average outcomes resulting, over a large number of periods, from different policy rules when maintained over these periods. Averages are represented analytically by unconditional expectations of relevant random variables. So, to conduct such a comparison, the analyst determines the value of some criterion such as $E(y_t - \bar{y}_t)^2$, pertaining to average outcomes, for one policy rule and then does the same for a different, alternative policy rule. Sometimes the comparison is, as in Section 11.2, for different values of a parameter (such as μ_1) with the rule's functional form unchanged, and sometimes different functional forms are considered. Either way, comparisons are made for a number of possible policy rules in order to determine which of these would be preferable, as judged on the basis of the relevant criterion [exemplified above by $E(y_t - y_t)^2$].

In making policy comparisons of this type, it is assumed implicitly that the same model of private economic behavior [e.g., equations (1) and (2)] is applicable under all of the different policy rules considered. If such were not the case, the comparisons would be invalid. Consequently, for policy analysis in dynamic stochastic settings it is necessary that the model of private behavior be one that is "structural," that is, *invariant* to the policy rule in effect. The implicit assumption that the model pertains for all the different policy rules must be justifiable; if relationships of the model were to shift with policy-rule changes, the necessary type of comparison could not be made.

The argument just developed may strike the reader as so obvious as to make the exposition unnecessary. But there are certain ways of constructing and using models that lead to violations of the requirement that the model's relations be structural. Indeed, one of the most famous articles of the past 20 years was one, published by Robert Lucas in 1976, which showed that a then-prevalent type of policy analysis involved violations of precisely this type. In particular, Lucas showed that the usual way of conducting policy analysis with the large econometric models of the day would be logically invalid if expectations were in fact formed rationally. Because Lucas's paper was entitled "Econometric Policy Evaluations: A Critique," the line of argument involved (and here summarized) has become known as the "Lucas critique."

To exemplify the nature of the Lucas critique, let us again make use of the example of Section 10.2, summarized in equations (1)–(3) of the present chapter. Again for simplicity let us treat $\bar{y}_t$ as a constant, $\bar{y}_t = \bar{y}$. In this model, equations (1) and (2) pertain to private-sector behavior, while (3) represents policy. Our previous analysis assumed that (1) and (2) are structural, that is, are invariant to changes in (3). For the sake of the present argument, let us suppose that that assumption is justified. But suppose that instead of (1) and (2), the analyst were to use as his model equation (1) and the following replacement for (2):

$$y_t - \bar{y} = \gamma_0 + \gamma_1 m_t + \gamma_2 m_{t-1} + \xi_t. \tag{20}$$

Now an equation of the form (20) is valid for the model at hand, in the sense that one could evaluate $E_{t-1} m_t$ from (3) as $\mu_0 + \mu_1 m_{t-1}$ and substitute into (2), thereby obtaining

$$y_t - \bar{y} = \beta_1 (m_t - \mu_0 - \mu_1 m_{t-1}) + v_t$$
$$= -\beta_1 \mu_0 + \beta_1 m_t - \mu_1 \beta_1 m_{t-1} + v_t. \tag{21}$$

Thus (20) obtains, with $\gamma_0 = -\beta_1 \mu_0$, $\gamma_1 = \beta_1$, $\gamma_2 = -\mu_1 \beta_1$, and $\xi_t = v_t$. But although (20) is a valid characterization of the relation between y_t and m_t, it is *not* a structural relation. Instead, its coefficients γ_0 and γ_2 will change in value with every change in the policy parameters μ_0 and μ_1. Consequently, comparative policy analysis based on a model consisting of equations (1), (20), and a policy rule would be invalid— would be subject to the Lucas critique.

The problem with equation (20) in the foregoing example is that it muddles together two types of behavior, the supply behavior summarized in (2) and the expectational or forecasting behavior summarized in the expression $E_{t-1} m_t = \mu_0 + \mu_1 m_{t-1}$. Whereas the former is by assumption policy invariant, the latter clearly is not: the forecast in $t - 1$ of m_t will depend (if individuals form expectations rationally) on the actual policy process. As its parameters pertain to both types of behavior, equation (20) will not be policy invariant.

The foregoing discussion provides an example of one of the most important types of model failure pointed out in Lucas's "critique" paper. Other types are also significant, and could possibly apply— contrary to the assumption made provisionally above—to our model's equation (2). It is conceivable, for example, that a change in policy could induce sellers to switch from price-setting behavior of type (5) to type (29) in Chapter 10, that is, from one-period to two-period price setting. If such a switch took place, then policy analysis as conducted in Section 11.2 would be misleading.

In general, there is no way of being certain that any model will not be open to the Lucas critique. Some economists, including Lucas (1976) himself, have stressed the benefits of using models based on explicit optimization analysis of individual agents' choices.[5] But while such a procedure is desirable, it can provide no guarantee of success; explicit optimization analysis will not help if the agent's objective function or constraints are misspecified. The true message of the Lucas critique is simply that the analyst must be as careful as possible to avoid the use of equations that will tend, for plausible reasons, to shift with policy changes.

11.4   Money Stock Control

The purpose of this section is to provide a second example of policy analysis in a dynamic stochastic model. The example to be developed here involves a return to the topic of Sections 4.4 and 4.5, namely, the monetary authority's choice among alternative operating instruments. Thus we concern ourselves—as in Chapter 4—with the fact that in most actual economics the central bank does not have direct control of the quantity of money in existence, but can only influence that quantity by manipulating some instrument such as high-powered (base) money, or another measure of bank reserves, or a short-term interest rate. Indeed, our example is designed to provide an explanation—as was promised in Section 4.6—of the operating procedure that was actually used by the Fed in the United States during the period 1979–1982.[6] In carrying out the analysis, we shall assume that the Fed was truly trying to hit money stock targets, that is, that its main objective was to induce m_t, the log of the money stock, to follow a target path described by m_t^*. Although this assumption perhaps overstates the Fed's concern for its official monetary targets, it is almost certainly the case that attempts to hit such targets were significantly more whole-hearted during the 1979–1982 episode than before or after.

The model to be utilized in our analysis is generally consistent with that of Section 4.5, but is more explicitly dynamic and is elaborated as

---

[5] A forceful and authoritative statement is provided by Sargent (1981).
[6] The precise period was, as mentioned in Chapter 4, from October 1979 to September 1982.

suggested in Chapter 10. It consists, to be specific, of four equations plus a specification of policy behavior. The four equations are *IS* and *LM* relations, an aggregate supply function like (2), and an equation of the type developed in Chapter 4 that pertains to the behavior of banks. The first three of these can be recorded without much explanation, as follows:

$$R_t = b_0 + b_1 y_t + E_{t-1}(p_{t+1} - p_t) + \eta_t, \tag{22}$$

$$m_t - p_t = c_0 + c_1 y_t + c_2 R_t + \varepsilon_t, \tag{23}$$

$$y_t - \bar{y} = \beta_1(m_t - E_{t-1}m_t) + v_t. \tag{24}$$

Here ε_t, η_t, and v_t are white noise disturbances, the latter being a linear combination of the first two (as suggested in Section 10.2). The fourth relationship is analogous to equation (20) of Chapter 4, but will be written here with h_t, the log of high-powered money, on the left-hand side. The purpose of that presentation is to emphasize that the relation may be interpreted as representing bank's demand for reserves:

$$h_t = d_0 + d_1 m_t + d_2 R_t + \zeta_t. \tag{25}$$

In the latter, $d_1 > 0$ and $d_2 < 0$, while ζ_t is a white noise disturbance that is assumed independent of the nonbank private-sector shocks ε_t, η_t, and v_t. Equation (25) can be described as positing that banks hold more reserves (and therefore the economy demands more high-powered money) when their deposits (and thus the money stock) are greater. For any given magnitude of m_t, however, the banks choose to hold lower reserves when the interest rate—and thus the cost of holding reserves—is higher.

Before turning to the 1979–1982 system itself, let us first rework in this setting the type of instrument-choice analysis conducted in Section 4.5. To begin with, let us suppose that the policy scheme is to use R_t as an instrument, setting its value each period at the level that is *expected* to make m_t equal to m_t^*. From (23) we then see that R_t should be set so as to satisfy

$$m_t^* - E_{t-1}p_t = c_0 + c_1 E_{t-1}y_t + c_2 R_t, \tag{26}$$

where we have taken expectations and set $m_t = m_t^*$. Subtracting (26) from (23) then gives the relation

$$m_t - m_t^* - (p_t - E_{t-1}p_t) = c_1(y_t - E_{t-1}y_t) + \eta_t. \tag{23'}$$

Next, we note that (24) implies that

$$y_t - E_{t-1}y_t = \beta_1 e_t + v_t, \tag{27}$$

where $e_t \equiv m_t - E_{t-1}m_t$. Furthermore, in the model at hand prices are preset so there are no one-period p_t surprises: in each period,

$p_t - E_{t-1}p_t = 0$. Consequently, substitution into (23') yields

$$m_t = m_t^* + c_1\beta_1 e_t + c_1 v_t + \varepsilon_t. \tag{28}$$

But since the control process is designed to make $E_{t-1}m_t = m_t^*$, we know that $m_t - m_t^*$ and e_t are equal. Therefore, (28) can be rearranged to give

$$m_t - m_t^* = \frac{1}{1 - c_1\beta_1}(c_1 v_t + \varepsilon_t) \tag{29}$$

as the analytical expression for the money stock control error provided by an operating procedure that used R_t as the instrument. The average square of this control error, the mean-squared error (MSE) for m_t, is therefore

$$E(m_t - m_t^*)^2 = \frac{1}{(1 - c_1\beta_1)^2} E(c_1 v_t + \varepsilon_t)^2. \tag{30}$$

Next we derive a comparable expression for a policy regime that attempts to hit m_t^* targets by means of a h_t instrument. In this case h_t is set so as to satisfy

$$h_t = d_0 + d_1 m_t^* + d_2 E_{t-1}R_t. \tag{31}$$

Subtraction from (25) then implies that

$$0 = d_1(m_t - m_t^*) + d_2(R_t - E_{t-1}R_t) + \zeta_t. \tag{32}$$

But relation (23) implies that the following must also be satisfied:[7]

$$m_t - m_t^* = c_1(y_t - E_{t-1}y_t) + c_2(R_t - E_{t-1}R_t) + \varepsilon_t. \tag{33}$$

So, by eliminating $R_t - E_{t-1}R_t$ and using (24), we obtain

$$(m_t - m_t^*)\left(1 + \frac{c_2 d_1}{d_2}\right) = c_1(\beta e_t + v_t) + \varepsilon_t - \frac{c_2}{d_2}\zeta_t.$$

The equality $m_t - m_t^* = e_t$ thus permits us to rearrange the latter and write

$$m_t - m_t^* = \frac{1}{1 - c_1\beta_1 + c_2 d_1/d_2}\left(c_1 v_t + \varepsilon_t - \frac{c_2}{d_2}\zeta_t\right). \tag{34}$$

The MSE value for this procedure is then[8]

$$E(m_t - m_t^*)^2 = \frac{1}{(1 - c_1\beta_1 + c_2 d_1/d_2)^2}\left[E(c_1 v_t + \varepsilon_t)^2 + \left(\frac{c_2}{d_2}\right)^2 E\zeta_t^2\right]. \tag{35}$$

---

[7] In writing (32) we have subtracted the expectation of (23) from (23) and have used the previously explained equalities $E_{t-1}m_t = m_t^*$ and $p_t - E_{t-1}p_t = 0$.
[8] Here we use the assumed independent of ζ_t from the other shocks.

Here, as in Section 4.5, we cannot definitely say whether the MSE is smaller with an interest rate or reserve instrument.

Now let us finally turn our attention to the control procedure actually utilized by the Fed during the 1979–1982 episode. As was mentioned in Chapter 4, under this procedure the Fed employed a variant of the h_t variable as its instrument, that variant being the nonborrowed component of bank reserves. Let us then assume that h_t in equation (25) pertains to that measure or, in other words, that (25) describes banks' demand for nonborrowed reserves. A second relevant feature of the 1979–1982 procedure is that at the time[9] the Fed's reserve requirements for banks pertained not to current deposits but to deposits held two weeks earlier. If we let our model's "periods" be interpreted as two-week intervals, then it would be appropriate to specify that required reserves in t depend on deposits in $t - 1$. Since the money stock is largely deposits, required reserves for period t therefore depended (during 1979–1982) primarily on m_{t-1}, not m_t. A better representation of nonborrowed reserve demand than (25) would accordingly be

$$h_t = d_0 + d_1 m_{t-1} + d_2 R_t + \zeta_t. \tag{36}$$

Let us then examine the consequences for money stock control of an operating procedure that uses h_t as the instrument when (36) represents reserve demand.

It will be noted that with (36) prevailing rather than (25), that relation itself provides no direct connection between the instrument h_t and the current money stock, m_t. In fact, the connection is in this case rather like that with an R_t instrument; the Fed manipulates h_t, which, because of banks' behavior as described in (36), affects R_t, which then influences the quantity of money demanded. Analytically, to solve for $m_t - m_t^*$ we begin with equation (23). The latter implies that

$$m_t^* - E_{t-1} p_t = c_0 + c_1 E_{t-1} y_t + c_2 E_{t-1} R_t \tag{37}$$

and the connection between m_t^* and the instrument h_t is provided by solving (37) for $E_{t-1} R_t$ and substituting into (36):

$$h_t = d_0 + d_1 m_{t-1} + \frac{d_2}{c_2} (m_t^* - E_{t-1} p_t - c_0 - c_1 E_{t-1} y_t). \tag{38}$$

Then by steps similar to those followed above,[10] it can be determined

---

[9] In 1984 the reserve requirements were changed to become more nearly contemporaneous in their effect. On this topic, see Goodfriend (1984).

[10] Specifically, (38) is subtracted from a combination of (36) and (23) from which R_t is eliminated. Thus (27) and $m_t - m_t^* = e_t$ are substituted and the resulting expression solved for $m_t - m_t^*$.

that in this case the m_t control error is

$$m_t - m_t^* = \frac{1}{1 - c_1\beta_1}\left(c_1 v_t + \varepsilon_t + \frac{c_2}{d_2}\zeta_t\right). \tag{39}$$

Thus the mean-squared m_t control error for the 1979–1982 procedure is

$$E(m_t - m_t^*)^2 = \frac{1}{(1 - c_1\beta_1)^2}\left[E(c_1 v_t + \varepsilon_t)^2 + \left(\frac{c_2}{d_2}\right)^2 E\zeta_t^2\right]. \tag{40}$$

The most striking fact about the result that we have obtained is that the MSE in (40) is unambiguously greater than in (30). That can readily be seen to be true, for the expressions are similar except for the inclusion of the extra term $(c_2/d_2)^2 E\zeta_t^2$ in (40), a term that is necessarily positive. Thus we conclude that, according to our model, typical control errors under the procedure adopted in 1979 should be larger than if the operating procedure consisted of the straightforward use of an interest rate instrument. This conclusion is rather striking, for the latter type of procedure was used by the Fed prior to October 1979, when a change was made ostensibly to improve money stock control! Analysis of the foregoing type would, if conducted earlier in 1979, have suggested that the procedure based on nonborrowed reserves would weaken monetary control, a suggestion that is entirely consistent with the facts described in Section 1.3.[11]

The other striking fact about our analysis is that expression (40) will also be larger than (35), provided that $c_1\beta_1 < 1$, so that the absolute value of $1 - c_1\beta_1 + c_2 d_1/d_2$ is greater than for $1 - c_1\beta_1$. With that provision, we find that when an h_t instrument is used, monetary control is less accurate with lagged reserve requirements than with contemporaneous requirements.[12]

It should be added that the foregoing conclusions are subject to the proviso that equations (22)–(25) are invariant to choice among the various operating procedures, that is, that the model is not in this regard subject to the Lucas critique. In fact, that is probably not a good assumption—on the contrary, it is likely that the parameters of the banks' reserve demand equation would probably be somewhat different under different operating procedures. The most significant difference, however, should be between the second procedure (with a reserve

---

[11] Readers are urged to study again, at this point, the material in Section 1.3. It should be admitted, however, that the procedure adopted in 1979 was helpful *politically*, for it enabled the Fed to disclaim responsibility for the high nominal interest rates that were *temporarily* necessary in the Fed's attempt to reduce inflation.

[12] The results of this section were developed, for a slightly different model, by McCallum and Hoehn (1983).

instrument and contemporaneous reserve requirements) and the other two.[13] By comparison, there should be little parameter sensitivity to the distinction between the first and third procedures. Consequently, the comparison between expressions (30) and (40) rests, it could be argued, on a fairly sound analytical basis.[14]

11.5 Conclusions

The purpose of this chapter has been to illustrate how policy analysis is conducted in dynamic, stochastic models. Instead of comparing values of endogenous variables—as with comparative static analysis of the type conducted in Chapter 5—the comparison is between the properties of stochastic processes for the endogenous variables, the different processes resulting from different behavior rules maintained by the policy authorities. But while Sections 11.2 and 11.4 provide two examples of policy analysis, the policy issues implicitly under consideration are very different. In the example of Section 11.4, the issue concerns the best type of operating procedure to be used given that the monetary authority wishes (for some unexplained reason) to set prespecified targets for the economy's money stock. In Section 11.2, by contrast, the focus is on the effects of money stock variations (achieved by some unspecified operating procedure) on real output. It should not be thought that there is any inconsistency between these two types of issues, or that one makes sense and the other does not. The appropriate perspective is that policymakers and analysts will sometimes be concerned with one type of question, and at other times with another. A thorough understanding of the two examples should help readers to see how to approach policy analysis in a dynamic model whatever the problem they wish to consider. In all cases it must be added, the analyst must be alert to the possibility that the model could be subject to the Lucas-critique difficulty explained in Section 10.3. By keeping alert to this potential problem, the analyst can do a better job of specifying a model so as to be relatively insensitive to the policy alternatives considered.

---

[13] The reason is that under this procedure, but not the others, the Fed is precommited as to the quantity of reserves to be made available to the banking system. That type of precommitment is more restrictive if the relevant measure of reserves is total reserves rather than nonborrowed reserves.

[14] To complete the present discussion, it should be mentioned that the Fed's main instrument since 1982 has been borrowed reserves. Various target variables have been used at different times, with very little attention devoted to M1 control.

Problems

1. Consider the model presented in Problem 3 of Chapter 9. Does that model have the monetary policy-ineffectiveness property?
2. Verify that equation (8) is implied by the model of Section 10.2 when it is modified to include $E_t(p_{t+1} - p_t)$ in the aggregate demand function.
3. Consider a model in which aggregate demand is $y_t = \beta_0 + \beta_1(m_t - p_t) + v_t$, with v_t white noise, and output is determined by the quantity demanded at the prevailing price with the latter given by $p_t - p_{t-1} = \theta(\bar{p}_t - p_{t-1})$. Here $\beta_1 > 0$, $\theta > 0$, and $\bar{p}_t$ satisfies $\bar{y} = \beta_0 + \beta_1(m_t - \bar{p}_t) + v_t$. Find the solution for output and determine whether the policy-ineffectiveness property prevails.
4. Verify equation (39) of Section 11.4.

References

Fischer, Stanley, "Long-Term Contracts, Rational Expectations, and the Optimal Money Supply Rule," *Journal of Political Economy* 85 (February 1977), 191–205.

Goodfriend, Marvin, "The Promises and Pitfalls of Contemporaneous Reserve Requirements for the Implementation of Monetary Policy," Federal Reserve Bank of Richmond, *Economic Review* 70 (May–June 1984), 3–12.

Lucas, Robert E., Jr., "Expectations and the Neutrality of Money," *Journal of Economic Theory* 4 (April 1972), 103–24.

Lucas, Robert E., Jr., "Econometric Policy Evaluations: A Critique," in *The Phillips Curve and Labor Markets*, Karl Brunner and Allan H. Meltzer, eds. (Amsterdam: North-Holland, 1976).

McCallum, Bennett, T., and James G. Hoehn. "Instrument Choice for Money Stock Control with Contemporaneous and Lagged Reserve Requirements," *Journal of Money, Credit, and Banking* 15 (February 1983), 96–101.

Sargent, Thomas J., "Interpreting Economic Time Series," *Journal of Political Economy* 89 (April 1981), 213–48.

Sargent, Thomas, J., and Neil Wallace, "'Rational' Expectations, the Optimal Monetary Instrument, and the Optimal Money Supply Rule," *Journal of Political Economy* 83 (April 1975), 241–54.

12

Rules Versus
Discretion in
Monetary Policy

12.1 Fundamental Distinctions

In this chapter we continue our investigation of monetary policy design by addressing a topic of long-standing interest to economists, namely, the relative merits of conducting policy on the basis of "rules" rather than the "discretion" of the policymaker. Although this topic has frequently been discussed at least since the publication of a famous essay by Henry Simons (1936), the nature of the dispute has been altered in recent years. In particular, it has only recently been recognized that the rules versus discretion issue is not the same as the issue of activist versus nonactivist policy.

To begin our explanation of the indicated distinction, suppose temporarily (and, of course, unrealistically) that a nation's monetary authority manipulates as its policy instrument the growth rate of the money stock, denoted Δm_t.[1] Suppose, in addition, that it sets Δm_t in each quarter according to the following formula, in which UN_t denotes the economy's unemployment rate (measured as a fraction) for

---

[1] In this chapter we again use M_t to denote the money stock in period t and define $m_t = \log M_t$. Thus Δm_t is the growth rate of M_t.

quarter t:

$$\Delta m_t = 0.01 + 0.5(UN_{t-1} - 0.05). \tag{1}$$

Thus the money stock is made to grow at a rate of about 1 percent per quarter (or about 4 percent per year) if the unemployment rate for the most recent quarter is 0.05 (i.e., 5 percent), and at a more or less rapid rate if unemployment has been greater or smaller (respectively) than 0.05. Now, for present purposes the significant feature of equation (1) is that it represents monetary policy that is *activist*, by which is meant that each period's setting of the instrument depends in a nontrivial or "active" manner on some aspect of the current state of the economy. In this example the relevant aspect is taken to be the unemployment rate, but it could be the inflation rate or an interest rate or some combination of such variables. By contrast, a formula such as

$$\Delta m_t = 0.01 \tag{2}$$

that specifies a constant value for the instrument setting, or even one such as

$$\Delta m_t = 0.01 + 0.0002t, \tag{3}$$

which makes the setting increase over time, is nonactivist. That is the case since neither (2) nor (3) incorporates any policy response to the state of the economy.

Now let us ask whether the activist policy behavior of equation (1) reflects an example of rules or discretion. Unfortunately, this question is a bit harder to answer. If equation (1) represents a formula that is implemented each period by the monetary authority, then it consists of a policy rule. But it is conceivable that (1) could instead be a representation of the outcomes of policymaking by discretion. Thus if no more is known about (1) than that it accurately describes the values of Δm_t that are generated by the policy authority in periods $1, 2, \dots$, then one cannot tell from the formula alone which type of policymaking is being followed. This difficulty exists because the rules versus discretion distinction centers on the *process* by which the Δm_t (or other instrument) values are determined, not what those values turn out to be.

Let us then consider different policy processes. Presumably, the monetary authority will, whichever way it proceeds, be attempting to optimize relative to some objective function and some perception of how the economy operates. But the attempt at optimization enters the policy process at different stages under the two different types of policymaking. Specifically, discretionary policy prevails when the monetary authority selects each period's value of Δm_t on the basis of a fresh optimization calculation.[2] Thus policy is discretionary when it is conducted on a period-by-period basis, with no necessary connection between the choices of different periods. By contrast, policymaking according to a rule exists when the policymaker merely *implements* in each period a rule or formula [such as (1)] that has been chosen to be applicable for a large number of periods, not just the one currently at hand. In the case of a rule, the authority's optimization efforts are exerted in the *design* of the formula to be utilized, not in the choice of any single period's action. So if the formula in equation (1) is one that was designed to be applicable for periods $t = 1, 2 \ldots$, then it constitutes a rule even though it reflects activist policy. The same type of reasoning indicates, moreover, that one cannot be certain that the Δm_t outcomes specified in equation (2) result from a policy rule, even though these outcomes are the same in each period.[3]

In summary, rule-type policymaking involves implementation in each period (or in each case) of a formula designed to apply to periods (or cases) in general, while discretionary policymaking involves freshly made decisions in each period (or case). This subtle but important distinction will be explored further, by means of an example, in the following section.

12.2   Rules Versus Discretion: An Example

The distinction between rules and discretion that we have outlined in Section 12.1 was first clearly developed in a paper by Kydland and Prescott (1977). With respect to monetary policy, that paper's discussion was based in large part on an important example, one that was later refined and extended by Barro and Gordon (1983). It will be useful for us now to consider a version of the Kydland–Prescott model.

To explain that model, let us first suppose that the monetary authority's policy objectives focus on the avoidance of inflation and unemployment. Specifically, the monetary authority (abbreviated MA)

---

[2] It is not necessary for this definition that the calculation be conducted in a formal manner on the basis of an explicit model. Instead, the policymaker can be relying on an informal model, that is, a nonexplicit but coherent view (or perception) of the way in which the economy works. Similarly, her objective function may be one that is not spelled out explicitly. In the analysis of policymakers, as well as households and firms, the agents' optimization problems are properly thought of in an "as if" fashion, not as a literal description of agents' thought processes.

[3] This point is substantiated by the example in Section 12.2.

wishes to keep the inflation rate close to zero and to keep the unemployment rate low.[4] In addition, let us also suppose that the MA believes that inflation rates are largely determined by money growth rates and that unemployment in any period is negatively related to that period's rate of *unexpected* money growth. The first of these beliefs is of course consistent with a prominent theme of the present book, while the second reflects the model of aggregate supply developed in Chapter 10. Under these suppositions, we can represent the MA's objectives in terms of the variables Δm_t and $\Delta m_t - \Delta m_t^e$, where the latter is the unexpected or "surprise" component of money growth. For concreteness, let us then adopt a specific functional form and assume that the MA's objective for period t is to minimize the value of

$$z_t = \frac{a}{2} \Delta m_t^2 - b(\Delta m_t - \Delta m_t^e), \tag{4}$$

where $a > 0$ and $b > 0$. Finally, let us assume that expectations are formed rationally, so that (in the notation of Chapter 8) $\Delta m_t^e = E_{t-1} \Delta m_t$.

Our object now is to determine what Δm_t values would be chosen by the MA, with the objective function (4), under rules and under discretion. Since the parameters a and b are constants, there is no reason for the chosen Δm_t values to differ from period to period, in the highly simplified setup at hand. Consequently, let us determine what constant value for Δm_t would be chosen if the MA were choosing a single value to prevail (as with a rule) over a large number of periods.[5] In making a choice of this type, the MA will take into account the fact that on average rational agents will neither overpredict or underpredict Δm_t.[6] Consequently, the second term of expression (4) will equal zero and the problem will reduce to finding the value of Δm_t that minimizes $(a/2) \Delta m_t^2$. But obviously, since $a > 0$ and squared values are nonnegative, that minimum will be obtained with the choice $\Delta m_t = 0$. Thus the rule chosen by the MA in this setting is $\Delta m_t = 0$ for all t.

Next we contrast that choice with those that would be made under discretion, that is, if choices were made on a period-by-period basis. In this case we imagine the MA to be making a choice of Δm_t at some specific point in time, say, $t = 4$. For example, the object might be to

---

[4] There is a variant of the model in which the aim regarding unemployment is to keep UN_t close to its natural-rate or market-clearing value. Also, the inflation-rate objective could be some number other than zero.

[5] This is a special case of a rule, one that is not activist.

[6] This is a fact under our assumption of rational expectations. But note that the condition necessary for the following argument is simply that $\Delta m_t^e = \Delta m_t$ on average, which is a less demanding condition than full rational expectations.

choose Δm_4 to minimize the value of

$$z_4 = \frac{a}{2} \Delta m_4^2 - b(\Delta m_4 - \Delta m_4^e). \tag{5}$$

The difference that characterizes this case is that Δm_4^e, the value of Δm_4 that private agents anticipate, has already been determined (at the end of period 3). From the perspective of the MA's choice problem Δm_4^e is therefore a fixed number. Consequently, the second term of (5) does not necessarily equal zero in the minimization calculation. Instead, the value of Δm_4 that minimizes (5) is found by calculating the derivative

$$\frac{\partial z_4}{\partial \Delta m_4} = a \Delta m_4 - b \tag{6}$$

and setting it equal to zero. Solving the resulting equation, we find that $\Delta m_4 = b/a$ is the optimal value. Under discretion, this value as calculated pertains only to period 4. However, when period 5 comes around, the situation will be the same in the sense that the objective $z_5 = (a/2) \Delta m_5^2 - b(\Delta m_5 - \Delta m_5^e)$ has the same form as (5). In addition, Δm_5^e will already have been determined and will be a fixed number from the MA's perspective. Consequently, the "optimal" value chosen for Δm_5 will be the same as for Δm_4, namely, b/a. Furthermore, it is clear that this same choice will be made in periods 6, 7, 8, and so on. Thus the sequence of Δm_t values chosen by the MA when conducting policy on the period-by-period basis is, in this example, $\Delta m_t = b/a$ for all t.

We have seen, then, that in the economy considered, policy conducted according to a rule (chosen to pertain to a large number of periods) would lead to a money growth rate of zero: $\Delta m_t = 0$ for all t. In the same economy and with the same policy objectives, by contrast, policy choices made in a discretionary period-by-period fashion would lead to $\Delta m_t = b/a$ for all t.

12.3   Effects of Rules Versus Discretion

Having seen that rules and discretion lead to different money growth rates in our example, let us now consider the desirability of these alternatives. In doing so, our criterion will be the value of z_t that results on average (over a large number of periods). The first step in our evaluation is to recognize that while Δm_t can be chosen in any single period to differ from Δm_t^e, on average Δm_t^e and Δm_t will be equal under both types of policymaking. This follows from the assumption that private agents' expectations are rational.[7] So, whichever type of policymaking is adopted, the average performance will involve $\Delta m_t - \Delta m_t^e = 0$. Thus the difference in outcome arises only because $\Delta m_t = 0$ with a rule and $\Delta m_t = b/a$ under discretion. But with the objective function as specified in (4), this result clearly favors the rule. Specifically, the average value of z_t, which the MA wishes to minimize, is zero when $\Delta m_t = 0$ and is $(a/2)(b/a)^2 = b^2/2a$ when $\Delta m_t = b/a$. Since $a > 0$, $b^2/2a > 0$ and the value of z_t is higher than under the rule.

In terms of the inflation and unemployment goal variables used to rationalize the specification of z_t, the foregoing result can be interpreted as follows. With either type of policymaking, rational private agents will form their expectations of money growth and inflation in a manner that yields an average expectational error of zero; the average value of $\Delta m_t - \Delta m_t^e$ will be (approximately) zero over any large number of periods. Thus the average effect of monetary policy on unemployment will be zero and the difference in the two policy approaches will consist of different amounts of inflation. But rule-type policymaking leads to zero inflation, while discretionary policymaking leads to positive inflation. Given the assumption that zero inflation is desirable, then, policy conducted according to a rule is superior.

The *reason* that discretionary policymaking is inferior in the foregoing example can be understood in the following way. In a typical period t, it is true that Δm_t^e is given and unalterable by policy action, so the MA is correct to believe that $\Delta m_t - \Delta m_t^e$ will be higher (and unemployment lower) the greater is the value chosen for Δm_t. Consequently, there is, *from the perspective of the period at hand*, a tradeoff between the reduced-unemployment benefits of faster monetary growth and the increased-inflation costs of faster growth. So the equating of marginal costs and benefits leads to a value of Δm_t that is a compromise between the zero-inflation value of $\Delta m_t = 0$ and higher values of Δm_t that would make $\Delta m_t - \Delta m_t^e$ even larger. But the discretionary emphasis on this particular outcome for the single period at hand fails to recognize the overall effects of the policy *process*. In particular, it fails to recognize that the value at which Δm_t^e is "given" is itself determined by the character of the ongoing policy process. The values of Δm_t that are chosen each period under discretion (i.e., $\Delta m_t = b/a$ for all t) themselves lead agents to believe that Δm_t values will equal b/a, and to form the expectation $\Delta m_t^e = b/a$. This effect of policy on expectations is not taken into account in period-by-period decision making. For that reason, the MA gives too much consideration under discretion to a variable—$\Delta m_t - \Delta m_t^e$ or unemployment—

---

[7] Or from the weaker assumption mentioned in footnote 6.

that it cannot affect on average. The advantage of decision making by rules is that it views the problem not as a sequence of unrelated decisions, but as the choice of an ongoing process that has desirable properties.[8]

It is interesting to note that one aspect of the advantage of rule-type decision making was recognized long before 1977 (the date of the Kydland–Prescott article). In a paper published in 1962, Milton Friedman suggested that "monetary policy has much in common with a topic that seems at first altogether different, namely, the Bill of Rights to the [U.S.] Constitution" (Friedman, 1962, p. 239). In this discussion, Friedman focused in particular on the first-amendment guarantee of individuals' rights to freedom of speech. He did so in response to a question that is often asked by critics of rules: "Why not take up each case separately and treat it on its own merits? ... One man wants to stand up on a street corner and advocate birth control; another, communism; a third, vegetarianism; and so on, ad infinitum." Indeed, *why not* consider each case on its own merits? Why tie the policymaker's hand? Friedman's answer goes as follows: "It is immediately clear that if we were to take up each case separately, a majority would almost surely vote to deny free speech in most cases. ..."[9] "But now suppose all these cases were grouped together in one bundle, and the populace at large was asked to vote for them as a whole; to vote whether free speech should be denied in all cases or permitted in all alike. It is ... highly probable, that an overwhelming majority could vote for free speech; that, acting on the bundle as a whole, the people would vote exactly the opposite to the way they would have voted on each case separately."

Then, after remarking on "our good fortune of having lived in a society that did adopt the self-denying ordinance of not considering each case of speech separately" (p. 241), Friedman contends that:

> Exactly the same considerations apply in the monetary area. If each case is considered on its merits, the wrong decision is likely to be made in a large fraction of cases because the decision-makers are ... not taking into account the cumulative consequences of the policy as a whole. On the other hand, if a general rule is adopted for a group of cases as a bundle, the existence of that rule has favorable effects on people's attitudes ... and expectations that would not follow even from the discretionary adoption of precisely the same [actions] on a series of separate occasions. (Friedman, 1962, p. 241)

---

[8] That this remains true, even if the MA's objection function takes account of future z_t values, is explained below.

[9] It should be kept in mind that this passage was written in 1961, when public attitudes toward several of the items mentioned were apparently different than they seem to be in the late 1980s.

Thus, while there are aspects of the Kydland–Prescott and Barro–Gordon analyses that Friedman did not foresee, he clearly recognized that treating cases as a group could lead to different outcomes than if treated separately, and that the bundled outcomes could be preferable because of favorable effects on agents' attitudes and expectations.

12.4   Extensions of the Basic Model

Section 12.3 has argued that discretionary monetary policymaking tends to result in more inflation than would obtain if policy were conducted in a rule-like fashion, and with no compensating reduction in unemployment. That conclusion would clearly be of great interest if it pertained to an actual economy, so it is important to consider its robustness or sensitivity to alterations in the model utilized. That is, we need to know whether the conclusion would continue to be valid if the model of Section 12.2 were modified in various ways.

The first thing to be noted in this regard is that the analysis would be exactly the same if the MA's objective function were

$$z_t = \frac{a}{2}(\Delta m_t - \overline{\Delta m})^2 - b(\Delta m_t - \Delta m_t^e) \tag{7}$$

rather than (4). Thus the analysis does not require that the desired average money growth or inflation rate be zero. Instead, this desired rate could be $\overline{\Delta m}$. If the objective were to keep Δm_t close to $\overline{\Delta m}$ rather than zero, (7) would be a preferable specification—but precisely the same conclusions as before would follow. Readers are asked to work out this point for themselves in Problem 1.

Next we ask, is it necessary for the first term of (7) or (4) to involve the *square* of $\Delta m_t - \overline{\Delta m_t}$? In this case the answer is that what is required is that this term have a derivative with respect to Δm_t that is an increasing function of Δm_t. In other words, the *marginal* cost of extra inflation (or Δm_t) must rise with the magnitude of inflation (or Δm_t).[10] This is not nearly as stringent a condition as requiring that the term involve a square; indeed, it is not an excessively demanding requirement.

Regarding the second term of z_t in (4) or (7), the situation is even more favorable. Specifically, all that is needed for our conclusion to hold is that z_t be a decreasing function of $\Delta m_t - \Delta m_t^e$ in the vicinity of

---

[10] It may be, of course, that this derivative or marginal cost is increasing with respect to Δm_t over some range of Δm_t values and not others. What is needed is that the derivative be increasing in the vicinity of $\Delta m_t = \overline{\Delta m_t}$.

$\Delta m_t - \Delta m_t^e = 0$. In terms of the unemployment rate interpretation, this amounts to the requirement that the monetary authority would welcome a reduction in unemployment, starting from the "natural" unemployment level that would obtain if the current value of the surprise term $\Delta m_t - \Delta m_t^e$ were zero. Given the stated policy objectives of actual national governments, it seems very likely that this condition is met in reality.

One objection that might be made to our formulation of Section 12.2 is that the objective function pertains only to the current period, thereby neglecting the future. But this feature was imposed on the model only for expositional simplicity. In the Barro–Gordon (1983) treatment it is assumed that at time t the policymaker seeks to minimize

$$z_t + \beta z_{t+1} + \beta^2 z_{t+2} + \cdots, \tag{8}$$

where β is a discount factor, with $0 \le \beta < 1$. Those authors show that the argument carries over to cases in which the monetary authority is concerned with the infinite future, as in (8).

In addition, Barro and Gordon (1983) explicitly demonstrated that the argument presented in Section 12.3 does not depend on the absence of random shocks or cyclical fluctuations. In other words, it continues to be true, in a setting that is otherwise similar but includes random disturbances and/or cyclical fluctuations, that with discretion the *average* inflation rate will be higher and the average unemployment rate no lower. The analysis of Section 12.3 pertains to central tendencies, or typical occurrences.

From the foregoing list of admissible modifications, ones that the model can accommodate without alteration of the basic rules versus discretion result, it seems reasonable to conclude that the argument of Section 12.3 is not excessively sensitive to specificational details. The message of that section thus warrants some confidence; it would appear to be applicable to actual economies, at least to some extent.[11]

12.5 Evidence

The argument to this point has, however, been entirely theoretical. It would accordingly be reasonable for the reader to wonder if there is any empirical *evidence* in support of the notion that discretionary monetary policy has an inflationary bias. As it happens, one of the most striking bits of evidence in that regard was discussed in this book's

---

[11] For other useful discussions of the material of Sections 12.1 to 12.4 the reader is referred to Barro (1985) and Cukierman (1986).

introductory chapter. Specifically, Section 1.2 emphasized the difference in the inflationary experience of the United States before and after World War II, a fivefold increase in the price level between 1946 and 1985 being contrasted with a negligible increase from 1776 up to 1940. And it was suggested that this remarkable difference was probably in some way related to the fact that the United States adhered to a commodity-money standard in the earlier period and has not had any such standard in recent years. Now the point of this contrast is that a commodity-money standard is one form of a monetary rule. In particular, it is a rule stating that the money price of the specified commodity—in this case, gold—be kept constant over time. This type of rule requires the monetary authority to manage the money stock in such a way that the specified money price of gold can successfully be maintained.[12]

Thus the fact that the United States had virtually zero inflation on average over the decades in which a monetary rule was in effect, and has by contrast experienced substantial inflation during the discretionary regime of the post–World War II era, is important evidence in favor of the conclusion of Section 12.3. In fact, the inflationary-bias argument is crucial to understanding why it is that the demise of the gold standard has seen *positive* inflation in each decade of the discretionary era. The mere absence of the commodity-money standard would appear to leave the door open for negative inflation—deflation—as much as for positive inflation. But, in fact, positive inflation has occurred regularly, just as predicted by the model of Section 12.2.

Other nations, too, have abandoned commodity-money standards in favor of discretionary monetary policy in the post–World War II period. Consequently, it is relevant to compare their recent inflationary experience with that of the gold standard era. In doing so, it will be better to use only the years before World War I to represent the gold standard era, for most nations except the United States abandoned that standard during World War I.[13] Furthermore, some of those nations that temporarily restored the standard in the 1920s did so at gold prices different from those that had prevailed prior to 1914.

The relevant facts are reported in Tables 12-1 and 12-2. In the former, general wholesale price indices are reported (on a basis of 100 for 1913) for four important European nations in addition to the United States. From these figures it is apparent that there was no inflationary tendency during the period covered: levels were roughly the same in 1913 as a century earlier. The main departure from price-

---

[12] An extensive discussion of the workings of a commodity-money standard is presented in Chapter 13.

[13] Even the United States left the standard briefly in 1917–1919.

Table 12.1. Wholesale Price Indices During the Gold Standard Era[a]

Year	Belgium	Britain	France	Germany	United States
1776		101			84
1793		120		98	100
1800		186	155	135	127
1825		139	126	76	101
1850	83	91	96	71	82
1875	100	121	111	100	80
1900	87	86	85	90	80
1913	100	100	100	100	100

Source: Data from B. R. Mitchell, *European Historical Statistics*, Columbia University Press, New York, 1979; and U.S. Bureau of the Census, *Historical Statistics of the United States, Colonial Times to 1970*, U.S. Government Printing Office, Washington, D.C., 1975.

[a] Indices equal 100 in 1913.

Table 12-2. Consumer Price Indices, Post–World War II

Nation	CPI[a] in 1950	CPI[a] in 1985	Ratio
Belgium	30.1	140.5	4.7
France	15.6	157.9	10.1
Germany	39.2	121.0	3.1
Italy	13.9	190.3	13.7
Netherlands	23.9	122.7	5.2
United Kingdom	13.4	141.5	10.6
United States	29.2	130.5	4.5

Source: International Monetary Fund, *International Financial Statistics* 60 (Yearbook, 1987).

[a] The index is 100 for 1980.

level stability occurred in the period around 1800, when the Napoleonic Wars were being fought. Because of stresses brought on by those wars, Britain temporarily suspended its commodity-money rule from 1797 to 1821, which explains the atypically high price level reported for Britain in 1800. Under the restored discipline of the rule, prices had returned to their pre-1797 values before 1850.

In the era since World War II, by contrast, there has been no effective commodity-money standard in place.[14] The experience of

---

[14] Until 1971 there were vestiges of the gold standard, but these were almost entirely ineffective. A brief description of the Bretton Woods arrangement that prevailed from 1948 until 1971 is provided in Chapter 15.

European countries has generally been similar to that of the United States—price levels have increased several times. Figures for a few important nations are reported in Table 12-2. There it will be seen that between 1950 and 1985 the general price level[15] increased by more than four times in Belgium, France, Italy, the Netherlands, and the United Kingdom. Even Germany, famous for its anti-inflationary policies, has seen its price level triple—which is quite unlike the experience recorded under a commodity-money standard.

Problems

1. Suppose that the monetary authority's objective is to minimize the value of z_t as specified in equation (7). What values for Δm_t would be chosen if choices were made on a period-by-period basis, with Δm_t^e taken as given in each period? What would be the outcome if a single value of Δm_t were chosen to be used over a large number of periods, as with a rule?

2. Attempt to redo the discretionary analysis of Problem 1 with $(\Delta m_t - \Delta m_t^e)$ used in place of $(\Delta m_t - \Delta m_t^e)^2$. What is the source of the difficulty that arises? Would it be overcome if the term were $(\Delta m_t - \Delta m_t^e)^\alpha$ with $\alpha > 1$?

References

Barro, Robert J., "Recent Developments in the Theory of Rules Versus Discretion," *Economic Journal* 95 (Supplement, 1985), 23–37.

Barro, Robert J., and David B. Gordon, "A Positive Theory of Monetary Policy in a Natural-Rate Model," *Journal of Political Economy* 91 (August 1983), 589–610.

Cukierman, Alex, "Central Bank Behavior and Credibility: Some Recent Theoretical Developments," Federal Reserve Bank of St. Louis, *Review* 68 (May 1986), 5–17.

Friedman, Milton, "Should There Be an Independent Monetary Authority?" in *In Search of a Monetary Constitution*, L. B. Yeager, ed. (Cambridge, Mass.: Harvard University Press, 1962).

Kydland, Finn E., and Edward C. Prescott, "Rules Rather Than Discretion: The Inconsistency of Optimal Plans," *Journal of Political Economy* 85 (June 1977), 473–91.

Simons, Henry, "Rules Versus Authorities in Monetary Policy," *Journal of Political Economy* 44 (February 1936), 1–30.

---

[15] Here represented by the consumer price indices of the various nations.

13

The Gold Standard: A Commodity-Money System

13.1 Introduction

In Chapters 1, 2, and 12 we have emphasized various ways in which commodity-money systems, which were widespread in the western hemisphere before World War II, differ in their operating principles and effects from fiat-money arrangements of the type that prevail today. In the present chapter we undertake a more extensive discussion of the workings of a commodity-money system. Since the international Gold Standard of the nineteenth century is the most famous and important of the commodity-money systems that have actually existed, we shall in most of the discussion refer to the commodity that serves as the monetary standard as "gold." The treatment here will be primarily analytical rather than historical, however: the purpose will be to understand how any commodity-money system works in a principle.[1] With this analysis as a backdrop, some actual historical experiences will then be considered in Chapter 15.

It was mentioned briefly in Chapter 2 that the purest form of a

---

[1] The reader interested in alternative analytical discussions is referred to classic treatments by Mill (1848, Bk. III, Chaps. 7–10) and Fisher (1911, Chaps. 6 and 7) and to recent contribution by Niehans (1978, Chap. 8) and Barro (1979). Useful background material, with a historical emphasis, is provided by Bordo (1981).

commodity-money system is one in which the economy's actual circulating medium of exchange is a commodity that would be valuable even if it were not used as money. In such a system the value of money is the price of that commodity relative to goods in general, which is a relative price that will be determined by supply and demand considerations in a manner similar to (though more complex than) that emphasized in standard microeconomic analysis. This pure form of a commodity-money system tends to be replaced in practice, however, by one in which the actual circulating medium of exchange consists partly or entirely of paper (or other token) claims to units of the monetary commodity. This "impure" type of system tends to arise for two reasons. First, it permits a smaller amount of the valuable monetary commodity (e.g., gold) to be devoted to monetary use, and thereby frees more of it for use as an ordinary commodity. Second, under modern conditions the physical management of the medium of exchange can be accomplished more satisfactorily when paper claims, rather than coins (or ungraded masses of gold), are passed from hand to hand.[2]

In the analysis that follows, accordingly, it will be assumed that the actual circulating medium of exchange consists—at least in part—of paper claims to gold. For reasons of familiarity, we shall refer to these paper claims as "dollars." Each paper dollar is then a claim to a certain specified quantity of gold. But since exchanges are conducted using dollars as the circulating medium, we presume that the prices of goods are normally quoted in terms of dollars.[3] Thus the requirement that each dollar constitute a claim to an unchanging quantity of gold may equivalently be expressed as the requirement that the (dollar) price of gold be kept constant. This is one way of describing the central feature of a commodity-money standard—as a requirement that the money price of the standard commodity be kept constant over time.

13.2 Basic Model

Let us begin by developing a simple model of an economy on a gold standard with a circulating medium consisting entirely of paper dollars. The model will initially be formulated for a closed economy but later

---

[2] The advantages of using coins, rather than ungraded masses of a metal, are apparent: standard quantities of convenient sizes can be established and the need for weighing and assaying (i.e., determining purity) can be avoided. But as long as counterfeiting can be prevented, the same advantages can be achieved to a greater extent with paper claims used in place of coins.

[3] As mentioned in Chapter 2, there is a strong tendency for the item that serves as the medium of exchange also to be used as the medium of account.

will be reinterpreted so as to be applicable in a multinational context. The model's notation and specification are to some extent based on those suggested in a useful paper by Barro (1979), but the exposition itself is rather different.

Let P_g denote the dollar price of a unit of gold. This is the price that must, for the gold standard to be maintained, be kept constant over time. It is, therefore, not a variable in our model but instead a fixed parameter—a potential variable that is kept constant by the central bank, by its willingness to buy or sell gold at the price P_g.

The first analytical constituent of the model is a demand function for the medium of exchange (i.e., dollars). Let M denote the quantity of paper dollars and P the price level, the dollar price of a unit of output. Also, let total output be denoted y.[4] Then the demand for dollars will be assumed to be of the form

$$\frac{M}{P} = L(y, \pi), \tag{1}$$

where the function L is increasing in y and decreasing in π, so that $L_1 > 0$ and $L_2 < 0$. Here π denotes the expected inflation rate, that is, the expected rate of change of P. The inflation rate, rather than an interest rate, is used as the opportunity cost of holding dollars as in the Cagan model of Chapter 7. Thus (1) depicts, in a manner with which the reader is by now familiar, a demand function for money that relates real balances demanded to a real transactions variable and to a measure of the opportunity cost of holding money.

Next consider the supply of paper dollars. In this regard it will be helpful to relate the quantity M to the monetary gold reserves that are held by the banking system, including the central bank, so as to be able to maintain the gold price P_g by selling gold to any citizen who wishes to acquire it at that price. Let G_m be the quantity of gold reserves thus held, measured in physical units. For concreteness, let us use "ounces" as our unit of measurement for gold, so that P_g is the dollar price of one ounce of gold and G_m is the number of ounces held as monetary reserves. Then $G_m P_g$ is the dollar value of monetary gold (i.e., gold reserves). Consequently, if we define the symbol λ as

$$\lambda = \frac{G_m P_g}{M}, \tag{2}$$

---

[4] The economy's output may include gold production, so P reflects (but to a small extent) the price of gold. That is, P is an index number in which P_g is accorded a positive but small weight.

λ will be the reserve ratio: the ratio of monetary gold reserves to the stock of (paper) dollars. Central bank policy can then be represented in terms of λ. The central bank can change its own reserve ratio and therefore that of the banking system at large.

In the economy in question, there is a derived demand for monetary gold—a demand "derived from" the demand for dollars to be used as a medium of exchange. In particular, the quantity of monetary gold demanded can be found by solving (2) for $M = G_m P_g / \lambda$ and substituting into (1). That step yields $G_m P_g / \lambda P = L(y, \pi)$, so that

$$G_m = \lambda \frac{P}{P_g} L(y, \pi) \tag{3}$$

is the derived demand function for monetary gold. It represents the demand for a stock, not a flow, of gold.

Gold is also desired for nonmonetary uses such as jewelry, dentistry, and industrial applications. To account for these uses, we assume that the demand for nonmonetary purposes—again a stock demand concept—can be represented by the function

$$G_n = f\left(y, \frac{P_g}{P}, \pi \right) \tag{4}$$

with $f_1 > 0, f_2 < 0$, and $f_3 < 0$. Thus, in a familiar way, the quantity G_n is assumed to be positively related to the economy's output or income and negatively related to its own (i.e., gold's) relative price which, in this case, is P_g/P. The third argument of f is also easy to understand. The idea is that the stock demand for nonmonetary gold is positively related to the expected future rate of change in the relative price P_g/P: if a durable good is going to go up in price, one would like to own more of it now. But P_g is constant over time, so an expected increase in P_g/P is equivalent to an expected fall in P (i.e., a deflation).[5]

The total stock demand for gold is equal to the sum of expressions (3) and (4). At any point in time, then, this sum will be equated to the total stock G of gold existing in the economy. If at some point in time that stock is G^0, the relative price of gold P_g/P will have to satisfy the following equation:

$$\lambda \frac{P}{P_g} L(y, \pi) + f\left(y, \frac{P_g}{P}, \pi \right) = G^0. \tag{5}$$

---

[5] Barro (1979) assumes that nonmonetary gold holdings adjust only gradually toward their "desired" values, with the latter given by an expression like (4). Under that type of assumption, the stock demanded at any point in time would depend not only on the desired stock, but also on the stock held in the recent past. Here we achieve a significant degree of simplification by assuming that stock demand adjustments are complete within each "period."

Of course, the latter is only one part of a complete macroeconomic model. But suppose that we take total output y to be determined, as in the classical model of Chapter 5, by conditions that are largely unaffected by monetary policy. And suppose that we also (as in Chapter 5) take inflationary expectations to be predetermined, in which case π is "given" for the purpose of current price determination. Then, if λ is set by the central bank's policy choice, there will be only one variable included in equation (5), since the stock quantity G^0 is given from a point-in-time perspective. That variable is P, the price level. Consequently, equation (5) can be viewed as a model of point-in-time price-level determination for an economy on a gold standard.

But point-in-time analysis is not the only type of analysis of interest in the context of the gold standard. Also of considerable importance is determination of the manner in which the economy's total stock of gold grows or shrinks as time passes. Thus we must consider *flow* supply and demand relations for gold. Since we are at present discussing a closed economy, flow additions to the stock of gold will take place by new production, that is, extraction from natural deposits by mining and refining operations, or perhaps creation from other basic elements by nuclear fission.[6] The rate at which such additions will be made by competitive producers will of course be positively related to the relative price of the commodity in question, so our model takes the flow supply of gold to be $g(P_g/P)$, where the function g is increasing: $g' > 0$.

Flow subtractions from the stock of gold are in principle of two types. First, gold stocks held for nonmonetary uses will be subject to "depreciation"—unavoidable losses that are roughly proportional in magnitude to G_n. Second, some industrial uses effectively destroy gold by breaking it up into such small pieces that its reassembly would be prohibitively costly. But the rate at which such usage takes place will presumably be related to y, P_g/P, and π in much the same way as with the stock demand: positively dependent on y and negatively dependent on P_g/P and π. Consequently, we are justified in assuming that the total of depreciation and industrial consumption of gold will be proportional to the stock demand. Taking δ as the constant of proportionality, we then obtain $\delta f(y, P_g/P, \pi)$ as our measure of flow subtractions from the existing stock of gold.

Finally, combining new production with flow usage, we see that the rate of change of the total stock G will be representable as follows:

$$\Delta G = g\left(\frac{P_g}{P}\right) - \delta f\left(y, \frac{P_g}{P}, \pi\right). \tag{6}$$

---

[6] Some colleagues have pointed out to me that this last type of production has thus far been quantitatively unimportant.

During any given period, then, the total stock of gold available for monetary and nonmonetary holdings will increase or decrease depending on whether $g(P_g/P)$ is greater or smaller than $\delta f(y, P_g/P, \pi)$.

The two equations (5) and (6) constitute a simple but effective depiction of price-level behavior in an economy with a gold standard. At any point in time, the price level P is determined (since P_g is fixed) by the interaction of stock demand as specified by (5) with the total stock of gold currently existing in the economy. But the relative price P_g/P implied will give rise, via relation (6), to a gradual change in the stock G in existence. Then, as that stock changes, the relative price P_g/P, and hence the price level P, will also change.

This process can be depicted graphically as in Figure 13-1. There the relative price P_g/P is plotted on the vertical axis. This axis applies to both the right-hand and left-hand sides of the diagram, which measure stock and flow magnitudes, respectively. The downward-sloping curve on the right-hand side of Figure 13-1 is a plot of the sum of the two expressions on the left-hand side of equation (5). This curve represents, then, the total stock demand for gold. If the stock in existence is G^0, the current price level will be the value P^0 that is implied by the relative price P_g/P^0 that is determined by the intersection of G^0 and the stock demand function. That, however, is not the end of the story. At the relative price P_g/P^0, the rate of new production $g(P_g/P)$ will, according to the curves shown in Figure 13-1, exceed the flow loss from depreciation and industrial consumption by the amount $g^{s^0} - g^{d^0}$. Consequently, the stock in existence will increase as time passes. After a

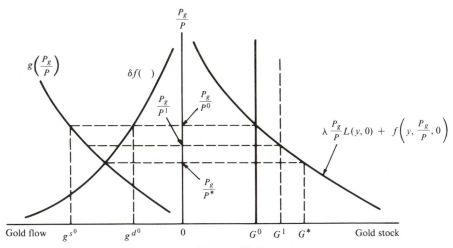

Figure 13-1

few periods the new stock might be G^1, for example.[7] In that case the relative price of gold would be P_g/P^1, implying a price level P^1 that is higher than P^0.

For a situation of full equilibrium, it is required that $g(P_g/P) = \delta f(y, P_g/P, \pi)$, so that the total stock of gold is neither increasing nor decreasing. For the relations drawn in Figure 13-1, that situation will prevail with the relative price P_g/P^*. That price, furthermore, will be attained when the gold stock is G^*, which gives rise to a price level of P^*. In the economy as depicted, therefore, there is a tendency for the gold stock to approach its full equilibrium level G^* as time passes, and for the price level to approach its full equilibrium value P^*.[8]

13.3 Analysis with Basic Model

Having constructed a model pertaining to the monetary aspects of an economy operating under the gold standard, let us now put it to use by analyzing the effects of a few hypothetical changes in conditions. As a first example, consider an increase in the flow supply of new gold—an outward shift in $g(P_g/P)$—that comes about from an improvement in gold refining technology or the discovery of new deposits for mining. Suppose that the initial situation before this shift in $g(P_g/P)$ is one of full equilibrium, indicated in Figure 13-2 by $G = G^0$, $P = P^0$, and $g^s = g^d = g^0$.[9] Then the new supply function would be depicted by the dashed line labeled S^1. Now the point-in-time effect on the price level of the shift in $g(P_g/P)$ is nil, for the stock demand function is unaffected and the passage of some time would be required for any substantial change in G to come about. But at the initial price level P^0, the relative price of gold is such that the flow production of gold will exceed $\delta f(y, P_g/P, \pi)$ after the shift, so the stock of gold will increase from G^0 as time passes. As this happens, the price level will rise until finally a new full equilibrium is attained at the relative price P_g/P^1 with

---

[7] The diagram has not been constructed so that flow magnitudes on the l.h.s. (left-hand side) can be used to infer quantitative changes in stock magnitudes on the r.h.s. The relationships should be interpreted only in qualitative terms: positive $g^s - g^d$ values lead to increases in G, and so on.

[8] A qualification must be added. Since the positions of the stock demand curve and the function $\delta f(y, P_g/P, \pi)$ both depend upon π, a full equilibrium situation will require that those curves be drawn for the value $\pi = 0$. Full equilibrium, that is, requires not only that the price level P be unchanging over time, but also that this zero rate of change be correctly anticipated.

[9] Here, and in the remainder of this section, we assume that $\pi = 0$, that is, that no inflation or deflation is expected. This was probably a fairly good approximation for the years during which the gold standard was in operation and actual inflation was in fact small. We shall, however, study expectational dynamics in Section 13.4.

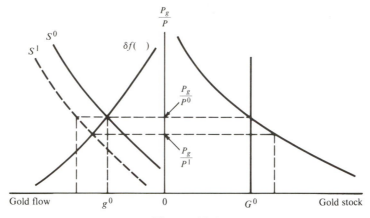

Figure 13-2

$P^1 > P^0$. Thus the increased facility for producing gold lowers its value relative to other commodities, and so lowers the value of money (i.e., raises the price level) in the ultimate equilibrium, although the immediate effects on P and G are negligible.

Next let us consider an entirely different type of change, one involving the central bank's reserve policy. In particular, suppose that the central bank lowers the quantity of gold reserves held in relation to the amount of paper dollars in circulation. This change is represented algebraically by a reduction in the value of λ, say from λ^0 to λ^1. Graphically, this would be depicted, as inspection of equation (5) will readily show, as a downward shift in the stock demand for gold. In Figure 13-3 that shift is indicated by the position of curve D^1 as compared with D^0. In this case, there is an immediate impact on the price level, as the decrease in stock demand entails a lower value of P_g/P for the given existing quantity of gold, G^0. That lower relative price P_g/P^1 amounts to a higher price level, $P^1 > P^0$. So the impact effect of the decreased reserve ratio λ is to raise the price level. But there is no change implied in either the flow supply function $g(P_g/P)$ or the demand for nonmonetary gold, $g^d = f(y, P_g/P, \pi)$, so the lowered relative price induces a situation in which $g^d > g^s$. As time passes, then, the total stock of gold in the economy will fall. Indeed, it will continue to fall until it reaches G^2, at which point $g^d = g^s$. An interesting aspect of this new full equilibrium is that the price level P^2 is the same as the value P^0 that prevailed before the reduction in λ. Thus we see that a change in the central bank's reserve policy has temporary effects on the economy's price level, but no effect on the ultimate equilibrium value of P.

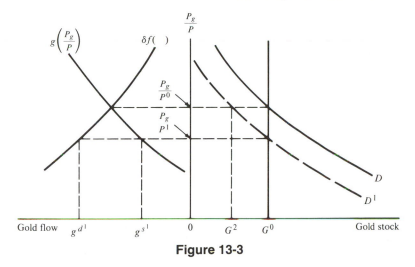

Figure 13-3

From this last result it might appear that an economy could function just as successfully under the gold standard with a reserve ratio of $\lambda = 0.1$ or $\lambda = 0.01$ as with a more conservative figure of, for example, $\lambda = 0.3$. Such a conclusion would not be warranted, however, for the analysis given above simply *assumes* that the monetary standard is successfully maintained. But if a central bank tried to operate with 1 percent reserves (i.e., with $\lambda = 0.01$), it is likely that it would be unable to fulfill its promise to buy and sell gold at the stipulated price P_g in whatever quantities are chosen by private agents. In response to some stochastic shock, then, private agents might choose to hold additional gold to an extent greater than the central bank's entire stock. The bank would be unable to meet this demand and would have to break its promise to buy and sell freely at P_g. While an occasional "suspension of convertibility" of this type might be accepted, frequent occurrences would destroy private agents' belief in the bank's promise and would bring the system to an end. Knowledge that the bank's reserve ratio was low could, moreover, lead to speculative attacks that would themselves tend to promote the breakdown. Thus we see that a successful gold standard operation requires that adequately high gold reserves be held by the banking system.[10]

There are many other exercises that could be conducted with our basic model, but most of these are closely related to the two discussed above. Rather than devoting space to such exercises, let us accordingly

---

[10] This paragraph has been worded as if all the monetary gold were held by the central bank. The reasoning can be extended to the more general case.

conclude this section by considering two extensions to the basic model. The first indicates how the basic model can be modified to become applicable to an open economy—one that engages in foreign trade. In fact, all that is required is a reinterpretation of the flow supply schedule, $g(P_g/P)$, so as to include the propensity of foreigners to trade gold for the nation's goods. When P_g/P rises, the price of "our country's" output becomes lower in terms of gold. So gold holders abroad will be inclined to purchase more of this output than before. Ordinary businessmen abroad will be more inclined to trade their goods to their fellow countrymen in order to acquire gold to make purchases in our country. The tendency for foreigners in these and other categories to purchase our goods with gold—that is, to supply gold on our market at a more rapid pace when P_g/P is higher—is precisely what is specified by the $g(P_g/P)$ schedule. So the analytical framework of Section 13.2 will be applicable to an open economy, provided that the $g(P_g/P)$ function is specified so as to reflect the foreign as well as (or instead of) the domestic flow supply of gold.[11] The first experiment of this section could, therefore, be interpreted as indicating the effects in our country of a gold mining discovery made in another part of the world.

The second extension also involves a reinterpretation. Specifically, although our discussion has been phrased in terms of an economy in which paper dollars are the actual circulating medium of exchange, with gold held as reserves by the banking system, the analysis pertains as well to an economy in which gold coin also circulates. To represent such an economy, all that is needed is to reinterpret λ as the ratio of gold to circulating media (including gold). In this case λ will not be directly under the central bank's control, as when λ refers to the central bank's reserve ratio, but it will still be influenced by central bank actions. As long as private money holders keep a constant fraction of their money in the form of gold, the central bank can raise or lower λ by increasing or decreasing its own reserves. If it lets its own reserves fall too low, however, the system will tend to break down in the same way as mentioned above.

13.4 Dynamic Analysis with Rational Expectations

In Sections 13.2 and 13.3 we have been concerned with comparative static analysis. Here our objective is to extend the gold standard model described above by developing a dynamic version that is capable of

---

[11] Strictly speaking, the value of P_g/P in the foreign country would be a second relevant determinant of gold flows into our country. Changes in that value are here being treated as a shift in the g function.

determining period-to-period movements in the price level and other variables. In dynamic models, as we have seen in previous chapters, expectational effects are usually important. In our present analysis it will be assumed, for reasons familiar from Chapter 8, that agents' expectations are formed rationally.

The difficult task of solving and manipulating a rational expectations model is, as readers may realize, much simpler when that model is linear in the recognized variables (which may be logarithms of "natural" variables). Consequently, we shall formulate our dynamic model of the gold standard in terms of linear equations. To do so requires some notational tricks and an important approximation, so the reader will want to note carefully details of the following setup.

Our model's first equation will describe the demand for monetary gold. In Section 13.2 this demand was specified in equation (3) as

$$G_m = \lambda \frac{P}{P_g} L(y, \pi).$$

In that expression both P_g and y are constants, not variables. Accordingly, they will not be explicitly recognized in what follows, but their value will influence the constant term of our new equation. The same is true, moreover, for the policy-controlled reserve ratio, λ. One genuine variable in (3) is the price level, P. Here we let $p_t = \log P_t$, in a familiar fashion, and use $E_t(p_{t+1} - p_t)$ to represent the expected inflation rate, π. In a notational step that is, by contrast, unorthodox, we denote $m_t = \log G_{mt}$. Thus m_t represents the log of the stock of monetary gold, not the log of the stock of paper dollars. Finally, we add a stochastic disturbance term ε_t and summarize the new version of (3) as

$$m_t - p_t = c_0 + c_1(E_t p_{t+1} - p_t) + \varepsilon_t, \tag{7}$$

where $c_0 > 0$ and $c_1 < 0$. Clearly, this equation is of the same form as a Cagan-style demand for money equation. Here, however, it pertains to the demand for monetary gold. It should be kept in mind that c_0 reflects, among other things, the value of λ. An increase in λ would be represented as an increase in c_0.

Next we consider the stock demand for nonmonetary gold. Above, the relevant function was written as

$$G_n = f\left(y, \frac{P_g}{P}, \pi\right), \qquad f_2 < 0, f_3 < 0$$

in equation (4). Here we adopt the symbol $q_t = \log G_{nt}$ and write

$$q_t = b_0 + b_1 p_t + b_2 E_t(p_{t+1} - p_t) + v_t. \tag{8}$$

By specifying $b_1 > 0$ and $b_2 < 0$, we get the same qualitative effects as in (4). The disturbance term v_t reflects random shocks to nonmonetary gold demand. For simplicity, let us assume that both ε_t and v_t are white noise.

Having specified in (7) and (8) stock demands for monetary and nonmonetary gold, we now need to account for flows. In the model of Section 13.2, these are summarized in (6), which we now repeat:

$$\Delta G = g\left(\frac{P_g}{P}\right) - \delta f\left(y, \frac{P_g}{P}, \pi\right).$$

Here ΔG denotes the change in the total gold stock. For our current system formulated in terms of logarithms, we note that the proportionate change in total gold can be approximated as $\theta \, \Delta m_t + (1 - \theta) \, \Delta q_t$, where θ is the fraction of total gold held in monetary form in full equilibrium.[12] The determinants of that total as indicated on the right-hand side of (6) are the relative price, which we now represent with the variable p_t, and the loss of gold due to depreciation, which we take to be a fraction of q_{t-1}. Accordingly, the counterpart of equation (6) in the present system can be written as

$$\theta \, \Delta m_t + (1 - \theta) \, \Delta q_t = a_0 + a_1 p_t + a_2 q_{t-1},$$

where $a_1 < 0$ and $a_2 < 0$. The latter can clearly be rearranged, moreover, to give

$$\Delta m_t + \psi \Delta q_t = \alpha_0 + \alpha_1 p_t + \alpha_2 q_{t-1},$$

where $\psi = (1 - \theta)/\theta$ and $\alpha_j = a_j/\theta$ for each of the α_j parameters. This equation, finally, can be written as

$$m_t + \psi q_t = \alpha_0 + \alpha_1 p_t + (\alpha_2 + \psi)q_{t-1} + m_{t-1}. \tag{9}$$

Our model consists, then, of equations (7), (8), and (9), which together serve to determine the dynamic evolution of p_t, m_t, and q_t. To obtain a solution, the procedure is to begin (in the manner familiar from Chapter 8) by recognizing the essential "state variables" or determinants of p_t, m_t, and q_t. Inspection of equations (7)–(9) indicates that these include the two lagged variables q_{t-1} and m_{t-1} plus the current

---

[12] This approximation may be derived as follows. First write the identity $\Delta G = \Delta G_m + \Delta G_n$ and then divide by G to get $\Delta G/G = \Delta G_m/G + \Delta G_n/G$. But the latter is equivalent to $(G_m/G) \Delta G_m/G_m + (G_n/G) \Delta G_n/G_n$. Next, by defining $\theta = G_m/G$, we obtain $\Delta G/G = \theta \Delta G_m/G_m + (1 - \theta) \Delta G_n/G_n$. Then the familiar fact that proportionate changes are approximately equal to changes in logarithms—recall Chapter 6—gives the expression $\theta \, \Delta m_t + (1 - \theta) \, \Delta q_t$ as the approximation to $\Delta \log G_t$. It is legitimate to treat θ as a constant, provided that the ratio G_m/G does not vary too much relative to its mean—which is used for θ—over the time periods studied.

shocks ε_t and v_t. Solution equations will then be of the form

$$p_t = \phi_{10} + \phi_{11}q_{t-1} + \phi_{12}m_{t-1} + \phi_{13}\varepsilon_t + \phi_{14}v_t, \tag{10a}$$

$$m_t = \phi_{20} + \phi_{21}q_{t-1} + \phi_{22}m_{t-1} + \phi_{23}\varepsilon_t + \phi_{24}v_t, \tag{10b}$$

$$q_t = \phi_{30} + \phi_{31}q_{t-1} + \phi_{32}m_{t-1} + \phi_{33}\varepsilon_t + \phi_{34}v_t. \tag{10c}$$

To evaluate the unknown ϕ_{ij} coefficients, we note that

$$\begin{aligned}
E_t p_{t+1} &= \phi_{10} + \phi_{11}q_t + \phi_{12}m_t \\
&= \phi_{10} + \phi_{11}(\phi_{30} + \phi_{31}q_{t-1} + \phi_{32}m_{t-1} + \phi_{33}\varepsilon_t + \phi_{34}v_t) \\
&\quad + \phi_{12}(\phi_{20} + \phi_{21}q_{t-1} + \phi_{22}m_{t-1} + \phi_{23}\varepsilon_t + \phi_{24}v_t) \tag{11}
\end{aligned}$$

and substitute (10) and (11) into (7), (8), and (9). Substitution into (7) yields an equation which, to be satisfied for all realizations, implies four conditions relating the ϕ's to the parameter values of the model [i.e., the parameters of (7)–(9)]. The same is true for substitution into (8) and for substitution into (9). Thus 12 conditions are implied, which can in principle be solved for the 12 unknown ϕ_{ij} coefficients.

Unfortunately, in the system at hand the 12 conditions to be solved involve some nonlinear relations. Consequently, a multiplicity of solutions is implied. This situation is like that described in Section 8.7, but in this case the crucial equation involved is a cubic rather than a quadratic equation. That implies that the task of determining which of the three solutions is free of bootstrap effects is quite complex. Accordingly, we shall not continue with the algebraic analysis of this full-fledged gold standard model. Instead, we shall content ourselves with the understanding that we have thus far developed and move on, for explicit analysis, to a simpler system.

The simpler system to be considered is one in which the total stock of gold in the economy is treated as fixed. Thus we ignore the possibility of augmenting or diminishing the economy's stock of gold by production and depreciation. Since the total stock can in practice be changed only slowly, this type of analysis should give some insight into the "short-run" dynamics of price behavior and the allocation of gold between monetary and nonmonetary uses, even though it will not reveal anything about long-run results of the type discussed in Section 13.3.

Formally, the model to be utilized includes the demand functions (7) and (8) but replaces the gold accumulation relation (9) with the following:

$$m_t + \psi q_t = k. \tag{12}$$

Here (12) specifies that the total stock of gold is constant. That fact might be clearer if we wrote $\theta m_t + (1 - \theta)q_t = \text{constant}$, but (12) is simply that equation divided by θ and is clearer to work with.

To analyze price-level behavior in the fixed-stock system (7), (8), and (12), let us begin by substituting (7) and (8) into (12). That step yields

$$p_t + c_0 + c_1(E_t p_{t-1} - p_t) + \varepsilon_t$$
$$+ \psi[b_0 + b_1 p_t + b_2 E_t(p_{t-1} - p_t) + v_t] = k. \tag{13}$$

Here the only relevant state variables are ε_t and v_t, so we conjecture that the bootstrap-free solution is of the form

$$p_t = \phi_0 + \phi_1 \varepsilon_t + \phi_2 v_t. \tag{14}$$

This implies that $E_t p_{t+1} = \phi_0$, so substitution back into (13) yields

$$(1 - c_1)(\phi_0 + \phi_1 \varepsilon_t + \phi_2 v_t) + c_0 + c_1\phi_0 + \varepsilon_t$$
$$+ \psi[b_0 + (b_1 - b_2)(\phi_0 + \phi_1 \varepsilon_t + \phi_2 v_t) + b_2\phi_0 + v_t] = k. \tag{15}$$

The implied conditions on the ϕ's are then

$$\phi_0 + c_0 + \psi b_0 + \psi\phi_0 b_1 = k,$$
$$(1 - c_1)\phi_1 + 1 + \psi(b_1 - b_2)\phi_1 = 0,$$
$$(1 - c_1)\phi_2 + \psi[(b_1 + b_2)\phi_2 + 1] = 0. \tag{16}$$

Solving these, we find that

$$\phi_0 = \frac{k - c_0 - b_0\psi}{1 + b_1\psi},$$

$$\phi_1 = \frac{-1}{1 - c_1 + \psi(b_1 - b_2)},$$

$$\phi_2 = \frac{-\psi}{1 - c_1 + \psi(b_1 - b_2)}. \tag{17}$$

With these values inserted, equation (14) describes the behavior of p_t. Since $b_1 > 0$ and $b_2 < 0$, while ψ is a fraction and $c_1 < 0$, it is clear that ϕ_1 and ϕ_2 are both negative. Thus we see that a positive shock to the demand for monetary gold (i.e., a realization with $\varepsilon_t > 0$) temporarily reduces the price level. Also, a positive v_t value tends to lower p_t. Those conclusions accord with common sense: an increase in the demand for gold raises its value and thereby the value of money, which amounts to a reduction in the price level.

From our solution for p_t, given by (14) and (17), we readily see that the variance of p_t about its mean value, ϕ_0, is

$$V(p_t) = \frac{\sigma_\varepsilon^2 + \psi^2 \sigma_v^2}{[1 - c_1 + \psi(b_1 - b_2)]^2} \tag{18}$$

provided that ε_t and v_t are uncorrelated. From this expression in (18) we can draw conclusions about the effects of different parameter values on the variability of p_t. For example, since the denominator in (18) is increased in magnitude for increased values of b_1, we can see that an increased elasticity of demand for nonmonetary gold (an increased value of b_1) will lead to reduced volatility of the price level for a given severity of shocks (i.e., for given values of σ_ε^2 and σ_v^2). Also, we can see that a change in the reserve ratio λ has no effect (assuming a fixed stock of gold) on $V(p_t)$. Readers are asked in Problem 5 to verify this last conclusion.

Armed with our solution for p_t, we can derive an expression for $E_t(p_{t+1} - p_t)$. Then we can insert these two solution expressions into (7) and (8) to obtain solutions for m_t and q_t. Thus the model can be used to explain dynamic adjustments in the quantities m_t and q_t, that is, to explain the allocation of the fixed stock of gold between monetary and nonmonetary uses.

13.5 Bimetallism

To this point our discussion of commodity-money systems has focused attention on the gold standard. Of course there is nothing in our formal analysis that would imply that the monetary commodity is gold rather than silver, brass, or quartz. But the analysis has implied that there is a *single* monetary commodity for the economy in question. During the centuries in which commodity-money systems held sway, however, there were many experiments with arrangements featuring *two* monetary commodities, typically gold and silver. In this section we shall, accordingly, touch on some of the issues raised by a bimetallic system, that is, one with two standard commodities. Throughout this discussion it will be presumed that coins made of the two metals, as well as paper "dollars," circulate as the economy's medium of exchange.

We begin by describing a basic problem that is inherent to any bimetallic system. Under such a system, the monetary authority is required to maintain the dollar price of both metals—both gold and silver. This it does by standing ready to buy and sell gold and silver at the prescribed "standard" prices. Any citizen is, in other words, free to exchange dollars for gold or vice versa at the dollar price P_g per ounce of gold. And he is also free to exchange dollars for silver, and vice versa, at the price P_s.

Now, for the sake of concreteness in our discussion, let us suppose that $P_g = 20.672$, that is, that the official price of an ounce of gold is \$20.672. Also suppose that the standard price P_s of silver is 1.292 dollars per ounce. Then the monetary authority is required to maintain dollar prices of the two metals that imply a relative price of 16, an ounce of gold being exchangable for 16 times as many dollars as an ounce of silver. But these two metals are valuable as nonmonetary commodities. So what happens if the relative value of gold (in terms of silver) in nonmonetary uses is less than 16? To develop an answer, let us suppose that this relative value is 15.9, which means that there are private businessmen who (because of their industrial needs) are willing to trade an ounce of gold for only 15.9 ounces of silver. Then rational individuals will be unwilling to use silver as money. For if someone had to make a payment of \$129.20, he could do so under the double standard by handing over 10 ounces of silver coin *or* $10/16 = 0.625$ ounces of gold coin. But the silver coin could be traded to the businessman for $10/15.9 = 0.628$ ounces of gold. So rather than paying 10 ounces of silver, the rational individual would first trade the silver for 0.628 ounces of gold, then make his payment with 0.625 ounces of gold and have 0.003 ounces of gold left over. Under such circumstances, that is, rational agents would not use silver to make payments; it would go out of monetary circulation and be transferred to nonmonetary uses.

In the same way, rational individuals would use silver but not gold as money if the relative value of gold in industrial uses were greater than 16. In a bimetallic system, then, only one metal will be used as money unless the official standard price ratio is just equal to the relative value of the metals in nonmonetary uses. But that nonmonetary relative value will naturally fluctuate over time in response to supply conditions and nonmonetary demand conditions for the two metals. So bimetallic systems have a strong tendency to break down, in the sense that only one of the two metals actually circulates as money, with the other being used only for nonmonetary purposes.

This tendency is often referred to by means of an aphorism known as "Gresham's law." The usual way of stating Gresham's law is as an assertion that *bad money drives out good money*. What is meant is that the metal which is relatively less valuable (the "bad money") in nonmonetary uses will drive the relatively more valuable metal ("good money") out of monetary circulation. But note that it is the relative value in nonmonetary uses in comparison with the relative value in monetary uses (given by the ratio of the standard prices) that is relevant. Gresham's law does not say that silver will drive gold out of monetary circulation just because the nonmonetary value of gold is greater. In fact, the situation in the United States between 1834 and 1860 was that of a bimetallic standard with the dollar prices mentioned above. But the industrial value of gold was less than 16 times that of silver, so gold was the "bad" money and it drove silver out of circulation. Only gold and paper (or other token) money actually circulated.

Now that the basic difficulty with a bimetallic standard has been outlined, it needs to be said that the official price ratio for the two metals does not have to be *precisely* "correct" for both metals to remain in circulation. To understand this qualification, suppose that the official gold/silver price ratio is 16, as above, and that the same relative value prevails in nonmonetary usage. Then suppose that non-monetary demand for silver increases slightly, enough to raise the relative value of silver from 1/16 to 1/15.99, given the initial stock of nonmonetary silver. Then silver will be converted from monetary to nonmonetary uses—driven out of circulation—as in the example above. But the resulting increase in the stock supply of silver will tend (given the new demand) to reduce its value. The possibility exists that the value will be driven back down to 1/16 before the entire stock of monetary silver has been converted to nonmonetary use. Thus there is a *range* of relative official prices that will keep both metals in circulation. It is probably a very narrow range—that would depend on various elasticities—but it is not literally a single precise value.[13]

Nevertheless, it remains true that an official bimetallic system is highly likely to degenerate into a *de facto* monometallic system. Why, then, should any sensible society choose to have a bimetallic system? At the level of theoretical principle the answer is that a *smaller* price-level change is required for a given shock to money demand if the system is bimetallic than if it were monometallic. This can be explained informally as follows. Suppose that money demand shifts upward. For given stocks of monetary gold and silver, this will require a fall in the price level, P. But since a fall in P raises both P_g/P and P_s/P, it will reduce nonmonetary demand for both gold and silver, permitting some of the existing stock of each to shift into monetary use. Because there are *two* stocks of metal to draw on in this fashion, it is likely that P will not have to fall as much, to satisfy the increased demand for money, as if there were only one metallic stock. Thus we conclude that ("short-run") price-level fluctuations in response to money demand shifts may

---

[13] Barro (1979) has suggested that although there is a range of suitable values from the perspective of point-in-time or fixed-stock equilibrium, from a long-run (full equilibrium) perspective there is no possibility of maintaining official prices even with unchanging conditions. That conclusion is, however, unwarranted. Barro's analytical result breaks down if agents' nonmonetary demands depend—as they surely do—on wealth, inclusive of gold and silver holdings.

be somewhat muted under bimetallism compared with a monometallic system.

It seems unlikely, however, that this small advantage would compensate for the disadvantage provided by the increased complexity of the system. The force that has probably motivated actual decisions to attempt bimetallic systems is quite different. Almost certainly, the true source of support for bimetallism has been a desire on the part of certain groups of citizens—usually debtors—for a higher price level. The switch from a monometallic to a bimetallic system will almost always result in an increased price level. Why? Well, if the new metal is "bad money," general prices are higher in terms of it than in terms of the old monetary metal. And "bad money drives out good money," so the new equilibrium will be one in which the higher dollar prices prevail. Whereas such a change would be undesirable or a matter of indifference to the rest of the community, it would be welcomed by anyone who is a net debtor in dollar terms.

Before concluding, brief mention should be made of an entirely different type of system involving two monetary metals. This system is known as *symmetallism* because that term was used by its inventor, Alfred Marshall. Marshall's proposal, put forth in an article published in 1887, is that the standard monetary commodity should be a unit consisting of a specified number of ounces of gold *and* silver. Thus, for example, the standard unit might consist of 0.0242 ounces of gold *plus* 0.3870 ounces of silver. And the monetary authority would be required to buy and sell such units (or bundles) at the price of one dollar. It should be clear that this is quite a different system from bimetallism. Detailed analysis of its workings will not be attempted here, but one point can be made as follows. If two goods can be included as part of the standard bundle, then so could three goods, or four goods, or more. Now suppose that the standard bundle consisted of a very large number of commodities in relative magnitudes corresponding to the weights used in calculating the Wholesale Price Index (from individual price movements). Then keeping fixed the dollar price of such a bundle would be equivalent to conducting monetary policy so as to stabilize the Wholesale Price Index! An extreme version of symmetallism, then, would provide stability (i.e., near constancy) to an index that is closely related to an economy's general price level. Recent proposals of alternative schemes of this general type have been put forth by Hall (1982) and by Yeager (1983).[14]

---

[14] For some criticisms of certain aspects of the Hall and Yeager schemes, but not of symmetallism in general, the reader is referred to McCallum (1985).

13.6 Conclusions

The purpose of this chapter has not been to praise or to criticize commodity-money systems, but only to develop an understanding of some analytical principles involved in their operation. To develop a reasoned view concerning the overall desirability of a commodity-money system, one would need both to understand these principles and to have considerable knowledge about the way such systems have actually worked in the past. To provide a start toward such knowledge, some actual historical experiences will be reviewed in Chapter 15.

One more analytical point needs emphasis, however, before we move on. That point concerns the resource cost of maintaining a commodity-money system that stems from the need to hold valuable commodities in monetary form—as circulating coins, possibly, but more likely as reserves. Some quantity of reserves must be held, since the dollar price of the standard commodity will not be maintained unless there is some agent that will sell and buy freely at the official price. The agent—probably the monetary authority—must hold reserves to be able to sell upon request at that price.

An interesting question, then, concerns the magnitude of this resource cost. What fraction of total income would it represent? To attempt a rough answer, let us start by noting that the ratio of M1 to annual GNP in the United States is currently about 0.15. If λ, the ratio of reserves to medium of exchange, were 0.3, the ratio of maintained reserves to annual income would be about 0.045. The opportunity cost of permanently holding commodities in this form, rather than investing them in a productive nonmonetary capacity, would then be 0.045 times the real rate of return on capital. Now suppose that the latter were 0.03 (i.e., 3 percent). Then the cost of maintaining commodity-money reserves, expressed as a fraction of income, would be 0.03 (0.045) = 0.00135. In other words, the resource cost would be 0.135 of 1 percent of total income, under our assumptions regarding λ and the real rate of interest. Higher values for those would imply a higher cost, and lower values would imply a lower cost. But even with substantially higher values, it would appear that the resource cost of a commodity-money system is not very large.

Problems

1. Using the analytical apparatus of Section 13.2, determine the impact and full equilibrium effects on the price level of an improvement in the payments technology of a gold standard economy, that is, a

reduction in the quantity of real money balances needed to facilitate transactions.

2. What would be the effects on the price level of an increase in agents' stock demand for nonmonetary gold?

3. Using the analytical apparatus of Section 13.2, determine whether the relative price of gold to other commodities in an economy depends on whether or not it is used as the monetary standard.

4. Reconsider the policy action analyzed in Figure 13-3. Suppose that, starting from the initial equilibrium, the central bank's action is to put into circulation a quantity of paper money that exceeds $P_g G^0$. Will the final equilibrium price level equal P^0, as it does in Figure 13-3? [For a classic analysis, see Mill (1848), Book III, Chapter XIII.]

5. In Section 13.4 it is stated that the reserve ratio λ has no influence on the variance of p_t in the dynamic model expressed by equations (7), (8), and (12). How can that statement be established from the equations developed in Section 13.4?

References

Barro, Robert J., "Money and the Price Level Under the Gold Standard," *Economic Journal* 89 (March 1979), 13–34.

Bordo, Michael D., "The Classical Gold Standard: Some Lessons for Today," Federal Reserve Bank of St. Louis, *Monthly Review* (May 1981), 2–17.

Fisher, Irving, *The Purchasing Power of Money*. (New York: Macmillan Publishing Company, 1911).

Hall, Robert E., "Explorations in the Gold Standard and Related Policies for Stabilizing the Dollar," in *Inflation: Causes and Effects*, R. E. Hall, ed. (Chicago: University of Chicago Press, 1982).

Marshall, Alfred, "Remedies for Fluctuations of General Prices," *Contemporary Review* 51 (March 1887), 355–75.

McCallum, Bennett T., "Bank Deregulation, Accounting Systems of Exchange, and the Unit of Account: A Critical Review," *Carnegie–Rochester Conference Series on Public Policy* 23 (Autumn 1985), 13–45.

Mill, John Stuart, *Principles of Political Economy*. (London: John W. Parker, 1848).

Niehans, Jürg, *The Theory of Money*. (Baltimore: The Johns Hopkins University Press, 1978).

Yeager, Leland B., "Stable Money and Free-Market Currencies," *Cato Journal* 3 (Spring 1983), 305–26.

14

Open-Economy
Monetary Analysis

14.1 Introduction

Up to this point our discussion has almost completely ignored interactions of the economy under study with the rest of the world. In reality, however, considerations involving international trade and finance are of great importance in the design of monetary policy. Even for the United States, which has traditionally been one of the most nearly closed (i.e., self-contained) of the major economies, balance-of-payments and exchange-rate ramifications have come to play a prominent part in policy deliberations. As a result, macroeconomists have become increasingly aware of the need to understand and take account of these open-economy influences, especially in policy-related empirical work.

In the present chapter, accordingly, we shall be concerned with the essential aspects of open-economy monetary analysis. In particular, we develop in Section 14.2 a rational expectations model of an open economy which has monetary arrangements that involve a market-determined or "floating" exchange rate. Properties of this model are explored in Section 14.3, while Section 14.4 is devoted to modifications that enhance its reality in certain respects. In Section 14.5 we alter the framework of Section 14.2 so as to be applicable to a monetary regime that involves a "fixed" exchange rate—that is, one pegged by policy interventions. Then in Section 14.6 we shall be concerned with basic balance-of-payments concepts and some special features of the official U.S. accounts. Finally, in Section 14.7 we provide a brief comparison of some aspects of fixed and floating exchange-rate systems.

Throughout this discussion it will be presumed that the "home" country—the one on which we focus—and its trading partners all have their own independent fiat-money systems. In each nation, that is, there is a paper currency (issued by the monetary authority) that circulates as the nation's principal medium of exchange for internal transactions. These currencies are denominated in different units, such as pounds, yen, marks, and so on, with "dollars" being the currency unit of the home economy. It is assumed, furthermore, that residents of the home economy have no use for foreign currencies in conducting their day-to-day business transactions and thus do not hold significant amounts. Similarly, we assume that foreign residents do not hold dollars. Accordingly, when an importing firm in the home economy wishes to purchase some item from a producer in another country, it must first purchase enough of that other nation's currency to make payment to the exporting firm in the latter's own currency. Thus the home country importer must exchange dollars for whichever currency is needed—yen, guilder, pounds, or whatever—on the foreign exchange market.[1] The price of one currency in terms of another is termed an *exchange rate*. Any such price can clearly be expressed in two ways: as the dollar price of a yen, for example, or as the yen price of a dollar. In this chapter the convention will be that exchange rates are expressed in terms of home-country prices. Thus the home-country–West German exchange rate will be reported as the dollar price of 1 mark.

Furthermore, as our object is to develop an aggregative macroeconomic model of an open economy, we shall invariably work with an *average* exchange rate, that is, an index reflecting the dollar price of a representative bundle of foreign currencies. Terminologically, we shall refer to this average as "the" exchange rate for our home country, just as we refer to the money price of a representative bundle of commodities as "the" price level within a nation.

Operationally, an average exchange rate of this type is computed for the United States by the Fed. What the Fed reports, to be more precise, is a weighted-average exchange value of the U.S. dollar relative to the currencies of 10 important nations, with weights based on the nations' respective volume of international trade. Since the measure reflects the foreign value of the dollar, it corresponds to the inverse of our measure of the U.S. exchange rate (i.e., the dollar price of foreign currencies). A plot of the Fed's index for the period 1947–

---

[1] In reality these markets—which consist of numerous banks and speciality dealers all linked by powerful telecommunications systems—exist in New York, London, Zurich, Tokyo, and other financial centers. The various centers also maintain telecommunications links with each other, so the market for foreign exchange is essentially a worldwide entity.

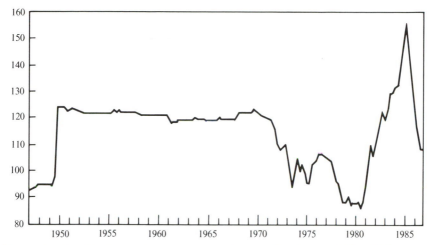

Figure 14-1 Foreign exchange value of the U.S. dollar, 1947–1986 (Index equals 100 in March 1973).

1986 is shown in Figure 14-1.[2] There one can see the major impact of the United Kingdom's devaluation of the pound in 1949 and observe the relative constancy of the exchange rate that prevailed otherwise up until 1971. Then in late 1971 the United States stopped its intervention to maintain the value of the dollar, and the latter effectively began to float relative to other currencies. After reaching a trough in 1980, the value of the dollar rose sharply through the years 1981–1984 and then began a dramatic decline in 1985. That greater variability obtains when the exchange rate is free to float is not surprising, although the extent of the difference shown in Figure 14-1 may be to some viewers. Whether this variability is undesirable is a difficult issue, which we touch on in Section 14.6.

14.2 Basic Open-Economy Model

We are now prepared to begin with the main task of this chapter, which is the construction of a dynamic, rational expectations model that is applicable to an open economy with a floating exchange rate. Our basic structure will be one that corresponds to the classical framework of Chapters 6 to 8, but extended so as to take account of trade and financial interactions with other nations. The first step in constructing

---

[2] Actually, the Fed's series dates back only to 1967. Earlier values were roughly estimated by the author.

the model is to consider the specification of a relationship that corresponds to the *IS* function of Chapter 5, that is, a relation that summarizes the interaction of saving and investment decisions. It will be recalled that our derivation of the *IS* function began with the national product identity for a closed economy, which we here write as $Y = C + I + G$.[3] With foreign trade recognized, the appropriate modification of that identity adds net exports, X, to the right-hand side:

$$Y = C + I + G + X. \tag{1}$$

Thus, to the extent that net exports are positive (i.e., exports exceed imports) domestic production must be greater than domestic "absorption" of goods for consumption, investment, and government purposes. Previously we have specified that private demands for C and I depend on the level of disposable income and the real interest rate, that is, that $C = \tilde{C}(Y, r)$ and $I = \tilde{I}(Y, r)$.[4] With respect to net exports, we now hypothesize that the magnitude of X will depend negatively on the price of export goods relative to import goods, denoted Q, and negatively on the level of domestic real income relative to incomes abroad, Y^*.

Specifically, we assume that

$$X = \tilde{X}\left(Q, \frac{Y}{Y^*}\right), \tag{2}$$

with the partial derivatives $\tilde{X}_1$ and $\tilde{X}_2$ both negative. Then, substituting into (1), we obtain a relation of the form

$$Y = \tilde{C}(Y, r) + \tilde{I}(Y, r) + G + \tilde{X}\left(Q, \frac{Y}{Y^*}\right), \tag{3}$$

which can in principle be solved for Y as a function of the remaining variables:

$$Y = D(r, Q, Y^*, G). \tag{4}$$

Comparison with equation (6) of Chapter 5 readily reveals the difference between closed-economy and open-economy versions of the *IS* function: the latter includes the relative price of domestic to imported goods and the level of real incomes abroad. Under standard assump-

---

[3] Here, in contrast with Chapter 5, we use uppercase letters to denote the following *real* variables: Y = production (income), C = consumption, I = investment, and G = government purchases. This leaves us notationally free to use lowercase versions of the same letters as logarithms of the corresponding variables.

[4] Here $\tilde{C}$ and $\tilde{I}$ are the names of functions that specify the dependence of C and I on the determinants Y and r. A similar notational convention is also used for X and $\tilde{X}$ in equation (2). For simplicity, we neglect any impact of taxes on disposable income.

tions the signs of the partial derivatives are as follows: $D_1 < 0, D_2 < 0,$ $D_3 > 0,$ and $D_4 > 0.$

Next, we need to formulate a version of equation (4) that will be usable in a dynamic model with rational expectations. Accordingly, we shall adopt a relationship that provides the best approximation possible within the class of relations that are *linear* in the relevant variables. To keep the number of variables as small as possible, we shall not express Y^* and G explicitly but shall include their influence as part of a stochastic disturbance term. Then, defining $y_t = \log Y_t$ and $q_t = \log Q_t,$ we write

$$y_t = b_0 + b_1 r_t + b_2 q_t + v_t.$$

Here $b_1 < 0$ and $b_2 < 0$, while the disturbance v_t reflects random movements in government spending and foreign income, as well as shocks to the home-country's saving and investment behavior.

Next it will be convenient to express r_t and q_t in terms of constituent variables. In the case of the former we have the familiar decomposition

$$r_t = R_t - E_t(p_{t+1} - p_t), \tag{6}$$

where R_t is the domestic nominal interest rate and $E_t(p_{t+1} - p_t)$ is the rate of inflation expected to occur between periods t and $t + 1$. In particular, p_t is the log of the domestic money price of domestic goods while $E_t p_{t+1}$ denotes, as in previous chapters, the rational expectation of p_{t+1} conditional upon information available in period t. That information, moreover, will typically be assumed to include all relevant variables dated t and earlier.

Turning to Q, the relative price of domestic goods, we begin by recognizing that imported goods will (since they are produced abroad) be priced by their producers in terms of their own national currencies. Suppose that P^* is the (average) price of imports in terms of those currencies. Then to express that price in terms of dollars, so as to be comparable with the dollar price of domestic goods, we must multiply P^* by the prevailing exchange rate as defined above (i.e., the dollar price of foreign currencies). Let us very briefly use E to refer to the exchange rate. Then the relative price of domestic to import goods will be expressed as $Q = P/P^*E.$[5] But as our model is being formulated in terms of the logarithms of those variables, the relevant expression for period t will be written as

$$q_t = p_t - (e_t + p_t^*), \tag{7}$$

where e_t is the log of the home-country's exchange rate and $p_t^* = \log P_t^*$. Now for the remainder of this chapter we shall typically use the

---

[5] Here we are abstracting from transportation costs.

logarithmic measure e_t to refer to the exchange rate in the context of algebraic expressions. That practice will leave us free to use the symbol E to designate expectations, as mentioned above.

Next we turn to the LM relationship specifying the behavior of money demanders in the home economy. In this regard our strategy will be to neglect certain complications implied by the open-economy setting and use again the log-linear relation familiar from Chapters 7 and 11, namely,

$$m_t - p_t = c_0 + c_1 y_t + c_2 R_t + \varepsilon_t, \qquad c_1 > 0, \quad c_2 < 0. \qquad (8)$$

Here, as before, m_t denotes the log of the (domestic) money stock, with the latter treated for the present as determined by the central bank or monetary authority. The complications that are being neglected are two in number. First, real money balances are here defined by deflating nominal money holdings by the price of domestic goods. This constitutes a shortcut, since it would be more appropriate to deflate by a price index that also takes account of imported goods that are domestically consumed. That inclusion would complicate the model, however, without strongly altering its properties. Use of p_t will be approximately correct, anyhow, if imported goods account for only a small fraction of expenditures. Second, the variable representing the volume of transactions should arguably reflect domestic expenditures $C + I + G$ rather than output $(C + I + G + X)$. But neither measure is literally correct,[6] and again it is likely that any error involved would be quite minor. Consequently, we use the familiar relation (8) in what follows.

The final component of our model involves the relationship between home-country and foreign interest rates, R_t and R_t^*. In this regard our assumption is that domestic and foreign securities are close substitutes—that lenders (i.e., bond purchasers) are nearly indifferent concerning the nationality of borrowers (bond sellers) and care only about the yields that will be received. Now this indifference does not imply that R_t and R_t^* will be equal, because domestic and foreign securities are denominated in different currencies. Also, the exchange rate expressing the relative value of these currencies can change between the time at which the loan is made (the bond is purchased) and the time at which it is repaid (the bond is redeemed). If the value of the foreign currency increases by 2 percent relative to the value of domestic currency over the time of the loan, for example, the effective (nominal) interest rate to a home-country resident lending abroad would be enhanced by two percentage points (or by 0.02 in fractional terms). Thus

---

[6] Both Y and $C + I + G$ are value-added measures that net out intermediate transactions. Such transactions are, however, quite relevant to the determination of money demand.

if such an appreciation in the value of foreign currency (i.e., a depreciation in the value of domestic currency) were expected, then a lender
would be indifferent between a foreign bond yielding R_t^* and a domestic bond yielding $R_t^* + 0.02$.

Generalizing the foregoing line of reasoning, our assumption is that
the behavior of lenders and borrowers in the international economy is
such that interest rates satisfy the following *interest–parity* relationship:

$$R_t = R_t^* + E_t(e_{t+1} - e_t). \tag{9}$$

In words, the domestic interest rate equals the foreign interest rate plus
the expected change in the log of the exchange rate.[7] If this relation did
not hold, the expected yield to domestic residents would be different on
domestic and foreign securities. Investors would then shift their funds
toward the source of the higher expected yield until the equality was
restored. Equation (9), therefore, will be utilized as one of the basic
relationships in our model.[8]

In our analysis, furthermore, it will be assumed that R_t^* is exogenous.
In other words, the (home) economy being studied is small enough in
relation to the entire international economy that its behavior has a
negligible impact on interest rates in the rest of the world. It could be
argued that in reality such would not be true for the United States. But
the assumption should certainly be appropriate for studying any other
nation and should not be seriously misleading even for the United
States. In any event, it must be emphasized that the assumption does
not imply that current-period values of R_t are dictated by external
conditions in a dynamic setting, for R_t and e_t are both variables that are
determined endogenously in our model.[9]

14.3 Properties of the Model

The model that we have specified in Section 14.2 is made up of equations (5)–(9). For the present we assume that the economy under
consideration is of the classical type, with flexible prices and wages, so

---

[7] Since e_t is the logarithm of the exchange rate, $e_{t+1} - e_t$ reflects the percentage
change (in fractional units) between periods t and $t + 1$.
[8] That (9) does in fact conform reasonably well with actual experience is shown by
results reported by Mussa (1979). It should be mentioned, incidentally, that the analysis
that follows would not be appreciably altered if a constant term, reflecting a risk
differential for home-country relative to foreign currencies, were included in (9). Thus
our implicit assumption is not that home and foreign currencies are subject to equivalent
risks of whatever type is relevant, but only that the risk differential is constant over time.
[9] With international monetary arrangements that maintained *fixed* exchange rates, as
considered in Section 14.5, R_t would be dictated by foreign conditions.

that output y_t is determined exogenously; thus we have $y_t = \bar{y}_t$, where $\bar{y}_t$ is the value that corresponds to labor-market clearing. Then with m_t, p_t^*, and R_t^* also determined exogenously, the five equations of the model have the task of explaining movements over time in the five variables p_t, R_t, r_t, q_t, and e_t. But while all five of these endogenous variables are of interest, analysis will be easier to conduct if we eliminate some of them by means of straightforward substitution. In particular, (6) and (7) can be inserted into (5) to express the IS relation in terms of price variables as follows:

$$\bar{y}_t = b_0 + b_1[R_t - E_t(p_{t+1} - p_t)] + b_2[p_t - e_t - p_t^*] + v_t. \quad (10)$$

In addition, the interest–parity relation (9) can be used in (10) and also in the LM function (8) to eliminate R_t from both. Those steps lead to the following pair of equations:

$$\bar{y}_t = b_0 + b_1[R_t^* + E_t(e_{t+1} - e_t) - E_t(p_{t+1} - p_t)] \quad (11)$$
$$+ b_2[p_t - e_t - p_t^*] + v_t,$$

$$m_t - p_t = c_0 + c_1\bar{y}_t + c_2[R_t^* + E_t(e_{t+1} - e_t)] + \varepsilon_t. \quad (12)$$

At a glance these may still appear somewhat complicated, but it must be kept in mind that $\bar{y}_t$ is given from outside the model, that p_t^* and R_t^* are exogenous to the economy under study, and that m_t is determined by the monetary policy authority. Thus the only endogenous variables appearing in the system (11) and (12) are p_t and e_t. We have developed, then, a highly compact model for the dynamic analysis of exchange rate and price-level behavior in an open economy. With movements of those two variables determined, one can then go back to equations (6), (7), and (9) to easily derive implications for q_t, R_t, and r_t.

  In discussing the properties of our model, it will be helpful to consider separately the responses of p_t and e_t to *anticipated* movements in the exogenous variables, on the one hand, and responses to random shocks, on the other hand. Let us begin the former type of investigation by suppressing the disturbance terms and considering steady-state behavior of the system. More specifically, for the moment we assume that $v_t = 0$ and $\varepsilon_t = 0$ for all t, while the domestic money stock grows at a constant rate $\Delta m_t = \mu$, output is constant ($\Delta \bar{y}_t = 0$), and foreign inflation proceeds at the constant rate $\Delta p_t^* = \mu^*$. The latter condition suggests, moreover, that R_t^* would remain constant at $R^* = r^* + \mu^*$. Finally, the steady-state requirement implies that expectations will be correct, in other words, that $E_t(e_{t+1} - e_t) = e_{t+1} - e_t$.

  Under the specified conditions, the model (11) and (12) can be first-differenced and written as follows:

$$0 = b_1[0 - 0] + b_2(\Delta p - \Delta e - \mu^*),\tag{13}$$

$$\mu - \Delta p = c_2(0).\tag{14}$$

Here, the zeros appear for changes in expected growth rates because of the steady-state restriction. As a consequence of these zeros, the results are very easy to comprehend. First, from (14) we see that the domestic inflation rate equals the rate of growth of the domestic money stock—an equality that would be modified, as explained in Chapter 6, if output were growing at a positive rate. Second, from (13) we see that $\Delta p - \Delta e - \mu^* = 0$. But with $\Delta p = \mu$, this implies that $\Delta e = \mu - \mu^*$. The rate of change of the exchange rate, in other words, equals the difference between money growth rates at home and abroad. If domestic money is growing faster ($\mu > \mu^*$), then Δe will be positive. In that case the domestic price of foreign currency will be rising through time, or, in other words, the dollar's value will be depreciating. Finally, since $q_t = p_t - e_t - p_t^*$, the last result implies that $\Delta q = 0$; that is, the relative price of imports (in domestic currency) will be constant through time in the steady state. In sum, we see that the model's steady-state behavior conforms to the sort of "classical" characteristics that one would expect from a system with flexible prices.

These characteristics are often represented in the form of a theory of exchange-rate movements that stems from some ideas known as the "purchasing power parity" doctrine, abbreviated PPP. This theory emphasizes the effect of relative inflation rates, as summarized in the relationship $\Delta e = \Delta p - \Delta p^*$. The latter obtains in the steady-state version of the model at hand, since it assumes that output growth rates are zero both at home and abroad (implying that $\Delta p = \mu$ and $\Delta p^* = \mu$). In fact, actual exchange rates do not conform at all closely to the relation $\Delta e_t = \Delta p_t - \Delta p_t^*$ in quarterly or annual data series, and do not conform very well even over periods of several years. This failure occurs because of various phenomena, including autonomous changes in real variables, some of which are discussed in Section 14.4. But the PPP doctrine can usefully be interpreted not as a complete theory of exchange-rate movements, but rather as a monetary *neutrality* proposition in the open-economy setting. The prediction of the PPP doctrine, under that interpretation, is that an expansion in the home country's money stock will (other things equal) ultimately bring about a proportionate increase in the price level and the exchange rate, leaving unchanged real variables including Q. Under this interpretation, the significance of changes in real conditions for e_t is recognized and emphasis is placed on ultimate (rather than impact) effects of monetary policy actions.

We now turn to the second type of experiment mentioned above, one concerned with the effects of random shocks. Since the previous investigation has given us some idea about the effects of anticipated growth in the exogenous variables, let us keep matters as simple as possible by specifying that p_t^*, R_t^*, and m_t do not change over time but are constant: $p_t^* = p^*$, $R_t^* = R^*$, and $m_t = m$. Then with the shocks restored, the system (11) and (12) can be written as

$$B = b_1[E_t(e_{t+1} - e_t) - E_t(p_{t+1} - p_t)] + b_2[p_t - e_t] + v_t, \quad (11')$$

$$-p_t = C + c_2(E_t e_{t+1} - e_t) + \varepsilon_t. \quad (12')$$

Here we have combined all the unchanging variables and parameters into the composite constants B and C.[10]

To solve the model (11') and (12'), we have to specify the nature of the stochastic processes generating v_t and ε_t. For simplicity, let us for the moment take these processes to be white noise. Thus we assume that v_t and ε_t are serially uncorrelated random variables with variances σ_v^2 and σ_ε^2. In addition, we assume that these two stochastic processes are independent, so that v_t and ε_t are uncorrelated.

With these assumptions, the only relevant state variables in the system (11') and (12') are the current values of u_t and ε_t, so we guess that solutions for p_t and e_t are of the form

$$p_t = \phi_{10} + \phi_{11}v_t + \phi_{12}\varepsilon_t, \quad (15)$$

$$e_t = \phi_{20} + \phi_{21}v_t + \phi_{22}\varepsilon_t. \quad (16)$$

Those relations imply that $E_t p_{t+1} = \phi_{10}$ and $E_t e_{t+1} = \phi_{20}$, so substitution into (11') and (12') yields the following pair of equations:[11]

$$B = b_1[-\phi_{21}v_t - \phi_{22}\varepsilon_t + \phi_{11}v_t + \phi_{12}\varepsilon_t]$$
$$+ b_2[\phi_{10} + \phi_{11}v_t + \phi_{12}\varepsilon_t - \phi_{20} - \phi_{22}\varepsilon_t] + v_t, \quad (17)$$

$$-(\phi_{10} + \phi_{11}v_t + \phi_{12}\varepsilon_t) = C + c_2(-\phi_{21}v_t - \phi_{22}\varepsilon_t) + \varepsilon_t. \quad (18)$$

Since these must hold for all possible values of v_t and ε_t, we can use each of them to derive three identities pertaining to the coefficients attached to v_t, ε_t, and 1. That will give us six equations to solve for the undetermined coefficients ϕ_{10}, ϕ_{11}, ϕ_{12}, ϕ_{20}, ϕ_{21}, and ϕ_{22}. For brevity, however, we will ignore the constant terms ϕ_{10} and ϕ_{20}, and thus need to write out only the identities implied by v_t and ε_t. For (17)

---

[10] Problem 1 at the end of this chapter asks you to derive the correct expressions for B and C.

[11] It should be noted that the solution procedure being utilized is a natural extension, designed to handle two endogenous variables at once, of the one developed in Chapter 8. It is easiest to handle the two variables at once in the present model because both $E_t p_{t+1}$ and $E_t e_{t+1}$ appear in equation (11').

they are

$$0 = b_1(-\phi_{21} + \phi_{11}) + b_2(\phi_{11} - \phi_{21}) + 1, \tag{19a}$$

$$0 = b_1(-\phi_{22} + \phi_{12}) + b_2(\phi_{12} - \phi_{22}), \tag{19b}$$

and for (18)

$$-\phi_{11} = -c_2\phi_{21}, \tag{20a}$$

$$-\phi_{12} = -c_2\phi_{22} + 1. \tag{20b}$$

These four equations can readily be solved to give $\phi_{11} = c_2/(1 - c_2) \times (b_1 + b_2)$, $\phi_{12} = 1/(c_2 - 1)$, $\phi_{21} = 1/(1 - c_2)(b_1 + b_2)$, and $\phi_{22} = 1/(c_2 - 1)$. From the specified signs of the parameters in (11) and (12), it can be inferred that ϕ_{11} is positive while ϕ_{12}, ϕ_{21}, and ϕ_{22} are all negative.

From those last conclusions we can determine how p_t and e_t will respond to shocks of either type. Thus as ϕ_{12} and ϕ_{22} are both negative, it follows that a positive value of ε_t will lower both p_t and e_t. Thus a greater desire for domestic residents to hold money drives up its value, that is, drives down the price level and the price of foreign currency. It should be noted, for subsequent use, that a positive ε_t could alternatively be interpreted as a negative shock to the money supply. Thus, if we had written $m_t = m - \varepsilon_t$ and left the shock off the demand function itself, equation (12) would have resulted just the same. So the foregoing responses can be interpreted as price level and exchange rate declines occurring in reaction to an unexpected decrease in the stock of money.

A positive value of v_t—a positive shock to the *IS* relation—will by contrast reduce the value of e_t but raise p_t, since $\phi_{22} < 0$ and $\phi_{11} > 0$. That these movements also conform to one's intuition can be seen as follows. Since a positive v_t represents a temporarily enhanced demand for home-country output, such a value will tend to raise the money price of that output (with an unchanged money supply) and lower the value of foreign currency. The effect on the relative price q_t can easily be found, moreover, from the definition in (7) (i.e., $q_t = p_t - e_t - p_t^*$). With p_t^* fixed by assumption, the per-unit response of q_t to a positive v_t shock is given by $(\phi_{11} - \phi_{21})$, which in the case at hand equals

$$\phi_{11} - \phi_{21} = \frac{c_2}{(1 - c_2)(b_1 + b_2)} - \frac{1}{(1 - c_2)(b_1 + b_2)} = \frac{-1}{b_1 + b_2}.$$

Since $b_1 + b_2 < 0$, this composite coefficient is positive. Thus we see that a positive shock to the demand for domestic goods raises their relative price—just as one would expect. But since $\phi_{12} - \phi_{22} = 0$, the effect on q_t of a positive ε_t shock is zero. That reflects a form of monetary "neutrality" in the present classical framework.

14.4   Extensions

Unfortunately, there are some important ways in which the properties of the model that we have just developed fail to correspond to actual experience with a floating exchange rate. In particular, three notable features of the post-1971 data that are not matched by our model are as follows:

  (i) The purely random component of exchange rate fluctuations is much greater than for national price levels.
 (ii) Exchange rates respond more promptly to shocks than do national price levels.
(iii) Relative prices of imported goods exhibit a great deal of persistence in their fluctuations.

In our model, by contrast, the value of the ϕ_{ij} applicable in (15) and (16) imply that the random component of p_t will exceed that for e_t unless $|c_2| \leq 1.0$,[12] that both variables respond fully to shocks within the period in which they occur, and that q_t fluctuates randomly about a constant mean.

That features (i) and (iii) pertain in the actual U.S. data can easily be documented. One way to do so for the former is to estimate time-series models in which p_t and e_t are related to past values of observable variables and then compare the variability of the portions of the fluctuations that are *not* explained by these statistical models. Doing so with U.S. quarterly data for 1971.3–1986.3, one finds that the standard deviation of the unexplained portion is almost 10 times as large for e_t as for p_t.[13] As for item (iii), one measure of the relative price q_t is plotted in Figure 14-2.[14] There it will be seen that the value does not fluctuate randomly from quarter to quarter about a constant value or even a smooth trend. Instead, there are periods of several years' length during which q_t remains significantly above or below "normal."[15] With regard to feature (ii), documentation is more difficult to develop and so will not be presented here. Many writers (e.g., Dornbusch, 1976) take the

---

[12] That the "long-run" value of $|c_2|$ is probably much greater than 1.0 is implied by most estimates of money demand functions. One way of reaching this conclusion is described by Flood (1981, pp. 234–35).

[13] Second-order autoregressions in the first differences Δp_t and Δe_t yield standard-error values of 0.0043 and 0.0364, respectively. These numbers are not strongly altered by use of more complex ARIMA models or vector-autoregression systems.

[14] The measure plotted involves the ratio of the U.S. GNP price deflator to the deflator for imported goods and services (with values for 1980 equal to 100). The log of this ratio is shown in Figure 14-2.

[15] Only the floating-rate period should be considered when reaching this conclusion, since the properties of a floating-rate model are under discussion.

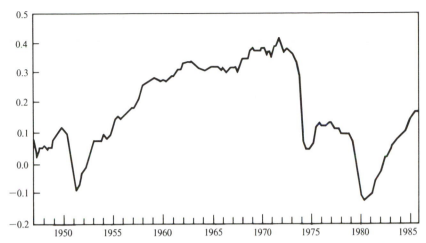

Figure 14-2 Log of U.S. price ratio for produced to imported goods and services, 1947–1985.

validity of item (ii) to be so obvious as to require no documentation. Careful though nonconclusive arguments are presented by Mussa (1986) and Meese (1984).

The question that naturally arises, then, is how the model of Section 14.2 needs to be modified to overcome these three weaknesses. Much recent research has been devoted to this difficult question; here we shall briefly describe two lines of attack that have attracted substantial support from experts in the field.[16]

The first line of work, described in nontechnical terms by Stockman (1987), emphasizes the importance of real shocks to technology or preferences, shocks that have the effect of altering the full equilibrium value of relative prices—in our model, of q_t. Such shocks are viewed, moreover, as being essentially *permanent* in their effects. As was mentioned in connection with shocks to normal output discussed in Section 10.3, it seems unlikely that the effects of a technological innovation (or a taste change) would be reversed after a single period; instead, they would be quite long lasting. In terms of the model (11) and (12), this hypothesis can be represented by specifying that the stochastic process generating v_t is of the random walk type rather than white noise. Thus the suggestion is that the *IS* disturbance v_t—which can be interpreted as representing real shocks to domestic and foreign production

---

[16] A fairly terse and wide-ranging analysis that is similar in spirit to ours is provided by Flood (1981).

conditions, as well as domestic tastes—should be specified as follows:

$$v_t = v_{t-1} + \xi_t. \tag{21}$$

Here ξ_t is purely random white noise; the expected value $E_t v_{t+1}$ is not zero but rather v_t. Thus $E_t(v_{t+1} - v_t) = 0$.

In our revised specification, it will be useful to make the LM equation's disturbance ε_t also conform to the random-walk assumption. In this regard, it is plausible to argue that taste or payments-technology shocks that affect the demand for money are long lasting, or alternatively that random components of the money supply process pertain to growth rates rather than levels. In either case, it is appropriate to assume that ε_t is generated according to

$$\varepsilon_t = \varepsilon_{t-1} + \zeta_t, \tag{22}$$

where ζ_t is white noise.

Let us now solve the model (11′) and (12′) with the revised stochastic specifications (21) and (22). It is still possible to use (15) and (16) to represent the solutions,[17] but now we have $E_t(p_{t+1} - p_t) = 0$ and $E_t(e_{t+1} - e_t) = 0$, so substitution into (11′) and (12′) yields

$$B = b_2(\phi_{10} + \phi_{11}v_t + \phi_{12}\varepsilon_t) - b_2(\phi_{20} + \phi_{21}v_t + \phi_{22}\varepsilon_t) + v_t \tag{23}$$

$$-(\phi_{10} + \phi_{11}v_t + \phi_{12}\varepsilon_t) = C + \varepsilon_t. \tag{24}$$

From these it is easy to verify that the implied values for ϕ_{ij} coefficients are $\phi_{11} = 0$, $\phi_{12} = -1$, $\phi_{22} = -1$, and $\phi_{21} = 1/b_2$. Thus the solutions for p_t and e_t can be written as

$$p_t = \phi_{10} - \varepsilon_t, \tag{25}$$

$$e_t = \phi_{20} + \frac{1}{b_2}v_t - \varepsilon_t. \tag{26}$$

From these expressions two relevant implications come forth readily. First, since ε_t has the same coefficient in both expressions while v_t appears in only the second, the variance of the random part of e_t must be strictly greater than for p_t. Furthermore, if the variability of v_t is sizable relative to that of ε_t, and if b_2 is a small number, the variability of e_t could be *much* greater. Both of these conditions are likely to pertain in actuality, according to the line of argument under review. Second, using (25) and (26) we can express the relative-price variable q_t as

$$q_t = \phi_{10} - \phi_{20} - \frac{1}{b_2}v_t. \tag{27}$$

---

[17] It would also be possible to include v_{t-1}, ξ_t, ε_{t-1}, and ζ_t as the relevant state variables. The solution obtained would be equivalent.

Thus q_t would also have a sizable variability if σ_v^2 were large and b_2 small. Furthermore, with v_t generated by a random-walk process, the same would be true for q_t. Thus q_t would have a form of stochastic behavior that permits it to remain substantially above or below any specified value for long spans of time.[18] So we see that the suggestion put forth by Stockman—that v_t is important and close to a random walk—converts our basic model into one that is consistent with features (i) and (iii) of the actual floating-rate data.

This improvement still leaves us, however, with a model in which p_t responds just as promptly as e_t to monetary shocks—to nonzero ε_t values. To mimic item (ii) on the list of features given above, it will then be necessary to alter the model more substantially. Indeed, it will be necessary to adopt some "sticky price" assumption, such as one of those discussed in Chapters 9 and 10. Since Chapter 10 developed one particular approach in detail, we shall now extend it so as to be applicable in the context of our open-economy model.[19]

Toward that objective, let us begin by rewriting the model of Section 14.2 once more, this time suppressing the p_t^* and R_t^* values but now recognizing y_t as a variable. Doing so gives us the expressions

$$y_t = B_1 + b_1[E_t(e_{t+1} - e_t) - E_t(p_{t+1} - p_t)]$$
$$+ b_2[p_t - e_t] + v_t, \tag{11''}$$

$$-p_t = C_1 + c_1 y_t + c_2 E_t(e_{t+1} - e_t) + \varepsilon_t. \tag{12''}$$

Next, let us define $\bar{p}_t$ as the market-clearing value of p_t that would be determined by the flexible-price system in which y_t is equated to $\bar{y}_t$. Then, as in Section 10.2, we specify that the price level for period t is preset, on the basis of information available from $t - 1$ and before, at the expected market-clearing level,

$$p_t = E_{t-1}\bar{p}_t. \tag{28}$$

Now, since we are retaining the random-walk assumptions for v_t and ε_t, values of $\bar{p}_t$ will be as given by equation (25). Thus we see that $E_{t-1}\bar{p}_t = E_{t-1}(\phi_{10} - \varepsilon_t) = \phi_{10} - \varepsilon_{t-1}$, and consequently that p_t is set to equal $\phi_{10} - \varepsilon_{t-1}$ in the present model. That implies that $E_t(p_{t+1} - p_t) = -\varepsilon_t + \varepsilon_{t-1}$, which helps to simplify the analysis.

Our next step is to substitute (11'') in for y_t in (12'') and use the

---

[18] Under this theory one would expect $\phi_{10} - \phi_{20}$ to be close to zero. With some tedious calculations it can be shown that our model indeed implies that $\phi_{10} - \phi_{20} = 0$.

[19] Theoretical models of exchange-rate behavior in which domestic prices are assumed to be sticky were pioneered by Dornbusch (1976). More satisfactory formulations have been provided by Mussa (1982) and Flood (1981). The latter's specification of the form of price stickiness is similar to that employed below.

expressions just obtained for p_t and $E_t(p_{t+1} - p_t)$. This gives

$$
-\phi_{10} + \varepsilon_{t-1} = C_1 + c_1[B_1 + b_1 E_t e_{t+1} - b_1 e_t + b_1(\varepsilon_t - \varepsilon_{t-1})
$$
$$
+ b_2(\phi_{10} - \varepsilon_{t-1}) - b_2 e_t + v_t]
$$
$$
+ c_2 E_t e_{t+1} - c_2 e_t + \varepsilon_t. \tag{29}
$$

Here we have an equation governing the dynamic behavior of e_t. Regrouping terms and using A_0 to designate the constant term, we have

$$
A_0 + (1 + c_1 b_1 + c_1 b_2)\varepsilon_{t-1} = (c_1 b_1 + c_2)E_t e_{t+1}
$$
$$
- [c_2 + c_1(b_1 + b_2)]e_t + c_1 v_t
$$
$$
+ (1 + c_1 b_1)\varepsilon_t. \tag{30}
$$

Our conjecture, then, is that the solution for e_t is of the form

$$
e_t = \phi_0 + \phi_1 v_t + \phi_2 \varepsilon_t + \phi_3 \varepsilon_{t-1}. \tag{31}
$$

But that implies that $E_t e_{t+1} = \phi_0 + \phi_1 v_t + \phi_2 \varepsilon_t + \phi_3 \varepsilon_t$. Thus substitution into (30) yields

$$
A_0 + (1 + c_1 b_1 + c_1 b_2)\varepsilon_{t-1} = (c_1 + b_1 c_2)[\phi_0 + \phi_1 v_t + (\phi_2 + \phi_3)\varepsilon_t]
$$
$$
- [c_2 + c_1(b_1 + b_2)][\phi_0 + \phi_1 v_t
$$
$$
+ \phi_2 \varepsilon_t + \phi_3 \varepsilon_{t-1}] + c_1 v_t + (1 + c_1 b_1)\varepsilon_t. \tag{32}
$$

Finally, from the latter the undetermined-coefficient procedure gives the values $\phi_1 = 1/b_2$, $\phi_2 = (1 - c_2)/[c_2 + c_1(b_1 + b_2)]$, and $\phi_3 = -[1 + c_1(b_1 + b_2)]/[c_2 + c_1(b_1 + b_2)]$. Thus we have derived the solution expression for e_t in our sticky-price model with randomwalk shocks.

To interpret the implications, we first note that ϕ_1 and ϕ_2 are unambiguously negative as before. Thus the exchange rate is again driven down by positive shocks to foreign production and domestic money demand. But now there is also a new implication that deserves to be emphasized. It depends on the assumptions that c_1 is fairly close to 1.0 and that the absolute value of $b_1 + b_2$ is much smaller than 1.0, both of which are realistic. If those conditions hold, inspection shows that the numerator term in ϕ_2 is of larger absolute value than the denominator. Thus we have that $\phi_2 < -1$. This is interesting, as it implies that the impact (i.e., first-period) effect of a monetary shock—a nonzero value of ε_t—is larger in absolute value than with flexible prices. This can be seen by comparison with equation (26). But that means that the exchange rate initially moves farther in response to a monetary shock than it would with flexible domestic prices. Then in succeeding periods it moves back so as to end up in the same final position as it would if prices were flexible; this is implied by the model, since ϕ_2 plus ϕ_3 equals -1. In the literature, this phenomenon—large impact responses of e_t that are later partially reversed—is referred to as exchange-rate "overshooting." It was brought to prominence by a famous article by Dornbusch (1976).

14.5 Fixed Exchange Rates

Thus far we have assumed that our home country has a floating exchange rate—that government policy leaves the exchange rate free to be determined by private supply and demand forces in the international market for currencies. In this section, by contrast, we consider briefly the nature of a policy regime in which the monetary authority of the home country intervenes in the foreign exchange market so as to maintain—in principle, permanently—a *fixed* value for e_t.[20]

To begin our analysis of this type of system, let us revert to the model summarized in equations (11) and (12). Thus we initially assume that domestic prices are flexible, which implies that $y_t = \bar{y}_t$ with $\bar{y}_t$ exogenous to the system under study. Then with $e_t = e$, the model can be written as

$$\bar{y}_t = b_0 + b_1[R_t^* - E_t(p_{t+1} - p_t)] + b_2[p_t - e - p_t^*] + v_t, \quad \textbf{(33)}$$

$$m_t - p_t = c_0 + c_1\bar{y}_t + c_2R_t^* + \varepsilon_t. \quad \textbf{(34)}$$

As before, the foreign interest rate R_t^* is exogenous while v_t and ε_t are stochastic shocks. We need to ask, then: what are the two endogenous variables that this two-equation system serves to explain? In previous sections they were p_t and e_t, but now the latter is a policy-determined constant. Inspection of equations (33) and (34), plus recognition that $\bar{y}_t$ and R_t^* are exogenous, clearly reveals that there is only one possible candidate to be determined endogenously in place of e_t, namely, m_t. But this simple fact amounts to an important conclusion, which is as follows: with a fixed exchange rate, it is not possible for monetary policy to be set "exogenously." More precisely, the conclusion is that monetary actions must be subordinated to the goal of maintaining the exchange rate at its specified par value. In other words, the condition

---

[20] It might be noted that such a regime has some similarities to a commodity-money standard. The possibility of exchange rates that are fixed, but not permanently, is considered briefly in Section 14.7.

$e_t = e$ becomes the *description of monetary policy* in a fixed-exchange-rate regime.[21]

To expand somewhat on this critical point, let us imagine a situation in which market forces threaten to drive e_t below its par value. Then since the monetary authority of the home country is committed to maintain e_t at par, it will be obliged to purchase foreign currencies in the exchange market, thereby bidding their price, e_t, back up toward its par value. But such an action by the monetary authority (i.e., exchanging dollars for foreign currencies) will have significant consequences for domestic monetary conditions. If the foreign currencies are purchased from domestic banks, to consider one possibility, those banks will find themselves with enlarged holdings of domestic monetary reserves (i.e., domestic currency or deposits with the monetary authority). That will induce, in the manner explained in Chapter 4, an expansion of the home country's money stock. If, on the other hand, the foreign currencies are purchased from dealers or from foreign banks, the action will leave those businesses with excessive holdings of dollars. If the business is a domestic dealer, its expanded holdings of dollars will directly constitute an increase in the domestic money stock. But if it is a foreign bank, the dollars will be traded (as foreigners have little use for them in transactions) to dealers or domestic banks for foreign currencies, which again leads to an expanded domestic money stock. In sum, one result of the monetary authority's purchase of foreign exchange is an enlarged domestic money stock—regardless of the identity of the sellers of foreign exchange. This illustrates that a policy of holding the exchange rate fixed requires the monetary authority to surrender control of the domestic money stock. The basic reason is that the latter has to be set equal to whatever value is determined by the economic forces described by equations (33) and (34), given the target e and the shock values that occur.

Despite this critical difference from a regime with a floating exchange rate, it remains true that the steady-state behavior of the system conforms to the relations (13) and (14). But whereas with a floating exchange rate those equations determine the values of Δp and Δe in response to exogenous values of $\Delta m = \mu$ and Δp^*, with a fixed value of e we have $\Delta e = 0$ necessarily. Thus in this case (13) indicates that Δp is required to equal μ^*, and (14) then determines Δm endogenously as

---

[21] In actuality there will of course be *some* latitude for day-to-day or week-to-week policy attention to other objectives. But that does not invalidate the point, namely, that dedication to a fixed exchange rate does not leave monetary policy free to pursue other goals (such as price-level stability).

equal to that same value.[22] With a fixed-rate system, in other words, the home country is required to accept an inflation rate equal to that occurring abroad, and the monetary authority is required to "validate" that inflation with the implied rate of monetary expansion. As was emphasized in writings of the 1970s by proponents of the so-called "monetary approach" to the balance of payments,[23] a commitment to a fixed exchange rate requires a nation to surrender control over its own inflation rate.[24]

The situation described above is frequently characterized in both textbook and professional literature by statements to the effect that "monetary policy is ineffective under a system of fixed exchange rates." But that way of describing the situation is rather misleading, since it is *not* the case that an expansion in the money stock would have no effect on nominal aggregate demand. What is true, instead, is simply that monetary policy cannot be used for the purposes that economists often have in mind when discussing the effectiveness of monetary policy; it cannot be used in that way because it is pledged to another duty.

But are matters different, one might sensibly inquire, if domestic prices are sticky? After all, equations (11) and (12) are predicated on an assumption of price flexibility, which may be inappropriate for actual economies. In considering this question, we note that y_t would be treated as an endogenous variable if the model were revised to reflect price stickiness and that another equation such as (28) would be added to the system. But with e_t fixed at e, m_t would still be an endogenous variable. Thus the monetary authority would still be required to provide the requisite quantity of money, or else have e_t depart from its par value.

In practice, one does not, of course, observe monetary authorities behaving in a fashion that indicates *total* subservience to the value of the exchange rate, even in regimes that are officially of the fixed-rate type. This is possible because governments have other policy tools at their disposal, including fiscal variables (government spending and taxation) and direct controls over international financial transactions. Such tools can, in actuality, be used to keep the exchange rate temporarily at its par value while monetary actions are being diverted to other

---

[22] It should be kept in mind that we are for simplicity assuming that $\Delta \bar{y}_t = 0$ (i.e., a zero growth rate for real output). More generally, Δm would be required to equal Δp minus $\Delta \bar{y}$ times the income elasticity of money demand.

[23] On this body of literature, see Frenkel and Johnson (1976).

[24] Some nations' political realities may be such that this type of commitment provides the best way of curtailing domestic inflation. But it should be clear that in this case the true function of the fixed exchange rate is to induce the monetary authority to create money at a pace that is not highly inflationary.

ends. But it should be clear that this type of approach cannot be sustained more than temporarily. Suppose, to the contrary, that a nation tried to maintain a fixed exchange rate while engaging in a monetary policy that kept the domestic inflation rate below that being experienced abroad.[25] To keep the value of e_t from falling, this country might pursue an expansionary fiscal policy and try to prevent net financial flows (foreign purchases of domestic assets) that would have the effect of increasing m_t. But the fiscal policy would have to be *increasingly* expansive each year, which cannot go on forever. Furthermore, participants in actual financial markets can find dozens of ways to avoid legislated restrictions. So eventually the value of this nation's currency would rise— its e_t would fall—unless the monetary authorities were to intervene by purchasing foreign currencies. Then its rate of monetary expansion would be forced to conform to the world rate, in the manner described above.

It might strike the reader as surprising that, except for one oblique mention, nothing has been said in this chapter about the concept of a nation's international *balance of payments*. In fact, our presentation has been designed so as to avoid that topic and others that are significant, yet inessential for our primary aim of constructing an open-economy model. But there are interesting connections between balance-of-payments concepts and the point that we have been developing, so a brief discussion is in order.

14.6   The Balance of Payments

Balance-of-payments (BOP) accounts are, as many readers will know, records that describe international transactions, that is, flows of goods, services, and financial claims between a nation's residents and those of the rest of the world. There are many ways in which these records can be classified, aggregated, and arranged. One possible breakdown that emphasizes the most important distinctions, but does not go into great detail, is illustrated in Table 14-1. There BOP figures are presented for the United States for a number of years, occurring at half-decade intervals, over the span 1965–1985. That span of time is long enough to include a major expansion in the volume of the nation's foreign trade and also some dramatic changes in its status in the world economy.

One prominent BOP measure is the *balance on current account*, which is defined as *net* exports of goods and services minus unilateral

---

[25] This example is relevant to the actual experience of West Germany during the fixed-rate decade of the 1960s.

Table 14-1. U.S. Balance-of-Payments Accounts (billions of dollars)

	1965	1970	1975	1980	1985
(a) Export of goods and services	41.1	65.7	155.7	342.5	359.5
(b) Imports of goods and services	32.7	59.9	132.7	333.0	460.6
(c) Unilateral transfers	3.0	3.4	4.9	7.6	15.3
(d) Balance on current account [(a) − (b) − (c)]	5.4	2.3	18.1	1.9	−116.4
(e) Change in private foreign holdings of U.S. securities	0.6	−0.5	8.7	42.6	131.0
(f) Change in private U.S. holdings of foreign securities	6.9	11.8	38.9	78.0	27.5
(g) Balance on capital account [(e) − (f)]	−6.3	−12.3	−32.2	−35.4	103.5
(h) Statistical discrepancy plus increase in SDRs	−0.4	0.6	5.9	26.1	17.9
(i) Official settlements balance [(d) + (g) + (h) = (j) − (k)]	−1.3	−9.4	−6.2	−7.5	5.0
(j) Change in U.S. official foreign reserves	−1.2	−2.5	0.8	8.1	3.9
(k) Change in foreign official dollar reserves	0.1	6.9	7.0	15.5	−1.1

transfers (i.e., gifts). This measure corresponds fairly closely to the variable X that appeared in our formal model of Section 14.2, but also includes net receipts of interest and dividend payments. (These can be viewed as payments for the export of services.) Line (d) of Table 14-1 shows that the U.S. balance on current account has been positive over most of the period 1965–1985, but that an enormous negative balance obtained in 1985. That figure reflects a large excess of imports over exports, which a more detailed breakdown would show to be in the form of merchandise rather than service flows.

A second important BOP concept, pertaining to financial flows, is termed the *balance on capital account*. This balance can also be defined in terms of net exports (i.e., net sales abroad) by the trick of considering the traded commodities to be financial *securities*. Thus a positive figure for the U.S. balance on capital account indicates that U.S. residents were selling more bonds, equities, and other financial claims to foreigners than they were buying from foreigners during the period in question. This was the case for the United States during 1985, as can be seen from line (g) of Table 14-1, again reversing the traditional pattern. In other words, more dollar-denominated U.S. securities were exported (sold to foreigners) than were imported (bought from foreigners): line (e) exceeds line (f).

To explore a bit further the nature of this capital account items, let us recall that the sale of a bond is equivalent to an act of *borrowing*, while the purchase of a bond constitutes lending. Thus to the extent that the 1985 capital-account figures represent bond transactions, the situation might be summarized as follows: in that year the United States was importing more goods and services than it was exporting and was financing the excess expenditure by borrowing from foreigners. Or, to the extent that the figures represent equity transactions, the United States was financing its current account deficit by selling ownership shares in U.S. firms.[26]

In principle, the balance on current account plus the balance on capital account should equal another measure that will be defined momentarily. In practice, however, the figures actually compiled will not do so because of accounting errors and omissions. These are shown in Table 14-1 under the heading "statistical discrepancy." For the sake of neatness, the figures reported in line (h) also include an item that is hard to classify and which usually equals zero, namely, the year's increase in the allocation of the U.S. "special drawing rights" with the International Monetary Fund.[27]

Our final concept adds together the balances on current and capital accounts plus line (h). This sum constitutes the excess of U.S. international sales over purchases, with all transactions included except those pertaining to central banks (or other official monetary agencies). Clearly, if U.S. sales are greater than purchases during some period, there will be a buildup in net U.S. foreign reserves. Such a buildup can come about either by an increase in the U.S. official holdings of foreign currencies or in a decrease in foreign official holdings of U.S. currency. Consequently, the sum is designated as the *official settlements balance*.

---

[26] Whether it was *sensible* for the United States to be importing more goods than it was exporting is not obvious. The excess of imports made possible increased current consumption, but the enhanced foreign debt will require lower consumption in the future.

[27] The International Monetary Fund (IMF) was set up to manage the system of fixed exchange rates that prevailed between 1948 and 1971. It continues in existence as an international central bank, but one with limited powers. A nation's special drawing rights with the IMF constitute ownership of a credit balances that can be used to make official payments to other members of the IMF, and thus are a form of foreign exchange reserves.

It is reported in Table 14-1 on line (i), with the two possible types of reserve changes shown in lines (j) and (k).

Some conceptual clarity regarding this last measure may be provided by momentarily thinking of a world in which all nations hold reserves only in the form of gold (and in which all gold is held in central bank reserves). Then the official settlements balance for a country would simply be the buildup of the gold stock held by the central bank, which would equal the net inflow of gold into the nation from its net exports of goods, services, and financial claims (current account plus capital account balance).

Returning to the reality of the 1980s, there are two features of Table 14-1 that must be mentioned. First, the BOP figures published by the U.S. government are not arranged in exactly the way that has been described. Instead, line (j) is lumped together with line (f) and line (k) is added in with line (e). This provides an arrangement in which the official settlements balance does not appear separately, but is included as one part of a financial-flows balance that also pertains to private financial transactions.[28] Specifically, the official figures are arranged (though with more detail) as indicated in Table 14-2. The U.S. government's justification for this unorthodox way of reporting BOP accounts concerns the unique role of the U.S. dollar as a currency that is widely held by many countries for settling foreign balances with other nations.

The second point to be made also concerns the special role of the dollar. In particular, it must be recognized that for most of the world's nations it is the case that foreign holdings of their currencies are extremely small. Consequently, for most nations the official settlements balance is virtually equivalent to its own buildup of foreign exchange reserves. For most countries, that is, the counterpart of line (k) is always approximately zero and the official settlements balance is approximately equal to line (j) alone.

With this bit of BOP accounting at our disposal, let us conclude the present discussion by emphasizing its importance for the theme of the preceding section, namely, the inability of a nation to control its own

---

[28] There are also other differences between the U.S. government's reporting format and ours. For example, the government reports imports with a minus sign attached and then adds these to exports to obtain net exports. This practice is logically equivalent to ours, but is expositionally different. Also, categories are specified with different words. Our reluctance to use official terms reflects our desire for greater clarity. One example of official terminology that seems unclear to the present author is "U.S. assets abroad, net." Does that term refer to U.S. holdings of foreign securities or to foreign holdings of U.S. securities? The experienced worker will know, of course, but the words themselves seem quite ambiguous.

Table 14.2. U.S. Balance-of-Payments Accounts, Official Arrangement (billions of dollars)

		1965	**1970**	**1975**	**1980**	**1985**
(d)	Balance on current account	5.4	2.3	18.1	1.9	−116.4
(l)	Change in foreign holdings of U.S. securities [(e) + (k)]	0.7	6.4	15.7	58.1	129.9
(m)	Change in U.S. holdings of foreign securities [(f) + (j)]	5.7	9.3	39.7	86.1	31.4
(n)	Capital balance including official transactions [(l) − (m)]	−5.0	−2.9	−24.0	−28.0	98.5
(h)	Statistical discrepancy plus increase in SDRs	−0.4	0.6	5.9	26.1	17.9
(o)	Sum of lines (d), (n), and (h)	0.0	0.0	0.0	0.0	0.0

money stock and inflationary experience under a policy regime with a fixed exchange rate. In terms of BOP concepts the basic point is that, with a fixed exchange rate, any surplus or deficit in the current and capital accounts together must be financed by an inflow or outflow of official monetary reserves. But these are, in effect, sales or purchases of foreign exchange made by the monetary authority. If the exchange rate were free to float, the official settlements balance would be zero— indeed, a truly pure float would involve no purchase or sale of foreign currencies by the home country's central bank; the exchange rate would adjust to bring the current and capital accounts together into balance. But with the monetary authority committed to keep the exchange rate at par, any surplus or deficit on current and capital account will require intervention (i.e., the sale or purchase of foreign exchange).[29] In turn, this intervention will bring about changes in the domestic money stock, and subsequent inflation rates, in the manner described in Section 14.5.

---

[29] There exists the possibility that the sales or purchases will be made by foreign central banks, in which case the domestic money supply might not be affected. But typically nations will have to assume the primary responsibility for their own exchange rate.

14.7   Fixed Versus Floating Exchange Rates

In March 1973, the policy of the United States toward its exchange rate shifted from a fixed-rate commitment to a stance permitting a relatively free float vis-à-vis other leading currencies.[30] As a glance at Figure 14-1 will confirm, the foreign-exchange value of the U.S. dollar has fluctuated quite severely since that time, with typical quarter-to-quarter and year-to-year changes being substantially greater than during the previous fixed-rate era of 1947–1971. In addition, fluctuations have also been noticeably greater under the floating-rate regime for the "real exchange rate," that is, the dollar price of foreign currency multiplied by the ratio of prices abroad to prices in the United States. One indication of variability in the real exchange rate is provided by the movements in our variable q_t, which are plotted in Figure 14-2.[31] From that figure one can see that swings have been more rapid since the advent of floating rates.

The increase in exchange-rate variability experience since 1973 has led some economists to argue that the floating-rate system has been counterproductive. It may be useful, accordingly, to conclude the present chapter with a very brief discussion of the desirability of reverting to a system of fixed exchange rates. In doing so, it will be useful first to consider the desirability of rates that are permanently fixed and then to take up the possibility of temporary fixity.

The most basic point that should be kept in mind is that exchange-rate fluctuations are not themselves fundamental "causes" of macroeconomic instability. The exchange rate is an endogenous variable, under a floating-rate regime, whose movements occur in response to shocks of macroeconomic relevance. These shocks might be unpredictable actions of the monetary authority or they might be private-sector

---

[30] The beginning of the floating-rate period is usually given as March 1973, which was the date of the final collapse of the Bretton Woods fixed-rate system. The breakdown had been under way for some time, however. Another important milestone was the .U.S. action of August 1971, which revoked the U.S. commitment to sell gold to foreign central banks at $35 per ounce. This step led to a substantial exchange rate realignment in December 1971. For more discussion of the breakdown, see Krugman and Obstfeld (1988, pp. 527–30).

[31] In examining movements in Figures 14-1 and 14-2, it should be kept in mind that the former pertains to the *inverse* of the exchange rate (the dollar price of foreign exchange) while the latter plots one measure of q_t, the *inverse* of the (log of the) real exchange rate, $e_t + p_t^* - p_t$. It might be mentioned that some analyses distinguish between goods that are exported and those that are produced and consumed in the same nation. In these analyses there is a distinction between the real exchange rate and a related concept known as the "terms of trade." In particular, the former is EP^*/P with P and P^* referring to national price levels while the latter interprets P and P^* as prices of home-country exports and imports.

shocks of the types represented in Section 14.2 by the random variables v_t and ε_t. But there is little reason to believe that the extent of private-sector disturbances (measured by σ_v^2 and σ_ε^2) would be different under floating- and fixed-rate regimes.[32] Moving to a fixed-rate system would have consequences for macroeconomic variables, but would not eliminate shocks stemming from the private sector and is unnecessary for the elimination of monetary policy shocks. Thus the fact that variability has been greater since 1973 does not constitute an adequate reason for attempting to restore fixed rates. Arguments emphasizing the greater post-1973 variability tend to overlook the related fact that the flexible-rate system was not the consequence of deliberate international design, but instead came about because the world's nations were unable, despite vigorous attempts, to maintain the previous sytem of fixed rates in the face of the disturbances that were occurring.

Another important point is that the increased variability of exchange rates experienced since 1973 has *not* led to a breakdown in international trade, as opponents of floating rates had feared. In fact, world trade in financial assets as well as goods and services has grown even more rapidly during the floating-rate era than before. Whatever the costs might be of exchange-rate variability, severe hampering of international trade does not appear to be one of them.

From these considerations it appears that one cannot settle the relevant question (i.e., whether fixed or flexible rates are preferable) without a model of the international economy upon which there is a substantial amount of agreement by the parties to the debate. But, as we have seen in Chapters 9 and 10, such agreement does not exist. There may be a considerable amount of agreement concerning the specification of *other* relationships, but regarding the extent and nature of price-level stickiness—the dynamics of aggregate supply—there is not. Instead, there is wide-ranging and extensive dispute.

Consequently, it is not possible to present any conclusive argument concerning the desirability of fixed or flexible exchange rates. It may be useful, nevertheless, to provide a very brief outline of the argument developed in a paper on the subject that has been both famous and influential, namely, Milton Friedman's essay entitled "The Case for Flexible Exchange Rates" (1953). In this paper, it should be noted,

---

[32] Some supporters of fixed rates would dispute this contention, arguing that with flexible rates there is an additional source of randomness provided by the stochastic component of expectations concerning future values of the exchange rate. Under the hypothesis of rational expectations, this position amounts to a claim that stochastic "bubble" or "bootstrap" effects, related to the type mentioned in Section 8.7, are quantitatively important. Professional controversy over this issue continues at present and is, unfortunately, too technical to permit any intelligible brief summary.

Friedman explicitly assumes the presence of a substantial degree of nominal price stickiness.

The gist of Friedman's argument can be summarized as follows. Suppose that, starting from a situation of balance in the official settlements account, there occurs some change in conditions—a substantial real or monetary shock. This shock will tend to throw the official settlements balance (OSB) into either deficit or surplus, depending on its nature. Accordingly, for balance to be restored (which will sooner or later be necessary) there must be an adjustment in some variable that significantly affects the OSB. The obvious candidate variables are e_t and p_t, the exchange rate and the domestic price level, so if e_t is fixed, there will arise the need for a nontrivial adjustment in p_t. But with sticky prices, this adjustment will not occur promptly. The burden of adjustment will then be thrown, in the interim before p_t completes its adjustment, onto real income and employment levels. Movements in those variables will eventually be reversed, at least in part, so their fluctuations are socially undesirable. Such fluctuations are also unpopular, so, in an attempt to avoid them, governments will often adopt quantitative controls and barriers to trade—which are themselves highly undesirable. But real fluctuations and quantitative controls could both be avoided if the exchange rate was free to adjust in response to the initiating shock.

The foregoing is Friedman's case for preferring a floating rate to one that is permanently fixed. As for an arrangement involving temporary fixity, with occasional changes in the officially supported value, Friedman's argument is that this option would be even worse than permanent fixity. The main reason is that it creates a self-destructive inducement toward speculative transactions.[33]

> Because the exchange rate is changed infrequently and only to meet substantial difficulties, a change tends to come well after the onset of difficulty, to be postponed as long as possible, and to be made only after substantial pressure on the exchange rate has accumulated. In consequence, there is seldom any doubt about the direction in which an exchange rate will be changed, if it is changed. In the interim between the suspicion of a possible change in the rate and the actual change, there is every incentive to sell the country's currency if a devaluation is expected ... or buy it if an appreciation is expected. (Friedman, 1953, p. 164)

---

[33] Friedman's position is not that speculative transactions are generally undesirable. Indeed, with flexible rates the activities of speculators, who attempt to purchase currencies when their values are low, and to sell them when their values are high, should tend to smooth and dampen fluctuations that do occur. The objection under discussion is concerned only with the undesirable consequences of a system that gives rise to one-way inducements for speculative behavior.

Thus speculation tends to undermine this system, in contrast to the case with a flexible rate. And "partly for this reason, partly because of their innate discontinuity, each exchange rate change tends to become the occasion for a crisis" (p. 163). "In short, the system of occasional changes in temporarily rigid exchange rates seems . . . the worst of two worlds" (p. 164).

If it were the case that domestic price levels were not sticky, the consequences of one arrangement rather than another would be less serious. Prices would adjust in response to shocks, even with fixed rates, so quantity adjustments would be minimal. The main difference would be, as mentioned above, that nations are able to choose their own average pace of inflation (or deflation) with a floating exchange rate but are required to conform to the world's pace if the exchange rate is fixed.

Reflection on that last implication leads to the conclusion that maintenance of a fixed exchange rate constitutes adherence to one form of a monetary *standard*. Such adherence can be helpful, as was emphasized in Chapter 12, in preventing the inflationary bias that tends to arise from period-by-period policymaking when the monetary authority believes that employment losses result from negative monetary surprises. But as we have seen, a fixed-exchange-rate standard will keep inflation low only if the other nations of the world are also avoiding inflation. Although adherence to *some* standard is desirable, it is far from clear that the fixed-exchange-rate standard is the best one. An alternative standard that seems more promising is discussed in Chapter 16.

If we express the problem in this way, it becomes apparent that it is misleading to pose the policy issue in terms of "fixed versus floating exchange rates." The actual issue is the choice of an appropriate rule for monetary policy.

Problems

1. Evaluate the constants B and C in equations (11') and (12') in terms of parameter values and variables that are assumed to be unchanging through time, namely, p^*, R^*, and m.
2. The floating exchange rate model of equations (11) and (12) can be further simplified by assuming that the relative price variable q_t in (7) is constant over time. Derive the bubble-free solution for e_t from (12) under that assumption. What other model, studied in an earlier chapter, is similar to this version?
3. Derive solution expressions for the two endogenous variables in the fixed-exchange-rate system given by the equations (33) and (34).

References

Dornbusch, Rudiger, "Expectations and Exchange Rate Dynamics," *Journal of Political Economy* 84 (December 1976), 1161–76.

Dornbusch, Rudiger, *Open Economy Macroeconomics*. (New York: Basic Books, Inc., Publishers, 1980).

Flood, Robert P., "Explanations of Exchange Rate Volatility and Other Empirical Regularities in Some Popular Models of the Foreign Exchange Market," *Carnegie–Rochester Conference Series on Public Policy* 15 (Autumn 1981), 219–49.

Frenkel, Jacob A., "Flexible Exchange Rates in the 1970s," in *Stabilization Policies: Lessons from the '70s and Implications for the '80s*. (St. Louis: Center for the Study of American Business, Washington University, 1980).

Frenkel, Jacob A., and Harry G. Johnson, eds., *The Monetary Approach to the Balance of Payments*. (London: Allen & Unwin, Ltd., 1976).

Frenkel, Jacob A., and Michael L. Mussa, "Asset Markets, Exchange Rates, and the Balance of Payments," in *Handbook of International Economics*, Vol. 2, R. W. Jones and P. B. Kenan, eds. (Amsterdam: North-Holland, 1985).

Friedman, Milton, "The Case for Flexible Exchange Rates," in *Essays in Positive Economics*, by Milton Friedman. (Chicago: University of Chicago Press, 1953).

Krugman, Paul R., and Maurice Obstfeld, *International Economics: Theory and Policy*. (Glenview, Ill.: Scott, Foresman and Company, 1988).

Meese, Richard A., "Is the Sticky Price Assumption Reasonable for Exchange Rate Models?" *Journal of International Money and Finance* 3 (August 1984), 131–39.

Mussa, Michael, "Empirical Regularities in the Behavior of Exchange Rates and Theories of the Foreign Exchange Market," *Carnegie–Rochester Conference Series on Public Policy* 11 (Autumn 1979), 9–57.

Mussa, Michael, "A Model of Exchange Rate Dynamics," *Journal of Political Economy* 90 (February 1982), 74–104.

Mussa, Michael, "Nominal Exchange Rate Regimes and the Behavior of Real Exchange Rates," *Carnegie–Rochester Series on Public Policy* 25 (Autumn 1986), 117–214.

Obstfeld, Maurice, and Alan C. Stockman, "Exchange Rate Dynamics," in *Handbook of International Economics*, Vol. 2, R. W. Jones and P. B. Kenan, eds. (Amsterdam: North-Holland, 1985).

Stockman, Alan C., "The Equilibrium Approach to Exchange Rates," Federal Reserve Bank of Richmond, *Economic Review* 73 (March–April 1987), 12–30.

15

Episodes in U.S. Monetary History

15.1 Introduction

In this chapter the principal objective is to illustrate some of the theoretical points developed in earlier parts of the book by reference to actual occurrences in U.S. history. It will not be possible, in the limited space available, to provide a well-rounded monetary history of the United States—not even a brief one. Instead, the strategy will be to concentrate on aspects of particular episodes that bear on specific points in a fairly direct and vivid manner. Enough of these episodes will be discussed, however, for the chapter to provide a condensed but reasonably complete outline of the various monetary *standards* that have prevailed during the nation's history.

In the discussion, emphasis will be given to episodes that took place relatively early in the nation's lifetime, and in particular to ones occurring before the establishment in 1914 of the Federal Reserve System. One reason for this somewhat unusual emphasis is that commodity money arrangements are unfamiliar to many of today's readers and can therefore derive special benefit from illustrative examples. A second reason is that these earlier episodes are relatively neglected in most textbooks and standard treatises pertaining to monetary economics. There is, consequently, a greater need for a short and accessible account.

15.2 Money in Colonial America

Some of the most unusual and interesting monetary experiences on record are those of the British colonies in North America—in particular, those of the 13 colonies that eventually joined to become the original United States of America.[1] These experiences were also rather confusing, for reasons that will be seen, and have led to considerable controversy.[2] In considering this colonial period, from (say) 1620 to 1776, it is important to keep in mind that the colonies in question were founded, chartered, and to some extent administered by the government of England. As a consequence, the monetary systems of the various colonies were strongly influenced by the English monetary regulations and practices of the day. In particular, in all 13 colonies the monetary units of account were the traditional British denominations of pounds, shillings, and pence. Thus prices were quoted and contracts specified in these units.[3] Initially, the meaning of a pound was 3.871 ounces of silver—this corresponds to a value of 5s 2d per ounce of silver—just as in England.[4] But as time passed, the meaning (and legal definition) of the units came to be different in the various American colonies. The Pennsylvania shilling (or pound) was, for example, worth only three-quarters as much silver as the Virginia shilling (or pound) after 1742—even according to law. Thus the same currency names meant different things in different places (and at different times for a single place). The colonies all issued paper money denominated in these local units, moreover, and in some cases the issues were so excessive as to undermine the silver standard altogether. It is instructive, therefore, to consider the extent to which the various colonial monetary systems conformed to the picture of a "normal" commodity-money arrangement provided by our model of Chapter 13.

The underlying reason for the development of different units, and other abnormal features of the colonies' arrangements, was a perpetual shortage of the world's principal medium of exchange at the time,

---

[1] Useful references for this period include Brock (1975), Ernst (1973), McCusker (1978), and Nettels (1934, 1963).

[2] A recent outburst is provided by Smith (1985a,b) and Michener (1987). The position of the latter is much more consistent with the account given here.

[3] Since the United Kingdom adopted a decimal-based system in 1970, it may be useful to mention that there were 20 shillings to the pound and 12 pence to the shilling (and, therefore, 240 pence to the pound). The written symbols for the three units were £, s, and d, so that, for example, the sum of 2 pounds, 12 shillings, and 8 pence was denoted as £2 12s 8d.

[4] Actually, England was on a bimetallic standard during the period in question, with its mint coining both gold and silver. But that complication will be ignored in this section; we shall discuss matters as if the English standard were silver alone. Some experiences involving bimetallism are discussed in Section 15.3.

silver. This shortage in turn resulted from a continuing deficit trade balance with England, a deficit that was at British insistence financed to the greatest extent possible by silver payments from the colonists to London exporters. In fact, the trade deficit was itself brought about in part by English regulations[5] whose purpose was the enhancement of England's stock of precious metals.[6] Now, under a fiat-paper-money system, a long-lasting shortage of money might be viewed as impossible because prices could fall and thereby increase the quantity of real money balances to whatever extent is necessary. But in an open economy the value of silver relative to other commodities has to be close to that prevailing in other parts of the world. Thus prices of goods in terms of silver cannot fall to an unlimited extent, under a silver standard, to provide larger real money balances (i.e., silver holdings) for conducting transactions.

During the early 1600s this money shortage was not as serious a problem as later because the colonial societies were so primitive—populated by small, largely self-sufficient communities—that the volume of market transactions was small and could be accommodated by barter and various credit arrangements. But by the late 1600s, the colonies in New England and the Mid-Atlantic region had developed to an extent such that the medium-of-exchange shortage was becoming seriously detrimental to their prosperity and further growth. Eventually, this shortage of metallic coin would lead to the circulation of paper claims, but since such systems had not yet been successfully utilized in Europe, the colonists' first attempts were directed toward schemes for attracting more silver to reside within their boundaries.

The colonists' principal scheme of this type was one that seems almost crazy to a monetary economist of the 1980s. For it relied, apparently, on the practice of legally declaring an ounce of silver (actually, a specified silver coin) to be worth more shillings in the colony in question than elsewhere. While the English value of silver was 5s 2d per ounce, for example, Massachusetts had by 1672 adopted regulations that made the local value greater than 6s 10d, so that an ounce of silver in Massachusetts corresponded to 1.333 times as many shillings as in England (or in other colonies retaining the English

---

[5] Some examples are England's restrictions that prohibited the colonies from producing goods that would compete with English exports, from selling tobacco to countries other than England, from creating a mint, and from acquiring and using English coins. On these and other practices, see Nettels (1934, 1973).

[6] During this time, before the publication of Adam Smith's *Wealth of Nations* (1776), prevailing opinion among social philosophers and practical men gave high priority to the "mercantilist" notion that the accumulation of gold and silver was crucial to a nation's well-being. Destruction of that idea was one of Smith's primary aims in writing his epochal classic.

standard).[7] The hope was that this device would induce profit seekers to bring silver to Massachusetts, where it was "more valuable." But of course the actual effect, perhaps after a period of adjustment, was that the meaning of "shilling" or "pound" units became different in Massachusetts. In effect, there were then different currency units, Massachusetts shillings and sterling (English) shillings. Prices in Massachusetts were quoted in the former, so these prices adjusted upward relative to sterling prices (so as to be equivalent in terms of silver). Similar attempts were made in the other colonies, moreover, so the outcome was the situation mentioned above: the words "shilling" and "pound" had different meanings in different colonies. In effect there were in the various colonies different units of account, even though all used the same words—similar to today's "dollars" of U.S., Canadian, and Australian origin (which have different values).

In short, the colonies' scheme of attracting or retaining silver by revaluation was a failure, leading simply to higher prices (in local units) and to no greater quantities of the metallic media of exchange. As the need for a circulating medium continued, other devices were accordingly attempted. Of these, the most important by far was that of issuing colonial government "bills of credit." Now these bills were colonial government debt—notes promising to repay the holder in silver at a certain specified time. But the bills were freely transferable without endorsement from holder to holder, were issued in convenient denominations, and were printed in a form somewhat similar to that of today's paper money. Consequently, these transferable paper claims to silver came to be generally acceptable as a medium of exchange. Of course, each colony's bills were expressed in the local units—the Massachusetts, or Pennsylvania, or Virginia, or whatever version of pounds, shillings, and pence. So, in effect, these bills were colonial currencies—paper money.

The monetary arrangement for any particular colony was therefore something like that described in Chapter 13, with silver serving rather than gold as the standard commodity and with bills of credit serving as the paper medium of exchange. There was, admittedly, a significant difference in that the colonies did not have central banks or other agencies committed to maintain the value of the paper currency by exchanging it for silver at the official standard rate. But the colonial governments took other steps designed to keep the value of currency

---

[7] The exact value in Massachusetts units of an ounce of silver is not stated here because it is not an integer number of pence. The reason for this is that the regulations were not expressed directly in terms of ounces of silver, but rather in terms of a silver coin—the Spanish peso (or "piece of eight")—which was the most important coin of the period. Specifically, the Massachusetts valuation of the peso was 6s as compared with the English figure of 4s 6d. (Thus in pence the ratio was $72/54 = 1.333$.)

constant in terms of silver. For one thing, the currency notes were at maturity convertible into silver, even if not convertible at earlier times. Furthermore, the notes were declared, by most of the colonial governments, to be *legal tender*. Thus there were colonial laws stating that a £100 debt could be paid with 100 pounds of colonial currency as well as with silver. So the implied silver value of currency was to some extent enforced by law.[8] And the colonists' need for a circulating medium was itself a big help, undoubtedly, in lending acceptability to the colonial bills of credit.

The commodity-money analysis of Chapter 13 should, accordingly, be useful in understanding price-level movements in colonial America. Data are not available on a sufficiently complete basis to permit application of the dynamic analysis of Section 13.4, but the static models of Sections 13.2 and 13.3 should be applicable in a general sort of way. In developing the application to individual colonies, it is important to keep in mind that these were not producers of silver (or gold) and that they were small open economies. Silver stock adjustments were therefore brought about by intercolony and international flows. Because of the colonies' small accumulated stocks of silver, furthermore, these adjustments should be thought of as occurring quite rapidly. Consequently, for understanding price-level movements it is probably best to focus attention on the full (stock) equilibrium analysis, as outlined in Section 13.3, rather than the temporary impact-effect analysis.

According to the relevant comparative static analysis, then, the price level in a given colony should have been fairly constant over time as long as there were no changes in the unit-of-account price of the standard metal (silver). But there were, as we have seen, occasional changes in this price—which corresponds analytically to the gold price P_g in our model of Section 13.2. And there is another possibility for significant and long-lasting price-level changes, namely, the possibility that issues of the paper medium of exchange would be so large as to displace *all* of a colony's monetary silver in the manner described in Problem 4 of Chapter 13. If such a displacement were to take place, the economy would have effectively abandoned the commodity-money standard. The price level in terms of the paper medium of exchange could then differ greatly from the value it would have if the standard had not been abandoned. Indeed, in such a case a fiat-money system would be in effect and arbitrarily large inflations (or deflations) would be possible.

---

[8] The British government periodically took steps to disallow these legal tender specifications, but not until after the bills of credit had come to be well established in most colonies as the primary currency.

As it happens, such events did take place during the American colonial experience. In particular, the New England colonies (Massachusetts, Connecticut, New Hampshire, and Rhode Island) departed from the silver standard during the period 1720–1750, while North and South Carolina had lapses beginning before 1720. As it is relatively well documented, let us briefly review the New England episode.

Although each of the four colonies of New England issued its own bills of credit, all of these currencies circulated routinely at par throughout the region during the period 1700–1750. Accordingly, it is appropriate to regard New England as a single monetary area over that period.[9] The relevant money stock, then, is that for the four colonies together. Unfortunately, there exist almost no data concerning the amount of silver coin (or other metallic media of exchange) present during those years. (The one exception will be mentioned shortly.) The total quantity of paper currency—bills of credit issued by the four colonial governments—has been estimated, however. The best figures are probably those of Brock (1975, pp. 591–93), which are reported in Table 15-1. Just a glance will show that there was an enormous percentage increase between 1703 and 1749, with the most rapid growth in absolute terms occurring in the late 1740s.

Also reported in Table 15-1 is a proxy measure for the price level in New England, namely, the price in Boston of English currency. More specifically, the last column reports the number of Massachusetts pounds required to purchase one sterling pound, via a bill-of-exchange arrangement, to be delivered in London. Despite carrying charges connected with the bill-of-exchange feature, this proxy should serve as a reasonably good measure of the exchange rate and thus—with England firmly on a silver standard—of the Massachusetts price level.

According to the summary statement given above, then, the theory of Chapter 13 should be interpreted as predicting that the Massachusetts price of sterling should increase when devaluations of the Massachusetts currency occurred (i.e., redefinitions) and when bills-of-credit issues were so great as to force New England off the silver standard. When it was off, moreover, prices and currency magnitudes should move roughly in proportion (for a constant level of transactions).

The values from Table 15-1 are plotted in Figure 15-1, with missing years filled in and some additional price-level statistics at the start. From this plot it can be seen that although the quantity of paper currency grew rapidly from 1703 to 1749, the price level did not begin

---

[9] After 1750, there was span of time during which the currency union was broken because Massachusetts restored a silver standard while the other three colonies did not.

Table 15-1. Currency and Prices in New England, 1701–1749[a]

Year	Bills of Credit Outstanding[b] (thousands of pounds)	Boston Price of Sterling Currency[c]
1701	na	1.36
1703	6.4	1.40
1705	29.4	1.35
1707	40.8	na
1709	69.4	1.51
1711	142	1.47
1713	219	1.50
1715	254	1.60
1717	310	1.70
1719	291	2.17
1721	307	2.26
1723	387	2.42
1725	446	2.89
1727	460	2.92
1729	507	3.13
1731	546	3.34
1733	660	3.50
1735	702	3.60
1737	724	5.17
1739	815	5.00
1741	1003	5.48
1743	1094	5.51
1745	2033	6.15
1747	3854	9.25
1749	4033	10.33

[a] na, not available.
[b] Denominated in Massachusetts pounds. Data from Brock (1975, pp. 591–92).
[c] Massachusetts pounds per pound sterling. Data from McCusker (1978, pp. 313–17).

to grow rapidly until about 1715, after which it increased at a rate fairly close to that of the money stock.[10] This pattern would suggest, in light of the theory at hand, that all silver was driven from circulation sometime around 1715–1720, after which the paper currency would consti-

---

[10] To be more precise, the price-level figures can be seen to increase somewhat less rapidly than the currency values, in proportionate (i.e., logarithmic) terms. This is in fact what the theory would call for, when account is taken of the population growth that is recorded and the income and transaction growth that must certainly have taken place.

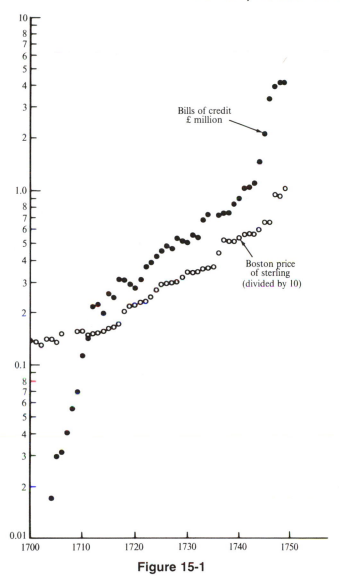

Figure 15-1

tute the bulk of the money stock. As it happens, there is one figure pertaining to holdings of monetary silver that enables us to conduct a rough test of this hypothesis. In particular, Brock (1975, pp. 23–29) reports that New England was estimated to possess about £200,000 of monetary silver in 1700, which dwindled to £130,000 in 1713 and thereafter disappeared. It is encouraging for the theory that not only is the timing correct, but also the quantity of bills of credit issued. The quantity, that is, of such bills came to roughly £250,000 by 1715 or £300,000 by 1718. Thus the quantity of paper money was slightly greater than the quantity of silver in circulation in 1700. Since the quantity of money demanded would have increased somewhat because of price increases and growth of spending, about the right amount of paper had been issued by 1718 to fully displace the preexisting stock of silver.[11]

In sum, the facts in Figure 15-1 correspond nicely to the implications of the Chapter 13 analysis: paper-money issues displace commodity money and have little effect on prices as long as the commodity standard remains in effect, but the latter collapses when all of the commodity has been displaced. After that, prices increase along with additional paper currency issues, with real money balances remaining fairly constant (unless total income grows). The experiment in question came to an end in 1750, when Massachusetts made a major change in its currency unit, began withdrawing bills of credit, and returned to a silver standard.

Experience in the Carolinas conformed reasonably closely to that of New England, although at different dates. Thus, after fruitless attempts to attract silver by means of unit-of-account redefinitions, North and South Carolina began issuing bills of credit on a large magnitude in the early 1700s, experienced severalfold increases in the price level, and then stabilized before 1750. For South Carolina some relevant figures are reported in Table 15-2.

In other colonies bills of credit were issued but not in such quantities as to displace all silver from circulation and force a departure from the silver standard. In these colonies, consequently, our theory suggests that major price-level changes should have occurred only when there were alterations in the local unit of account. Such redefinitions took place frequently in Pennsylvania during the period before 1742, to take one example. Accordingly, the price level—proxied in Table 15-3 by the Philadelphia price of sterling pounds—fluctuated around these varying par values. But the Pennsylvania paper-currency issues, which began in 1725, did not entirely displace silver from the colony, so the silver standard did not break down. As a result, there are no major price-level movements reported in Table 15-3 of a magnitude comparable to those of New England or South Carolina.

---

[11] For future reference it will be useful to calculate the quantity of silver per person in 1700. With an estimated population for New England of 93,000, the £200,000 amounts to £2.15 per person in terms of Massachusetts units or 2.15/1.39 = £1.55 in terms of sterling (English) units. (The population estimate comes from U.S. Bureau of the Census, *Historical Statistics of the United States*, 1975, p. 1168.)

Table 15-2. Currency and Prices in South Carolina, 1703–1774[a]

Year	Paper Currency Outstanding[b] (thousands of pounds)	Charleston Price of Sterling[c]
1703	4	1.50
1707	12	1.50
1711	20	1.50
1712	56	1.50
1716	90	na
1720	100	4.00
1723	120	6.75
1727	107	7.00
1731	212	7.00
1735	na	7.00
1740	na	7.96
1745	na	7.00
1749	133	7.26
1753	152	7.00
1755	221	7.00
1756	312	7.14
1757	542	7.00
1758	595	7.00
1760	864	7.00
1764	585	7.18
1768	482	7.00
1770	424	7.17
1774	259	7.00

[a] na, not available.
[b] Denominated in South Carolina pounds. Data from Smith (1985b, p. 1190).
[c] South Carolina pounds per pound sterling. Data from McCusker (1978, pp. 313–17).

That silver coin continued to circulate in Pennsylvania throughout most of the period is reported in records from the time—see Brock (1975, pp. 83, 386). Since the Pennsylvania population was relatively large—about 31,000 in 1720, 52,000 in 1730, 86,000 in 1740, 120,000 in 1750, and 184,000 in 1760—it is not surprising that the currency issues indicated in Table 15-3 for years prior to 1756 would leave silver in circulation. But those of the late 1750s were quite large. Nevertheless,

Table 15-3. Currency and Prices in Pennsylvania, 1721–1775

Year	Bills of Credit Outstanding[a] (thousands of pounds)	Philadelphia Price of Sterling[b]
1721	0.0	1.37
1723	15.0	1.40
1725	38.9	1.39
1727	38.9	1.50
1729	68.9	1.49
1731	68.9	1.53
1733	68.9	1.67
1735	68.9	1.66
1737	68.9	1.70
1739	80.0	1.70
1741	80.0	1.46
1743	80.0	1.60
1745	80.0	1.75
1747	85.0	1.84
1749	85.0	1.71
1751	84.0	1.70
1753	82.5	1.68
1755	81.0	1.69
1757	262.5	1.66
1759	433.6	1.53
1761	438.1	1.72
1763	286.3	1.73
1765	302.4	1.70
1767	263.9	1.66
1769	230.5	1.58
1771	184.5	1.66
1773	154.1	1.66
1775	316.6	1.61

[a] Denominated in Pennsylvania pounds. Data from Brock (1975, pp. 83, 386).

[b] Pennsylvania pounds per pound sterling. Data from McCusker (1978, pp. 313–7).

the largest quantity of paper outstanding was £486,000 in 1760. This amounts to 486/184 = 2.64 pounds per person in local currency units or 2.64/1.59 = 1.66 pounds in terms of sterling. But this figure is roughly the same as the quantity of silver per person held in New England in 1700—recall footnote 11—when the volume of transactions would presumably have been smaller. It is then easy to accept the hypothesis that some positive amount of silver remained in circulation in Pennsylvania even through the period 1756–1762.

Other colonies were also able to issue paper currency in quantities modest enough that they could maintain some silver in circulation; New York and Virginia are two examples.[12] Indeed, except for the New England and Carolina experiences described above, there were no major price-level inflations during the colonial period. In part, it should be said, this was due to restraints placed on colonial paper currency issues by the authorities in England: major restrictive acts were passed by Parliament in 1751 and in 1764.

The purpose of the foregoing sketch, it should be emphasized, has not been to develop praise or criticism for monetary arrangements of the colonial period, but to describe the experiences as illustrative of some analytical points pertaining to commodity-money arrangements. In particular, the experiences of the colonies illustrate nicely that major price-level movements will not occur, even with substantial issues of paper currency, provided that the commodity money standard remains in effect. If more paper is issued than is desired by money holders at the standard price, however, the monetary commodity will be driven from the economy and the standard will be destroyed. Further paper issues will bring about price-level changes, just as with other fiat-money systems.

15.3 From the Revolution to the Civil War

The United States of America declared their independence in Jefferson's eloquent document of 1776, then had to fight a long war to establish that independence. How was the war financed? How, that is, were the soldiers paid and supplies purchased? Nettels (1963) has described the ex-colonists' predicament as follows:

> But how was the Congress to raise money . . . ? It could not levy taxes; it could not at first commandeer property (lest it turn the people against the American cause); and it could not obtain adequate funds on loan from men of wealth. Many of the richest men, as loyalists, were unwilling to lend . . . while cautious capitalists feared to lend to the United States while the outcome of the war was in doubt. Should Britain win, all such loans would be repudiated. . . . The United States had no common currency,

---

[12] Virginia may have been driven off briefly, and to a relatively small extent, in the early 1760s.

either paper or metallic; there were no banks which could extend credit to the government; and the supply of foreign coins and state paper money, thanks to Britain's imperial currency policy, was woefully inadequate for financing an extended war. (p. 673)

The outcome, as the reader may have guessed, was that the war was financed largely by the issue of bills of credit—that is, paper money. Between June 1775 and December 1779 the Continental Congress issued a total of $191,500,000. Meanwhile, the states were putting out bills and notes of their own to the extent of about $250,000,000. A question that immediately arises is: How do these sums compare with the previously existing stock of money? To answer, we must first consider the meaning of the *dollar* unit, symbolized above in the now-familiar way. In fact, the "dollar" in question was the colonists' term for the Spanish peso or "piece of eight," whose equivalent in sterling was 4s 6d. Thus in terms of English units the wartime issues mentioned above would amount to $(54/240)$ $(441,500,000) = £99,337,500$. To make a crude comparison with the preexisting stock of money, let us recall that the estimates in Section 15.2 were in the vicinity of £2 sterling per person in the early 1700s, so we might use a generous figure of £3 to £4 per person as of 1775. But the colonies' population was about 2,500,000 in 1776 (including slaves), so the wartime issues amounted to almost £40 per person, more than 10 times the preexisting stock!

As might be expected, the value of the paper currency declined sharply. One index of price movements in Philadelphia is given in Table 15-4. From the reported figures it will be seen that the value of currency declined even more than the increase in its volume would suggest, as citizens feared that the bills would be repudiated by the government and become entirely worthless. In fact, in 1780 Congress ceased its issue of bills and called upon the states to accept its outstanding bills in payment of taxes at the value of 40 paper dollars to one silver dollar. After the redemption period (lasting until 1783) Congress's bills were to have no legal standing whatsoever. Accordingly, they did become nearly valueless and gave rise to the phrase "not worth a Continental" (Nettels, 1963, p. 674).[13]

Reflection on the figures in Table 15-4 might lead an alert reader to wonder how prices could be brought down so dramatically between 1781 and 1782. In particular, he might wonder if the series is actually consistent or if, instead, a redefinition of the paper "dollar" was involved. Indeed, the above-mentioned scheme of calling in bills and

---

[13] Bills of credit issued by the states were handled in a somewhat similar way, with some states giving even less that 1/40 of the face value in credit toward tax obligations.

Table 15-4.   Wholesale Price Index
for Philadelphia, 1770–1789

Year	Index, 1850–59 = 100[a]
1770	80.0
1771	84.9
1772	98.2
1773	90.9
1774	84.3
1775	78.0
1776	108.0
1777	329.6
1778	598.1
1779	1,969.1
1780	10,544.1
1781	5,085.8
1782	139.6
1783	119.1
1784	112.7
1785	105.0
1786	105.1
1787	103.9
1788	97.4
1789	94.0

[a] Data from *Historical Statistics of the United States*, p. 1196.

granting only 1/40 of their face value does amount to a redefinition. This observation might then lead an alert reader who also has a good memory to object to the claim made in Section 1.2 that the U.S. price level in 1940 was only 1.3 times its level as of 1776. The index numbers on which that claim is based should actually show a huge rise in prices between 1776 and 1800 (or any year subsequent to 1780). In fact, such an objection would have much merit. In defense of our use of these numbers in Section 1.2, it could be said that the comparison would have been legitimate if 1786 (rather than 1776) had been used as the starting date. Thus the moral of the story would have been the same, but its dramatic impact would have been lessened.

From 1781 until adoption of the Constitution in 1787 the monetary situation was one in which the "dollar" unit again referred to the quantity of silver in a Spanish peso, namely, 0.871 ounces. A considerable amount of silver coin was available for circulation, thanks to gifts and loans to the new nation from France and Spain, although this stock was run down badly on import expenditures following the end of the war. Some states issued paper money, but not enough to be destructive.[14]

The Constitution, it will be recalled from Chapter 2, gave to Congress the sole right to "coin Money and regulate the Value thereof" and forbade the states to "coin money; emit Bills of Credit; (or) make anything but gold and silver coin a Tender in Payment of Debts." These provisions were clearly intended to place the new nation firmly on a metallic standard. But no details were spelled out in the Constitution. Indeed, operational provisions for the nation's monetary standard were specified only with the passage of the Coinage Act of 1792 and the opening, in 1794, of a national mint in Philadelphia.

We must now turn our attention to the subject of bimetallism, for the Coinage Act of 1792 defined the dollar in terms of both gold and silver, and provided for free coinage of both. In particular, the unit of 1 dollar was specified as pertaining to 371.25 grains of silver or 24.75 grains of gold, these weights implying a ratio of precisely 15 to 1.[15] By "free coinage" was meant the following: if a person brought gold or silver bullion to the mint, the latter would without charge produce for him coins of the specified weight. In principle, these gold and silver coins were planned to serve jointly as the money—the circulating medium of exchange—for the nation. Prices and contracts were supposed to be expressed in dollars, with smaller amounts specified via a decimal system (which was the world's first).

Unfortunately, the world market price of silver was at the time closer to 1/15.5 than to 1/15 times that of gold. And this discrepancy was too large to be eliminated by a mechanism like that mentioned in Section 13.5. Consequently, silver was the "bad money"—the metal that was relatively less valuable in nonmonetary uses—so in accordance with Gresham's law it drove gold out of circulation. No one wanted to make dollar payments with gold, since they could as well be made with a quantity of silver that was less valuable in nonmonetary uses. In sum, only silver was brought to the mint for coinage; gold served no useful monetary role.

That situation was altered, however, by a new Coinage Act passed in 1834. That act reduced the gold equivalent of a dollar from 24.75 to 23.2 grains, thereby altering the silver-to-gold equivalence ratio from 15 to $371.25/23.2 = 16.002$. The ratio was adjusted in 1837 to $371.25/23.22 = 15.988$, but was still too far from the market valuation ratio of about 15.5. Consequently, gold became the "bad money," the

---

[14] On this topic, and indeed the entire period from 1775 to 1815, the reader could usefully consult Nettels (1962).

[15] There are 480 grains to the ounce, so the dollar could as well be described as constituting 0.7734 ounces of silver or 0.05156 ounces of gold. The latter figure was later changed, as we shall see.

metal that was overvalued at the mint and of relatively less value in nonmonetary uses. Accordingly, it became profitable to coin gold and to melt silver. Thus the U.S. monetary standard, while officially bimetallic, was *de facto* a silver standard before 1834 and gradually became a gold standard after. The overvaluation of gold in its monetary use was increased, moreover, by the California gold discoveries of the 1840s, which lowered its market price relative to all commodities, including silver.

But while the monetary standard was changed in a major fashion only once between 1792 and 1860, banking institutions underwent a period of development that was both rapid and tumultuous. As banking practices and regulations are critically important for money stock determination, an outline of their evolution is accordingly necessary. It is unfortunate that our account must be brief, for the detailed story is a lively and colorful one.[16]

Although the Constitution forbade the states to issue money, it did not prohibit their chartering of private banks. Such institutions were established, consequently, with three in existence in 1791 and 88 by 1811. These banks added to the circulating media by the issue of bank notes, which were ostensibly claims to specie (i.e., silver or gold) and therefore widely acceptable in payment. As their notes were supposed to be convertible into specie upon demand, the private banks needed to hold specie reserves. But the quantity of reserves could safely be a fraction (say, 0.2 or 0.3) of the notes outstanding, so the volume of the nation's medium of exchange was enhanced by the existence of banks—just as today's money stock is several times as large as the monetary base. In a young and vigorous society such as that of the times, there was of course a tendency for these banks to overissue notes in relation to reserves, since the proceeds could be lent at interest. And there were also possibilities for fraud. Consequently, in times of difficulty convertibility was frequently suspended—the banks refused to convert bank notes into specie, as promised. A complete breakdown of this type would, it should be noted, constitute a temporary abandonment of the metallic standard.

An important force for sound banking practices was, according to most accounts, provided by the first Bank of the United States, a national organization granted a 20-year charter by Congress in 1791. This was an exclusive charter; there were no other national banks. The Bank of the United States functioned like any commercial bank in the sense that it accepted deposits, issued notes, and made loans. But in

---

[16] Two standard reference on the topics are Temin (1969) and Hammond (1957). Useful short accounts are provided by Nussbaum (1957), Klein (1982), Hammond (1963), and the Gold Commission report (1982).

addition it was unusually well capitalized, provided some clearinghouse services, and had a special relationship with the federal government as its fiscal agent. In its operations the Bank not only followed sound banking practices and kept its notes convertible, but also exerted pressures on state banks to do the same. These pressures were made possible by its clearinghouse role and its role as a collector of specie for the federal government, which accepted state bank notes in payment for taxes (and then turned them over to its agent for collection).

Table 15-5. Wholesale Price Index, 1800–1859 (1910–1914 = 100)

Year	WPI[a]	Year	WPI
1800	129	1830	91
1	142	1	94
2	117	2	95
3	118	3	95
4	126	4	90
5	141	5	100
6	134	6	114
7	130	7	115
8	115	8	110
9	130	9	112
1810	131	1840	95
1	126	1	92
2	131	2	82
3	162	3	75
4	182	4	77
5	170	5	83
6	151	6	83
7	151	7	90
8	147	8	82
9	125	9	82
1820	106	1850	84
1	102	1	83
2	106	2	88
3	103	3	97
4	98	4	108
5	103	5	110
6	99	6	105
7	98	7	111
8	97	8	93
9	96	9	95

[a] Series compiled by Warren and Pearson, reported in *Historical Statistics of the United States*.

The latter activities were socially useful but unpopular with state banks, which would rather not have specie claims placed on them. Also, the unique position of the Bank of the United States made it a target for political attacks. As a consequence, its charter was not renewed when it expired in 1811.

The timing of this expiration was unfortunate, for the War of 1812 placed strong fiscal demands on the federal government. The services of the Bank of the United States were missed during the years of the war, and convertibility was suspended by banks outside New England in 1814. The price level rose, as can be seen from the wholesale price index figures reported in Table 15-5. This inflation was partly responsible for a shift in attitudes sufficient to lead to a new 20-year charter, granted by Congress in 1816, to the second Bank of the United States. Its functions were similar to those of its predecessor, but the Second Bank was larger and was poorly managed during its early years. Later it was operated in a useful manner, but its president (Nicholas Biddle) became embroiled in a semipersonal "war" with Andrew Jackson, the nation's president. This had the predictable outcome of leading to the Second Bank's demise. After 1836—actually, the breakdown came in 1834 when Jackson shifted Treasury deposits to other banks—there were no national banks until the 1860s.

During this era, the ostensibly convertible paper notes of state-chartered banks served as a major component of the nation's circulating medium, but they did so in a rather unsatisfactory way. Each bank's notes were its own, somewhat different in appearance and reliability from others. Even during periods of convertibility, they would circulate at values below par in regions distant from the bank of issue or if the latter's reputation was slight or shaky. And the absence of a nationwide coordinating agent arguably made the system's response to shocks more severe than it might have been. Thus major banking crises, with widespread suspensions of convertibility, occurred in 1837 and 1857. The former led to a sharp contraction in the money stock and a sharp decline in prices.

Various aspects of the banking system during this era would warrant discussion in a more lengthy historical treatment, but must be neglected here.[17] One topic that will be mentioned, in response to a recent outburst of interest, is that of the "Free Banking" experience of the years 1838–1861. During this period many states, beginning with New York, enacted laws that did away with the need for banks to obtain

---

[17] Of special interest are the Independent Treasury System (under which the U.S. Treasury held its own specie, rather than bank deposits), the Suffolk System (a New England arrangement for promoting adequate member bank reserves), and the New York and Boston clearinghouse organizations (for check clearing and the settlement of bank balances).

charters in the traditional manner. Instead, any group of persons was free to open a bank and circulate notes provided that it deposited a certain required volume of state and/or federal government bonds with the state's comptroller. There seems to be little clear-cut evidence that this practice was substantially better or worse than the traditional chartering requirements. In any event, an important point to recognize is that the system was not actually one of laissez-faire money creation. Instead, there were regulations not only concerning bond deposits, but also (in some cases) with regard to reserve requirements and centralized printing of the banks' notes. Most important, the system presumed a commodity-money standard: convertibility of bank notes into specie was required by law in all cases with heavy penalties imposed for any failure.

To put matters regarding the pre-1961 banking arrangements into perspective, it may be helpful to conclude this discussion with a statis-

Table 15-6. Composition of U.S. Money Stock, 1842–1859[a,b] (millions of dollars)

End of Year	Specie in Circulation[c]	Bank Notes	Bank Deposits	Money Stock
1842	44.8	46.4	49.3	140.5
1843	50.1	65.4	72.1	187.6
1844	57.0	79.8	75.7	212.5
1845	55.7	95.9	81.8	233.4
1846	58.0	89.2	77.9	225.1
1847	75.3	112.3	93.0	280.6
1848	78.6	91.9	90.5	261.0
1849	118.1	107.4	100.8	326.3
1850	162.0	146.7	100.7	409.4
1851	na	na	na	na
1852	208.6	175.4	137.3	521.3
1853	247.0	179.2	160.2	586.4
1854	277.9	158.5	163.1	599.5
1855	274.9	166.3	187.6	628.8
1856	299.3	182.7	201.2	683.3
1857	281.6	129.8	166.6	578.0
1858	268.2	170.0	227.2	665.4
1859	272.6	174.3	225.4	672.3

[a] Figures on specie and sum of bank notes plus deposits are taken from Stevens (1971). The division between notes and deposits is based on data in Friedman and Schwartz (1970), Table 13.
[b] na, not available.
[c] This figure includes Treasury holdings, which were substantial. Year-to-year changes in specie circulation are unreliable.

tical tabulation indicating the composition of the nation's money stock in the period just preceding the Civil War. Table 15-6 presents such a tabulation, one based on the work of Stevens (1971) and Friedman and Schwartz (1970). From the figures we see that in 1859 the nation's money stock was about 40 percent specie (coin plus bullion), 27 percent state bank notes, and 33 percent bank deposits. Our discussion to this point has virtually ignored bank deposits, but by the 1850s the establishment of the New York and Boston clearinghouses had made deposits subject to check an important component of the medium of exchange.

From the figures in Table 15-6 we can see the impact of the California gold discoveries—the stock of specie in circulation began to grow rapidly after 1848. The specie totals in the first column do not include specie held in banks as a reserve.[18] It is therefore worth mentioning that the magnitude of banks' specie reserves fluctuated, according to Stevens's work, in the vicinity of 20 to 35 percent of notes and deposits.

15.4 From the Civil War to World War I

The American Civil War was an event of enormous impact in many respects. In the area of money and banking it brought forth severe disruptions of a temporary nature and also lasting changes in institutions. In this section we review the more important of these effects as well as the general evolution of U.S. monetary arrangements up until 1914.

In 1861 the U.S. government's intention was to finance its war expenditures primarily by borrowing. Thus, although its early fund-raising activities in 1861 did involve a $50 million issue of non-interest-bearing "demand notes," they emphasized the selling of interest-bearing bonds. A major customer for these bonds was a group of banks located in Boston, New York, and Philadelphia. Rather than leave the loan proceeds on deposit with these banks, the Treasury chose to make massive specie withdrawals quickly, thereby endangering the banks' reserve position. To restore reserves, the banks attempted to resell a portion of the government's bonds to the public. In this attempt they were only partially successful, so reserve positions did deteriorate significantly. This led the public to fear a suspension of convertibility,

---

[18] The first-column figures do, however, include specie holdings by the Treasury. This inclusion is not consistent with current practices with regard to definition of the money stock.

and accordingly to make specie withdrawals—which exacerbated the problem. By January 1862, in consequence, most U.S. banks had suspended specie payments.

About the same time, moreover, the government had also revoked the convertibility aspect of their "demand notes." Finally, in early 1862 Congress passed its first Legal Tender Act, which authorized the issue of the famous notes known as "greenbacks." These were non-interest-bearing notes denominated in dollar units and declared to be legal tender. In other words, the greenbacks were by law acceptable for payment in any transactions conducted in terms of "dollars." Furthermore, there were only distant provisions for convertibility into specie. Consequently, the nation was effectively disengaged from any commodity-money standard. Greenbacks were essentially fiat money, although there was a presumption that the situation was not to be permanent.

Additional issues of greenbacks followed in 1863 and 1864, bringing the volume issued up to $450 million. In addition, there were other Treasury securities sold that had legal-tender status. But the innovation of the greatest lasting significance was the creation, beginning in 1863, of a network of national banks—banks chartered by the federal Comptroller of the Currency. Although this step was no doubt partially motivated by the weaknesses of the existing banking structure and had the benefit of introducing a uniform national paper currency, it also had the effect of providing loan funds for the U.S. government in yet another way. The mechanism was simple: national banks were required to hold $111.11 worth of government bonds for each $100.00 of bank notes issued. As the government bonds paid interest, this was an attractive proposition for the newly formed national banks. Their notes, it should be said, were not legal tender but were attractive to the public because of their uniformity and their safety—they were required to be convertible into "lawful money" (at the time, greenbacks!) and were guaranteed by the Treasury. Together, these stipulations gave rise to a National Banking System whose successor remains with us today.

Before continuing with our discussion of the Civil War experience, let us pause briefly to continue the story of the creation of the National Banking System. Despite the advantages to member banks, many existing state banks preferred to continue with their state charters rather than to move into the national system, because the capitalization and reserve requirements of the latter were more stringent. The growth of the national system was therefore disappointing to its supporters. Consequently, in 1865 Congress imposed a tax of 10 percent on any newly issued notes by state banks! This step brought about the end of state bank notes and drove some more banks into the National Banking

Table 15-7. Prices During the Civil War

Year	WPI[a] (1910–1914 = 100)	WPI[b]	Dollar Price of Gold[c]
1859	95	—	—
1860	93	—	—
1861	89	—	—
1862	104	98	1.016
1863	133	118	1.371
1864	193	148	1.562
1865	185	200	2.019
1866	174	172	1.404
1867	162	172	1.414
1868	158	158	1.400
1869	151	158	1.375

[a] Index of Warren and Pearson (1933).
[b] Index reported by Kindahl (1961); base year unstated.
[c] Reported by Kindahl (1961).

System. But many chose to remain state banks, providing exchange services by way of their checkable deposits.

The effect on the nation's money supply of all of the various governmental devices for financing the Civil War was dramatic. The amount of U.S. currency outstanding in 1862 was over $600 million, not including notes or deposits of the new national banks. Given the magnitudes in Table 15-6, it seems safe to say that the money stock doubled in roughly three years. What happened to prices? Prices continued to be quoted in "dollars," but now the term referred to a greenback rather than 23.22 grams (0.0484 ounces) of gold.[19] One would guess that prices would rise, and indeed they did. The Wholesale Price Index doubled between 1861 and 1864, according to the Warren and Pearson (1933) figures, while the greenback-dollar price of gold doubled between 1862 and 1865. Details are shown in Table 15-7, together with an alternative measure of the WPI reported by Kindahl (1961).

At the end of the war, the Treasury began to retire greenbacks as part of a program to bring prices back down to a level that would permit a return to the metallic standard, with gold priced as before at $20.67 per ounce. From 1865 to 1869 there was essentially no growth in the money stock, with declines occurring in three of the five years. Prices were falling—as Table 15-7 indicates—as the program required, but this was not popular with all segments of the population. The issue

---

[19] Except on the West Coast, where prices continued to be quoted in terms of gold.

Table 15-8. Prices, Income, and Money, 1870–1914

Year	WPI,[a] (1910–1914 = 100)	Nominal[b] GNP (billions of dollars)	Real GNP,[b] 1972 Prices	Money[c] Stock
1870	135	7.83	36.0	1.83
1	130	7.80	35.3	2.03
2	136	9.02	42.9	2.18
3	133	9.00	43.4	2.19
4	126	8.79	42.8	2.23
5	118	8.74	43.6	2.33
6	110	8.84	46.2	2.28
7	106	9.13	49.5	2.24
8	91	9.04	53.0	2.14
9	90	9.65	58.4	2.26
1880	100	12.14	66.7	2.76
1	103	12.13	68.0	3.31
2	108	13.10	71.1	3.57
3	101	12.79	70.3	3.79
4	93	12.44	72.2	3.79
5	85	11.66	72.4	3.89
6	82	12.06	76.0	4.21
7	85	12.56	78.3	4.49
8	86	12.48	76.4	4.61
9	81	12.96	78.9	4.88
1890	82	13.65	84.8	5.31
1	81.4	14.02	88.6	5.54
2	76.2	14.82	97.2	6.00
3	77.9	14.40	92.4	5.78
4	70.0	13.12	89.9	5.80
5	71.2	14.47	100.5	6.01
6	67.8	13.78	98.4	5.90
7	68.0	15.18	107.9	6.29
8	70.8	16.00	110.2	7.13
9	76.2	18.05	120.4	8.26
1900	81.8	19.40	123.5	8.96
1	80.7	21.47	137.9	10.14
2	85.9	22.39	139.1	11.08
3	87.0	23.80	146.1	11.77
4	87.1	23.78	144.2	12.54
5	87.7	26.07	155.0	13.89
6	90.2	29.88	173.0	15.02
7	95.1	31.59	175.6	15.73
8	91.8	28.80	161.2	15.55
9	98.6	33.39	180.9	17.25
1910	102.7	35.26	186.0	18.12
1	94.7	35.98	191.9	19.21
2	100.8	39.34	201.5	20.54
3	101.8	39.54	203.4	21.34
1914	99.4	38.84	196.0	22.21

[a] Data from Warren and Pearson (1933).
[b] Data from Gordon (1986).
[c] Data from Gordon (1986). This measure includes all bank deposits, and therefore pertains to the M2 concept of the money stock.

of when and whether to resume convertibility became a major political issue, but eventually legislation was passed in early 1875 that specified resumption of convertibility at the start of 1879. This legislation was almost overturned, but remained on the books and prices fell enough so that a successful resumption was in fact accomplished on schedule.[20]

For the next three years prices rose, but then in 1883 a decline began that continued for more than a decade. Thus between the Civil War and the turn of the century the United States experienced over 30 years of almost continual deflation. The Warren and Pearson price level was in 1896 only 35 percent of its value for 1864! This highly unusual experience provides a good opportunity for investigating the validity of the natural-rate hypothesis (mentioned in Chapter 9), which asserts that output performance is virtually independent over long spans of time of the average trend of nominal variables—a hypothesis that contrasts sharply with the popular notion that continued monetary stringency and deflation must bring about poor performance in terms of real output levels and growth rates. Estimates of real GNP for the period are provided in Table 15-8. From the reported figures, we see that the solution for b in the equation $\log(123.5/0.36) = 30b$ is 0.0408, which implies an output growth rate of 4.08 percent per year during the 30-year span 1870–1900. That figure is, of course, *above* the 3 percent rate that economists have come to regard as "normal" for the U.S. economy. The discrepancy is perhaps due to unusually rapid population growth during the period, but even taking account of the latter leaves about 2 percent per year output growth in per capita terms. That represents very good performance and tends to support the natural-rate viewpoint against the more popular notion mentioned above.

Despite this healthy rate of real economic growth, there was unhappiness concerning the price-level decline among a significant segment of the population. Debtors, of course, dislike deflation, as it requires them to repay loans with dollars that are more valuable than before in real terms. There was a political party, the Greenback Party, formed in 1875 to fight against resumption and campaign instead for more money creation and higher prices. The party elected 14 members of Congress in 1878, but declined thereafter.

A related campaign for "free silver" went on longer, however. Indeed, it provided the main platform plank in the presidential attempts of William Jennings Bryan in 1896 and 1900 and gave rise to the charge that a certain piece of coinage legislation constituted an act that should be known as the "crime of 1873." Let us consider the nature of this charge.

---

[20] The Warren and Pearson WPI values for 1878 and 1879 were 91 and 90, respectively, as compared with 89 for 1861 (see Table 15-8).

As explained above, silver had been more valuable as a commodity than as money since 1834. Thus there was in 1872 extremely little silver coinage in circulation even though the silver dollar was legal tender and the mint would coin one if someone would bring in 371.25 grains of fine silver. To put this in another way, the mint would buy (with "dollars") unlimited amounts of silver at the bimetallic standard price of $1.29 per ounce.[21] But the market price of silver stayed above $1.32 per ounce from 1850 until 1872, so few persons chose to have silver coined—that is, to sell silver for $1.29 per ounce.[22]

Then in February 1873 the Coinage Act in question was passed. At least on the surface, this act was designed primarily for tidying up the coinage laws and reorganizing the administrative structure of the mints and assay offices. But one bit of "tidying up" was the deletion of the standard 371.25-grain silver dollar from the list of the coins that the mint was obliged to produce. Since many adults had never even seen a silver dollar, and since the nation was not on a metallic basis at the time, this deletion attracted very little attention and consideration.

But silver production was expanding and Germany was in the process of switching from silver to gold coinage. Consequently, within a very few years the market price of silver had fallen below the $1.29 value that had previously been implied (see Table 15-9). Indeed, by the mid-1880s the price was substantially below $1.29. Now, if the silver dollar had not been deleted from the mint's list of coins, silver producers would have been able to sell all of their output to the mint at $1.29 rather than accept the lower prices that actually prevailed. But of course the effect would have been not only to make silver producers better off, but also to add substantially to the nation's stock of money. Prices would have declined less—indeed, probably would have risen— over the period and debtors, including prominently farmers of the South and the West, would have benefited. What the "free silver" movement wanted, then, was the free and unlimited coinage of silver at $1.29 per ounce, as would have prevailed in the absence of the "crime of 1873."[23]

---

[21] Note that 371.25/480 equals 0.7734 ounces per dollar, which implies $1/0.7734 = 1.293$ dollars per ounce.

[22] Coins of less than a dollar—so-called fractional coins—contained some silver, but less than enough to make their commodity value as high as their declared monetary value.

[23] Was there any "crime" in the sense of a *deliberate* attempt to avoid the coinage of the surging production of silver? O'Leary (1960) makes a rather convincing case that a man named H. R. Linderman, not a congressman but rather an assistant to the Comptroller of the Currency, knew exactly what he was doing when he drafted the legislation for congressional consideration. Linderman's motivation, according to O'Leary's account, was to keep the United States effectively on a gold standard. O'Leary's argument has been questioned, it should be said, by Friedman and Schwartz (1963).

Table 15-9. U.S. Silver Production and Market
Price, 1850–1900[a,b]

Year	Production (million ounces)	Price (dollars per ounce)
1845	0.05	na
1850	2.4	1.32
1855	2.7	1.34
1860	2.2	1.35
1865	2.6	1.34
1870	12.4	1.33
1871	17.8	1.32
1872	22.2	1.32
1873	27.6	1.30
1874	28.9	1.28
1875	24.5	1.24
1880	30.3	1.15
1885	39.9	1.06
1890	54.6	1.05
1895	55.7	0.65
1900	57.6	0.61

[a] Data from *Historical Statistics of the United States*, p. 606.
[b] na, not available.

It is interesting to consider the magnitude of the monetary effect that free-silver legislation would have had. A very rough estimate can be obtained by summing silver production from (say) 1873 through 1890, and valuing that total at $1.29 per ounce.[24] Doing so yields a figure of (653) (1.29) = 842 million dollars. As of 1890, the actual stock of high-powered money was about $1200 million, so it is clear that the monetary effect would have been substantial—and indeed probably would have led to the demonetization of gold in accordance with Gresham's law.

As it happens, legislation was adopted in 1878 and in 1890 calling for the Treasury to purchase certain specified quantities of silver at the $1.29 price, but not opening the mint to unlimited amounts. The second of these pieces of legislation, the Sherman Silver Purchase Act,

---

[24] Not all production would have gone into money creation, of course, and some did anyhow. But while those effects tend to make our estimate too large, there is another omitted consideration that would work in the other direction: a price of $1.29 would have induced more production.

specified a large volume of silver purchases—almost equal to the current rate of production—and led to some uncertainty among the public as to the future of the gold standard. This uncertainty may have contributed to a serious bank panic, involving currency withdrawals and bank failures, which took place in 1893.[25] In any event, President Grover Cleveland quickly called on Congress to repeal the silver purchase provisions of the Sherman Act. It did so, and the panic subsided.

Cleveland's party, the Democratic Party, nevertheless nominated the free-silver candidate Bryan for president in 1896 and 1900. He was defeated on both occasions, however, by the Republican William McKinley. In 1900, moreover, a currency act was passed which has become known as the Gold Standard Act, for it eliminated any residual element of bimetallism in the nation's monetary standard. Thus the battle for silver monetization came to an end and the nation was for the first time on a full and explicit gold standard. This remained the case until 1933.

In 1907 another bank panic occurred, one that led to widespread suspension of convertibility and to a short but sharp recession—note the real GNP value for 1908 in Table 15-8. This episode, following as it did other serious panics in 1873, 1884, and 1893, led to widespread agreement that some reform of the nation's banking institutions was needed. One consequence of that sentiment was the formation of a National Monetary Commission, consisting of members of Congress and chaired by a skillful and dedicated senator named Nelson W. Aldrich. After a major study, this commission made recommendations that eventually led to the Federal Reserve Act of 1913 and to the establishment in the following year of the institution that eventually became the nation's first full-fledged central bank, that is, the Fed. A few aspects of this establishment process will be mentioned briefly in the next section.

15.5 From 1914 to 1944

At the time of its creation, as today, the Fed's structure featured 12 regional Federal Reserve Banks plus a Washington-based supervisory body, initially named the Federal Reserve Board. But, unlike today, the regional Federal Reserve Banks were originally intended to possess the primary powers for management of the nation's monetary conditions. There was no counterpart of today's Federal Open Market

---

[25] For a much more detailed account of this period, as well as the one covered in Section 15.5, the reader is referred to the classic study of Friedman and Schwartz (1963).

Committee, and even after a counterpart was formed in 1923 the regional banks were for a while able to carry out their operations in a manner that was not highly coordinated. This sort of decentralized structure was a political necessity of the times, as there existed considerable hostility to the concept of a European-style central bank.

The purposes for which the Fed was established are summarized in the full title of the legislative document itself: "An Act to provide for the establishment of Federal reserve banks, to furnish an elastic currency, to afford means of rediscounting commercial paper, to establish a more effective supervision of banking in the United States, and for other purposes." Of particular importance here is the phrase concerning "an elastic currency." That term seems a bit vague, and indeed there are two distinct ideas that the founders probably had in mind. One of those ideas concerns responsiveness of the money stock to the economy's needs; it was felt that the previous arrangements "did not provide for the needed seasonal, cyclical, or secular variation in currency" (Klein, 1982, p. 198). By contrast, the second idea concerns the responsiveness of the *composition* of a given volume of money to altered desires—in particular, desires of individuals to hold more currency (specie or legal-tender paper) relative to deposits than they would normally. Elasticity in this sense is of special importance at times of incipient panic.

As Friedman and Schwartz (1963, pp. 168–73) have emphasized, the objectives to which these two meanings correspond are very different. In the second case the objective is well conceived, and elasticity in the relevant sense is clearly desirable; for if the public is confident of its ability to convert deposits into currency, then it will not rush to make conversions in a manner that itself tends to induce panic in a fractional-reserve banking system. But the desirability of currency elasticity in the first sense is more questionable. Is it good to have the volume of money unusually large at business cycle peaks, or would it be better for the volume to move countercyclically? Do the same considerations apply in the case of regular seasonal fluctuations? Whatever the answer is to these difficult questions, it is clear that the creation of the Federal Reserve System had a dramatic influence on currency elasticity with respect to seasonal movements. Before 1914 short-term interest rates exhibited much seasonal variability and reserves little; after 1914 exactly the reverse was true. It also seems clear that there was a tendency for policymakers to confuse the two distinct concepts of currency elasticity.

Another difference between the policy role of the Fed at the time of its creation and today concerns the monetary standard. In 1913, to be specific, it was taken for granted that maintenance of the gold standard would be an important aspect of, or constraint on, monetary policy.

Quickly, however, that situation was modified by the arrival of World War I. As the United States did not itself enter the war until 1916, and sold supplies in large volume during 1914–1916, the nation's stock of monetary gold increased rapidly. During those years, moreover, the gold standard was abandoned by most of the nations involved in the war. At no time during the war did the United States suspend convertibility domestically, but exports of gold to foreigners were curtailed by order of President Wilson between September 1917 and June 1918. Then in the early postwar period the United States was one of the very few major nations to provide convertibility of its currency into gold. Its buildup of gold during the war years led to rapid growth of the money stock and sizable increases in the price level during 1918–1920. Consequently, in the first half of 1920 the Fed twice tightened policy in response to a situation of declining reserves. (The Fed was required by law to hold gold reserves equal to at least 40 percent of its Federal Reserve notes outstanding.) This step led to a cyclical downturn, marked by an extremely sharp price-level decline in 1921. These movements can be seen in the data series reported in Table 15-10, and the price-level drop appears even more clearly in figures for the wholesale price index; the latter fell by 37 percent between 1920 and 1921!

Throughout the rest of the decade, until late 1929, the money stock expanded at a moderate rate, output grew steadily, and prices stayed nearly constant. Then, of course, came the start of the Great Depression of 1929–1940. The magnitude of that macroeconomic calamity has been mentioned above in Chapters 1 and 9, and is in any case probably a familiar topic for most readers. Rather than review well-known material, then, let us consider some facts and hypotheses concerning the role of monetary policy during these years.

The most basic of the relevant facts, one forcefully stressed by Friedman and Schwartz (1963), is that the money stock fell by almost 30 percent between 1929 and 1933.[26] It is the contention of Friedman and Schwartz that the cyclical downturn that began in 1920 would not have become so serious—would not have turned into the Great Depression—if this contraction in the stock of money had been prevented. Although controversial when first put forth, that contention today commands fairly widespread support among monetary and macroeconomic specialists, even though the profession lacks any widely accepted theory of the mechanism by which monetary shocks are turned into real fluctuations. Other aspects of the Friedman and Schwartz account of the period remain controversial, however, includ-

---

[26] Friedman and Schwartz usually describe the fall as "more than one-third." The apparent discrepancy arises only because they refer to the M2 measure of money whereas our figures pertain to M1.

Table 15-10.   Money, Prices, and Output, 1915–1946[a]

Year	M1 Money Stock (billions) of dollars)	GNP Price Deflator (1972 = 100)	Real GNP 1972 Prices
1915	12.2	20.7	193.6
6	14.4	23.2	208.2
7	16.7	28.6	211.4
8	18.6	31.3	244.3
9	21.4	36.8	229.0
1920	23.0	42.7	214.2
1	20.7	34.8	199.9
2	21.2	32.3	229.5
3	22.3	33.6	254.1
4	23.3	33.1	256.4
5	25.2	33.8	276.0
6	25.4	33.3	291.8
7	25.5	32.4	293.3
8	25.7	32.8	296.2
9	25.8	32.8	315.7
1930	24.8	31.7	285.5
1	22.8	28.9	263.5
2	20.1	25.7	227.0
3	19.1	25.1	222.1
4	21.6	27.3	239.1
5	25.2	27.9	260.0
6	29.0	28.0	295.5
7	29.6	29.3	310.2
8	29.8	28.7	296.8
9	33.6	28.4	319.8
1940	39.0	29.1	344.2
1	45.8	31.2	400.4
2	56.1	34.3	461.8
3	72.6	36.1	531.7
4	85.7	37.0	569.1
5	98.3	37.9	560.2
6	104.8	43.9	478.3

[a] All data from Gordon (1986, pp. 781–85).

ing their suggestion that the course of events would have been more favorable if the monetary institutions present *before* the creation of the Fed had remained in place.[27]

---

[27] A review of controversies concerning the Friedman and Schwartz volume is provided by Bordo (1988).

Table 15-11. Bank Suspensions, 1921–1946[a]

Year	Number of Banks	Deposits (millions of dollars)
1921	505	172
1922	367	93
1923	646	150
1924	775	210
1925	618	168
1926	976	260
1927	669	199
1928	499	143
1929	659	231
1930	1352	869
1931	2294	1691
1932	1456	725
1933	4004	3601
1934	61	37
1935	32	13
1936	72	28
1937	83	34
1938	80	60
1939	72	160
1940	48	142
1941	16	19
1942	23	19
1943	5	12
1944	2	1
1945	1	5
1946	2	1

[a] Data from *Historial Statistics of the United States*, pp. 1038–39.

Another basic fact concerns the extent of bank failures during the crucial years 1930–1933. The number of bank suspensions—that is, the number of banks closed to the public by supervisory authorities or because of financial difficulties—is shown for each year from 1921 to 1946 in Table 15-11, where the years 1930–1933 stand out dramatically. These bank failures[28] were brought about by attempts by depositors to make withdrawals—to convert their deposits into coin or Federal Reserve notes—in excess of the banks' available volume of reserves. The critical effect of these failures was to contribute to the contraction

[28] Most of the banks with suspensions during this period never reopened.

in the money stock that was taking place. In this regard there were two channels at work. First, there was the direct effect on the money stock of the elimination of the failed banks' deposits, which amounted to almost $7 billion. Second, the failures led to a reduction in the public's confidence in the banking system and thereby to an increase in the public's chosen ratio of currency to deposits. As such an increase implies a smaller money stock for any given value of high-powered money—recall the analysis of Section 4.2—this channel provided additional contractionary effects of an indirect type.

Thus it appears that the banking panics and bank failures of 1930–1933 were largely responsible for the contraction in the stock of money that took place between 1929 and 1933.[29] Now a major purpose in creating the Federal Reserve System was precisely to prevent banking panics, and it can be argued that the Fed possessed the policy tools necessary.[30] Consequently, Friedman and Schwartz (1963) have strongly criticized the Fed for its behavior, suggesting that the term "inept" amounts to "a plain description of fact" (p. 407).

In response to the last and worst of the banking panics, the newly elected president, Franklin Roosevelt, ordered all banks closed during March 1933—the famous nationwide banking "holiday." After a week, most banks were reopened gradually—others were liquidated—and some institutional changes were initiated, which were then enacted over the next two years. Of these changes, three were of lasting significance and deserve brief discussion. First, the Banking Act of 1933 authorized the creation, as of January 1, 1934, of the Federal Deposit Insurance Corporation (FDIC). All member banks of the Federal Reserve System were required to have their deposits insured by the FDIC, and other banks could obtain deposit insurance if certain conditions were met. The existence of such insurance is designed to give depositors confidence that their deposits would not be lost even if the bank holding them were to fail. This confidence would in turn keep depositors from rushing to make withdrawals at times of crisis, and should thereby help to prevent bank panics from ever arising. Within six months, over 97 percent of all commercial bank deposits had been insured, and subsequently bank failures declined sharply relative to their pre-1930 levels (see Table 15-11). This creation of a federal deposit insurance program has been widely praised by economists. It is regarded by Friedman and Schwartz as "the structural change most

---

[29] The contraction can certainly not be attributed to external events causing gold outflows, for the nation's stock of monetary gold was (very) slightly larger in 1933 than in 1929 ($4.036 billion as compared with $3.997).

[30] There is some dispute over this point; the opposing position is discussed by Friedman and Schwartz (1963, pp. 399–406).

conducive to monetary stability since state bank note issues were taxed out of existence immediately after the Civil War" (1963, p. 434).[31]

Second, the Banking Act of 1935 provided for some significant organizational changes within the Fed—the board was renamed the Board of Governors of the Federal Reserve System and the Federal Open Market Committee was reconstituted. Also, the Fed was given increased powers, including the authority to vary reserve requirements imposed on member banks.

Third, there were major changes concerning the role of gold in the monetary system. To begin with, the entire U.S. stock of gold was *nationalized* in 1933–1934: private holders were required to sell all their nonnumismatic gold to the Treasury at $20.67 an ounce and were forbidden to hold gold privately thereafter. In addition, after a brief period of floating, the dollar price of gold was on February 1, 1934, set at $35.00 per ounce, a figure that was maintained until 1972. In other words, the Treasury became committed to buy gold from any seller at $35.00 per ounce, but it would sell gold (at that price) only to the monetary authorities of other nations. Without attempting to understand the (partly ill-conceived) reasons for adopting these new arrangements, let us consider the question: Did they leave the United States with a monetary system that should be thought of as constituting a gold standard? The answer is not obvious because, although the dollar price of gold was fixed, U.S. citizens were not permitted to *buy* gold at that price. Nevertheless, it would be appropriate to regard the system as constituting a gold standard if it was so designed that the nation's money supply would be adjusted so as to yield a price level that would make the relative price of gold—P_g/P in the notation of Chapter 13—tend to approach the value implied by full stock equilibrium. In principle, that sort of adjustment could take place even though gold would be sold only to foreign governments. The mechanism would work as follows. If the U.S. price level were too high, P_g/P would be below its full equilibrium value. Citizens of other nations would want to increase their holdings of gold at that relative price, so they would purchase gold from the U.S. Treasury through the intermediary of their national monetary authority. The U.S. stock of gold would then fall when the U.S. price level was too high. If this led invariably to a monetary restriction that would lower P and increase P_g/P, then the system would constitute a gold standard: the price level would be driven toward the value necessary for P_g/P to be at its equilibrium level given the fixed P_g.

---

[31] Recently, it has become clear that the charges for insurance that a bank must pay to the FDIC are not adequately related to the riskiness of the bank's loan portfolio, a failing that induces banks to engage in undesirably risky investments.

Whether such a system was in effect in the United States during the late 1930s and early 1940s is difficult to determine, for the world situation was such that there were no major outflows of gold from the United States until the 1950s.[32] Until then, there was no opportunity to observe whether the system in operation was one that would result in a monetary restriction designed to lower the price level when gold outflows occurred. The reaction that did occur in the postwar period is described briefly in the next section.

After 1934, the economy gradually began to recover from the depths of the depression. This recovery was interrupted, however, by a significant downturn in 1937–1938; see the real GNP figures in Table 15-10. That downturn is attributed by Friedman and Schwartz (1963, Chap. 9) to an action taken by the Fed: a doubling of banks' reserve requirements that was carried out in three steps in 1936 and 1937. This led, they suggest, to a marked slowdown in the growth rate of the money stock and that in turn to the output decline. Whatever the validity of that argument, after 1938 the money stock and real income again began to grow strongly. The outbreak of World War II in Europe in 1939 intensified the pace of recovery from the Great Depression and the output/employment expansion carried on until 1944.

15.6 Conclusion

The period since World War II will be at least moderately familiar to all readers, and a few episodes have been mentioned elsewhere in this book. Accordingly, it will not be discussed here, except to bring up to date our account of the evolution of the nation's monetary standard. That story is a brief one, moreover, as basically it amounts to little except the creation and demise of the Bretton Woods system.

The international monetary system created at the Bretton Woods Conference of 1944 was one in which nations other than the United States kept the dollar price of their currencies—their exchange rates with the United States—fixed.[33] The United States, in turn, was to continue to keep the dollar convertible into gold at the price of $35.00 per ounce. Together, these two provisions would place all the cooperating nations on a gold standard, a variant under which dollars were used as the main exchange medium for international transactions. In

---

[32] A detailed review of the course of events is provided by the Gold Commission report (1982, pp. 66–81).

[33] There were provisions for occasional adjustments in the par values, which were to take place only in the event of "a situation of fundamental disequilibrium."

addition, the participating nations were to become members of the International Monetary Fund, which would administer the exchange-rate system, and were to avoid restrictions on international trade while gradually reducing impediments to international financial transactions.

For reasons that will not be explored here, the United States had current-account deficits with the rest of the world year after year beginning in the early 1950s. These deficits were financed by the payment of gold and dollars to other nations; under the system in place those nations would accept dollars to a considerable extent because of the dollar's role as an international transaction medium. But with the United States committed to maintain gold at $35.00 an ounce, these dollars held abroad amounted to claims on the U.S. gold stock. As time passed, the stock of claims outstanding became large relative to the stock of gold. Eventually, other nations wished to add to their own gold supplies and so began to draw down the U.S. stock of gold. Maintenance of the gold standard would then have required the United States to contract its money supply so as to drive down its price level, thereby raising P_g/P to a value that would not induce gold outflows. But the United States was unwilling to undergo the massive deflation that would have been necessary: by 1971 the U.S. price level was well over twice its value as of 1944. Consequently, in a series of steps taken over the period 1968–1973, the Bretton Woods system was abandoned in favor of floating international exchange rates, with the monetary arrangements of the United States no longer tied to gold in any way whatsoever.

With that brief account in mind, we can now return to the question posed in Section 15.5, that is, whether the U.S. arrangements of the late 1930s constituted a gold standard. In that previous discussion we suggested that the answer should depend on whether the system was one that forced the price level to adjust so as to make the price of gold relative to other commodities move toward the value determined by nonmonetary forces—gold production possibilities and nonmonetary flow demands. We recognized that a long time should be permitted for these adjustments to take place, as the situation in 1933 was clearly far from one of full equilibrium. But the postwar record is one that shows very few indications of any attempt to make the U.S. price level adjust so as to move P_g/P toward its full equilibrium level. The opportunity for private foreign citizens to purchase gold from the United States was not truly present until 1958, when several European nations removed their wartime restrictions on the acquisition of foreign currencies, and by 1960 the price of gold on the London gold market was significantly above $35.00 per ounce. Almost immediately the U.S. government began with a series of further restrictions on private actions, altered regulations, and international agreements—all designed to try to somehow maintain the $35.00 price *without* a U.S. or world deflation.[34] Thus in retrospect it seems clear that there was no genuine commitment by the U.S. government to make its monetary policy behavior conform to the constraints implied by a gold standard. Perhaps there was some such commitment present in the attitude of the authorities and the political system during the late 1930s, but if so it seems to have been gone by the end of World War II. For that reason, one must conclude that the United States was not on a gold standard following World War II, but precisely when it left the standard—when the latter's political support disappeared—is impossible to determine.[35]

Problems

1. About how much paper currency was held per capita in South Carolina in 1770? Does the answer conflict with the conjecture of Section 15.3 that per capita money holdings in the early 1770s were about £2 sterling per person? Explain.
2. By June 1781, the bills of credit issued by the Continental Congress had become nearly valueless and had ceased to circulate. Does this fact constitute a failure of Gresham's law? Discuss.
3. In late 1875, the annual rate of interest on five-year loans was around 7 percent. What was the real rate of interest on these loans? Briefly justify your answer.
4. An important influence on the legislation that established the Federal Reserve System was a line of thought known as the "real bills doctrine." The main point of this doctrine was the idea that a *sufficient* condition for desirable monetary policy is that all banks, including the central bank, restrict their lending to nonspeculative loans secured by "real" collateral, that is, inventories and other tangible productive property. Suppose that producers desire credit from the banking system in an amount equal to 20 percent of a year's output and that banks pass their demand on in the form of collateralized demand for central bank credit. Under these circumstances, what limitation is placed on the nominal stock of high-powered money by adherence to the real bills doctrine? Would the answer be affected by recognition that loan demands depend on interest rates?

---

[34] On this topic, again see the Gold Commission report (1982).
[35] That is the reason for the vagueness, concerning the demise of the gold standard, in our discussion in Section 1.2.

References

Bordo, Michael D., "The Contribution of *A Monetary History of the United States, 1867–1960* to Monetary History," in *Money in Economic Perspective*, M. D. Bordo, ed. (Chicago: University of Chicago Press, 1988).

Brock, Leslie V., *The Currency of the American Colonies, 1700–1764*. (New York: Arno Press, 1975).

Commission on the Role of Gold in the Domestic and International Monetary Systems, *Report to the Congress*, Vol. 1 (Washington, D.C.: U.S. Congress, 1982).

Ernst, Joseph A., *Money and Politics in America, 1755–1775*. (Chapel Hill: University of North Carolina Press, 1973).

Friedman, Milton, and Anna J. Schwartz, *A Monetary History of the United States*. (Princeton, N.J.: Princeton University Press, 1963).

Friedman, Milton, and Anna J. Schwartz, *Monetary Statistics of the United States*. (New York: National Bureau of Economic Research, 1970).

Gordon, Robert J., ed., *The American Business Cycle: Continuity and Change*. (Chicago: University of Chicago Press, 1986).

Hammond, Bray, *Banks and Politics in America from the Revolution to the Civil War*. (Princeton, N.J.: Princeton University Press, 1957).

Hammond, Bray, "Banking Before the Civil War," in *Banking and Monetary Studies*, ed. D. Carson. (Homewood, Ill.: Richard D. Irwin, Inc., 1963).

Kindahl, James, "Economic Factors in Specie Resumption: The United States, 1865–79," *Journal of Political Economy* 69 (February 1961), 30–48.

Klein, John J., *Money and the Economy*, 6th ed. (Orlando, Fla.: Harcourt Brace Jovanovich, Inc., 1982).

McCusker, John J., *Money and Exchange in Europe and America, 1600–1775: A Handbook*. (Chapel Hill: University of North Carolina Press, 1978).

Michener, Ronald, "Fixed Exchange Rates and the Quantity Theory in Colonial America," *Carnegie–Rochester Conference Series on Public Policy* 27 (Autumn 1987), 233–308.

Nettels, Curtis, *The Money Supply of the American Colonies Before 1720*. (Madison: University of Wisconsin, 1934).

Nettels, Curtis, *The Emergence of a National Economy, 1775–1815*. (New York: Holt, Rinehart and Winston, 1962).

Nettels, Curtis, *The Roots of American Civilization: A History of American Colonial Life*, 2nd ed. (New York: Appleton-Century-Crofts, 1963).

Nussbaum, Arthur, *A History of the Dollar*. (New York: Columbia University Press, 1957).

O'Leary, Paul M., "The Scene of the Crime of 1873 Revisited: A Note," *Journal of Political Economy* 68 (August 1960), 388–92.

Ratner, Sidney, James J. Soltow, and Richard Sylla, *The Evolution of the American Economy*. (New York: Basic Books, Inc., Publishers, 1979).

Smith, Adam, *An Inquiry into the Nature and Causes of the Wealth of Nations*. (London: W. Strahan and T. Cadell, 1776).

Smith, Bruce D., "American Colonial Monetary Regimes: The Failure of the

Quantity Theory and Some Evidence in Favor of an Alternate View," *Canadian Journal of Economics* 18 (August 1985a), 531–65.

Smith, Bruce D., "Some Colonial Evidence on Two Theories of Money: Maryland and the Carolinas," *Journal of Political Economy* 93 (December 1985b), 1178–1211.

Stevens, Edward J., "Composition of the Money Stock Prior to the Civil War," *Journal of Money, Credit, and Banking* 3 (February 1971), 84–101.

Temin, Peter, *The Jacksonian Economy*. (New York: W.W. Norton and Co., Inc., 1969).

Timberlake, Richard H., Jr., *The Origins of Central Banking in the United States*. (Cambridge, Mass.: Harvard University Press, 1978.

U.S. Bureau of the Census, *Historical Statistics of the United States, Colonial Times to 1970*. (Washington, D.C.: U.S. Government Printing Office, 1975).

Warren, George F., and Frank A. Peason, *Prices*. (New York: John Wiley & Sons, Inc., 1933).

16

A Strategy for Monetary Policy

16.1 Basic Considerations

In this concluding chapter, our object is to consider an approach to the formulation of monetary policy, one that recognizes the latter's importance and also its limitations. The discussion is intended to serve a double purpose: not only will it provide a framework for thinking about policy, but it should also be useful as a review, for it relies on results and arguments developed in several of the previous chapters.

One of the most significant results that we have developed above concerns the desirability of a policy regime in which actions of the monetary authority are carried out in accordance with a maintained policy *rule*. Specifically, the analysis of Chapter 12 indicates that "discretionary" or period-by-period decision making tends to produce more inflation than desired, when outcomes are averaged over a long span of time, and with no additional output or employment generated in compensation. But this undesirable tendency can be overcome, it was shown, by adherence to a suitably designed rule—a contingency plan for policy actions chosen to pertain over a large number of periods. In addition, it was emphasized that such a rule can in principal be activist—that is, responsive to recent economic conditions. In Sections 16.2 and 16.3 we develop an explicitly specified rule of this type and explore its properties.

But before beginning, it will be useful to recognize that adherence to a monetary rule amounts to one form of a monetary *standard*. Thus it is relevant to recall that the monetary standard of the greatest historical importance was the gold standard. In that regard, the analytical principles pertaining to a gold standard—in fact, to any commodity-money standard—were explored in Chapter 13, while actual experience with gold and bimetallic systems was outlined in Chapters 12 and 15. From the material in those chapters most scholars would conclude that, while a metallic standard tends in practice to prevent the occurrence of long periods of rapid inflation or deflation, it does not prevent fairly sustained price movements or moderately severe cyclical fluctuations. Furthermore, a commodity standard works by requiring the monetary authority to create or destroy money so as to keep the money price of the standard commodity constant at some specified value. It would seem, consequently, that some alternative rule for the creation and destruction of money could be devised which would prevent severe inflation (or deflation) on a secular basis, yet also provide a diminished magnitude of cyclical fluctuations.[1]

In principle, one would logically want to design such a rule by adopting explicit objectives for the policymaker and then using an accurate model of the economy to determine which rule would most nearly achieve those objectives. But in practice there is one extremely important problem with that strategy. In particular, as was emphasized in Chapters 9 and 10, current knowledge of the dynamics of aggregate-supply or Phillips-curve behavior is inadequate for the construction of an accurate model. Specifically, the mechanism by which monetary policy actions have their effects on real output and employment is not well understood by macroeconomists. Consequently, the design of a policy rule cannot sensibly be based on any particular model of the nominal-to-real mechanism. Consequently, it would be more sensible to choose a rule that has the property that it works reasonably well under a wide variety of specifications concerning this mechanism. Thus the rule should be able to provide adequate performance if the economy actually works as hypothesized by Lucas (1972), or by Fischer (1977), or by Taylor (1979), or by the "real business cycle" theorists (e.g., Kydland and Prescott, 1982).

But while economists' knowledge of the period-by-period dynamics of the nominal-to-real interaction is poor, knowledge concerning *average* behavior over long periods of time is much better. In particular, both theory and evidence tend to support the classical notion embodied in the steady-state analysis of Chapter 6: over extended periods, real

---

[1] A fixed exchange rate also constitutes a monetary standard for an individual economy. Statements similar to those just made concerning the gold standard are also applicable to a fixed-exchange-rate standard. A small bit of additional discussion on this topic appears in Section 16.3.

output and employment levels are virtually independent of the rate of growth of monetary variables. Thus, whether inflation proceeds on average at 1 percent per year or at 10 percent—or indeed at 100 percent or minus 10 percent—the average growth of output and employment will be about the same.

Together, these two propositions concerning knowledge and ignorance of monetary effects on real variables suggest that a sensible monetary strategy would aim for a zero inflation rate on average and would not attempt to be highly ambitious with regard to its effect on cyclical variation of real variables. Most important in that regard, it would seem, is the avoidance of abrupt changes in conditions due to monetary policy itself.

On the basis of considerations somewhat similar to these, Milton Friedman put forth many years ago a well-known argument[2] suggesting that a desirable monetary strategy would be to make the stock of money grow at a *constant* rate designed to yield zero inflation.[3] The monetary authority should not attempt to mitigate cyclical fluctuations, according to Friedman's argument, but should keep the growth rate of the money stock the same year by year, "month by month, and indeed, so far as possible, day by day" (Friedman, 1962, p. 54). Friedman's original guess at the appropriate rate was about 4 percent per year, so as to accommodate real growth of about 3 percent per year with a 1 percent annual decline in velocity.[4]

In recent years it has become clear that there are two problems with Friedman's suggestion. The first of these is that the money stock is not itself a controllable *instrument* but is instead, as emphasized in Chapter 4, a variable that the monetary authority can manipulate only indirectly

---

[2] Friedman's argument for a constant money growth rate was first developed in Friedman (1960), as a modification of a proposal for automatic variation in the rate of monetary growth put forth in a much earlier paper (1948). The constant-growth-rate proposal has been emphasized in many of Friedman's influential writings, including *Capitalism and Freedom* (1962) and his American Economic Association presidential address (1968).

[3] It might legitimately be asked why the target should be zero inflation rather than the mild deflation suggested by the analysis of Section 6.7. One possible reason is that price indices may overstate inflation to some extent because they take inadequate account of product improvements that occur over time. Or "political feasibility" might be invoked, despite its unattractiveness to an analytical economist. In any event, any rule that is applied so as to yield zero inflation can easily be modified to yield some other value instead. The same principles of design would be applicable, so the analysis of this chapter would remain relevant.

[4] At the time, Friedman believed that the elasticity of money demand with respect to real expenditures was greater than unity. In this case, velocity would decrease as time passes under steady-state conditions, assuming (as he did) no continuing improvement in payments technology. This conclusion can be obtained by combining the result expressed in equation (15) of Section 6.6 with the velocity discussion of Section 3.5.

and with some significant quarter-to-quarter errors.[5] Thus Friedman's rule is not fully operational, that is, capable of being executed. Second, the existence of significant technical progress in the payments industry, and the random occurrence of this technical progress, makes it difficult to know *how much* money growth will lead to zero inflation on average. Over the 32-year span from 1954 through 1986, for example, M1 velocity increased in the United States at an average rate of about 2.5 percent per year. Consequently, a 4 percent growth rate for M1 would have led to about 3.5 percent inflation over that period, even with a 3 percent growth rate for real output.

Because of these two weaknesses in Friedman's scheme, it would appear that a better monetary rule could be devised. In the following section, one that has been previously investigated by the present author (McCallum, 1987, 1988) will be discussed.

16.2 A Specific Rule

For a monetary rule to be fully operational, it must be expressed in terms of a variable that the monetary authority can accurately control. In the United States, accurate control is possible for short-term nominal interest rates (such as Treasury bill rates and the federal funds rate) and for reserve aggregates (including total reserves and nonborrowed reserves). Another variable in this category is the monetary base (i.e., reserves plus currency in the hands of the public). A rule that specifies settings for any of these variables would therefore be operational— that is, could feasibly be put into operation by the Fed.

But although rules pertaining to an interest rate are operational,[6] they are highly undesirable. The problem is that interest rates are extremely poor indicators of the state of monetary policy—that is, whether it is "tight" or "loose." To appreciate that problem, readers might quickly ask themselves whether *high* interest rates indicate that monetary policy is restrictive or expansionary. Now, as readers of newspapers and observers of television news programs will know, the media's commentators on economic affairs take it as obvious that "high interest rates" is synonymous with "restrictive monetary policy." But

---

[5] It should be recognized that Friedman (1960) also proposed major institutional changes in banking regulations that would have made the M1 money stock controllable. These proposed changes (e.g., 100 percent reserves) have not been adopted and do not appear likely to be adopted in the foreseeable future.

[6] In what follows, the interest rates being discussed are nominal interest rates. Real rates are, of course, not controllable by the monetary authority.

readers of this book will know, from the discussion in Chapter 6, that high interest rates are largely a consequence of the public's expectation of a high inflation rate, and also that the latter results primarily from a rapid (and sustained) rate of growth of the money stock. So the presumption of the media commentators is highly misleading. Yet it is not entirely incorrect, either, for the *temporary* impact effect of an abrupt and unexpected tightening of monetary policy is an increased nominal interest rate.[7] Thus the sign of the relationship between nominal interest rates and monetary policy tightness depends on the time horizon involved: monetary tightening is reflected by a temporary increase in interest rates followed by a longer-lasting reduction. This pattern, to come to the point, makes any interest rate an ambiguous and potentially misleading indicator of monetary policy.

For that reason, we conclude that a policy rule should be formulated in terms of the behavior of a quantitative magnitude—either a reserve measure or the monetary base. There is something to be said for each of these possibilities,[8] but in the work to be described below the monetary base is the chosen instrument. Thus the rule to be studied specifies quarterly[9] settings for the variable Δb_t, where $b_t = \log B_t$ and B_t denotes the average value during quarter t of the monetary base.[10]

In the spirit of Friedman's suggestion, one possibility would be to specify a constant value for Δb_t, that is, to set Δb_t equal to 0.01 or 0.005 (for example) for each quarter.[11] But since the rate at which the payments technology will improve over the next few decades is currently unknown—that is the second weakness of Friedman's rule mentioned above—it would seem to be preferable to use a rule that incorporates some built-in adjustments. In the previous studies conducted by the author, this has been accomplished as follows. First, let V_t be defined as the base "velocity" for period t, that is, $V_t \equiv X_t/B_t$, where

---

[7] This is illustrated in Problem 2.

[8] Advocates of a reserve measure instead of the base emphasize that the latter is largely composed of currency, and they conjecture that much of the currency outstanding is held by drug dealers and other participants in illegal economic activities. If the money-holding behavior of these participants does not respond in the normal manner to economic stimuli, the base might be an unreliable instrument for effecting monetary policy. But in fact the base seems to be more closely related than reserves to nominal GNP and other measures of economic activity.

[9] In principal, the definition of time periods used in the study could be a month or some other duration. It is the author's guess that a quarter is the most useful definition for the analysis of macroeconomic phenomena and the conduct of monetary policy.

[10] The symbol H_t was used in Chapter 4, where we now use B_t. One reason for the switch in notation is that the following investigation uses a measure of the base, constructed by the Federal Reserve Bank of St. Louis, that makes adjustments to compensate for any changes that occur in reserve requirements.

[11] Note that a figure of 0.01 for Δb_t would amount to growth rate of roughly 4 percent over a year (i.e., four quarters).

X_t = nominal GNP in period t.[12] Then using lowercase letters for logarithms, we have $v_t = x_t - b_t$ and the growth rates are related according to

$$\Delta v_t = \Delta x_t - \Delta b_t. \tag{1}$$

Next, let us suppose that it is known that *real* GNP will grow on average at about 3 percent per year over the foreseeable future.[13] Then, to get zero inflation on average, we would want nominal GNP also to grow at that rate. In terms of quarterly values, that is, we would want to have Δx_t equal 0.00739 on average, since 0.00739 corresponds to a 3 percent annual growth rate.[14] So if the future growth rate of velocity were known to be Δv, we would then have the rule

$$\Delta b_t = 0.00739 - \Delta v. \tag{2}$$

Now, of course, we do not know what values will prevail for Δv_t in the future, even on average. But since technical progress occurs in a fairly smooth and regular fashion, a reasonably good forecast for the near future can be based on recent actual values of Δv_t. Thus if we let $\overline{\Delta v_t}$ denote the average value at time t of velocity growth over a few recent periods, we might reasonably opt for a rule of the form

$$\Delta b_t = 0.00739 - \overline{\Delta v_t}. \tag{3}$$

More specifically, an average of Δv_t over the previous 16 quarters (four years) would seem appropriate, since use of a smaller number of quarters would imply an averaging period that would include cyclical effects on velocity growth, as well as the technical-change effects that we wish to incorporate. Let us therefore interpret $\overline{\Delta v_t}$ in what follows as a 16-quarter average of Δv values for periods $t - 1, t - 2, \ldots, t - 17$. With that interpretation, we have in equation (3) a formula expressing a monetary rule that is similar in spirit to Friedman's, but which is not open to the two problems mentioned above.

It seems very likely that if the rule in equation (3) were followed by the Fed, the United States would experience roughly 3 percent annual growth in nominal GNP over any extended period of time and therefore would experience approximately zero inflation. Even if real growth averaged only two-thirds as much as the postulated 3 percent, the inflation rate would be only 1 percent per year. So this rule should

---

[12] Recall the definition of the term *velocity* provided in Chapter 3.

[13] In fact, over the past 100 years, real GNP in the United States has grown at about a 3 percent annual rate over most intervals of 20 years or more, provided that neither initial nor final date in the comparison is taken from the depression of the 1930s or during a major war.

[14] Specifically, if $x_t - x_{t-1} = \log X_t - \log X_{t-1} = 0.00739$, then $\log x_t - \log x_{t-4} = 0.002956$ and $X_t/X_{t-4} = 1.03$.

work rather well—probably as well as the gold standard—in terms of preventing inflation (or deflation) over extended periods of time.

But what about the prevention of cyclical fluctuations? There is only so much that monetary policy can do in that regard, but it is nevertheless important that most of whatever is feasible be accomplished. In trying to decide what is feasible, we are thrown up against the difficulty emphasized above—inadequate knowledge of the nature of the period-by-period connection between monetary and real variables. It seems likely, nevertheless, that cyclical fluctuations in real output and employment would be kept small if fluctuations in *nominal* GNP were minimized.[15] Consequently, one is led to consider whether rule (3) could not be modified so as to yield a nominal GNP growth path that stays close to a 3 percent target path in each period, as well as on average.[16]

With that aim in mind, let us now define x_t^* as the target value of (the log of) nominal GNP for period t and specify that these x_t^* targets grow steadily at a 3 percent annual rate. In terms of quarterly logarithmic variables, this implies that x_t^* should increase by the amount 0.00739 each period, as mentioned above. Now suppose that the actual x_t value exceeds the target value x_t^* in some period, because of private-sector shocks. Then to get x_{t+1} closer to x_{t+1}^* than it would be if rule (3) were followed, the monetary authority could decrease the setting for Δb_{t+1}. Similarly, Δb_{t+1} values could be made greater than those specified by rule (3) when x_t falls short of x_t^*. To accomplish this sort of adjustment would not constitute abandonment of policymaking according to a rule, but would call for the addition of another term involving $x_t^* - x_t$ in the adopted rule. In particular, the approach at hand could be implemented by adoption of the following rule, in which λ is a positive constant:

$$\Delta b_t = 0.00739 - \overline{\Delta v_t} + \lambda(x_{t-1}^* - x_{t-1}). \qquad (4)$$

According to the formula specified in (4), the growth rate of the monetary base would be augmented when the most recent value of nominal GNP lies below its target path, and would be diminished when nominal GNP exceeds the target value.

To complete the specifications of rule (4), a particular numerical value needs to be assigned to the parameter λ. This value must be

---

[15] One reason for believing this is that quarterly growth rates in nominal and real GNP are highly correlated. During the sample period 1954–1985, for instance, the correlation for the U.S. values is greater than 0.8.

[16] For expositional simplicity, our discussion proceeds as if it were established that the long-term average growth rate of real output were 3 percent per year. The rule could easily be modified to take account of a different number or even a process whereby the "permanent" growth rate is frequently re-estimated.

chosen with some care, for values that are too small or too large would have undesirable consequences. Specifically, λ values that are too small would provide too little in the way of corrective adjustments and thus result in only minor improvements over formulation (3). Values for λ that are too large, on the other hand, can create a system that is dynamically *unstable* in the sense defined in Chapter 7. As dynamic instability—explosive oscillations, in the case at hand—is the more serious problem, one should aim to err on the low side (if at all) in choosing λ.

Previous work by the author suggest that a value of approximately 0.25 should be appropriate for λ. But this work also suggests that rule (4) would work reasonably well with a broad range of λ values. A brief description of the work in question will be provided in the next section.

16.3   Performance of Proposed Rule

Our objective here is to determine how nominal GNP would behave in an actual economy—such as that of West Germany, Canada, or the United States—if its monetary authority were to conduct policy by setting the monetary base in each quarter in accordance with the policy rule proposed above, which we now write as

$$\Delta b_t = 0.00739 - \overline{\Delta v_t} + 0.25(x_{t-1}^* - x_{t-1}). \tag{5}$$

But how can such a question be studied?

In answer, let us consider the example of the United States. Then to determine whether rule (5) would lead to desirable behavior—that is, smooth growth of nominal GNP at a 3 percent rate—there are two ways to proceed. One is to experiment with the actual economy, while the other is to experiment with a reliable model. As it is beyond our power to pursue the former course, we are forced to experiment with a model. An attractive type of experiment is to estimate how the economy would have behaved in the past *if* the rule had been in effect. Now this course is also problematical, for—as emphasized above—we do not possess adequate knowledge about some aspects of the economy. But we would nevertheless possess evidence in support of our rule's desirability if we found that it would have yielded good results *in a wide variety of different models*. In fact, some evidence of precisely that type has been developed and presented in a recent paper (McCallum, 1988). To explain the logic of the study, which considers the period from 1954 through 1985, let us begin with one extremely simple model of the economy and then bring in evidence relating to the variety of models.

For the sale of exposition, then, we temporarily consider the following estimated model of nominal GNP determination:

$$\Delta x_t = \underset{(0.002)}{0.00740} + \underset{(0.079)}{0.262\,\Delta x_{t-1}} + \underset{(0.120)}{0.488\,\Delta b_t} + e_t,$$

$$R^2 = 0.23, \qquad SE = 0.010, \qquad DW = 2.11. \tag{6}$$

Here the rate of growth of nominal GNP Δx_t is determined by its own past value Δx_{t-1} and the current growth rate of the monetary base Δb_t. The coefficient values shown in (6) were obtained by least-squares regression using U.S. quarterly data (seasonally adjusted) for 1954–1985. In the displayed relation, the residuals e_t represent estimates of the disturbances or shocks to the relationship. The reported SE and DW values indicate that the variance of these shocks is about $0.01^2 = 0.0001$ and that they involve very little (first-order) serial correlation.

To estimate how nominal GNP would have evolved in the United States over the period 1954–1985 if the policy rule (5) had been in effect, we use equation (5) together with the model (6) to generate simulated values for x_t and b_t, beginning with initial conditions pertaining to the start of 1954 and with the estimated shock values e_t fed into the system in each period. The results of this simulation exercise are shown in Figure 16-1, where TAR denotes the target path x_t^* and LX

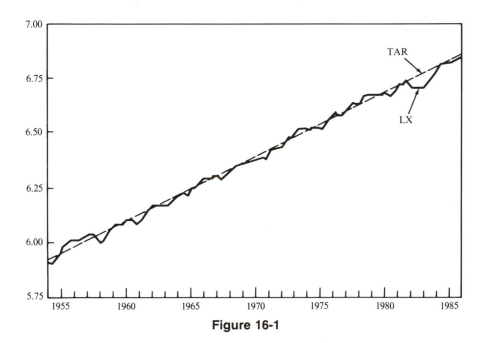

Figure 16-1

denotes the simulated values for x_t. From this figure it is evident that the rule (5) would have worked quite well according to model (6); the simulated values stay quite close to the target path despite the disrupting influence of the new e_t shocks that arrive in each period.

The "model" in equation (6) is extremely simple and, in any event, is only one particular model. Consequently, exercises of the type just described have also been conducted with three more fully specified— but still very small—models of the U.S. macroeconomy. These three models are estimated statistical representations of three different theories regarding the nature of cyclical fluctuations. Since the main disagreement among economists concerns the nature of aggregate-supply or Phillips–curve relations,[17] three different versions of that portion of the model were used together with one common specification of aggregate demand behavior.[18] The three aggregate supply models used are ones representing the real business cycle (RBC) hypothesis described in Section 9.7, the monetary misperception theory discussed in Section 9.4, and a more "Keynesian" model that is related to (but somewhat different than) the theories of Sections 9.5 and 9.6.[19]

For all three of these more detailed models of the macroeconomy, the simulation exercises give results with nominal GNP values that follow the 3 percent target path even more closely than in Figure 16-1. Instead of presenting additional plots, which look much like Figure 16-1, it will be useful to tabulate summary statistics pertaining to the *control errors*, $x_t^* - x_t$. In particular, the root-mean-square error (RMSE) values[20] are as follows:

Model	RMSE Value
Equation (6)	0.0197
Real business cycle	0.0160
Monetary misperceptions	0.0161
Keynesian	0.0191

From these figures it is clear that with each of these three models the performance of the monetary policy rule (5) is superior, in terms of nominal GNP control, to that illustrated in Figure 16-1.

---

[17] This point was emphasized, and alternative theories described, in Chapter 9.

[18] That common model is an operational version of the aggregate demand equation in Problem 1 of Chapter 10.

[19] For more discussion of these models, the reader may consult McCallum (1988).

[20] The RMSE statistic is the square root of the mean value (over the 128 periods 1954.1–1985.4) of the $(x_t - x_t)^2$ values. It corresponds to the square root of the MSE measures used in Chapters 4 and 11, but here the variable in question is nominal GNP.

Table 16-1. RMSE Values with Different Models and Alternative Values of λ

Model	Value of λ in Rule (4)			
	0.0	0.1	0.25	0.50
Illustrative, Eq. (6)	0.0488	0.0249	0.0197	0.0162
Real business cycle	0.0281	0.0200	0.0160	0.0132
Monetary				
misperception	0.0238	0.0194	0.0161	0.0137
Keynesian	0.0311	0.0236	0.0191	0.0174
Vector autoregression	0.0479	0.0216	0.0220	0.1656

In addition, simulations have been conducted using alternative values of the policy coefficient λ, with magnitudes of that parameter ranging from 0 to 0.5. These results are reported in Table 16-1. There it will be seen that for the four models described thus far, the RMSE values are smaller with $\lambda = 0.5$ than with $\lambda = 0.25$. In other words, stronger responses of monetary base growth to recent target misses helps to keep x_t closer to the x_t^* target path. The final line of Table 16-1 gives results for another type of model, however, a "vector autoregression" model that relies more heavily on purely statistical relationships and less heavily on restrictions suggested by theoretical considerations.[21] In that line it will be seen that the RMSE value is much greater when λ is set at the value 0.5 than when more modest feedback responses are used. In fact, a plot of the simulated x_t values for this case indicates that explosive oscillations are encountered, reflecting dynamic instability. This result suggests, then, that smaller values of λ would be safer.

It should be emphasized, nevertheless, that the policy rule (4) provides rather good performance of nominal GNP for a sizable range of λ values even in the VAR case. And for such values, with λ between, say, 0.1 and 0.3, the rule leads to smooth noninflationary growth of nominal GNP according to a variety of macroeconometric models. Consequently, the exercise reported provides evidence strongly in

---

[21] A vector autoregression (VAR) model consists of a set of regression equations that "explain" each of the system's variables by means of lagged values of all of the system's variables. In the particular VAR model reported, values for $t - 1$, $t - 2$, $t - 3$, and $t - 4$ were used for each of the four included variables, which were (1) the growth rate of real GNP, (2) the growth rate of the price level, (3) the growth rate of the monetary base, and (4) the interest rate on three-month U.S. Treasury bills.

favor of the idea that a simple monetary policy rule such as (4) could result in desirable macroeconomic performance. With the path of nominal GNP kept close to a steady 3 percent trend line, the economy would not experience any significant amount of inflation or deflation when experience is averaged over an extended period of time.[22] Furthermore, real fluctuations might be smaller than those actually realized in the postwar era, although that conclusion is more questionable since knowledge regarding the source and nature of such fluctuations is inadequate. In any event, a rule such as (4) would eliminate monetary policy surprises as a potential source of fluctuations and would provide a stable and noninflationary monetary environment for producers and households. Such a rule would appear to provide improved monetary performance, as compared with the discretionary policymaking of the postwar era or the commodity-money standards of the more distant past.

There are two points regarding the foregoing analysis that should be mentioned before we move on to our concluding section. First, the point of footnote 16 should be expressed in a more prominent location. It should be emphasized, that is, that a rule such as (4) can easily be modified to be applicable in cases in which the long-term rate of output growth is not 3 percent per year. Indeed, the rule could be formulated so as to permit periodic revisions in the estimated value of the average future real growth rate.[23]

Second, the analysis of this chapter is applicable to an open economy, despite the absence of any reference above to exchange rates or international trade. The basic argument is simply that the principal job of a nation's monetary authority is to keep nominal demand for its output growing in a smooth and noninflationary fashion, because doing so will help to prevent demand-induced fluctuations in real output and employment (as well as preventing inflation). This statement is not affected by the recognition of international trade in goods and securities. If the position is accepted, it follows that—since monetary policy can only be directed at one target—exchange rates should be left free to be determined by market forces.

---

[22] To avoid possible misunderstanding, it should be emphasized that the simulation experiments reported do not show that smooth, 3 percent growth of nominal GNP would lead to good performance of inflation and real growth variables; that conclusion is based on other theoretical and empirical analyses that support the natural-rate hypothesis. What the simulation experiments do indicate is that the operational policy rule (5) would lead to smooth 3 percent growth of nominal GNP.

[23] An example, stimulated by a policy rule proposed by Meltzer (1987), is considered in McCallum (1988).

16.4   Conclusions

In conclusion, let us turn our attention to a question that might arise rather naturally in response to the analysis of the previous three sections.[24] That analysis is not highly technical, nor difficult to comprehend. The question, then, is this: If the case for conducting monetary policy according to a rule such as (4) is so strong, as claimed, why do so few actual monetary authorities choose to use such a rule?[25] Why do they instead operate in a "discretionary" manner and claim in their public statements that policymaking *flexibility* is preferable to any rule?[26] In response to this natural and important question, we begin by considering the attitude of the central bank itself—or its officials—and then touch on the attitude of the voting public at large.

One possible reason for the objection of most central bankers to proposals for a monetary rule is the existence of a genuine misunderstanding. Until recently, academics as well as practical men had in mind, when discussing monetary rules, specifications of the nonactivist type which incorporates no responses to the state of the economy. Indeed, with many monetary experts the term "rule" still gives rise to visions of a Friedman-type constant-money-growth rule that takes no account of changing conditions and evolving institutions. Many of these people have developed over time an antagonism to Friedman-type rules that is applied indiscriminately to rules of a more responsive variety.

But this logically invalid sort of position is unlikely to be the major source of central-bank antipathy to rule-based policymaking. Of more fundamental importance, probably, is a matter of individual and institutional self-interest. In that regard, reflection makes it clear that actual central-bank organizations have a certain incentive to prevent the adoption of a rule governing monetary policy. For example, if such a rule were in effect, the Chairman of the Federal Reserve's Board of Governors would not be described by the press as the "second most powerful man in America," for it is the belief that his *decisions* regarding policy strongly affect the welfare of millions of citizens that leads the press to make such statements. Furthermore, it is important to recognize that this prestige does not accrue only to the chairman, but

---

[24] Indeed, the question *has* been brought up by students in various classes taught by the author.

[25] As of 1988, there is only one actual central bank that conducts policy by adherence to a rule, namely, the Swiss National Bank. [On this, see Rich (1987).] Interestingly, the OECD country with the lowest average inflation rate over the last 30 years is Switzerland.

[26] For an example of such a statement, see Volcker (1983).

rather to many persons in the organization. In other words, the feeling of self-importance of hundreds of Federal Reserve employees might be diminished substantially if policy were conducted in accordance with an automatic rule. And the interest of the financial, business, and political communities in Fed employees would also plunge, quite possible affecting their opportunities for positions with alternative employers (e.g., Wall Street financial firms desirous of information about Fed operations). Basically for this reason, it would seem clear that actual central banks naturally have a significant institutional aversion to the idea of a monetary rule.[27]

But why, to press the issue farther, does not the public in a democratic society *impose* some type of rule-type policymaking procedure on its monetary authority, its central bank? This is an interesting but difficult question in *political economy* that has recently begun to attract the attention of researchers.[28] We will not attempt to explore the matter at all deeply here, for the subject is highly technical and also unsettled. Instead, we shall conclude with a pair of observations that go some way, at a commonsense level, toward an explanation. First, the subject of monetary economics is not well understood by most members of the voting public—or even by their national representatives, such as congressmen and members of parliament. There is much remaining for economists to accomplish in the way of explaining and articulating basic monetary principles. Second, the monetary experience of most North American and European nations, since the advent of "discretionary" policymaking, has not been terrible. Although it has been argued above that better performance is possible—lower inflation with no less real growth and no more variability—it must be recognized that during the 40-year period from 1947 to 1987 there has been no major depression comparable to that of the 1930s, no breakdown in world trade, and no hyperinflation involving a major currency. By historical standards, the record of discretionary policymaking has actually been rather good in most respects. Consequently, there has not developed any groundswell of public opinion in favor of potentially improved methods of conducting monetary policy. The occurrence of an event of the type mentioned—a depression or hyperinflation, for example—would focus attention more strongly on questions involving monetary

---

[27] It is conceivable, nevertheless, that a central bank could choose to conduct policy in a rulelike fashion—abstaining from period-by-period attempts to exploit given expectations—and yet retain the public image of a powerful decision-making institution. For that reason, the author retains some optimism about the likelihood of central bank support for policymaking in accordance with a rule.

[28] For a useful survey of work in the area of political economy as applied to macroeconomic phenomena, see Alesina (1988). An insightful discussion focusing on the Fed and the U.S. Congress is provided by Hetzel (1986).

standards and institutions. It is, however, probably better (for every-one except monetary economists) to continue without that type of impetus.

Problems

1. Carefully derive the conclusion mentioned in footnote 4, namely, that a money demand expenditure elasticity in excess of unity tends to result in a secular decrease in velocity.
2. To determine how the nominal interest rate responds to a monetary policy shock, consider the following simplified version of the model of Section 10.2:

$$y_t = \beta_0 + \beta_1(m_t - p_t) + \beta_2 E_{t-1}(p_{t+1} - p_t),$$

$$y_t = \bar{y} + \beta_1(m_t - E_{t-1}m_t),$$

$$m_t = \mu_0 + \mu_1 m_{t-1} + e_t.$$

Here we have assumed that the v_t shocks are absent and that $\bar{y}_t = \bar{y}$. In this model, recall from Section 10.1, the interest rate satisfies

$$R_t = b_0 + b_1 y_t + E_{t-1}(p_{t+1} - p_t),$$

where $b_1 < 0$. Obtain a solution for R_t of the form $R_t = \phi_0 + \phi_1 e_t + \phi_2 m_{t-1}$ and determine the sign of ϕ_1.
3. Consider a situation in which loving parents are confronted with an instance of misbehavior by their child, whose happiness and conduct are both important to them. Should they punish the child for the misbehavior, thereby inflicting disutility upon themselves as well as the child? Or should they refrain in this instance, while promising punishment for any future misbehavior? What does all this have to do with monetary economics?

References

Alesina, Alberto, "Macroeconomics and Politics," in *NBER Macroeconomics Annual 1988*, S. Fischer. ed. (Cambridge, Mass.: MIT Press, 1988).

Fischer, Stanley, "Long-Term Contracts, Rational Expectations, and the Optimal Money Suupply Rule," *Journal of Political Economy* 85 (February 1977), 191–205.

Friedman, Milton, "A Monetary and Fiscal Framework for Economic Stabil-ity," *American Economic Review* 38 (June 1948), 245–64. Reprinted in Friedman's *Essays in Positive Economics*. (Chicago: University of Chicago, Press, 1953).

Friedman, Milton, *A Program for Monetary Stability*. (New York: Fordham University Press, 1960).

Friedman, Milton, *Capitalism and Freedom*. (Chicago: University of Chicago Press, 1962).

Friedman, Milton, "The Role of Monetary Policy," *American Economic Review* 58 (March 1968), 1–17.

Hetzel, Robert L., "A Congressional Mandate for Monetary Policy," *Cato Journal* 5 (Winter 1986), 797–820.

Kydland, Finn E., and Edward C. Prescott, "Time to Build and Aggregate Fluctuations," *Econometrica* 50 (November 1982), 1345–70.

Lucas, Robert E., Jr., "Expectations and the Neutrality of Money," *Journal of Economic Theory* 4 (April 1972), 103–24.

McCallum, Bennett T., "The Case for Rules in the Conduct of Monetary Policy: A Concrete Example," Federal Reserve Bank of Richmond, *Economic Review* 73 (September–October 1987), 10–18.

McCallum, Bennett T., "Robustness Properties of a Rule for Monetary Policy," *Carnegie–Rochester Conference Series on Public Policy* 29 (Autumn 1988), 173–203.

Meltzer, Allan H., "Limits of Short-Run Stabilization Policy," *Economic Inquiry* 25 (February 1987), 1–14.

Rich, Georg, "Swiss and United States Monetary Policy: Has Monetarism Failed?" Federal Reserve Bank of Richmond, *Economic Review* 73 (May–June 1987), 3–16.

Taylor, John B., "Staggered Wage Setting in a Macro Model," *American Economic Review Papers and Proceedings* 69 (May 1979), 108–13.

Volcker, Paul A., "Statement Before the House Committee on Banking, Finance, and Urban Affairs," *Federal Reserve Bulletin* 69 (August 1983), 617–21.

Index

Adaptive expectations formula, 13, 137–139,
  142–143, 145
Aggregate demand
  classical model and, 93–96, 97, 106
  function, 85–89
  Keynesian model and, 100–101, 103, 106
  maximization analysis and, 102–107
  money demand and, 83–85
  saving-investment behavior and, 78–82
Aggregate supply
  classical function, 89–93
  classical model and, 93–96, 97, 106
  Keynesian function, 96–99
  Keynesian model and, 100–101, 103, 106
  maximization analysis and, 102–107
  model, 201–218
    monetary policy and, 221–228
    multiperiod pricing and, 211–214
    normal output and, 208–211
    price stickiness and, 214–215
    shocks and, 209–211, 212–213
  unemployment and inflation and theories of.
    See Inflation
Alesina, Alberto, 349n
Anticipated inflation. *See* Inflation
ATS accounts, 19, 20
Augmented Phillips curve, 181–185
Average exchange rate, 270–271

Bailey, Martin J., 103n, 113, 125
Balance on capital account, balance of
  payments and, 289–290
Balance on current account, balance of
  payments and, 288–289
Balance of payments, 288–292
Bank of the United States, 315
Banks
  central, 348–350; *see also* Federal Reserve
    System
  chartering national, 313–315
  commercial, 55, 56, 57, 58
  Great Depression and, 328–330
  National Banking System, 318–319

Barro, Robert J., 35n, 36n, 42n, 47n, 51n,
  102n, 103, 104, 113, 122n, 144n, 148,
  184n, 213, 239, 245, 245n, 249n,
  251n, 252n, 265n
Barter, 17
Baumol, William J., 35n, 38n, 48
Baumol–Tobin inventory model, 35, 44n,
  48–53
Bimetallism, 6n, 263–266, 312–313
Bivariate distributions, 165–166
Blinder, Alan S., 12n
Bordo, Michael D., 249n, 327n
Bretton Woods System, 293n, 331–332
Broaddus, Alfred, 10, 55
Brock, Leslie V., 299n, 303, 304, 305, 307,
  308
Brunner, Karl, 12n, 102n, 103n
Bryan, William Jennings, 321, 324
Bryant, Ralph C., 12n
Bubble (bootstrap) effects, rational
  expectations and, 158–160

Cagan, Phillip, 133–144, 251
Campbell, John V., 210
Cannan, Edwin, 25n
Capital stock growth, output growth and,
  122–123
Central bank, rule-based policymaking and,
  348–350; *see also* Federal Reserve
  System
Checkable deposits, 19, 20, 56
Civil War, money and, 317–321
Classical aggregate supply function, 89–93
Classical model, 93–96, 97, 106
  inflation in, 113–117
  as static, 77–78
Coins, 19, 222
Colonial America, money in, 299–309
Commercial banks, money stock and, 55, 56,
  57, 58
Commodity-money standards, 22–23, 24,
  249–267; *see also* Gold standard;
  Monetary history

bimetallism, 6n, 263–266
  cost of, 267
  inflation and, 246–248
  monetary rule and, 336–337
  symmetallism, 266
Conditional density, 167
Conditional distributions, 167, 169, 170
Consumer Price Index (CPI), 5n
Consumer surplus analysis, welfare cost of
    inflation and, 125
Consumption function, aggregate demand
    and, 78–82
Continuous random variable, 162–163
Continuous-time concept, 110
Control errors, 68, 232–234
Correlation measure, 170
Covariance, 170
Credit, 26–27
Credit-card transactions, 20
Cukierman, Alex, 245n
Currency, 19, 20
Currency-to-deposit ratio, 56–57, 59, 329

Demand. *See* Aggregate demand; Money
    demand
Deposits, 19, 20, 56–58, 231, 328–329
Density function, 161, 166
Discount window borrowing, 57
Discrete probability distribution, 162
Discrete random variable, 161
Discretionary policymaking. *See* Monetary
    policy
Dollar; *see also* Commodity-money standards
  gold standard and, 6, 250
  value of, 5, 6
Domestic nonfinancial debt, 26–27, 28
Dornbusch, Rudiger, 35n, 42n, 47n, 175n,
    280, 283n, 285
Dotsey, Michael, 216n
Durbin–Watson statistic, 213–214
Dynamic stability, 139–142

Employment, labor supply and demand and,
    91–92; *see also* Unemployment
Employment Act of 1946, 6–7
Endogenous variable, 94
Ernst, Joseph A., 299n
Excess reserves, 58
Exchange rates, 270
  average, 270–1271
  fixed, 285–288, 293–296
  floating, 271–285, 293–296
Exchange-rate overshooting, 285
Exogenous variable, 94
Expectations, 13; *see also* Rational
    expectations
  adaptive, 137–139, 142–143
  mathematical, 146, 160–171
Expectations-augmented Phillips curve. *See*
    Augmented Phillips curve
Expected values, 164–165

Federal funds rate, 65
Federal Reserve Act, 324
Federal Reserve notes, 6, 19, 22

Federal Reserve System, 4, 21, 324–330
  average exchange rate and, 270–271
  gold standard and, 325–326
  inflation and, 9–12
  monetary policy and, 6–9
  money stock and, 19, 55, 56, 57, 60–65, 71,
      230–235
  notes, 6, 19, 22
  rule-based policymaking and, 348–350
Feldstein, Martin, 130
Fiat money, 12, 23–24
Financial intermediation, 27–29
Fischer, Stanley, 35n, 42n, 47n, 51n, 122n,
    175n, 189–192, 211, 225n, 337
Fisher, Irving, 249n
Fixed exchange rates, 285–288, 293–296
Floating exchange rates, 271–285, 293–296
Flood, Robert P., 139n, 280n, 281n, 283n
Flow supply, for gold, 253–254, 255–256
Foreign exchange market. *See* Open-economy
    monetary system
"Free Banking" experience, 315–316
"Free silver," 321–324
Frenkel, Jacob A., 287n
Friedman, Benjamin M., 26n, 142n
Friedman, Milton, 10n, 12n, 21, 137, 181–185,
    243–244, 294–296, 316n, 317, 322n,
    324n, 325, 329–330, 338–339, 340

Garber, Peter M., 139n
GNP, monetary rule and, 340–349
Gold; *see also* Gold standard
  bimetallism and, 6, 263–266, 312–313
  symmetallism and, 266
Gold Commission report, 313n, 331n, 333n
Gold standard, 6, 23, 250–263
  Bretton Woods and, 331–332
  Federal Reserve and, 325–326
  Great Depression and, 330–331, 332–333
  history of, 324
  inflation and, 246–248
  model of, 250–258
  rational expectations and dynamic analysis
      of, 258–263
Gold Standard Act, 324
Goldfeld, Stephen M., 45n
Goodfriend, Marvin, 10, 47n, 233n
Gordon, David B., 239, 245
Gordon, Robert J., 6n, 8n, 183n, 213n, 320
Great Depression, 326–331
Greenbacks, 318, 319
Greenspan, Alan, 4
Gresham's law, 264, 312
Growth rate, 109–112

Hall, Robert E., 185, 188, 191, 266
Hammond, Bray, 313n
Harrod-neutral technical progress, 123
Henderson, James M., 79n
Hetzel, Robert L., 349n
High-powered money, money stock and,
    56–60, 64–66, 67–70; *see also*
    Monetary base
Hoehn, James G., 71n, 234n
Hyperinflation. *See* Inflation

Independence, probabilistic, 167–168, 169–170
Inflation
  Cagan model of hyperinflation and, 133–144
    adaptive expectations formula and,
      137–139, 142–143
    dynamic stability and, 139-142
    rational expectations and, 148–151
  discretionary monetary policymaking and,
    241–248
  hyperinflation, 13; *see also* Cagan model of
    hyperinflation
  monetary rule and, 340–342
  money held during, 18, 118
  money stock and zero, 338–339
  1979–1982, 9–12
  postwar, 5–9
  rate of, 26
  steady (anticipated), 109–131
    classical model and, 113–117
    growth rates and, 109–112
    output growth and, 122–124
    real versus nominal interest rates and,
      112–113
    real-balance effects and, 120–122
    steady-state equilibrium and, 109, 111,
      112, 117–120
    welfare cost of, 124–131
  unemployment and, 174–200
    augmented Phillips curve and, 181–185
    Keynesian model and, 174–177
    monetary misperceptions theory (Lucas)
      and, 185–188
    Okun's law and, 184–185
    original Phillips curve and, 177–181
    real business cycle theory and, 192–196
    relative-prices theory (Taylor) and,
      188–189
    sticky-wage theory (Fischer) and, 189–192
Instrument, money stock control and, 64–66
Interest rates, 21
  monetary policy and, 339–340
  money stock and, 64–66, 70–71
  1979–1982, 9–12
  real versus nominal, 112–113
Interest-parity relationship, 275
International Monetary Fund (IMF), 290, 332
Investment, saving-investment behavior and
  aggregate demand and, 78–82
IS function, aggregate demand and, 78–82
Iterated-expectations, law of, 147, 170–171

Johnson, Harry G., 287n

Kahn, Moshin S., 139
Keynes, John Maynard, 175–176
Keynesian aggregate supply function, 96–99
Keynesian model, 100–101, 103, 106
  dynamics and, 174–177
  inflation and unemployment and, 174–177
  monetary policy rule and, 345–346
  as static, 77–78
Kindahl, James, 319
King, Robert G., 187n, 192, 216n
Klein, John J., 313n, 325
Krugman, Paul R., 293n
Kydland, Finn E., 192, 194, 195, 239, 337

Labor supply and demand, 91–92; *see also*
  Aggregate supply; Employment;
  Unemployment
Lagged variables, rational expectations models
  with, 157–158
Lagrangian technique, 38
Law of iterated expectations, 147, 170–171
Legal tender, 12, 24–25
Lieberman, Charles, 44n
LM function, aggregate demand and, 83–85
Lucas, Robert E., Jr., 37n, 148, 185–188, 189,
  214, 225, 228–230, 337
Lucas critique, 228–230, 234

McCallum, Bennett T., 18n, 71n, 158n, 184n,
  215, 234n, 266n, 339, 343, 345n, 347n
McCusker, James J., 299n, 304, 307, 308
Mankiw, N. Gregory, 210
Marginal product of capital, 80
Market-clearing model, 102, 103; *see also*
  Classical model
Market-clearing output. *See* Aggregate supply
  model
Marshall, Alfred, 266
Marty, Alvin L., 129n
Mathematical expectation, 146, 160–171
Maximization analysis, *IS–LM* framework
  and, 102–107
Mean, 161
Mean-square error (MSE), 68
Medium of account, money as, 17–18
Medium of exchange, money as, 17, 18, 19, 37
Meese, Richard A., 281
Meltzer, Allan H., 12n, 102n, 103n, 347n
Mercantilism, 300n
Michener, Ronald, 299n
Mill, John Stuart, 16, 249n
Mishkin, Frederick S., 213n
Mitchell, B. R., 247
Monetarist economists, 9–10
Modigliani, Franco, 131
Monetary base, 21–22; *see also* High-powered
  money
  monetary rule based on, 340–349
Monetary history, 298–333
  Bretton Woods system, 293n, 331–332
  from Civil War to World War I, 317–324
  colonial America, 299–309
  in late 1930s, 332–333
  from 1914 to 1944, 324–331
  pre- and post-World War II, 4–9
  recent, 9–12
  from Revolution to the Civil War, 309–317
Monetary misperception theory, 185–188, 214
  monetary policy rule and, 345–346
Monetary neutrality, 96, 106
  open economy and, 277–279
Monetary policy; *see also* Policy analysis
  aggregate supply model and, 221–228
  description of, 286
  and fixed exchange rate, 286
  postwar, 6–9
  rules versus discretion in, 237–248, 336–351
    central bank and, 348–350
    distinctions in, 237–239
    effects of, 241–244

example of, 239–241
inflation and, 241–248
Monetary standards. *See* Commodity-money
standards
Money
functions of, 16–18, 37
output and. *See* Aggregate supply model
Money demand, 33–53
aggregate demand and, 83–85
Baumol–Tobin inventory model of, 35, 44,
48–53
empirical functions for, 42–47
shopping-time model of, 35–41, 52–53
uncertainty and, 41–42
velocity and, 47–48
Money demand function, 39–40
Money standard. *See* Commodity-money
standards
Money stock, 55–72
Cagan model of inflation and, 133–142
commercial banks and, 55, 56, 57, 58
control of, 60–71, 230–235
empirical measures of, 19–22
Federal Reserve System and, 19, 55, 56, 57,
60–65, 71
high-powered money and, 56–60, 64–66,
67–70
interest rates and, 64–66, 70–71
M1, 19–20, 22
M2, 20–21
M3, 21
1979–1982 targets, 9–12, 230–235
zero inflation and, 338–339
Money supply. *See* Money stock
Multiperiod pricing, aggregate supply model
and, 211–214
Multivariate distributions, 165–166
Mussa, Michael, 275n, 281, 283n
Muth, John F., 148

Napoleonic Wars, legal tender and, 25
National Banking System, 318–319
National banks, chartering, 313–315
Nationalization of gold, 330
Natural-rate hypothesis, 189, 206, 348n
Nelson, Charles R., 210
Nettels, Curtis, 299n, 300n, 309, 310, 312n
Neutrality of money. *See* Monetary neutrality
Niehans, Jürg, 249n
Nominal GNP, monetary, rule and, 340–349
Nominal interest rate, 112–113
Nominal prices, aggregate supply model and,
214–215
Nominal variables, 26
NOW accounts, 10, 19, 20
Nussbaum, Arthur, 313n

Obstfeld, Maurice, 293n
Official settlements balance, balance of
payments and, 290–291
Okun, Arthur, 184, 214
Okun's law, 184–185
O'Leary, Paul M., 322n
Open-economy monetary analysis, 269–297
balance of payments, 288–292

fixed versus floating exchange rates and,
293–296
gold standard and, 258
rational expectations model and
for fixed exchange rate, 285–288
for floating exchange rate, 271–285
Operating instrument. *See* Instrument
Original Phillips curve, 177–181
Other checkable deposits, 19, 20
Output
money and. *See* Aggregate supply model
steady inflation and growth in, 122–124
Overlapping generations model of money, 52n

Patinkin, Don, 100n, 121n
Pearson, Frank A., 5n, 314n, 319, 320, 321,
321n
Phelps, Edmund, 181–185
Phillips, A. W., 177–178
Phillips curve
augmented, 181–185
original, 177–181
Pierce, James L., 71n
Plosser, Charles I., 192, 210
Point-in-time price-level determination, for
gold standard economy, 253–254,
255–256
Policy analysis, 221–236; *see also* Monetary
policy
aggregate supply model and, 221–228
Lucas critique and, 228–230, 234
money stock control and, 230–235
Policy process, 150–151
Poole, William, 71n, 144n
Population growth, output growth and, 122
Portfolio balance relation, 40
Prescott, Edward C., 192, 194, 195, 239, 337
Price level, 26
Cagan model of inflation and, 133–142
history of, 4, 5, 246–248, 302–309, 315,
319–322
Price rigidity. *See* Aggregate supply model
Price stickiness
aggregate supply model and, 214–215
fixed exchange rates and, 287
floating exchange rates and, 283
Probability theory, concepts of, 146, 160–171
Purchasing power parity doctrine (PPP), 277

Quandt, Richard E., 79n
Quantity-theory property, of Cagan model,
155

Random variable, 160
mathematical expectation of, 163–164
Random walk process, 154n, 210n
Random walk with drift, 154n
Rational expectations, 143, 145–160; *see also*
Open-economy monetary analysis
Cagan model, and, 148–151
gold standard and, 258–263
mathematical expectations and, 146,
160–171
monetary policy and, 225, 240–243
properties of, 145–148

Rational expectations (*Continued*)
  solutions
    examples of, 155–157
    with lagged variables, 157–158
    multiple, 158–160
    procedures, 151–153
    properties, 153–155
Real bills doctrine, 333
Real business cycle theory (RBC), 192–196, 337
  monetary policy rule and, 345–346
Real interest rate, 112–113
Real wage, 90–93
Real-balance effect, steady inflation and, 120–122
Relative-prices theory, 188–189
Required reserves, 58, 233, 316, 331
Reserve ratio, gold standard and, 256–257
Reserve-to-deposit ratio, 56–57, 58–59, 317
Revolutionary War, money during, 309–310
Rich, Georg, 348n
Rule-type policymaking. *See* Monetary policy
Rush, Mark, 213

Sargent, Thomas J., 91n, 102n, 148, 184n, 225, 230n
Saving-investment behavior, aggregate demand and, 78–82
Schwartz, Anna J., 21, 316n, 317, 322n, 324n, 325, 326–327, 329–330
Sherman Silver Purchase Act, 322–324
Shocks
  aggregate supply model and, 209–211, 212–213
  floating exchange rate and, 276–279, 281–285
Shopping-time model, 35–41, 52–53
Silver, 299–309
  bimetallism and, 263–266
  free, 321–324
  symmetallism and, 266
Simons, Henry, 237
Smith, Adam, 300n
Smith, Bruce D., 299n, 307
Solow, Robert M., 123, 124n, 183n
Stability analysis, 139–142
Standard deviation, 162
Standards, fiat money and, 23–24; *see also* Commodity-money standards
State variables, rational expectations solutions and, 158–160

Steady inflation. *See* Inflation
Steady-state equilibrium, 109, 111, 112, 117–120
Stevens, Edward J., 316n, 317
Sticky-wage theory, 189–192; *see also* Price stickiness
Stock demand, for gold, 252
Stockman, Alan C., 281, 283
Store of value, money as, 18, 52n
Symmetallism, 266

Taylor, John B., 185, 188–189, 211, 337
Technical progress, output growth and, 123
Temin, Peter, 313n
Terms of trade, 293n
Thomson, Thomas D., 71n
Tobin, James, 27–28, 35n, 42n, 48
Tower, Edward, 125n
Travelers checks, 19, 20
Treasury-issued notes, 19n

Uncertainty, money demand and, 41–42
Unconditional (marginal) density functions, 166
Unemployment, 175–176; *see also* Inflation
  monetary policy and, 6–9
  1979–1982, 9–12
Unit of account, 17n
U.S. Constitution
  commodity-money standards and, 24
  money and, 311–312, 313
Univariate marginal densities, 166

Varian, Hal R., 125n
Variance, 161–162
Vector autoregression (VAR) model, 346
Velocity, 47–48, 340–341
Volcker, Paul A., 3–4, 9, 348n

Wallace, Neil, 52n, 225
War of 1812, money and, 315
Warren, George F., 5n, 314n, 319, 320, 321, 321n
Weintraub, Robert E., 9n
Welfare cost, of steady inflation, 124–131
White, Lawrence H., 18n
Wholesale Price Index (WPI), 5n
World wars, money and, 4–9, 324–331

Yeager, Leland B., 266